COMPUTER ANIMATION SERIES

W0071822

Nadia Magnenat Thalmann
Daniel Thalmann (Eds.)

Models and Techniques in Computer Animation

With 200 Figures, Including 85 in Color

Springer Japan KK

Prof. Nadia Magnenat Thalmann
MIRALab, Centre Universitaire d'Informatique
University of Geneva
24 rue du Général-Dufour
CH-1211 Geneva 4
Switzerland

Prof. Daniel Thalmann
Computer Graphics Lab.
Swiss Federal Institute of Technology
CH-1015 Lausanne
Switzerland

Cover picture:
Design: Hans Martin Werner, from the film "Fashon Show", MIRALab,
University of Geneva and CGL, Swiss Federal Institute of Technology,
Lausanne

ISBN 978-4-431-66913-5   ISBN 978-4-431-66911-1 (eBook)
DOI 10.1007/978-4-431-66911-1

Printed on acid-free paper

© Springer Japan 1993
Originally published by Springer-Verlag Tokyo in 1993

Preface

by

Andries van Dam
Brown University

As the power of computers and display hardware have steadily increased, interaction has come to computer animation. Until recently, the term **computer animation** referred mostly to frame-by-frame, batch-computed recordings, in which the computer was used to model the geometry of time-varying scenes, execute camera motion, compute in-between interpolation of key frames and create photorealistic renderings. The end result of such a process, a movie or videotape, is then displayed to passive users who may have at most the standard controls over speed and direction of playback.

The reasons that computer animation has been primarily a batch phenomenon are twofold. First, to achieve the necessary precise artistic control over modeling, camera motion, and rendering, animation professionals had to experiment until the desired effects were achieved, using relatively low-level tools such as procedural scripting languages that required a considerable training period. Second, the various processing tasks were far too compute-intensive to be done in real time on readily available hardware.

Fortunately, hardware improvements continue unabated (increased processor speed, memory size, and rendering speed and quality via such techniques as antialiasing, alpha blending, texture mapping, and global illumination), and software tools continue to become both more powerful and easier to use. Thus previewing and sometimes even final animation of simple scenes can now be done with reasonable pseudo-realism rather than in wireframe mode only. When geometric, behavioral and rendering fidelity are critical, or at least more important than interaction, frames are computed with the newest modeling and photorealistic rendering algorithms, still in batch mode . Indeed, batch animation will not disappear: As technology improves, expectations increase commensurately, and there will always be simulation, animation and rendering effects that cannot be achieved in realtime.

Traditional interactive graphics applications have also benefitted from steady hardware and software evolution. While most graphics applications still involve creating and viewing static 2D or 3D objects or data, computer graphics is increasingly concerned with modeling time-varying behavior, not just geometry. At the same time, interactive exploration of synthetic worlds, using both desktop and more immersive virtual reality environments, is becoming more common to visualize engineering and industrial designs and scientific and mathematical phenomena, and for teleoperation (e.g., remote operation of robots and vehicles, telesurgery), as well as art and entertainment. We are experiencing a coming together, even a partial merging of technologies, including those of traditional CAD-centric graphics, flight simulators, virtual environments, teleoperation, and computer simulation and animation.

The common goals at the intersection of these efforts are to create detailed models of geometry and behavior and to allow realtime user control of all aspects of the scene and its visualization, using as many channels of human-computer communication as possible. Such control is certainly necessary for the author/producer of a model, and although more constrained modes of contr ol are probably appropriate for other users who are primarily consumers of a predefined model, even such users need more interactive control then just flying through a pre-modeled scene. The mouse and keyboard-based WIMP (Windows, Icons, Mice, Pointing) graphical user interfaces now standard in desktop productivity tools are insufficient for this more demanding new environment, and high-bandwidth, multimodal interaction using speech, head- and hand-tracking, and touch and force feedback haptic devices will become increasingly common. A new generation of post-WIMP interfaces is being developed that use multiple simultaneous channels of communication, input devices with more than two degrees of freedom, and realtime gesture recognition. These interfaces implement various forms of direct manipulation of 3D objects and indirect manipulation by 3D widgets that are first class objects in the scene.

What does **computer animation** mean in this far more dynamic and interactive world? Flying logos, morphing, character animation and other "classical" computer animations done by professionals will not disappear. There is no substitute for a well-crafted "narrative" designed and implemented by professionals, which the reader/consumer has minimal control over beyond a speed control. But increasingly this largely passive experience will be augmented by more interactive animation. Educators, students, industrial designers, scientists and engineers will be able to experiment with parameterized models or even modify models on the fly, as the models are simulated and animated in real time. Animation for such situations will come to mean realtime, user-controlled, model-driven simulation and animation. Again, such models may be largely created by designers, who will have far more control than typical consumers need or want, but, in principle, the degree of control will be a matter of design and not induced by technology limitations.

Many research and engineering problems remain to be solved before this more ambitious type of animation becomes common. Among these are issues in input and output device technology, software and systems integration, and 3D user interfaces for interacting with 3D time-varying scenes. Fundamental problems remain in both geometrical (shape) modeling and behavioral modeling and its simulation (e.g., physically based modeling), and in 3D interfaces to specify and control the models. Furthermore, it is no longer sufficient to consider a single user at a workstation controlling the synthetic world; protocols for multi-user interactions with the time-varying synthetic worlds must be developed, especially for large numbers of simultaneous participants.

In earlier days, animators used command languages or WIMP interfaces to design static models and then used animation scripts with low-level, direct commands to specify the batch animation of geometric objects, lights and cameras. Now we must learn to integrate higher-level procedural, declarative and rule-based control with direct interactive control by multiple simultaneous users, of more intelligent, self-sufficient objects. Specifying what kind of (constrained) behavior is appropriate to individual objects and collections of interacting objects is still very difficult, as is specifying constraints on user interaction. Indeed, these problems are as hard as those of doing the behavior simulations themselves efficiently.

Techniques for all these problems rarely scale up efficiently, and the desire for ever greater scene and behavior complexity will continue to outpace the expected hardware and software improvements for the foreseeable future. Yet, as the papers in this volume clearly show, enormous progress has been made in the past decade. Pixar's famous early eighties "Road to Point Reyes" image was a quest, as the pun on Point Reyes implied, to "Render Everything You Ever Saw". These papers illustrate today's quest, not so neatly expressed in an acronym, to "Animate Everything You Ever Imagined." It is easy to imagine that in the remainder of the current decade hitherto largely passive users will be empowered to experience their computers as an "exploratorium" populated with responsive objects and humanoid or artificial agents.

Table of Contents

Part I
Advanced Techniques in Animation

Living Pictures

LANCE WILLIAMS

ABSTRACT

Although computer animation has applied techniques from many branches of science and engineering, it has important roots in the art of animation. There have been many efforts to incorporate the art of animation, and the traditional performing arts, into the emerging medium of computer animation. Adapting computing to the arts is primarily a matter of providing interfaces artists can use, and means for utilizing art in traditional forms. Our experience suggests that pictures provide a broad and flexible basis for such an interface, and that film or video sequences -- "moving pictures" -- can be used to accommodate the lively arts as well.

Keywords: computer animation, graphical interface, rotoscoping, motion capture.

1. INTRODUCTION

Computer animation was provided much of its initial impetus by research directed toward flight simulators. Real-time visual simulation proved such a demanding computational task that many simplifying stylizations were made, some quite specific to the pilot-training task. Subsequent research has emphasized enhancing the details of the visual simulation, rather than the scope and expressive power of the stylizations. This neglected latter path is more in the direction of traditional animation, however, which has long used simplified, stylized representations to communicate form and motion.

Enhancing the realism of a visual simulation for animation purposes may mean deepening and elaborating nonvisual simulations -- elastic collisions, gravity fields, dynamics of linkages, fluid flow and continuum mechanics -- which drive the pictures. All of this is grist for the computer scientist's mill, which grinds out refined and enriched numbers according to the details of the numerical techniques employed. It also represents a convenient and unlimited computational sink for succeeding generations of newer and more powerful computers.

On the other hand, one's goal in animating on a computer may be to make something like a film. People make films to persuade, educate, entertain, and market, to inform or deceive, and these goals require more than the semblance of physical interactions. If this were not so, it would be easy to make films in the real world, where the laws of nature are very strenuously enforced, at no expense to the studio.

Of course, animators and creators of film special effects may labor long and hard, and with mixed success, to produce spectacles that seem "natural" to the audience. It is only reasonable to provide meta-physical tools by which algorithms supplement the realism affected by the artist, and it is hard to quarrel with this trend. Such realism is constantly subverted for dramatic purposes in narratives of all sorts, however, and will not in itself assist us with the problems of narrative.

Films begin and end with pictures. They are sequences of pictures, and pictures are frequently used by film makers in the process of making a film, to communicate set design, camera set-ups, and staging. More and more live-action films are now "storyboarded" like animated features prior to production.

The work described here can be seen as an effort to extend the use of pictures in the creation of computer animation. Pictures can be used to define three-dimensional models, to represent such models in the absence of any three-dimensional information, and to specify and control motion. This approach will ultimately achieve closure with the development of computer vision at the level of broad and robust segmentation, recognition, and tracking of moving imagery. In the meantime, simpler conventions of image interpretation permit pictures to convey a great deal of "graphical" information to the computer, just as interactive graphics has been used to convey information from the computer to its users.

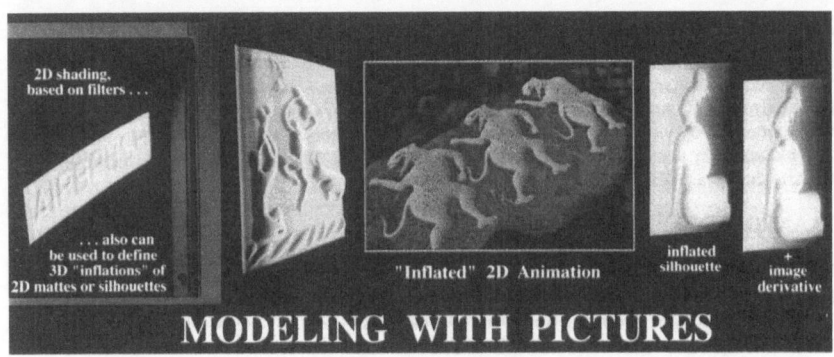

2D shading, based on filters . . .

. . . also can be used to define 3D "inflations" of 2D mattes or silhouettes

"Inflated" 2D Animation

inflated silhouette

+ image derivative

MODELING WITH PICTURES

2. MODELING WITH PICTURES

From childhood, we are taught to interpret a flat rectangular map of a spherical world, a world which is moreover not perfectly spherical, but richly detailed with surface features at many levels of scale. Thus it does not seem to be asking too much of the expressive power of such maps to suggest that they might be used in combination to model complex objects and environments. "Bump" and displacement mapping have traditionally been used in computer graphics to represent detail at the finer levels of scale, the coarser underlying shape being considered the "model" proper. This division is somewhat arbitrary; less arbitrary is the specification of the underlying topology, which might be considered the bare bones of the model. This is the graph on which the maps are draped.

In a computer animation system, we might easily expect to interact with some kind of "skeleton" representation, a kind of stick figure which stands in for the fully fleshed-out model. Traditional animators often work out their ideas with simple stick figure drawings, evaluating the general motions before drawing in the minute particulars. We shall return to this idea of skeletons later. In this section, we consider creating and editing the displacement maps which flesh these skeletons out.

As far as interfacing to traditional artists is concerned, the most successful programs in computer graphics have been interactive drawing and painting programs. Graphic artists who do commercial work for television or print, to whom the limitations of accessible computer output media are no deterrent, are particularly happy with interactive graphics on small computers. Many programs are marketed, vast libraries of "clip art" are available, and high-resolution color scanning makes work created by more traditional means easy to adapt and apply.

A special video display, similar to the luminance display on a video waveform monitor, can be used to view a video signal as a relief surface. This permits painting and illustration programs to be used to create and edit surfaces (Williams 1990). Such simple relief surfaces are the natural product of laser scanners or other scanning rangefinders, and traditional image processing as well as interactive painting has proved valuable in editing such range images. The images which define these surfaces can then be divided into patch meshes, which reparametrize the displacement maps.

Such "painting" of relief surfaces is not the only way that a 2D picture can be used to define a 3D model. Contour triangulation, extrusion of outlines (contours of a thresholded matte), and "sweeps" of interpolated profiles along space curves, are all traditional means of operating on 2D specifications to produce 3D forms. Where they apply, they are especially valuable, for they can be defined by pictures and are hence self-documenting. In the form of pictures, they are also subject to all software for the creation and editing of pictures, which becomes 3D modeling software by extension.

3. ANIMATING PICTURES

One example of such image processing is the low-pass filtering used to create the effect of airbrush shading on a matte (Williams 1991). Viewed as a relief surface, the matte can be "airbrushed" so as to become an inflation of the silhouette. An interesting approach to automatically creating a 3D model from a picture and an associated matte is to "inflate" the matte as a displacement map, then blend into this map a small percentage of a first derivative or high-pass filter applied to the picture.

The original goal of this filtering process, however, was to directly simulate a shaded object without an intervening 3D description. This is an example of pictures being used as graphic primitives; in this case, a shading rule is defined based on two dimensional shape. Such shading is a natural extension of the soft drop-shadows often used with type. A soft shadow (opposite the direction of light) is dropped inside the silhouette to be shaded, and a soft highlight (on the side facing the direction of light) mattes in a highlight color (once again, confined to the interior of the silhouette).

Another way in which pictures can be used as graphic primitives can be illustrated by any two-dimensional animation system. If the system is used to interpolate a drawing depicting the front of a three-dimensional object to another drawing depicting the object from the side, an apparent 3D rotation is produced. This rotation will be more convincing if more drawings are used to interpolate the ninety degrees from front to profile. The important thing is that the drawings, interpolated in image space, serve to represent objects in a three-dimensional world.

Range images were introduced as "images" in the previous section, and their use as graphical primitives is well-established. Since they have a range coordinate at every point, surface normals can be derived, and the surface can be shaded. These surfaces, optionally reflected about the image plane, really are 3D objects from the standpoint of the traditional graphics pipeline. As relief surfaces (functional surfaces, height fields) they are a special case, for which fast shading and transformation algorithms can be developed (Venolia 1990).

4. PICTURE-DRIVEN ANIMATION

Tensor product "deformations" have been introduced as 3D modeling tools (and applied to 3D animation) only relatively recently. More general 2D deformations were applied to the body parts of cartoon characters for animation purposes by Computer Image Corporation in the early 1970's (Harrison, Honey, Tajchman and Parker, 1973; Tajchman 1974). Once a set of animated deformations were created, they could be applied to any character whose body parts could be placed within the undeformed rectangles used to define the motion. Such "hierarchical" animation, seldom applied in practice by the group that developed the idea, is an important conceptual contribution. It is one avenue by which "clip motion" (libraries of previously developed animations, in analogy to "clip art") might become useful to film makers.

Shortly after the picture-driven animation methods of Computer Image were developed, deformations based on the movements of an underlying "skeleton" were applied to 2D animated drawings (Burtnyk 1976). This powerful and productive idea has subsequently been used in 2D animation with a smoother interpolant (Overveld 1990), and has also served as the basis for two-dimensional "morphing" (Beier 1991). The most elaborate extension of this sort of simple skeleton is a smooth three-dimensional interpolant which permits "skeleton" animation of 3D characters (Chuang 1990). Once again, this is an important approach to reusable motion libraries, since the motion defined for a skeleton can be applied to any model in which the skeleton is embedded. Using the same formulas by which skeletons control bodies, one skeleton can "drive" another (even if they are topologically quite different). In any of these contexts, the spatial remapping described by Patterson, Litwinowicz and Greene (1991) can be used to refine the geometric conformation of skeletons and bodies of differing proportions.

It is clear in discussing these techniques that "picture-driven" animation is a term that can easily be applied to animation of matted images "shaded" in 2D, or to animation created by deforming pictures, as Computer Image and Overveld have done. It also obviously applies to morphing between pictures, since the impression of a metamorphosing three-dimensional form is conveyed by an interpolation between images. These possibilities have many useful applications in film making, and we have gained considerable experience with the use of pictures as animation primitives with the "Inkwell" animation testbed (Litwinowicz 1991).

"Picture-driven" animation was a locution originally applied to computer interpolation of keyframe drawings, because the specification input to the computer was strictly drawings (rather than scripts, or lists of parameter values), although some of these drawings were paths for motions to follow, and some were hand-drawn graphs of control functions (such as acceleration along a path). A surprising number of authors on the subject have contrasted keyframing, which is the archetype of picture-driven animation, with physical simulation. This curious misunderstanding should have been laid firmly to rest by simulation programs which take key frames as input (Isaacs and Cohen 1987; Witkin and Kass 1988; Cohen 1992). The real contrast here is between picture-driven and script-driven animation. It is straightforward for an interactive graphics system to output its frames in the form of text, although this is difficult for pictures in general. In the form of text, the frames can be interpreted and edited by human beings, and can be manipulated by the wealth of software developed for "word processing." It is equally straightforward to turn these simple, unambiguous text descriptions into pictures with a rendering program. What is not so simple is using text at the level of a movie script, from which only a small minority of human beings can produce a satisfactory performance.

As deformations, and skeletons, become three-dimensional, what could be meant by "picture-driven" animation? We might simply be speaking of an interactive 3D keyframing system, where the user interacts with a computer generated "picture" of the scene, but perhaps the word "picture" connotes an image without an accompanying 3D model. We might mean the use of an image to define a flow field, which controls the motion of a flurry of snow or the flight of a flock of bats. But there is another important sense in which 3D animation may be "picture-driven": when moving pictures are the input, and the animated subject is controlled by tracking motion in a sequence of pictures.

4.1. Recording Motion

The work of Marey, Muybridge and the Gilbreths introduced the graphical and photographic recording of human and animal motion, in the former two cases, before the use of motion pictures (Marey 1873; Muybridge 1887; Gilbreth & Gilbreth 1917). This pioneering technology is still quite relevant to the communication and representation of motion in images; different methods of depicting a sequence in a single image were essayed which can be meaningfully applied in our animation interfaces today.

The invention of the rotoscope made the application of recorded motion to animation practical. Although its significance is often understated by traditional animators, the rotoscope has been used extensively in virtually every successful animation of human figures. Snow White, for example, was animated from very extensive film studies, including the use of the rotoscope. The actor's performance is captured by the film, with all its emotional nuance, along with physics of flawless plausibility. Less human, more fanciful characters have less to learn from filmed human motion. A human performance would have to be adapted to the idiosyncrasies of the cartoon universe to be helpful in this context, but this is a development which can now be seriously considered.

The Disney "imagineers" deserve credit for developing both three-dimensional keyframing (using wireframe 3D models on a vector-display, with linear interpolation between keys) and 3D recording of human motion using linkages of goniometers on the actor. Both of these developments occurred in the 1960's, but neither was used for animation. These systems were developed for control of the robot "audio-animatrons" which were gradually populating the Disney theme parks. In the animation arena, Computer Image Corporation once again deserves credit for pioneering work. One of their early brochures shows animator Chuck Jones in harness, wearing a goniometric rig which permits an (analog!) computer-animated character to reflect his movements on a CRT screen, in real time.

The mechanical linkages used to record a performer's motion were reliable but clumsy. Subsequent efforts in this direction (which originates in the work of Marey) have included multiaxis "Waldos" for computer-aided puppetry (Robertson 1988), waist-up goniometric rigs used to control animation at PDI, and the VPL Data Glove and Data Suit. This technology has already become a consumer product in the form of the Mattel "Power Glove" (Gardner 1989).

Graphs of forces and angles are graphical representations, and can be used to mediate interactions in computer animation systems. Of more direct relevance to our subject are motion recording systems based on image capture. An early venture of this sort in the computer animation field, DeWitt's "pantomation" (DeWitt 1982), performed realtime tracking of multiple colored spots in the view of a video camera. The coordinates of the tracked spots could be used to control simple animations in real time, or to mediate other realtime interactions (playing music under the control of the subject's gestures, for example).

Capturing motion data from a live performer addresses one of the fundamental problems of physical simulation: it cannot model volition. For "actuator" systems, where the forces and torques of the physical system are constantly modified by volition, physical simulation solves only the strictly mechanical portion of the task. Since the arm can adapt to an unexpectedly heavy cup by increasing the force to lift it, tasks are performed by planning trajectories and adapting actuator outputs to achieve them; the result is far closer to 3D keyframing, with or without physics, than it is to any action expressible in forward dynamics. Even in "goal directed" control systems, the goals of the system must be expressed in terms of its physical states. Emotional states -- critical for dramatic purposes -- are more elusive. A relatively early paper on the integration of different types of motion control calls for, "creation of a knowledge base containing parameter values of physical systems which provide reference animation sequences . . . the actuator forces and torques needed to produce the reference motion either obtained by descriptive models or by image analysis, can be computed through inverse dynamics." (Hegron, Palamidese, and Thalmann 1989). Besides emphasizing the usefulness of such libraries of motion parameters with or without the estimates of mass matrices, etc. necessary for dynamic simulation, it is worth observing that motion libraries of human beings will contain information of another type. From the reference cited, ". . . psychological aspects are very important and the subtleties of motion should be dependent on the character's personality." These psychological aspects are the very bread and butter of traditional character animation. The animator, with human empathy, can involve the emotions of the audience with the actions of the animated character. To imagine that we can embody the "psychology" of a human character in an algorithm is to take a very long view. It can confidently be expected that text-to-speech algorithms will be performing dramatic readings of poetry before our animated characters can be outfitted with elaborate "psychologies." If this is the goal, however, it can be achieved only by collating the physical correlates of human emotion with human judgments of that emotion. There is no physical measurement that can quantify happiness or sadness; we can correlate physical measurements only with human (and intrinsically subjective) assessments of the emotions experienced. If we want, ultimately, not only to make a character stand up and walk across the room (which any extra from central casting, some trained animals, and a few robots, can do), but also to display "personality," our task begins with recording and categorizing the characteristic motions of different personalities.

It would seem that capturing motion from nature would be similar to scanning texture maps or the shape of objects from nature, an obviously useful incorporation of data from the real world. In the case of texture maps, many painting, warping, and image processing utilities are available to adapt a scanned texture to the requirements of a particular model or scene. For 3D models, and for motions, the adaptive utilities are not so widespread or easily available. A number of 3D deformation schemes have been applied to scanned models for purposes of animation, and these distortions can also be employed to adapt a model's shape for other purposes. In the realm of motion capture, we are only beginning to see the sort of warping, remapping, interpolation, composition, and enchainement which will provide libraries of captured motion their expressive and dramatic power (Schultz, 1988; Maiocchi and Pernici, 1990; Patterson, Litwinowicz, and Greene 1991).

Expanding the control systems of computer animation to handle motion data acquired from nature seems a difficult but rewarding undertaking. Such software will range from very low-level function editing, to inference of the parameters of dynamic models from the data. Kalman filters will play an important role in data acquisition and adaptation. Techniques from the world of computer music, particularly timbre synthesis and the control of time, should prove valuable. High-level abstractions of physical processes, like the "lag, drag, and wiggle" filters described in (Litwinowicz 1991), or the concept of "dynamic similarity" (Alexander 1991), will offer simple encapsulations of complex adaptations. Skeleton and deformation techniques will support the application of motions from one model to another, animation of objects for which no dynamic model exists, or for which the simulation is applied only to the simple skeleton (Overveld 1990). All of these approaches lead us to considerations quite outside the literature of control systems, robotics, or literal mechanics. Ultimately, they are the same sort of considerations to be observed in transposing a musical key, adapting the steps of a dance to a tune of a different measure, or tailoring the proportions of a fountain to a courtyard. Perhaps the most difficult accomodations are made in adapting the prancing of a goat to a dancer with only two legs, a swordfight to a staircase, or a bicycle ride to the constraints of the tightrope. In adaptation, the lively arts may serve as our most enduring and instructive model.

REFERENCES

Alexander, R.M., (1991) How dinosaurs ran. Scientific American, April, 1991, pp.130-136.

Biomechanics, Inc., 200 N. Cobb Parkway, Suite 142, Marietta, GA 30062, U.S.A. (404) 424-8195.

Brennan, S., (1982) Caricature generator. MS thesis, Visual Studies, School of Architecture, Massachusetts Institute of Technology, Cambridge, MA.

Burtnyk, N., and Wein, M., (1976) Interactive skeleton techniques for enhancing motion dynamics in key frame animation. Communications of the ACM, volume 19, no. 10, October 1976.

Chuang, R. (1990) The DOT character animation system developed at Pacific Data Images, Sunnyvale, CA, U.S.A. Personal communication with the author.

Cohen, M. (1992) Interactive Spacetime Control for Animation. Computer Graphics 26, 2, Proceedings of SIGGRAPH 1992, July 26-31, Chicago, IL, pp. 293-302.

DeWitt, T., and Edelstein, P. (1982) Pantomation: a system for position tracking. IEEE 1982 Symposium on Small Computers in the Arts, Philadelphia, PA

Frizot, M. (1984) Etienne-Jules Marey. Paris, FR: Centre National de la Photographie.

Gardner, D.L. (1989) The power glove. Design News, December 4, 1989, pp. 63-668.

Gilbreth, F.B., and Gilbreth, L.M., (1917) Applied motion study. Sturgis & Walton Co., NY, 1917.

Goodell, J.D. (1984) Computer created actors. Screen Actor, Screen Actors' Guild, Inc., August 1984, pp. 68-73.

Harrison, L., Honey, F.J., Tajchman, E.J., Parker, M.M. (1973) Digitally Controlled Computer Animation Generating System. United States Patent No. 3,747,087, July, 1973.

Hegron, G., Palamidese, P., and Thalmann, D. (1989) Motion control in animation, simulation, and visualization. Computer Graphics Forum 8, North-Holland, pp. 347-352.

International Olympic Committee, (1991) First IOC world congress on sport sciences. Institut Nacional d'Educacio Fisica de Catalunya (INFC), Barcelona.

Isaacs, P.M., and Cohen, M.F. (1987) Controlling dynamic simulation with kinematic constraints, behavior functions, and inverse dynamics. Computer Graphics 21, 4, Proceedings of SIGGRAPH 1987, July 27-31, Anaheim, CA, pp. 215-224.

Lee, M.W., and Kunii, T.L. (1991) Animation Design: A Database-oriented animation design method with a video image analysis capability. In: Magnenat-Thalmann, N., and Thalmann, D., (ed) Computer Animation '91. Springer-Verlag, Tokyo, pp. 97-112.

Litwinowicz, P., (1991) Inkwell: a 21/2-D animation system. Computer Graphics 25, 4, Proceedings of SIGGRAPH 1991, Las Vegas, NV, pp.113-122.
Maiocchi, R., and Pernici, P. (1990) Directing an animated scene with autonomous actors. The Visual Computer, 6, pp. 359-371.

Marey, E.J., (1873) La machine animale, locomotion terrestre et aérienne, Paris, 1873.

Marey, E.J., (1874) Animal mechanism. The International Scientific Series, volume XI, London and New York, 1874.

Motion Analysis Corp., 3650 N. Laughlin Road, Santa Rosa, CA 95403, U.S.A.

Muybridge, E.M. (1887) Human and animal locomotion. Dover Books, 1979; republication of: Animal locomotion; an electro-photographic investigation of consecutive phases of animal movements, University of Pennsylvania, Philadelphia, 1887.

Overveld, C.W.A.M. (1990) A technique for motion specification in computer animation. The Visual Computer, 6, pp. 106-116.

Patterson, E., Litwinowicz, P., and Greene, N., (1991) Facial animation by spatial mapping. In: Magnenat-Thalmann, N., and Thalmann, D., (ed) Computer Animation '91. Springer-Verlag, Tokyo, pp. 31-44.

Robertson, B. (1988) Mike, the talking head. Computer Graphics World, July, 1988.

Sabiston, W.R., (1991) Extracting 3D motion from hand-drawn animated figures. MS thesis, Media Arts and Sciences Section, School of Architecture and Planning, Massachusetts Institute of Technology, Cambridge, MA.

Schultz, A., (1988) Generating parameterized gaits from recorded kinematic data. MS thesis, Computing Science, University of Waterloo, Waterloo, Ontario.

Shawn, T., (1954) Every little movement. Dance Horizons, Inc., Brooklyn, NY.

Simgraphics Engineering Corp., 1137 Huntington Drive, Suite A1, South Pasadena, CA, U.S.A. (213) 255-0900.

Tajchman, E.J. (1974) Computer Aided Animation Utilizing a Mapping Process. Ph.D. dissertation, Dept. of Electrical Engineering, University of Denver, Denver, CO, April, 1974.

Venolia, D., Williams, L., (1990) Virtual integral holography. Proceedings of the SPIE 1259-11, Extracting Meaning from Complex Data: Processing, Display, Interaction, February, 1990, Santa Clara, CA, pp. 99-105.

Witkin, A., and Kass, M. (1988) Spacetime constraints. Computer Graphics 22, 4, Proceedings of SIGGRAPH 1988, August 1-5, Atlanta, GA, pp.159-168.

Williams, L., (1990) Performance-driven facial animation. Computer Graphics 24, 4, Proceedings of SIGGRAPH 1990, August 6-10, Dallas, TX, pp.235-242.

Williams, L., (1990) 3D Paint. Computer Graphics 24, 2, 1990 Symposium on Interactive 3D Graphics, Snowbird, UT, pp. 225-233.

Williams, L., (1991) Shading in two dimensions. Proceedings of Graphics Interface '91, June 3-7, Calgary, Alberta, pp. 143-151.

Lance Williams is a research scientist at Apple Computer, Inc. He studied computer graphics at the University of Utah, and went on to the New York Institute of Technology's Computer Graphics Lab in 1976. At NYIT, Williams developed a range of special effects technologies now in wide use. Creative work included the script for a prototype 3D computer animated feature, "The Works." Williams left the New York Institute of Technology in 1986, after serving briefly as president of CGL Studios. After leaving NYIT/CGL, he worked as an independent consultant for GLOBO television in Rio de Janeiro, and for Henson Associates (the muppet people) in New York. In October 1988, he joined the Advanced Technology Group at Apple Computer, Inc., where he is researching interactive computer animation. Feature film credits include "Lensman," a Japanese animated feature, and "Lawnmover Man," a science-fiction film on the theme of virtual reality.

Address: Apple Computer, MS: 301-3J
          1 Infinite Loop, Cupertino, CA 95014 U.S.A.
          email: lance@apple.com fax: (408) 862-5520

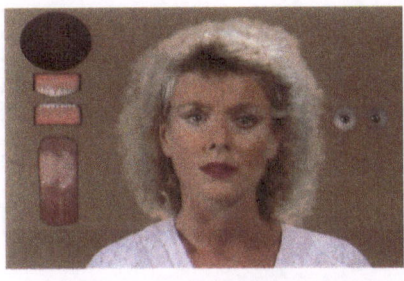

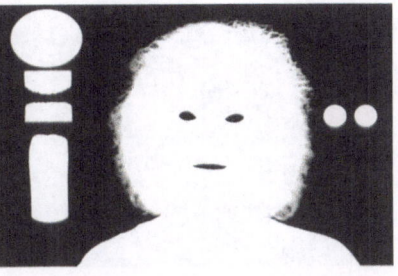

A face to be animated is divided into parts, and the parts assigned a rendering priority

Although the parts are rendered as meshes of irregular shape, mattes capture edge details

ANIMATING PICTURES

    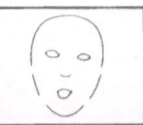

The top row of line drawings control the animation process. These keyframes were derived from a recorded subject. Mapped to corresponding features of the faces in the first column, the same key drawings drive the expressions of the animated characters in the lower 3 rows.

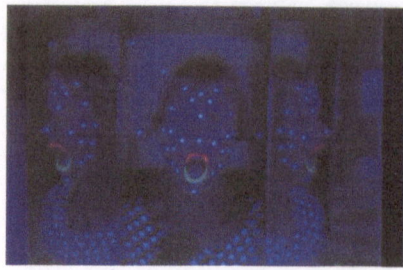

Mirrors reflect the subject's flourescent dots and lips from two sides as well as a front view, permitting 3D digitization

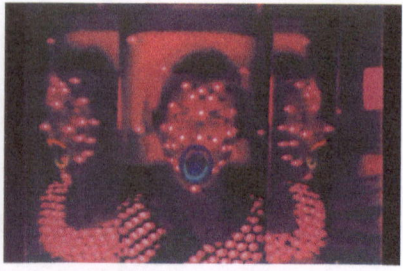

Image enhancement outside the region of the subject's mouth provides a better view of the motion-capture set-up.

PICTURE-DRIVEN ANIMATION

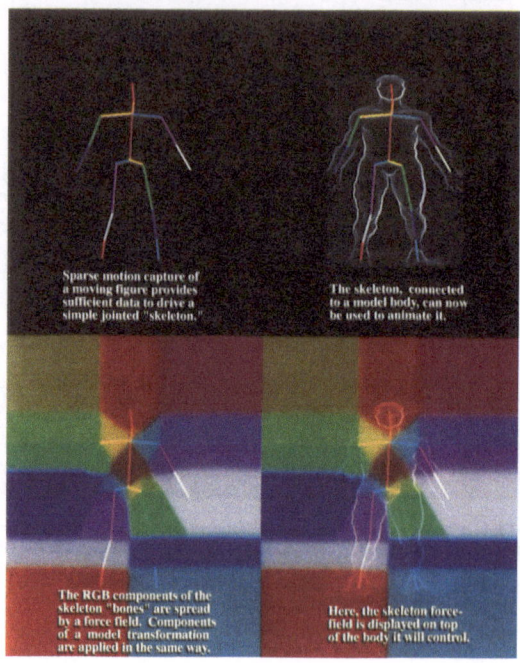

Sparse motion capture of a moving figure provides sufficient data to drive a simple jointed "skeleton."

The skeleton, connected to a model body, can now be used to animate it.

The RGB components of the skeleton "bones" are spread by a force field. Components of a model transformation are applied in the same way.

Here, the skeleton force-field is displayed on top of the body it will control.

Simplex Based Animation

HERVÉ DELINGETTE, YASUHIKO WATANABE, and YASUHITO SUENAGA

ABSTRACT

We propose a methodology for animating complex models based on simplex mesh representation and deformation. A simplex mesh is characterized by a connectivity between vertices of three and can be obtained by duality from a triangulation. In addition to their generality of representation, simplex meshes have a compact and unambiguous shape description, related to the notion of mean curvature.

We devised a physically-based metamorphism algorithm that rests on the intrinsic shape representation of these meshes. This algorithm handles transformations between objects of different topology or boundary conditions. Various simplex mesh shapes were extracted from range images or some triangulated data and then metamorphosed by applying generalized mesh transformations.

Keywords: object representation, duality, triangulation, modeling, metamorphism.

1 INTRODUCTION

Physically based techniques use a large set of nodes to represent objects which makes them well suited for generating complex shapes. Each node is moved independently according to Newton's law of motion. A "cohesion" force is used to correlate the displacements of neighboring nodes thereby constraining the freedom of the surface. Physically based modeling gives the model a dynamic behavior resulting in a more intuitive interaction.

First introduced by Terzopoulos, Kass and Witkin[10][20] to extract contour or axial-symmetric surfaces from video images, elastically deformable models have been extensively used both in computer vision and computer graphics[4][6]. The equations of motion are derived by minimizing quadratic elastic energies such as the bivariate generalized spline functionals[18], through some variational principals. Solutions are computed over time by using finite differences with explicit [6] or semi-implicit[4] schemes, or finite-element analysis[2]. External constraints have been designed to fit range-data[6][20], to enhance the user interface or to simulate physical phenomena such as object contact, viscoelasticity or animated characters.

Though appealing for their clay-like behavior, elastic models are difficult to manipulate because they do not respond to global constraints. Shaping an object with local constraints such as assigning node positions or normal orientations requires too many operations and is practically ineffective. Welch and Witkin[21] proposed a framework where curves can be attached to a tensor-product spline surface while minimizing some objective function. Curves

13

provide a natural boundary condition of surface models and handling curves instead of surfaces leads to improved interfaces since three-dimensional curves can be directly input.

Our modeling system is physically-based as well, but a different surface representation is introduced. Simplex meshes are general enough to represent surfaces of all topology and boundary conditions. In particular they overcome the pole problem that arise when representing a closed object with tensor-product splines. Moreover, we can add or remove nodes from the mesh structure in a natural manner without perturbing the mesh continuity and connectivity. Internal constraints may be defined in terms of intrinsic parameters without great computational cost. Unlike most elastic deformable models algorithms, internal constraints are achieved through the minimization of some local energy. Therefore, we can consider a simplex mesh as a network of independant particles with fixed connectivity. Global interaction is handled though contours similarly to Welch and Witkin[21].

Section 2 introduce the concept of simplex mesh while Sections 3 and 4 describe surface and contour internal constraints. Range data interaction and mesh transformation operations are discussed in Sections 5 and 6.

2 SIMPLEX MESH

2.1 Definition

Among all the possible surface representations, polyhedra are of wide use in computer graphics. Most polyhedral representations employ either triangular or rectangular patches. Triangulation handles planar patches, therefore, surface normals may be computed along the surface without ambiguity. On the other hand, rectangular grids can be interpreted as a tensor product of two splines which decreases the complexity of the representation. Both representations share the same geometric property as to yield a regular tessellation of the plane.

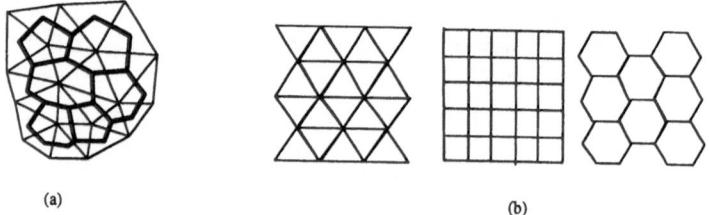

(a)   (b)

Figure 1:   (a) Dual of triangulation; (b) the three regular tessellation of plane

However, there is a third regular tessellation pattern (see Figure 1(b)) based on hexagons which can be developed from the duality of regular triangulation. The duality of polyhedra associates faces with vertices and edges with edges and plays an important role in the field of regular polytopes.

We introduce another powerful polyhedral representation of three-dimensional surfaces which is characterized by a connectivity between vertices that is equal to three and that are dual triangulations (see Figure 1 (a)). We coined the word "Simplex Mesh" to describe a mesh representing a surface in dimension n for which each node is linked to n neighbors.

Therefore in a simplex mesh, we can define around each vertex a n-simplex made of $n + 1$ nodes. In particular, for a three-dimensional surface, a tetrahedron, the 3-simplex, is defined at each node. Table 1 summarizes the connectivity of the three representations and their dual nature.

	Vertex to Vertex Connectivity	Face to Face Connectivity	Regular Tessellation
Triangulation	$n \geq 3$	3	Equilateral Triangles
Rectangular Grid	4	4	Squares
Simplex Mesh	3	$n \geq 3$	Regular Hexagons

Table 1: Properties of triangulation, rectangular grid and simplex mesh

We will consider only closed meshes for which the three-connectivity is valid at each node. The Euler relation links the number of vertices V, the number edges E, the number of faces F and the genus g of the surface :

$$F - \frac{V}{2} = 2 * (1 - g) \qquad E = \frac{3V}{2} \qquad (1)$$

A simplex mesh $\mathcal{M}$ is fully described by its n vertices $\{P_i\}$ and by the $3n/2$ vertex to vertex relations $\{(P_i, P_j)\}$. From this, vertex to face and edge to face relations can be derived and each face can be consistently oriented. We will write $N_j(i)$ as the index of the $j^{th}, (j = 1, 2, 3)$ neighbor of node number $i, (i = 0, .., n - 1)$ so that $P_{N_1(i)}, P_{N_2(i)}, P_{N_3(i)}$ are the three nodes connected to P_i.

The advantage of the simplex-mesh is that a normal vector can be defined at each node by considering the normal at the plane defined by its three-neighbors. Furthermore we can associate each tetrahedron with a circumscribed sphere which provides a measure of mean curvature of the surface. This is in contrast to triangulated mesh that provide a measure of gaussian curvature through the spherical-excess of dihedral angles[11].

Simplex meshes like triangulations can represent all orientable surfaces. This is in contrast with rectangular grids that exhibits poles for closed surfaces of genus 0.

Simplex-meshes have a vertex to vertex connectivity of three but each face consists of a variable number of vertices. We define a *p-face* as a face consisting of p vertices. Meshes whose faces have the same number of vertices are called regular. If the surface has one handle (genus strictly positive), it is possible to build a regular hexagonal simplex-mesh with a variable number of nodes. On the other hand, for closed surface without handles, there are only three regular models : tetrahedron, cube and dodecahedron.

Another advantage of simplex meshes is the possibility of introducing the notion of *End* or "empty face". A face is labeled as an end when we want to create a hole in the surface. The numbers of ends and handles are powerful characteristics for classifying surfaces. For example, a cylinder has two ends while a sphere has none; both have no handles. On the other hand, a torus has one handle but no ends.

Precise rendering of simplex meshes is difficult since each face is actually wedged and normals are impossible to define at each face. The current solution is to build a triangulated model by associating the center of a p-face with each vertex. The face center is computed as the centroid of the p vertices which tends to flatten the overall shape.

2.2 Equation of Motion

The dynamics of each vertex is given by a newtonian law of motion:

$$m\frac{d^2 P_i}{dt^2} = -\gamma\frac{dP_i}{dt} + \vec{F_{int}} + \vec{F_{ext}} \tag{2}$$

where m is the mass unit of a node and γ is the damping factor. $\vec{F_{int}}$ is the force created to make the surface continuous while $\vec{F_{ext}}$ corresponds to external constraints defined by either the user or some three-dimensional data.

Time is discretized as $t_i = t_0 + i * \Delta t$ and Equation (2) is integrated over time using finite differences with explicit scheme. A more stable though more complex implementation would use semi-implicit schemes[4]. If P_i^t is the position of vertex i at time t then the discretized law of motion is :

$$P_i^{t+1} = (1 - \gamma)(P_i^t - P_i^{t-1}) + \vec{F_{int}} + \vec{F_{ext}} \tag{3}$$

$\vec{F_{int}}$ and $\vec{F_{ext}}$ are computed at time t.

3 SHAPE FUNCTIONALS

The internal forces of a physically-based model determines the model's response to external constraints. Such response should be both intuitive and invariant by isometries.

Researchers have proposed a wide variety of elastic energy terms. Energies proportional to the squared curvature[12][9][1] have the advantage of being physically meaningful but they do not accept circles[5] or spheres as optimum. Moreton et al.[14] introduced a fairness measure proportional to the squared derivative of curvature which yields spheres, tori and cylinders as optimum shape.

Curvature-based energies lead to complex non-linear expressions of $\vec{F_{int}}$. Linear elastic energies where the curvature is approximated by second order derivatives have been extensively used in the computer-aided-geometric design field[7] as well as for deformable modeling [21][2][6][20]. In the generalized formulation, the energy is composed of a stretching term and a bending term. Some weights can be adjusted to take into account surface discontinuities and normal discontinuities. Linear elasticity has proved to be efficient but there is no guarantee that fair shapes will be delivered since they are not expressed in terms of intrinsic parameters. They have a tendency to consistently flatten high curvature parts and do not accept circles or spheres as optimum[5].

Our framework does not derive $\vec{F_{int}}$ from the minimization of some global elastic energy. Instead we associate with each node P_i a local energy S_i that characterizes the state of local tetrahedron $(P_i, P_{N1(i)}, P_{N2(i)}, P_{N3(i)})$. More precisely the position of P_i can be determined from the position of its three neighbors by the relation:

$$P_i = \underbrace{\epsilon_{1i}P_{N_1(i)} + \epsilon_{2i}P_{N_2(i)} + \epsilon_{3i}P_{N_3(i)}}_{F} + L(r_i, d_i, \phi_i)\vec{N_i} \tag{4}$$

where

- F is the foot of P_i.

- r_i is the radius of the circle circumscribing $(P_{N_1(i)}, P_{N_2(i)}, P_{N_3(i)})$.

- d_i is the distance between F and the circle's center.

- ϕ_i is the simplex angle at P_i.

- $L(r_i, d, \phi_i)$ is the function described in appendix A.

- $\vec{N}_i$ is the normal vector at plane $(P_{N_1(i)}, P_{N_2(i)}, P_{N_3(i)})$.

Figure 2 shows the relation in the local tetrahedron:

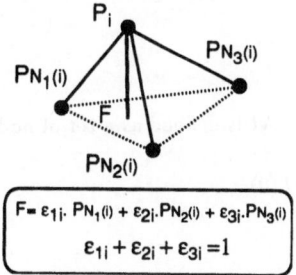

Figure 2: Curvature definition for a simplex angle ϕ_i

The simplex angle ϕ_i characterizes the mean curvature at P_i. With each node P_i we associate a simplex angle $\phi_i^\star$ for which the local tetrahedron $(P_i, P_{N_1(i)}, P_{N_2(i)}, P_{N_3(i)})$ is in its rest position. $\phi_i^\star$ corresponds to the natural state of the local tetrahedron or its state of minimum energy. If we write $P_i^\star$ as the position of node P_i if the simplex angle was $\phi_i^\star$ then the energy $\mathcal{S}_i$ of the local tetrahedron is:

$$\mathcal{S}_i = \tfrac{\alpha_i}{2} P_i P_i^{\star 2} \qquad (0 \le \alpha_i \le 0.5) \tag{5}$$

$\vec{F_{int}}$ is the gradient of this energy and since $P_i^\star$ is independant of P_i:

$$\vec{F_{int}} = \alpha_i \, \overrightarrow{P_i P_i^\star} \qquad (0 \le \alpha_i \le 0.5) \tag{6}$$

In this framework each node can be seen as an independant particle that interacts with its three neighbors and their surrounding nodes. Interacting sets of particles have been used in computer graphics to model viscous fluids [13] or thermoplasticity[19]. Szeliski[17] used particles that tended to align their orientations to interpolate 3D data without a priori knowledge of connectivity or topology. There is one important difference between simplex mesh and particles system in that simplex meshes constrain nodes connectivity to three which restricts the generality of representation but leads to smoother shapes and more efficient computation.

Different constraints are set depending on the computation of $\phi_i^\star$. We define three types of constraints applicable to any part of a simplex mesh.

The first constraint enforces smoothness along the surface and corresponds to a default option when no underlying shape is known. Resulting surfaces are piecewise C^2 continuous and their fairness is guaranteed since the laplacian of mean curvature over the mesh is null: $\Delta H = 0$. Spheres, cylinders, cones satisfy this equation as well as minimal surfaces for which $H = 0$. Minimal surfaces are of great interests in computer-aided design since they minimize the surface area spanned between two curves.

The second constraint is related to the notion of rest shape to which the model converges when no external constraints are applied. A representation of simplex meshes invariant by rotation, translation and scale is used to describe the underlying shape.

The third constraint concerns the adding of surface normal discontinuities in order to model sharp edges or conic points.

4 CONTOURS

4.1 Definition

A contour $\mathcal{C}$ attached to a mesh $\mathcal{M}$ is defined as a set of nodes $\{P_{L(i)}\}, (i = 0, l)$ such that:

- $L(-1) = L(l), L(l+1) = L(0)$
- $\forall i, \exists j, L(i+1) = N_j(L(i))$
- $\forall i, \forall j, P_{L(i)} \neq P_{L(j)}$

Therefore, $\mathcal{C}$ is a closed curve with consecutive nodes connected in mesh $\mathcal{M}$. The third condition states that $\mathcal{C}$ does not self-intersect (see Figure 3). When a contour encloses a p-face, the face is labelled as an end and the surface is trimmed along the contour. A contour is managed as an entity independantly from the mesh it is attached to. A node is attached to no more than one curve.

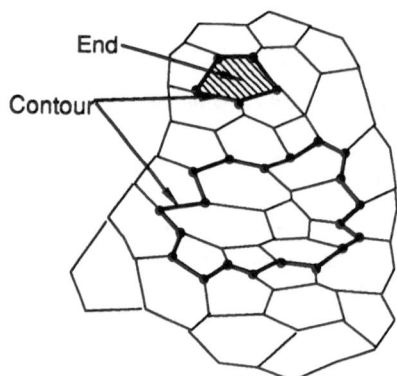

Figure 3: Two contours attached to a simplex mesh.

A contour is handled independently of the surface mesh and is also subjected to internal and external constraints. The only difference in terms of implementation is that internal force $\vec{F_{int}}$ at each node $P_{L(i)}$ is computed in order to ensure the elastic behavior of the contour instead of the surface model.

We propose an elastic functional that does not entail any shrinking effect and that exhibits stable behavior. Under this internal constraint contours are smoothed and converge toward their stable shape, circles. The expression of $\vec{F_{int}}$ is a generalization of functionals described in [5] and previous section.

4.2 Boundary Conditions

Boundary conditions describe how contours are embedded inside a mesh and are therefore important control parameters for shaping a model. The simplex mesh provide a simple way of set boundary conditions by controlling simplex angles $\phi_{L(i)}$ at each node of curve $\{P_{L(i)}\}$. The underlying assumption is that smoothness forces apply to surface nodes located around each contour. We defined two types of surface-contour constraints:

Curvature Constraint : Mean curvature is constrained at nodes surrounding a contour.

Tangent Constraint : The angle between the tangent plane and the contour normal as measured around the contour tangent vector, intuitively corresponds to the angle between the surface and contour. This angle can be controlled through the value of $\phi_{L(i)}$

Figure 9 shows a vase created from a cylinder and five contours. Two contours are defined by interpolation of four non-coplanar points and have tangent constraints of $\pi/4$ and $-\pi/4$ respectively while the three others are circles with null curvature constraints. Tangent constraints guarantees a C^1 continuity across a contour while curvature constraints leads to C^0 continuity only.

5   DATA CONSTRAINT

Three dimensional ranging device have gained popularity in computer graphics for building realistic models of existing objects. Physically based modeling systems are well suited for this task since data is often noisy or incomplete. The fitting process is performed by a potential field that drags the surface model close to the three dimensional data while the interpolating capability results from the internal smoothness constraints. Local minima may arise especially when models are initialized far from the data. We avoid this problem by interactively positionning and scaling the initial mesh as to get a reasonable estimate of the object shape. The mouse may be used also to drag a mesh out of a local minimum.

We follow a similar formulation as in [6] where the potential field has a limited range. For each mode P_i we determine the closest point in the data structure $P_{Cl(i)}$ and compute the attracting force as:

$$\vec{F_{ext}} = \beta_i G \left(\frac{\| \overrightarrow{P_i P_{Cl(i)}} \|}{D} \right) (\overrightarrow{P_i P_{Cl(i)}} \cdot \vec{N_i}) \vec{N_i} \qquad (7)$$

where $\vec{N_i}$ is the surface normal at P_i and $G(x)$ is the function of Figure 4. D is the maximum distance at which some data points attracts a node point and is computed as a function of the overall mesh size. The function $G(x)$ is designed such that the force is linear when data is within a distance D of the surface model but decreases sharply otherwise. A bounded range potential field is important in order to limit the influence of outliers or to models objects with narrow shapes. In order to get a smooth deformation in presence of sparse data, the force is projected on the normal surface vector.

The search for the closest point $P_{Cl(i)}$ is theoretically in $O(m^2)$ for a $m \times m$ range image but we were able to decrease the complexity to $O(m)$ by restricting the search along one image line.

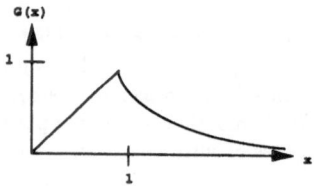

Figure 4: Function $G(x)$.

6 MESH TRANSFORMATION

6.1 Definition

A mechanism for mesh refinement is important to provide the maximum of flexibility to a modeling system. Simplex mesh structures can be locally altered without exhibiting any irregularity in the mesh connectivity. Therefore, nodes may be added or deleted locally without perturbing geometric continuity and a mesh is handled as an indefinitely expendable surface.

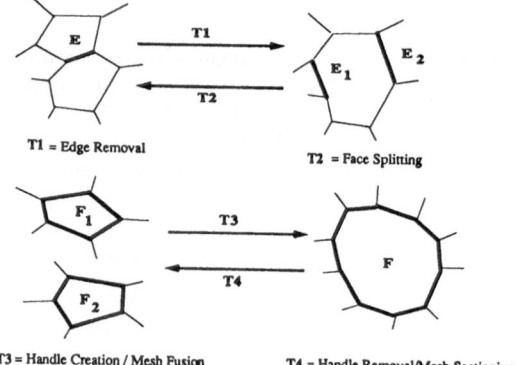

Figure 5: The four basic mesh transformations

We define four basic mesh transformation operations (see Figure 5). The first two, T_1 and T_2, are the inverse of each other and can be interpreted as, respectively, edge removal and face splitting operations. These transformations do not change the mesh topology but instead decrease or increase the density of nodes. T_3 is interpreted as a handle creation operation if both faces belong to the same mesh or as a mesh fusion operation otherwise. In the latter case the number of handles of the resulting mesh is the sum of the two handle numbers. T_4 amounts to cutting a mesh along a contour and results in either removing a handle or sectioning a mesh into two parts.

The general mesh transformation T that transforms a mesh $\mathcal{M}_1$ into $\mathcal{M}_2$ is an ordered set of the four basic operations :

$$T = \{T_{f(0)}, T_{f(1)}, .., T_{f(q)}\} \quad with \quad f(i) \in \{0, 1, 2, 3, 4\}$$

A transformation from $\mathcal{M}_2$ to $\mathcal{M}_1$ is:

$$T = \{T_{Inv(f(q))}, T_{Inv(f(q-1))}, .., T_{Inv(f(0))}\}$$

where $Inv(x)$ a function defined as:

$$Inv(1) = 2 \quad Inv(2) = 1 \quad Inv(3) = 4 \quad Inv(4) = 3$$

In particular, there are two important macro-transformations, T_5 and T_6 that respectively increase and decrease locally the mesh resolution by duplicating and removing a face (see Figure 6). Both can be decomposed into combinations of T_1 and T_2.

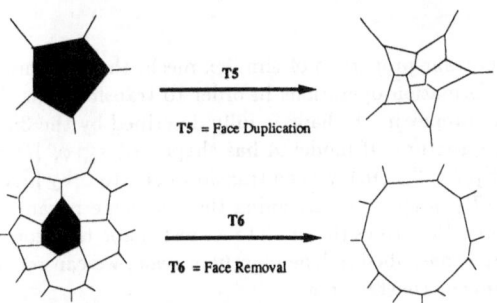

Figure 6: Mesh resolution transformations

7 EXAMPLES

We present two examples of models build from different range images. The three dimensional data with associated texture were provided by a Cyberware digitizer[16]. The modeling process can be decomposed into two stages. In the first stage, the model is initialized as a generic shape, either an ellipsoid, a cylinder or a plane, and then fit to the range data. In the second stage the mesh is refined as parts of high curvature and is eventually attached with another simplex mesh.

The first example shows how to build a hand model given two range images, one for each side of the hand (see Figure 10). The palm and fingers are first modeled separately and then connected to each other with several T_3 operations. We then compensate the finger displacement between two images by rigidly moving eighteen contours to their correct position while constraining the surface to keep the same curvature. The final model has about 8000 nodes and uses the texture of the two range data.

The second examples combines six range images of some body parts taken either from a mannequin or from a real person (see Figure 11). Junctions between the several meshes are smoothed until they reaches C^2 continuity.

8 INTERFACE

We designed an interface that provides the ability to interactively select a node, a face or a part of a mesh and then assign it some property. In addition to setting internal and external constraints, user may "nail" some nodes or use the mouse to drag both surface and contour nodes. Viewing point as well as contours and surfaces may be rotated, translated or scaled. Range images can be displayed as well providing a quick way to check the goodness of fit.

Constraint visualization is possible by attaching color patches to each node. Computational time is proportional to the number of mesh nodes but is, in most cases, small enough to provide real time feedback.

9 ANIMATION

9.1 Metamorphism

We combine two important properties of simplex mesh, their intrinsic shape representation and their mesh transformation operations in order to transform an object $\mathcal{A}$ into an object $\mathcal{B}$ (see Figure 13). A simplex mesh shape is fully described by the $3n$ values $\{\epsilon_{1i}, \epsilon_{2i}, \phi_i\} (i = 0, .., n)$ and its mesh structure. If model $\mathcal{A}$ has shape $\{\epsilon_{1i}^A, \epsilon_{2i}^A, \phi_i^A\} (i = 0, .., n)$ and model $\mathcal{B}$ has shape $\{\epsilon_{1j}^B, \epsilon_{2j}^B, \phi_j^B\} (j = 0, .., m)$, we can transform $\mathcal{A}$ into $\mathcal{B}$ by first applying a generalized mesh transformation $T_{\mathcal{A} \rightarrow \mathcal{B}}$ and then assigning the $3m$ shape parameters to each node. The internal constraint force F_{int} brings the mesh to its rest shape that corresponds to the shape of object $\mathcal{B}$. Since shape is described independantly of scale, we can render object deformations with a constant volume or constant area.

In the current status, all objects are either extracted from a range image or from some triangulated data. Given a simplex mesh representing an object $\mathcal{A}$, we fit the mesh on object $\mathcal{B}$ and modify its structure in order have a precise rendering of the object. We record and store the list of basic transformations as the generalized mesh transformation $T_{\mathcal{A} \rightarrow \mathcal{B}}$. Future extension would directly compute $T_{\mathcal{A} \rightarrow \mathcal{B}}$ from the two simplex meshes without having the fitting stage.

9.2 Articulated simplex mesh

Rotational joints are widely used especially to animate human parts models. A common approach is to consider hierarchical layered models with the lowest layer representing the bones and the upper layer the human skin[8][3]. Bones are rigidly rotated around some predefined axis while the skin is of elastic nature. Interaction between layers constrains the skin to closely surrounds the bones.

Layered models are closely related to the human physiology, but some magic parameters tune-up is necessary to render realistic animation. We propose an algorithm that simply and efficiently animates articulated simplex meshes. A joint is uniquely defined by two contours, one face and two vertices (see Figure7).

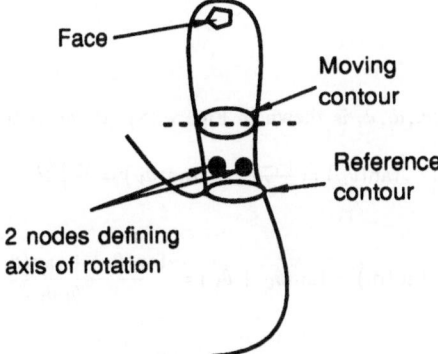

Figure 7: Rotational joint definition

The first contour is the moving contour where the surface is articulated. A contour splits a mesh into two parts and therefore a face indicates which part of a mesh is supposed to rotate. The two vertices defined the axis of rotation and the rotation angle is measured between the two segments that join the center of the moving contour to respectively the center of the face and the center of the second contour called refence contour. When the user changes the articulation angle of $\delta\theta$, all nodes on the moving side of the articulation contour are rotated of the same amount $\delta\theta$ while the contour is rotated around its center of the amount $\delta\theta/2$. This relation indicates that the contour bisects the angle between the moving part and the reference part which in general gives a natural effect. Surfaces nodes are constrained to keep constant curvature which results in a natural smoothing of the joint. More realistic effects such as the formation of wrinkles could be rendered by setting tangent end conditions at the moving contour instead of curvature constraints.

We have build a twenty degrees of freedom articulated hand from the model shown in Figure 10. We created four joints per finger following the same taxonomy as [15]. Joints are created fully interactively by selecting the five items. Figure 12 shows the model with the twenty articulations as seen from the interface. User may select each joint and set its rotation angle.

10 CONCLUSION

In this paper we have presented a physically based modeling system that represents three-dimensional surfaces as simplex meshes. By combining the notion of ends, mesh transformations, contours, smoothness and curvature constraints, our system's framework gives the user a large freedom of action at a local as well as a global level. Range images are handled as additional shape constraints and resulting models may be merged to render realistic images. An interactive interface that provides the ability to select a node, a face or a part of a mesh and to assign it some property was designed. We have developed in this perspective an animation scheme directly related to simplex mesh structures that simulates a rotational joint at a given contour. A twenty degrees of freedom hand model was thus created from the mesh as Figure

12. Current limitations include the lack of a continuous surface representation associated with a simplex mesh and a computational cost too high for interactively manipulating large models.

Appendix A

The relation between L, r_i, d_i, ϕ_i is shown in Figure (8). If we write θ_U as $\angle UP_iF$ and θ_V as $\angle VP_iF$ then :

$$\tan(\theta_U) = \frac{(r_i - d_i)}{L} \qquad \tan(\theta_V) = \frac{(r_i + d_i)}{L}$$

Since $\phi_i = \pi - \theta_U - \theta_V$,

$$-\tan(\phi_i) = \tan(\theta_U + \theta_V) = \frac{\tan(\theta_U) + \tan(\theta_V)}{1 - \theta_U \theta_V}$$

Finally,

$$L(r_i, d_i, \phi_i) = \frac{(r_i^2 - d_i^2).\tan(\phi_i)}{\epsilon.\sqrt{r_i^2 + (r_i^2 - d_i^2).\tan^2(\phi_i)} + r_i} \tag{8}$$

$$\epsilon = 1 \quad if \quad |\phi_i| < \pi/2$$
$$\epsilon = -1 \quad if \quad |\phi_i| > \pi/2$$

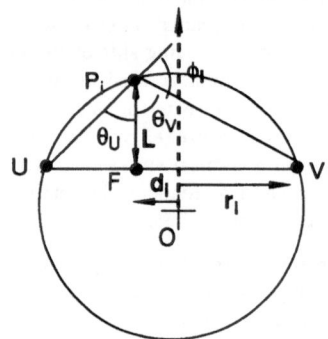

Figure 8: Computation of $L(r_i, d_i, \phi_i)$

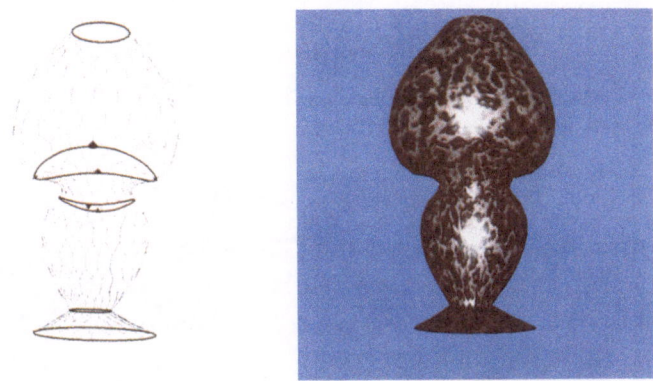

Figure 9: Vase created from a cylinder with five contours

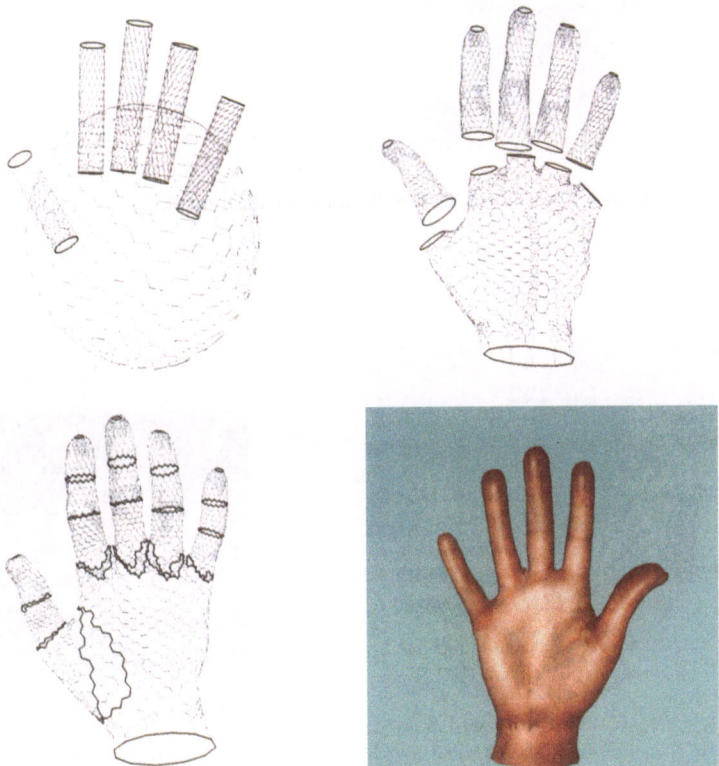

Figure 10: (a) Initialization of palm and fingers models; (b) All meshes are fit to the first range image; (c) Final model; (d) Texture display

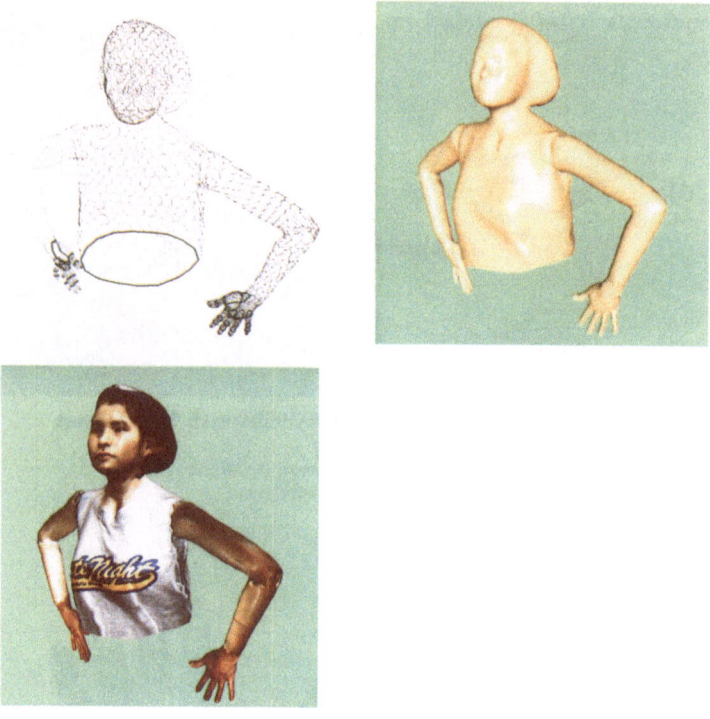

Figure 11: Depth Cued, Solid and textured display of bust model.

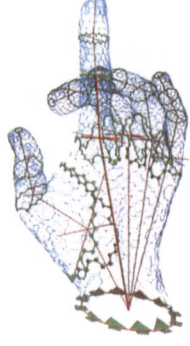

Figure 12: Articulated hand

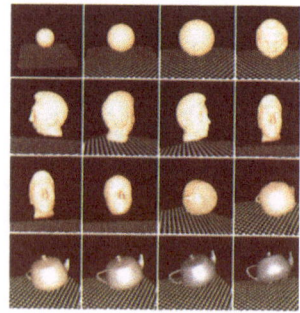

Figure 13: Metamorphism

References

[1] A. Blake and A. Zisserman. *Visual Reconstruction*. MIT Press, 1987.

[2] G. Celniker and D. Gossard. Deformable curve and surface finite-elements for free-form shape design. In *Computer Graphics (SIGGRAPH'91)*, pages 257–266, July 1991.

[3] J. Chadwick, D. Haumann, and R. Parent. Layered construction for deformable animated characters. In *Computer Graphics (SIGGRAPH'89)*, pages 243–252, July 1989.

[4] K. F. D. Terzopoulos. Deformable models. *The Visual Computer, 4,6*, pages 306–331, 1988.

[5] H. Delingette, M. Hebert, and K. Ikeuchi. Energy functions for regularization algorithms. In *Geometric Methods in Computer Vision*, San Diego, August 1991. SPIE.

[6] H. Delingette, M. Hebert, and K. Ikeuchi. Shape representation and image segmentation using deformable surfaces. In *IEEE Computer Vision and Pattern Recognition (CVPR91)*, pages 467–472, June 1991.

[7] G. Farin. *Curves and Surfaces for Computed Aided Geometric Design*. Academic Press, 1989.

[8] J.-P. Gourret, N. Magnenat Thalmann, and D. Thalmann. Simulation of object and human skin deformations in a grasping task. In *Computer Graphics (SIGGRAPH'89)*, pages 21–30, July 1989.

[9] H. Hagen and G. Schulze. Automatic smoothing with geometric surfaces patches. *Computer Aided Geometric Design*, 4:213–236, 1987.

[10] M. Kass, A. Witkin, and D. Terzopoulos. Snakes: Active contour models. *International Journal of Computer Vision*, 1:321–331, 1988.

[11] J. J. Koenderink. *Solid Shape*. MIT Press, 1990.

[12] E. Mehlum. Nonlinear splines. *Computer Aided Geometric Design*, pages 173–207, 1974.

[13] G. Miller and A. Pearce. Globular dynamics a connected particle system for animating viscous fluids. In *Computer Graphics (SIGGRAPH'89), Course 30 notes: Topics in Physically-based Modeling*, pages R1–R23, Boston, MA, August 1990. ACM.

[14] H. P. Moreton and C. H. Sequin. Functional optimization for fair surface design. In *Computer Graphics (SIGGRAPH'88)*, pages 167–176, July 1992.

[15] H. Rijpkema and M. Girard. Computer animation of knowledge-based human grasping. In *Computer Graphics (SIGGRAPH'91)*, pages 339–347, July 1991.

[16] Y. Suenaga and Y. Watanabe. A method for the synchronized acquisition of cylindrical range and color data. *IEICE Transactions*, E 74(10):3407–3416, October 1991.

[17] R. Szelinski and D. Tonnesen. Surface modeling with oriented particle systems. In *Computer Graphics (SIGGRAPH'92)*, pages 185–194, July 1992.

[18] D. Terzopoulos. Computing visible-surface representation. Technical Report Artificial Intelligence Memo 800, M.I.T., 1985.

[19] D. Terzopoulos, J. Platt, and K. Fleisher. From goop to glop: Heating and melting deformable models. In *Graphics Interface*, pages 219–226, June 1989.

[20] D. Terzopoulos, A. Witkin, and M. Kass. Symmetry-seeking models for 3d object reconstruction. *International Journal of Computer Vision*, 1(3):211–221, 1987.

[21] W. Welch and A. Witkin. Variational surface modeling. In *Computer Graphics (SIGGRAPH'92)*, pages 157–166, July 1992.

Hervé Delingette is currently a Ph.D. student at the Epidaure group of INRIA, France. He received the Diplome d'Ingénieur from the Ecole Centrale de Paris in 1989. Since 1989 he joined as a visiting scholar, the vision group of Carnegie-Mellon University and the Vision and Graphics group of Nippon Telegraph and Telephone. His research interests include image processing, object recognition and computer graphics.
Address: Groupe Epidaure, INRIA, 20004 Route des Lucioles B.P. 93, 06902 Sophia-Antipolis, France. E-mail: hdeling@sophia.inria.fr

Yasuhiko Watanabe is Senior Research Engineer in the Vision and Graphics Group of NTT Human Interface Laboratories. He is presently engaged in research on 3D model based coding systems. Since joining the Electrical Communications laboratories, NTT, in 1981, he has been working on facsimile communication systems and computer graphics research. He received the Bachelor degree from Niigata University, Niigata, Japan, in 1981. He is a member of the Information Processing Society of Japan.
Address: NTT Human Interface Laboratories, 1-2356 Take Yokosuka-shi, Kanagawa 238-03, Japan. E-mail: watanabe@nttcvg.ntt.jp

Yasuhito Suenaga is Senior Research Engineer, Supervisor, Vision and Graphics Group at the Nippon Telegraph and Telephone Human Interface Laboratories, Yokosuka, Japan. He leads a research project of computer analysis and synthesis of human images. He was born in Nagoya, Aichi prefecture, Japan in 1945. He received his B.S., M.S. and Ph.D. degrees in electrical engineering from Nagoya University, Nagoya, Japan in 1968, 1970 and 1974 respectively. Since joining the Electrical Communications Laboratories, Nippon Telegraph and Telephone Corporation in 1973, he has been engaged in the research of image processing. From 1985 to 1986, he was a visiting researcher at MIT Media Laboratory, Massachussets Institute of Technology. He received the younger engineers award from the Institute of Electronics, Information, and Communication Engineers (IEICE) in 1979, and the NICCOGRAPH'89 best paper award from the Nippon Computer Graphics Association in 1989. He is a member of the Information Processing Society of Japan.

Address: NTT Human Interface Laboratories, 1-2356 Take Yokosuka-shi, Kanagawa 238-03, Japan. E-mail : suenaga@nttcvg.ntt.jp

Animation of a Blooming Flower Using a Family of Complex Functions $M_{\zeta,\alpha}(z) = \exp(-\alpha\frac{\zeta+z}{\zeta-z})$

HYOUNG SEOK KIM, YOUNG BONG KIM, HO KYUNG KIM, HWANG SOO KIM, HONG OH KIM, and SUNG YONG SHIN

ABSTRCT

Recently, Kim et. al.(1992) addressed the properties of a family of complex functions $M_{\zeta,\alpha}(z) = \exp(-\alpha\frac{\zeta+z}{\zeta-z})$ where $\alpha > 0$ and $|\zeta| = 1$. When Newton's method is applied to solve $M_{\zeta,\alpha}(z) - 1 = 0$, the basins of attraction for its roots show flower-like self-similar structures which vary according to the value of α. From an artistic point of view, we explore those self-similar strucures for an animated sequence of flower blooming by extending $M_{\zeta,\alpha}(z)$ for $\alpha \neq 0$.

Keywords: Fractal geometry, Complex functions, Newton's method, Animation.

1. INTRODUCTION

Fractal images, generated by iterating complex functions such as $f(z) = z^2 + \lambda$ and $e(z) = \lambda \exp(z)$, have attracted much attention [Norton 89]. These functions generate very interesting fractal images called the Mandelbrot set and Julia sets for the parameter λ [Barnsley 88, Mandelbrot 82, Richter 86, Saupe 88]. The self-similarity of such images is often exploited for computer animation [Devanley 89, Hubbard 90, Peitgen 90].

Recently, Kim et. al.(1992) investigated dynamical behavior of a family of functions,

$$M_{\zeta,\alpha}(z) = \exp(-\alpha\frac{\zeta + z}{\zeta - z})$$

where $\alpha > 0$ and $|\zeta| = 1$. The equation $M_{\zeta,\alpha}(z) - 1 = 0$ has infinitely many roots on the unit circle and a singular point at ζ. Each root plays the role of an attractor of Newton's method for the equation [Kim 92, Motyka 90]. Since the point at infinity is also an attractor (an attracting fixed point), its Julia set is contained in a bounded region, say $|z| < 2 + \frac{4\alpha}{1-e^{-\alpha/2}}$. The Julia set consists of infinite-corner points where infinitely many basins of attraction of roots meet, and has the shape of self-similar flowers formed by these basins of attraction. Each of these flowers consists of infinitely many other ones of similar shape and different size. In fact, it does not quite look like a real flower of any kind. However, it gives a rather aesthetic flower-like image from an artistic point of view. The same properties can be shown to hold true for $\alpha < 0$. When $\alpha = 0$, $M_{\zeta,\alpha}(z)$ degenerates to a constant and thus does not give any interesting image. If $\alpha = 0$ is properly avoided, the shape of a flower nicely changes according to the value of α, which provides a possibility for generating a sequence of images to animate a blooming flower in an artistic sense.

In this paper, we consider a family of functions $M_{\zeta,\alpha}(z)$, where the parameter α is allowed to take a non-zero real number. In order to animate a blooming flower, we generate a sequence of time-varying images of the flower by properly computing its corresponding sequence of the parameter α. As α is getting smaller, its corresponding shape evolves into a flower in full bloom. However, the size of a flower is inversely proportional to its degree of blooming, which is not intuitive. We present a method for determining the size of a window and its location in each image to compensate this effect.

2. FRACTAL IMAGE GENERATION BY NEWTON'S METHOD

In this section, we first compute a bound of the Julia set for $\alpha < 0$. This bound together with the one for $\alpha > 0$ gives a condition for testing the divergency of a Newton sequence starting from an initial value. We also present how to generate fractal images by Newton's method for solving the equation

$$M_{\zeta,\alpha}(z) - 1 = 0, \tag{1}$$

where α is a nonzero real number.

2.1 Bound of Julia Sets

For $\alpha \neq 0$, the roots ξ_k of equation (1) satisfy

$$\alpha \frac{\zeta + \xi_k}{\zeta - \xi_k} = 2\pi k,$$

where k is an integer. If we set $\zeta = e^{i\phi}$, then the roots have the form $\xi_k = e^{i\theta_k}$, where

$$\alpha \cot(\frac{\theta_k - \phi}{2}) = 2k\pi,$$

i.e., $\qquad \theta_k = \phi + 2\cot^{-1}(\frac{2k\pi}{\alpha}) \qquad$ for an integer k. $\tag{2}$

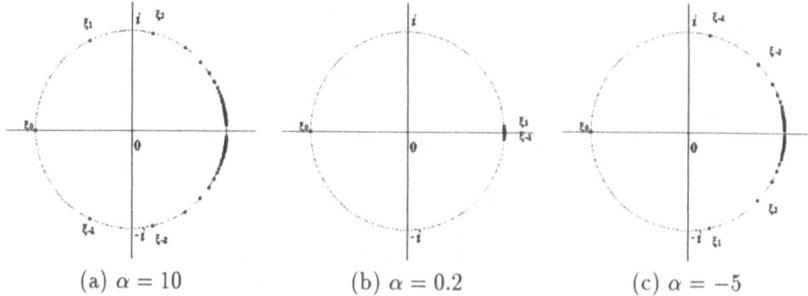

(a) $\alpha = 10$ (b) $\alpha = 0.2$ (c) $\alpha = -5$

Fig. 1. Roots of $M_{\zeta,\alpha}(z) - 1 = 0$

Therefore, equation (1) has infinitely many roots $\xi_k = e^{i\theta_k}$ on the unit circle. These roots are symmetrically located on the unit circle about the singular point ζ. That is, for an integer m, ξ_m and ξ_{-m} are symmetrical about the ray of angle ϕ. We can also observe that as $|\alpha|$ decreases the corresponding roots ξ_k get closer to the singular point ζ as shown in Fig. 1.

The explicit form of Newton's method for solving equation (1) is

$$N(z) = z + \frac{(\zeta - z)^2}{2\alpha\zeta}(1 - \exp(\alpha\frac{\zeta + z}{\zeta - z})), \tag{3}$$

where α is a nonzero real number. The simple roots ξ_k of equation (1) are attractive fixed points of $N(z)$, and they act as attractors of Newton's method since $N'(\xi_k) = 0$ [Barnsley 88, R.L. Devaney 89, D. Saupe 88]. That is, Newton sequence $\{z_k\}$ converges to a root of equation (1) if an initial value z_0 is properly chosen. For a simple root ξ_k, the set of initial values whose Newton sequences converge to ξ_k is called the basin of attraction of ξ_k. For the function $N(z)$, the point at infinity also plays the role of an attractor since $T(0) = 0$ and $T'(0) = 0$, where $T(z) = 1/N(1/z)$. Hence, its Julia set is located in a bounded region. In order to find its bound and the criterion for testing the divergency to infinity for an orbit, it is required to determine the region of starting points whose orbits definitely go to infinity. A bound for the case $\alpha > 0$ is given by Kim et. al. (1992). That is, the Newton sequence $\{z_k\}$ of an initial value z_0 in the region

$$|z| > 2 + \frac{4\alpha}{1 - \exp(-\alpha/2)}. \tag{4}$$

diverges to infinity. Therefore, the Julia set is contained in the complement of the region given by inequality (4) when $\alpha > 0$.

Now, we derive a similar bound for the Julia set when $\alpha < 0$. For $|z| \geq 3$,

$$
\begin{aligned}
|\exp(\alpha\frac{\zeta + z}{\zeta - z})| &= \exp(\alpha\mathrm{Re}\frac{\zeta + z}{\zeta - z}) \\
&= \exp(-\alpha\frac{|z|^2 - 1}{|\zeta - z|^2}) \\
&\geq \exp(-\alpha\frac{|z| - 1}{|z| + 1}) \\
&\geq \exp(-\alpha/2) \\
&\geq 1. \tag{5}
\end{aligned}
$$

From expression (3) and inequality (5), we have

$$
\begin{aligned}
|N(z)| &\geq \frac{|\zeta - z|^2}{2|\alpha\zeta|}|1 - \exp(\alpha\frac{\zeta + z}{\zeta - z})| - |z| \\
&\geq \frac{(|z| - 1)^2}{2|\alpha|}(\exp(-\frac{\alpha}{2}) - 1) - |z| \\
&= |z|(\frac{\exp(-\alpha/2) - 1}{2|\alpha|}|z| - \frac{\exp(-\alpha/2) - 1 + |\alpha|}{|\alpha|}) + \frac{\exp(-\alpha/2) - 1}{2|\alpha|} \\
&\geq |z|(\frac{\exp(-\alpha/2) - 1}{2|\alpha|}|z| - \frac{\exp(-\alpha/2) - 1 + |\alpha|}{|\alpha|}) \\
&> |z|.
\end{aligned}
$$

provided

$$
\begin{aligned}
|z| &> 2 + \frac{4|\alpha|}{\exp(-\alpha/2) - 1} \\
&= 2 + \frac{4\alpha}{1 - \exp(-\alpha/2)}. \tag{6}
\end{aligned}
$$

Since the right hand side of inequality (6) is always greater than 3, we obtain $|N(z)| > |z|$ for any z in the region satisfying inequality (6). Therefore, the Newton sequence $\{z_k\}$ for an initial value z_0 in the region diverges to infinity. The bounds in inequalities (4) and (6) have the same expression on α, which we denote by

$$L(\alpha) = 2 + \frac{4\alpha}{1 - \exp(-\alpha/2)}.$$

$L(\alpha)$ can be used as a threshold value for testing the divergency of a Newton sequence $\{z_k\}$. The basins of attraction of roots of equation (1) are contained in the bounded region: $|z| \leq L(\alpha)$.

2.2 Graphic Image Generation

We will utilize the image generation method introduced in Kim et. al.(1992). For self-containment of this paper, we first summerize their result. Equation (1) has infinitely many roots lying on the unit circle. Therefore, it is not possible to identify all of them in image generation. As shown in Fig. 1, most of the roots cluster near the singular point ζ. In fact, experiments show that the basins of attraction of these clustered attractors are too small to appear in a computer-generated image. They also provide the fact that the basin of attraction of an attractor tends to be smaller if the attractor gets nearer to ζ. Hence, we first choose, as attractors, the point at infinity and twenty nine roots farthest from ζ than the others to generate graphics images. The remaining infinitely many roots near ζ are considered to be the artificial attractor. Since it is hard to determine the maximum number N of iterations, we empirically choose N to be 100.

Let $\{z_j\}$ be a sequence of complex numbers generated by Newton's method with an initial value z_0. Suppose that $\{z_j\}$ has a value z_i near an attractor ξ_k such that $i \leq N$ and $|z_i - \xi_k| < \epsilon$ for a small positive real number ϵ. The first such ξ_k , encountered by Newton's method , is taken as the attractor of z_0. If Newton's sequence does not converge to such ξ_k within N iterations, the attractor of z_0 is assumed to be either the artificial attractor or the point at infinity unless $\{z_j\}$ has a point sufficiently close to ζ. Letting z^* be a point in a sequence $\{z_j\}$, the attractor of z_0 is the point at infinity if $|z^*|$ exceeds a positive real number $L(\alpha)$. Otherwise, its attractor is considered to be the artificial attractor. Suppose that $\{z_j\}$ has a point z_i such that $|z_i - \zeta| < \delta$, where δ is chosen to be a small positive real number. If Newton's method does not stop with an attractor until its full iteration, $\{z_j\}$ is considered to contain ζ. In this case, z_0 is not thought to have any attractor. Fortunately, the effect of the singular point ζ is negligible in fractal images shown later in this section. In order to test the convergency of an orbit to an attractor, we empirically choose $\epsilon = 10^{-7}$ and $\delta = 10^{-7}$.

The RGB color system is adopted to present graphics images. In order to generate a fractal image by Newton's method for $\alpha > 0$, the basins of attraction of the thirty attractors including the point at infinity are painted with three colors, red, blue, and green. The $i + 1^{st}$ farthest roots ξ_i and ξ_{-i} from the singular point ζ always appear in pair for $i = 1, 2, \dots , 14$. The basins of attraction of these twenty eight roots and the artificial attractor have the red color. The blue color is assigned to the basin of attraction of the farthest root ξ_0, and the remaining color is assigned to the basin of attraction of the point at infinity. By this assignment, we have an image as shown in Fig. 2. This image exhibits the basins of attraction of Newton's method for $M_{1,10}(z) - 1 = 0$. There appear infinitely many flower shapes. In particular, one of them is located around $\zeta = 1$. As such an example, Fig. 3 shows a zoomed image of the rectangular region in Fig. 2. The figure defined as "flower" in [Kim 92] is symmetrical about the real axis and gives three structural components forming a flower; the region colored with red corresponds to the petals of a flower, the green region is the trunk, and the blue region is considered as the background. A petal is helmet-shaped and bends toward its corresponding attractor from the singular point ζ. This petal mostly lies outside of the unit circle, and thus the image looks like a closing flower. In order to enhance its visual presentation, the small isolated green region in Fig. 3 near each petal will be painted blue from now as shown in Fig. 10.

Now, suppose that $\alpha < 0$. If we assign the three colors by the same strategy as the case for $\alpha > 0$, then the red region correctly corresponds to petals. But the color for the basin of attraction corresponding to the trunk is blue, and the region corresponding to the background is colored green. Hence, the image shows the background with green color and the trunk with blue color. To avoid this color discontinuity, we reverse the color assignment for $\alpha < 0$ so that the green and blue colors are assigned to the basins of attraction of ξ_0 and the point at infinity, respectively. Figure 4 shows the fractal image of Newton's method for $M_{1,-5}(z) - 1 = 0$. The image in Fig. 5 is obtained by zooming out the rectangular region in Fig. 4. In this image, every petal is mostly contained in the unit circle, and the image looks like a flower in full bloom. Since petals are located in the opposite side of the unit circle compared to the case for $\alpha > 0$, there is a discontinuity at $\alpha = 0$. In order to smoothly animate a blooming flower as the value of α goes from positive to negative, we reflect the images for $\alpha < 0$ on the line $\text{Re } z = 1$ as shown in Fig. 6.

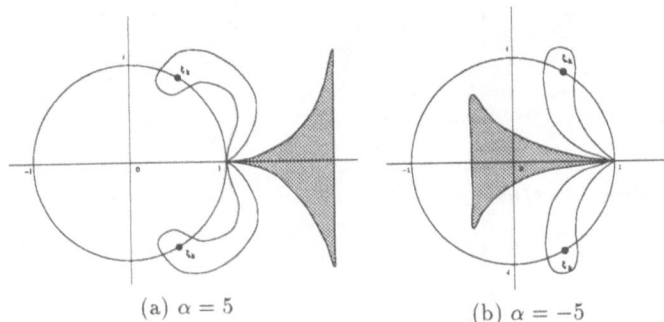

(a) $\alpha = 5$ (b) $\alpha = -5$

Fig. 6. The Basic shapes of petals

3. ANIMATING A BLOOMING FLOWER

In this section, we investigate the dynamics of petals as α varies and define an opening angle which measures the degree of blooming. We first present how to choose a sequence $\{\alpha_k\}$ of α at which its corresponding fractal image is generated. Then, a method for rotating a fractal image is given. We finally propose a method for controlling the size of a blooming flower and its location. We assume that $\zeta = 1$ unless otherwise stated.

3.1 Dynamics of petals

The fractal image obtained by Newton's method for $M_{\zeta,\alpha}(z) - 1 = 0$ exhibits many flower shapes near the boundary of each basin of attraction. One of them is always located around the point at 1 regardless of the value of α. The shape and size of this flower depend on the value of α. Each petal of the flower corresponds to the basin of attraction for a root on the unit circle and looks like a helmet such that its shape is bent toward its attractor from the point at 1. The most exterior pair of petals of the flower are related with the basins of attraction of the second farthest pair of roots $\xi_1 = \exp(i\theta_1)$ and $\xi_{-1} = \exp(i\theta_{-1})$, respectively. The next pair of petals correspond to the basins of attraction for the pair of roots ξ_2 and ξ_{-2}, and succesive pairs correspond to the basins of attraction for ξ_3 and ξ_{-3}, ξ_4 and ξ_{-4}, ... , and so on. The locations of roots ξ_1 and ξ_{-1} mostly affect both the degree of blooming for a flower and its size. The argument θ_k of each root ξ_k is given as a function of α:

$$\theta_k(\alpha) = 2 \cot^{-1} \frac{2k\pi}{\alpha} \qquad \text{for } k \neq 0.$$

Since $|\theta_k(\alpha)|$ decrease as $|\alpha|$ approaches 0 as shown in Fig. 7, most of roots are clustered near the singular point $\zeta = 1$. As $|\alpha|$ gets larger, they move away from ζ along the unit circle. Hence the size of the most exterior pair of petals becomes smaller as $|\alpha|$ approaches zero.

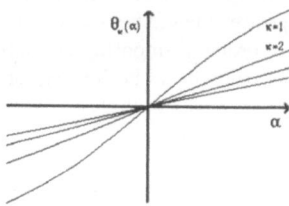

Fig. 7. $\theta_k(\alpha) = 2\cot^{-1}(2k\pi/\alpha)$

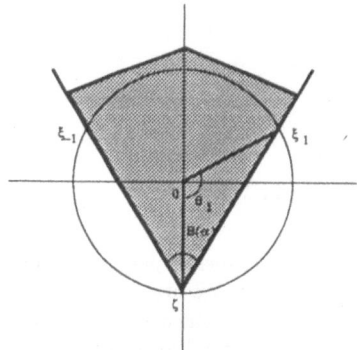

Fig. 8. The definition of $B(\alpha)$

Now, we are ready to explain how the sequence of images representing a blooming flower can be obtained by properly changing the value of α. The angle $\angle\xi_{-1}\zeta\xi_1$ is called the opening angle $B(\alpha)$ of a flower and is given as follows (see Fig. 8):

$$
\begin{aligned}
B(\alpha) &= \angle\xi_{-1}\zeta\xi_1 \\
&= 2\angle O\zeta\xi_1 \\
&= \pi - \theta_1(\alpha) \\
&= \pi - 2\cot^{-1}\frac{2\pi}{\alpha} \quad \text{(radian)},
\end{aligned}
$$

where O is the center of the unit circle. This angle is smaller than π for $\alpha > 0$ and greater than π for $\alpha < 0$. $\theta_1(\alpha)$ decreases as the value of α diminishes, and thus the opening angle gets wider as represented in Fig. 9. It is quite natural that the opening angle gets wider as a flower gradually blooms. Therefore, $B(\alpha)$ measures the degree of blooming of a flower. For example, compare the shape of flowers in Fig. 10 and their corresponding opening angles:

$$
\begin{aligned}
&B(10) = 1.121964, \quad B(5) = 1.797274, \\
&B(-3) = 4.032508, \quad \text{and} \quad B(-5) = 4.485911.
\end{aligned}
$$

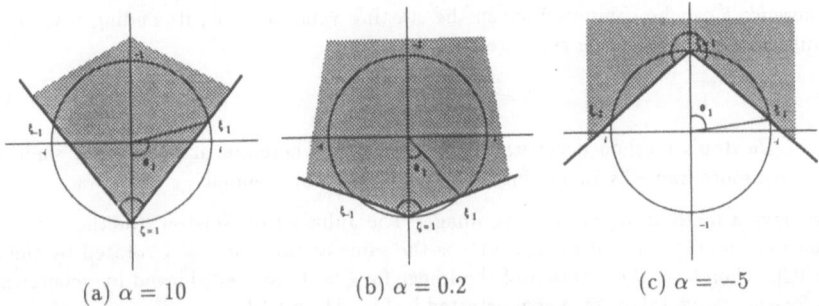

(a) $\alpha = 10$ (b) $\alpha = 0.2$ (c) $\alpha = -5$

FIg. 9. The opening angle $B(\alpha)$

The flowers for $\alpha = 10$ and -5 look like a closed bud and a full bloom, respectively. Their in-between images well interpolate an opening flower. Therefore, we hereafter fix the range of α as

$$-5 \leq \alpha \leq 10.$$

If we consider α as the time parameter, it is rather counter-intuitive, since a flower reversely blooms as time passes. Thus, we have to interpret that $-\alpha$ is the time variable.

Figure 10 shows another counter-intuitive phenomenon concerning the size of a flower. That is, the size of a flower is getting smaller as the flower blooms for $\alpha > 0$. The same is true for $\alpha < 0$. Since Newton's method degenerates when $\alpha = 0$, it does not even give any flower. Those anomalies will be overcome later in this section by introducing a function of α to smoothly interpolate the size of a flower and by properly choosing a sequence of α.

3.2 Generating the Sequence of α

It is clear that α plays the role of time in animating a blooming flower. Therefore, it is important to determine an appropriate sequence of α for creating a smoothly-opening flower. We choose the sequence α_k so that the difference between opening angles of successive flowers is constant. This can physically be interpreted to take each frame at a discrete time α_k in sequence such that a flower constantly evolves from a frame to its successive one.

Let b be the difference between two successive opening angles $B(\alpha_k)$ and $B(\alpha_{k-1})$, i.e.,

$$b = B(\alpha_k) - B(\alpha_{k-1}).$$

From section 3.1,

$$\begin{aligned} B(\alpha) &= \pi - \theta_1(\alpha) \\ &= \pi - 2\cot^{-1}(\frac{2\pi}{\alpha}). \end{aligned}$$

Hence,

$$\begin{aligned} b &= B(\alpha_k) - B(\alpha_{k-1}) \\ &= 2\cot^{-1}(\frac{2\pi}{\alpha_{k-1}}) - 2\cot^{-1}(\frac{2\pi}{\alpha_k}). \end{aligned}$$

Therefore,

$$\alpha_k = \frac{2\pi}{\cot(\cot^{-1}(\pi/\alpha_{k-1}) - b/2)}. \tag{7}$$

The difference b can be computed, given the starting value α_s of α, its ending value α_e, and the number Λ_f of frames to be generated;

$$b = \frac{B(\alpha_e) - B(\alpha_s)}{\Lambda_f - 1}.$$

Note that Newton's method degenerates when $\alpha = 0$. Therefore, if $\alpha_k = 0$ for some k, we generate one more frame by increasing Λ_f by 1 to avoid this anomaly.

Now, we give a method for rotating an image. The Julia set of Newton's method for solving the equation $M_{\zeta,\alpha}(z) - 1 = 0$ with $\zeta = e^{i\phi}$ is the same as that for $\zeta = 1$ rotated by the angle ϕ [Kim 92]. Therefore, the rotation of the image for $\zeta = 1$ can be achieved by generating the images for successive values of ϕ as illustrated in Fig. 11 and 12.

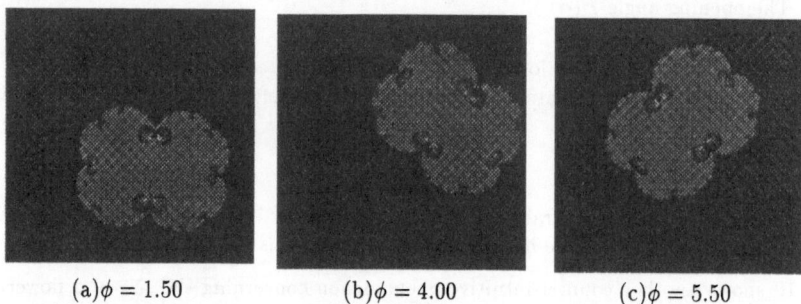

| (a)$\phi = 1.50$ | (b)$\phi = 4.00$ | (c)$\phi = 5.50$ |

Fig. 11. The rotation of a Julia set image when $\alpha > 0$

| (a)$\phi = 1.50$ | (b)$\phi = 4.00$ | (c)$\phi = 5.50$ |

Fig. 12. The rotation of a Julia set image when $\alpha < 0$

3.3 Window Size and Location

For ease of image generation, let the viewport for displaying images be a fixed square. Then, the square window uniformly scales the size of a flower according to the ratio of sizes between these two squares. Therefore, every window containing a flower is also assumed to be a square in the following discussion.

Since a fractal image has a very complicated structure, it is hard to analytically determine a tight square containing a flower in the image. In order to derive an experimental function $h(\alpha)$ for determining the size of a bounding square for a given α, we interactively construct bounding squares at sampled values of α. From the plot of sampled data, which looks linear when $\alpha > 0$ and quadratic when $\alpha < 0$, we obtain the following least square fit for the bound function $h(\alpha)$:

$$h(\alpha) = \begin{cases} 1.03299\alpha, & \alpha > 0, \\ -0.0842928\alpha^2 - 1.01206\alpha, & \alpha < 0. \end{cases}$$

$h(\alpha)$ and the plot of sampled data are shown in Fig. 13.

Suppose that $h(\alpha)$ is used to give the size of a window. Since the viewport is the same for all images, all flowers thus generated have more or less the same size. However, a natural flower gets bigger as it blooms. With the viewport fixed, we can imitate this phenomenon by adjusting the window size. That is, we need to make the window size smaller as a flower blooms.

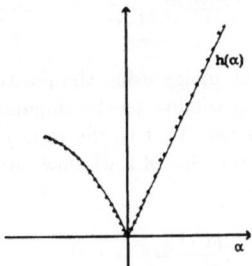

Fig. 13. Plotting of the value of height of a bounding square and approximated bound function $h(\alpha)$

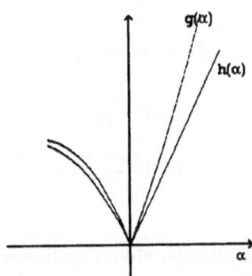

Fig. 14. The relation of $g(\alpha)$ and $h(\alpha)$

Let $g(\alpha)$ be the window size function which gives the length of an edge of the square window containing a flower. The ratio $h(\alpha)/g(\alpha)$ measures how much the flower occupies the viewport. That is, if the ratio gets larger, then the flower grows. Hence, a growing flower can be animated by controlling the ratio. This can be done by adjusting $g(\alpha)$ since $h(\alpha)$ has already determined. We assume that $h(\alpha)/g(\alpha)$ linearly depends on α. If the initial and final ratios are given, the $g(\alpha)$ can be determined. Since $-5 \leq \alpha \leq 10$, we take the initial flower image (bud) at $\alpha = 10$ with the ratio r_s and the final flower image (full bloom) at $\alpha = -5$ with the ratio r_f. The corresponding $g(\alpha)$ can then be determined from the following equation:

$$\frac{h(\alpha)}{g(\alpha)} = A\alpha + B \quad \text{for} \quad -5 \leq \alpha \leq 10.$$

The unknown constants A and B can be decided by the boundary conditions:

$$r_s = 10A + B,$$
$$r_f = -5A + B.$$

Hence,

$$\frac{h(\alpha)}{g(\alpha)} = \frac{r_s - r_f}{15}\alpha + \frac{r_s + 2r_f}{3}.$$

Therefore, the resulting $g(\alpha)$ is given in Fig. 14. by

$$g(\alpha) = \begin{cases} \frac{1.03299\alpha}{(r_s-r_f)\alpha/15+(r_s+2r_f)/3}, & 0 < \alpha \le 10, \\ \frac{-0.0842928\alpha^2-1.01206\alpha}{(r_s-r_f)\alpha/15+(r_s+2r_f)/3}, & -5 \le \alpha < 0. \end{cases}$$

Finally, we place the window in the image using the position function $p(\alpha)$, which gives the distance from the bottom edge of a window to the singular point ζ when the ray of angle ϕ coincides with the bisector of the edge. That is, the ratio $p(\alpha)/g(\alpha)$ gives a relative height of the singular point ζ from the bottom edge of a window. Assuming that the trunk of a flower linearly grows as it blooms,

$$\frac{p(\alpha)}{g(\alpha)} = C\alpha + D$$

where C and D are unknown constants. If the initial ratio at $\alpha = 10$ and the final ratio at $\alpha = -5$ are given by ρ_s and ρ_f, respectively, then we can determine C and D. The resulting position function $p(\alpha)$ is given as follows:

$$p(\alpha) = (\frac{\rho_s - \rho_f}{15}\alpha + \frac{\rho_s + 2\rho_f}{3})g(\alpha), \qquad -5 \le \alpha \le 10.$$

Therefore, the center of a window should be at the point

$$1.0 + p(\alpha) - \frac{g(\alpha)}{2} = 1.0 + g(\alpha)(\frac{\rho_s - \rho_f}{15}\alpha + \frac{\rho_s + 2\rho_f}{3} - 0.5) \qquad \text{for} \quad \alpha > 0,$$

$$\text{and} \quad 1.0 - p(\alpha) + \frac{g(\alpha)}{2} = 1.0 - g(\alpha)(\frac{\rho_s - \rho_f}{15}\alpha + \frac{\rho_s + 2\rho_f}{3} - 0.5) \qquad \text{for} \quad \alpha < 0.$$

Figure 15 shows an example for animating a blooming flower. We choose $\Lambda_f = 6, r_s = 0.5, r_f = 0.95, \rho_s = 0.1925$, and $\rho_f = 0.5$. Here, the flower for $\alpha = 10$ is excluded since it has already shown in Figure 10(a).

4. CONCLUDING REMARKS

Fractal images, generated by Newton's method for the equation $M_{\zeta,\alpha}(z) - 1 = 0$ where $\alpha \ne 0$ and $|\zeta| = 1$, show self-similar flowers whose shapes change according to the value of α. As α decreases from a positive value to a negative value, the shape of the flower evolves from a closed bud into a full bloom. From these properties, we compute an appropriate sequence of α which can animate a blooming flower in an artistic sense by considering the parameter α as a time variable. We also control the size of a window containing the flower and its location to imitate the growth of a flower. In the future, we will investigate the method to obtain $3D$ shape of a flower from $M_{\zeta,\alpha}(z)$ and thus animate a three dimensional flower.

ACKNOWLEDGEMENTS

This research was partially supported by TGRC.

REFERENCES

Alan Norton (1989), Julia set in the Quaternions, *Computer & Gr aphics*, Vol 13, No. 2, pp. 267-278.

B. B. Mandelbrot (1982), *The Fractal Geometry of Nature*, W. H. Fr eeman and Company, New York.

H. O. Kim and H. S. Kim (1991), Iteration, Denjoy-Wolff point and ergodic properrties of point-mass singular inner functions, *J. of Mathematical Analysis and Applications*, (to appear).

H.-O. Peitgen, H. Jurgens, and D. Saupe (1990), *FRACTALS: AN ANIMATED DISCUSSION*, Science Television, W. H. Freeman and Company, New York.

H.-O. Peitgen and D. Saupe (Eds) (1988), *The Science of Fractal Images* , Springer Verlag, New York.

H.-O. Peitgen and P.H. Richter (1986), *The Beauty of Fractals*, Sprin ger Verlag, New York.

H. S. Kim, Y. B. Kim, H. O. Kim, and S. Y. Shin (1992), Infinite-corner-point Fractal Image Generation by Newton's Method for Solving $\exp(-\alpha\frac{\zeta+z}{\zeta-z}) - 1 = 0$, *computer & graphics*, (to appear).

John H. Hubbard (1990), *The Beauty of Complexity of the Mandelbrot se t: University Edition*, Science Television, Times Square Station, New York.

M. A. Motyka and C. A. Reiter, Chaos and Newton's Method on Systems , *Computer & Graphics* , 14(1), pp. 415-418.

M. Barnsley (1988), *Fractals Everywhere*, Academic Press, New York,

R. L. Devaney (1989), *An Introduction to Chaotic Dynamical Systems*, Addison-Wesley, Menlo Park.

R. L. Devaney (1989), *CHAOS, FRACTAL, AND DYNAMICS: Computer Experiments in Mathetmatics* , Science Television, Times Square Station, New York.

R. L. Devaney (1989), *TRANSITION TO CHAOS: The Orbit Diagram and the Mandelbrot Set*, Science Television, Times Square Station, New York.

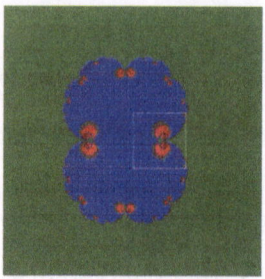

Fig. 2. Basins of attraction of Newton's
method for $M_{1,10} - 1 = 0$

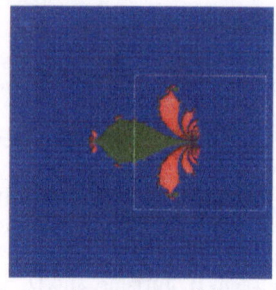

Fig. 4. Basins of attraction of Newton's
method for $M_{1,-5} - 1 = 0$

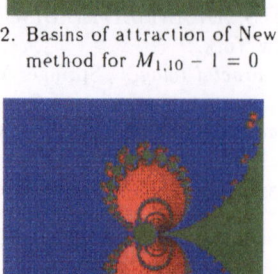

Fig. 3. A magnification of the rectangle
in Fig. 2

Fig. 5. A magnification of the rectangle
in Fig. 4

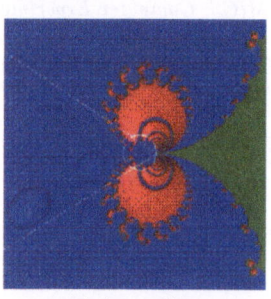

(a) $\alpha = 10$

(c) $\alpha = -5$

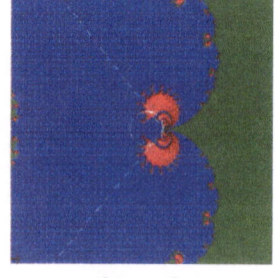

(b) $\alpha = 5$

(d) $\alpha = -3$

Fig. 10. Opening angles of a flower

41

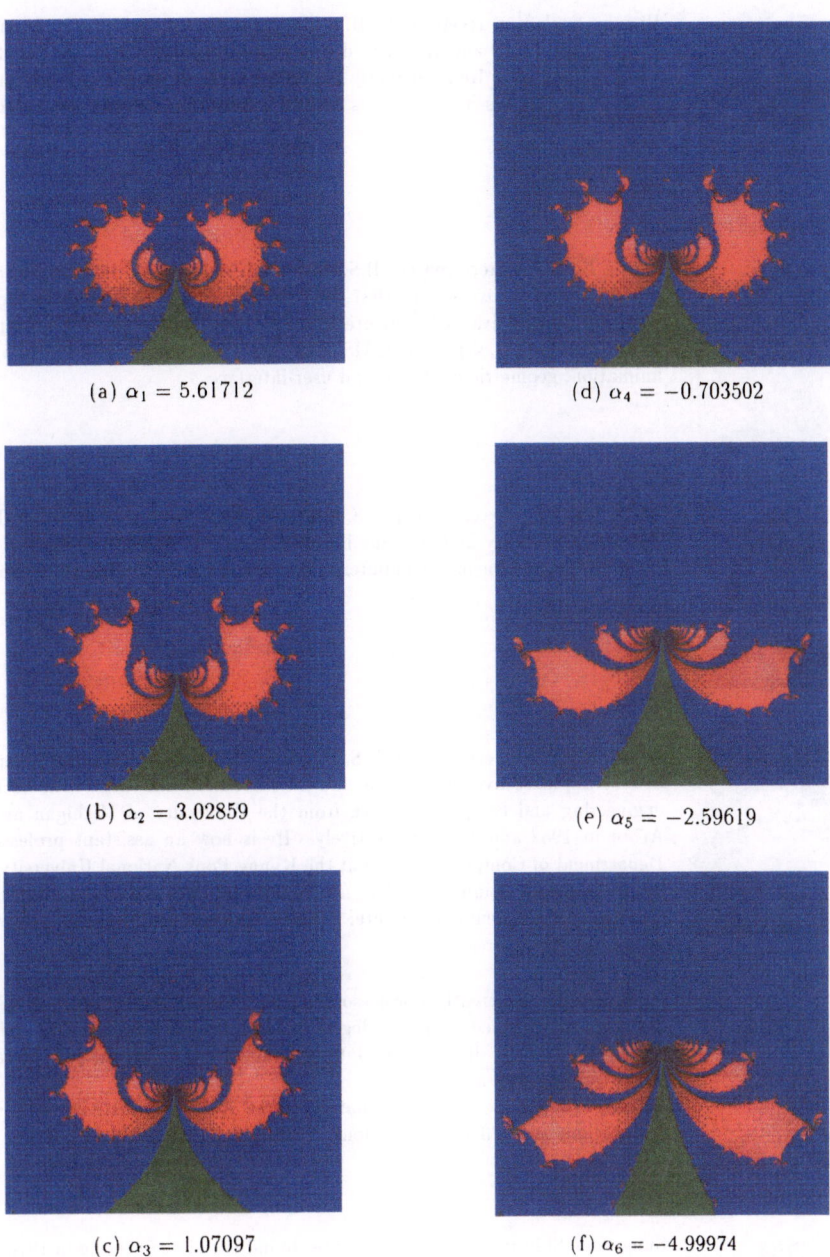

(a) $\alpha_1 = 5.61712$

(b) $\alpha_2 = 3.02859$

(c) $\alpha_3 = 1.07097$

(d) $\alpha_4 = -0.703502$

(e) $\alpha_5 = -2.59619$

(f) $\alpha_6 = -4.99974$

Fig. 15. A blooming flower

Hyoung Seok Kim received the B.S. degree in Mathematics from the Yonsei University in 1990 and the M.S. degree in Mathematics from the KAIST in 1992, respectively. He is currently pursuing his Ph.D. degree in Mathematics at KAIST. His research interests include geometric modeling and complex analysis.

Young Bong Kim received the B.S. degree in Computer & Statistics from the Seoul National University in 1987, and the M.S. degree in Computer Science from the Korea Advanced Institute of Science and Technology. He is currently pursuing his Ph.D. degree at KAIST. His research interests include computer animation, geometric modeling and user-interface.

Ho Kyung Kim received her B.S. degree in Computer Science from Ewha Womans University in 1992. She is currently a M.S. student at KAIST. Her research interests include computer animation and human-body modeling.

Hwang Soo Kim received the B.S. degree in electrical engineering from the Seoul National University in 1975, and the M.S. and Ph.D. degrees in electrical engineering and computer science from the University of Michigan at Ann Arbor in 1982 and 1988, respectively. He is now an assistant professor in Department of Computer Science at the Kyung Pook National University. His interests include computer vision, neural networks, and computer graphics.
Address: Department of Computer Science, Kyung Pook National University, Taegu 702-701, Korea.

Hong Oh Kim is currently a professor in Department of Mathematics at KAIST of Korea. He received his Ph.D. degree in Mathematics from the University of Wisconsin in 1982. His research interests include complex analysis, iteration theory and applied analysis.
Address: Department of Mathematics, Korea Advanced Institute of Science and Technology, 373-1, Kusong-dong, Yusung-gu, Taejon 305-701, Korea.

Sung Yong Shin received the B.S. degree in industrial engineering in 1970 from Hanyang University, Seoul, Korea, and the M.S. and Ph.D. degrees in industrial and operations engineering from the University of Michigan, Ann arbor, USA, in 1983 and 1986, respectively. He is presently an associate professor in Department of Computer Science at KAIST. His research interests include computer graphics and computational geometry.
Address: Department of Computer Science, Korea Advanced Institute of Science and Technology, 373-1, Kusong-dong, Yusung-gu, Taejon 305-701, Korea.

Interference Detection Between Curved Objects for Computer Animation

MING C. LIN[1] and DINESH MANOCHA[2]

Abstract: We present algorithms for collision detection between curved objects moving in a dynamic environment and modeled using B-spline or piecewise algebraic surfaces. The problem of contact determination is formulated using algebriac constraints and the resulting algorithms are based on the geometry of the models. In particular for a convex surface, the algorithms use polyhedral approximations and proceed by keeping track of closest features between the polyhedral approximations, thereby utilizing geometric coherence between successive time steps in a dynamic environment. In general, the performance of the algorithm is independent of the combinatorial complexity of the polyhedral mesh. For general spline surfaces, the algorithm for contact determination uses the geometric formulation of surfaces along with algorithms for solving algebraic equations.

Key Words: Contact Determination, Spline Patches, Geometric Coherence, Collision Detection, Dynamic Environments

1 Introduction

In computer animation and physical simulation the actual motion is constrained by interactions among various objects. These interactions are modeled by controlling object motion, simulating contact constraints and impact dynamics (Sturman 1987, Moore and Wilhelms 1988, Hahn 1988, Barzel and Barr 1988, Baraff 1990, Pentland and Williams 1990). *Collision* or *geometric contact* is an important type of interaction among objects. Since the contact information is crucial to simulate impact response in a timely fashion, an efficient collision detection algorithm is fundamental for realistic dynamic simulation or computer animation in a virtual world (computer simulated environment).

The problem of collision detection between moving objects has been extensively studied. Its literature covers the field of robotics and computational geometry (Boyse 1979, Cameron and Culley 1986, Canny 1986, Gilbert and Hong 1989). In the last few years it has received a great deal of attention in computer animation, physical based modeling and graphics as well (Pentland and Williams 1990, Baraff 1990, Hahn 1988, Moore and Wilhelms 1988, Pentland 1990, Herzen et. al. 1990). Most of the work has been on the problem of collision detection between convex polyhedra. Earlier algorithms in computational geometry use the fact that there is a separating plane between the two non-colliding polyhedra, and it can be computed using linear programming. Good algorithms for linear programming are known as well (Megiddo 1983, Seidel 1990). Other algorithms in the literature exist for computing distance between convex polytopes (Gilbert and Hong, 1989) and collision detection between a number of convex polytopes (Moore and Wilhelms 1988, Hahn 1988). For dynamic applications, algorithms utilizing geometric coherence between successive collision detection problems

---
[1]Supported by David and Lucile Packard Fellowship and National Science Foundation Presidential Young Investigator Award (# IRI-8958577).

[2]Supported in part by a Junior Faculty Award

are found to be quite effective (Baraff 1990, Lin and Canny 1991). Local properties have been used in the earlier motion planning algorithms by Donald (1984), Lozano-Pérez and Wesley (1979) and later by Lin and Canny (1991), when two objects come into contact.

In most environments corresponding to computer animation and physical simulation, the objects cannot be modeled only by convex polytopes (Pentland and Williams 1990, Baraff 1990). When it comes to nonconvex and curved objects, an algorithm for time-dependent parametric surfaces has been presented in (Herzen et. al. 1990) and for implicitly defined surfaces in (Duff 1992). Both these algorithms expect a closed form expression of motion as a function of time and use subdivision based methods for collision detection, which can be slow in practice. An algorithm for implicitly defined models has been described by (Pentland and Williams 1989). It is based on testing samples of points and is not robust. Overall no good algorithms for collision detection are known for general curved object models and in many simulated environments collision detection can be a major bottleneck (Hahn 1988).

In this paper, we describe an efficient algorithm for collision detection between object models undergoing rigid motion described by Bézier, B-spline patches and algebraic surfaces. The set of parametric and implicit surfaces described in terms of polynomial equations is currently considered to be the state of class for modeling physical objects (Hoffmann 1989, Farin 1990). The algorithm does not expect the motion of the objects to be expressed as a closed form function of time. Rather it makes use of the coherence between successive time steps, algebraic and geometric properties of these surface formulations and hierarchical representations for non-convex objects. The simplest algorithm for convex surfaces uses a polyhedral approximation and keeps track of the closest features between two polytopes using local geometric properties described in (Lin and Canny 1991). Although the combinatorial complexity of the resulting polytope can be high, it does not affect the running time of the collision detection algorithm and the expected time is constant between successive time steps. Eventually the exact contact point is determined by solving a system of algebraic equations. The algorithm for general curve objects uses hierarchical representation, global methods for solving polynomial equations and tracing solutions for determining contact points. It involves finding all solutions to a system of algebraic equations, which is done only once (as part of preprocessing) and locally updating these solutions at run time efficiently. This algorithm is part of a general purpose system for collision detection between multiple objects, described using linear and curved object models, and undergoing rigid motion (Lin, Manocha and Canny 1993).

The rest of the paper is organized in the following manner. In Section 2 we review some techniques from geometric and solid modeling used in the algorithm. Section 3 briefly describes the constant time algorithm for surfaces with linear boundaries. In Section 4, we analyze the problem of collision detection between spline patches using algebraic methods and highlight how we can use coherence along with local and global methods to solve a system of algebraic equations. The complexity of these algebraic systems is analyzed as well. In Section 5, we combine the almost constant time algorithm for convex polytopes with algebraic approaches to describe an overall efficient algorithm for collision detection and contact point determination. Finally, in Section 6 we conclude by describing the algorithm's main features and highlighting areas for future research.

2 Background

When several objects are moving around in a simulated environment, it is possible for them to collide and interpenetrate. In a realistic world, this is an undesired state; therefore, the current computer animation and physical simulation systems have to deal with two issues: (a) collision detection (b) collision response.

In this paper we deal with the first problem only for objects described by spline models. Furthermore, we restrict the problem to rigid motion between various objects. However, we do not assume that the motion of the object is expressed as a closed form function of time. Many solutions to the problem of responding to collision are proposed in (Moore and Wilhelms 1988, Pentland and Williams 1990, Baraff 1990).

2.1 Object Models

Most of the earlier animation and simulation systems have been restricted to polyhedral models. However, modeling with surfaces bounded by linear boundaries turns out to be a major restriction in these systems. Currently most geometric and solid modeling systems use piecewise spline patches and surfaces described using rational functions (these include piecewise algebraic surfaces, Bézier patches etc.) to model physical objects (Hoffmann 1989, Farin 1990). Therefore, they are natural choices for models in the animation environments.

Typically spline patches are described geometrically by their control points, knot vectors and order continuity (Farin 1990). The control points have the property that the entire patch lies in the convex hull of these points. Most commonly used surfaces like spheres, ellipsoids, cylinders, tori can all be described in terms of rational spline patches. We also allow the objects to be described implicitly as algebraic surfaces. For examples, the quadric surfaces like spheres and cylinders can be simply described as degree two algebraic surfaces.

Our algorithm assumes that each surface model has been represented as piecewise Bézier patches or piecewise algebraic surfaces. Each Bézier patch is described using homogeneous coordinates as:

$$\mathbf{F}(s,t) = (X(s,t), Y(s,t), Z(s,t), W(s,t)). \tag{1}$$

We also need the geometric description in terms of control points. In case of algebraic surfaces, they are described as zero set of an equation, i.e. $f(x, y, z) = 0$.

2.2 System of Algebraic Equations

Our algorithm for interference detection between curved surfaces uses system of algebraic equations to express the constraints. Given a system of n algebraic equations in n unknowns:

$$
\begin{aligned}
F_1(x_1, x_2, \ldots, x_n) &= 0 \\
F_2(x_1, x_2, \ldots, x_n) &= 0 \\
&\vdots \quad \vdots \\
F_n(x_1, x_2, \ldots, x_n) &= 0.
\end{aligned}
$$

Let their degrees be d_1, d_2, ..., d_n, respectively. We are interested in computing all the solutions in some domain (like all the real solutions to the system).

Current algorithms for solving polynomial equations can be classified into local and global methods. Local methods like the Newton's method or optimization routines need a good initial guess to each solution in the given domain. Their performance is a function of the initial guesses. If we are interested in computing all the real solutions of a system of polynomial, solving equations by local methods requires that we know the number of real solutions to the system of equations and good guesses to these solutions.

The global approaches do not need any initial guesses. They are based on algebraic methods like resultants, Gröbner bases or purely numerical techniques like the homotopy methods. In the context of finite precision arithmetic, two useful approaches are based on resultant and matrix computations (Manocha 1992) and continuation methods. A recent survey on continuation methods is given in (Morgan 1992). The recently developed algorithm based on resultants and matrix computations has been shown to be very fast and accurate on many geometric problems and is reasonably simple to implement using linear algebra routines (Manocha 1992). The global methods compute all the solutions to the given equations in the complex space. The total number of solutions, say N, is bounded by the product of the degrees of the given equations. The complexity of the resultant based approach is $O(N^3)$ (Manocha 1992). In our algorithm for collision detection we use both the local and global methods for solving equations.

3 Polyhedral Collision Detection Algorithm

In this section, we present a simple and efficient collision detection algorithm for convex polyhedra by tracking the closest points between them. The method works by finding and maintaining the pair of closest features (vertex, edge, or face) on the two convex polyhedra, in order to calculate the Euclidean distance between them to detect possible collision. The method is applicable in static environment, but is especially well suited to dynamic domains as the objects move in a sequence of small, discrete steps. We take advantage of the empirical fact that the closest features change only infrequently as the objects move along finely discretized paths. By preprocessing the polyhedra, the algorithm runs in almost *constant time* if the objects are not moving very swiftly. Even when the environment is changing rapidly, the algorithm takes only slightly longer.

3.1 Preliminaries

Each polyhedron data structure has a field for its features (faces, edges, and vertices) and Voronoi regions. Each feature is described by its geometric parameters. Its data structure also includes a list of its boundaries, coboundaries, and *Voronoi regions*. A vertex's coboundaries are the edges which cobound it; an edge's coboundaries are its right and left faces; as for a face, the coboundary is the polyhedron which contains it.

Definition: A *Voronoi region* associated with each feature is a set of points closer to that feature than to any others (Preparata and Shamos 1985).

Based on the geometric properties of convex sets, *applicability criteria* that each feature-pair must satisfy to be the closest feature pair are established. These criteria are based on *Voronoi regions*. The data structure associated with each Voronoi region has a corresponding feature and a set of constraint planes with pointers to neighboring cells (which share the same constraint planes with it) in its data structure.

3.2 Overview

The distance computation algorithm by finding the closest feature pair is carefully described in (Lin and Canny 1991). Please refer to it for more detailed description. Here we only give a general overview of the algorithm.

Our method is straightforward in its conception. We start with a candidate pair of features, one from each polyhedron, and check whether the closest points lie on these features. Since the objects are convex, this is a local test involving only the boundary and coboundary of the candidate features. If the features fail the test, we step to a neighboring feature of one or both candidates, and try again. With some simple preprocessing, we can guarantee that every feature has a boundary and coboundary of constant size. This is how we can verify the closest feature pair in constant time.

When a pair of features fails the test, the new pair we choose is guaranteed to be closer than the old one. So when the objects move and one of the closest features changes, we usually find it after one or two iterations. Even if the closest features are changing rapidly, say once per step along the path, our algorithm takes only slightly longer. In this case, the running time is proportional to the number of feature pairs traversed in this process. It is *not* more than the product of the numbers of features of the two polyhedra, because the Euclidean distance between feature pairs must always decrease when a switch is made, which makes cycling impossible.

3.3 Applicability Test

The applicability test is a simple checking process that verifies whether a point lies inside the Voronoi region of a given feature. With preprocessing procedures that guarantee every feature has a constant size of boundary and coboundary to establish its Voronoi region, each applicability test is only a local test which runs in constant time. When a point fails the applicability test of a given feature, the pointer associated with each constraint plane provides a new, closer feature which shares

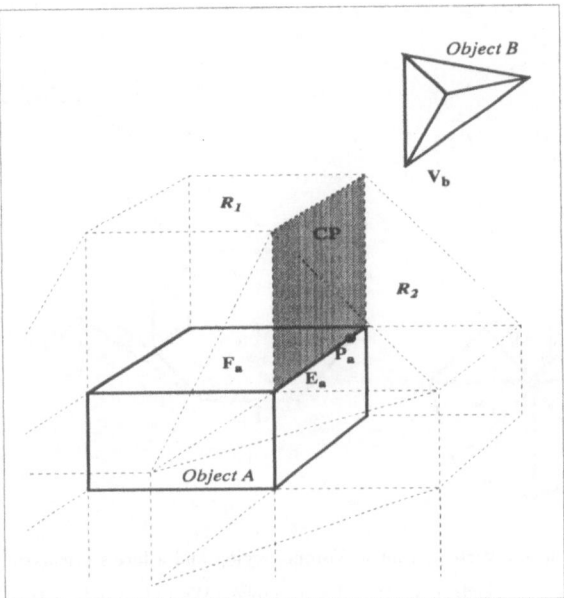

Figure 1: Applicability Test: $(F_a, V_b) \rightarrow (E_a, V_b)$ since V_b fails the applicability test imposed by the constraint plane CP. R_1 and R_2 are the Voronoi regions of F_a and E_a respectively.

the same constraint plane with the previous cell. See Fig.1

For a given pair of features, $feature_A$ and $feature_B$, on objects A and B, we first find a pair of nearest points, $point_A$ and $point_B$, between these two features. Then, we need to verify that $feature_B$ is truly the closest feature on B to $point_A$ (i.e. $point_A$ lies inside the Voronoi region of $feature_B$) and $feature_A$ is truly the closest feature on A to $point_B$ (i.e. $point_B$ lies inside the Voronoi region or of $feature_A$). If either check fails, a new and closer feature (which is usually one of the boundaries or coboundaries of the previous features) is substituted, and the new pair of features is checked. Eventually, we must terminate with the closest pair, since the distance between the feature pair is strictly decreasing through each iteration.

This verifying process is demonstrated in Fig. 1 where the previous closest feature candidate pair is (F_a, V_b), P_a and V_b are the two nearest points on these two given features. Though P_a satisfies the applicability of V_b (i.e. P_a lies inside of V_b's Voronoi region), V_b fails F_a's applicability test imposed by the constraint plane CP. Therefore, a new candidate pair (E_a, V_b), which is closer in distance, is returned. Then, the algorithm is called again upon (E_a, V_b) to verify whether this is the closest feature-pair, iteratively, until the nearest points on two features both satisfy the applicability tests of each other. Then, the algorithm stops and return with the closest feature-pair.

3.4 Implementation Issues

In general, each feature of a polyhedron has a low complexity of boundary or coboundary. To ensure that each feature has a constant size boundary and coboundary to achieve expected constant run time, the Voronoi region associated with each feature is preprocessed by subdividing the whole region into smaller cells. In Fig. 2, R_a, the Voronoi region of V_a which has 8 edges cobounding it, is subdivided into R_1, R_2, and R_3; R_b, the Voronoi region of F_b which has 8 edges in its boundary, is subdivided into R_4, R_5, R_6. This subdivision procedure is a simple calculation which can be done in linear time.

In order to minimize online computation time, we do all the subdivision procedures and build all the Voronoi regions first as one-time precomputational cost. We do *not* need reconstruct all the

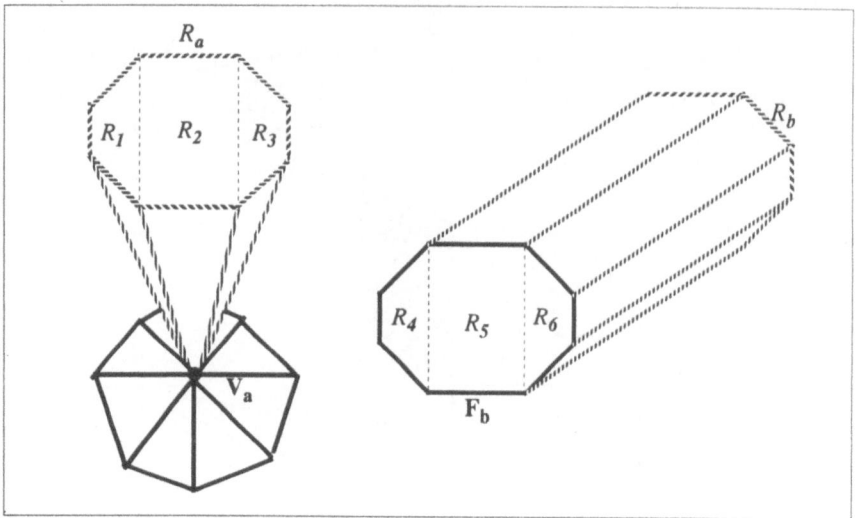

Figure 2: Subdivision of a vertex's conical Voronoi region and a face's prismatic Voronoi region

Voronoi regions for each polyhedron as the objects move. We only need to transform the closest feature candidates and recompute the nearest points, since *local* applicability constraints are all we need for tracking the closest pair of features. That is, we transform the point coordinates using *relative homogeneous transformation matrices* (which are available from either dynamic calculations or motion transformations) and leave constraint plane equations fixed.

4 Contact Determination for Curved Surfaces

In this section, we outline our approach based on algebraic methods for determining whether two curved surfaces described by spline models collide with each other. Our algorithm is based on geometric properties of these spline patches, formulation of constraints in terms of algebraic equations and computing the solutions of the system of algebraic equations.

4.1 Surface Intersection

In geometric and solid modeling, the problem of computing the intersection of surfaces represented as spline patches or algebraic surfaces has received a great deal of attention (Hoffmann 1989, Manocha and Canny 1991). Given two surfaces, the problem corresponds to computing all components of the intersection curve robustly and accurately. However, for collision detection we are actually dealing with a restricted version of this problem. That is, given two surfaces we want to know whether they have a geometric contact.

In dynamic environments we are dealing with rigid model of surfaces undergoing rigid motion. To account for the motion, we compute the new representation of the surface by applying that rigid motion transformation (represented as a 4×4 matrix multiplication) to its control points (Lin, Manocha and Canny 1993). The problem of collision detection reduces to checking, whether the two transformed spline patches described by their control points have a geometric contact. However, we are only interested in knowing whether the surfaces intersect and the possible contact points.

In general, given two spline patches, there is no good and quick solution to the question on whether they intersect or have a common geometric contact. For a few special objects such as two spheres or two cylinders this can be easily verified. A common approach for spline patches is based on utilizing the convex hull of control points corresponding to the surface formulation. If the convex hulls do not intersect, neither do the two surfaces. Otherwise, subdivide the surface and test the resulting control polytopes for intersection. However, this approach can be slow for simulated environments. Consider the case when the two surfaces are just touching each other at a contact point. In this case, the algorithm continues to subdivide the surfaces, until the volume of the convex hull is below a given threshold, thereby reaching such a conclusion. The subdivision algorithm results in linear convergence to the solution and generates a lot of intermediate data, which slow down the algorithm.

4.2 Algebraic Formulation

In this section we formulate the problems of contact determination between two surfaces using algebraic equations. In principle, it is possible to keep track of closest features between two curved surfaces as well, as we do for polyhedral objects. However, the problem of finding all the closest features between two curved objects can have a high computational complexity (Lin, Manocha and Canny, 1993). Furthermore, the closest features may correspond to points on the boundary of each model or curves on the boundary, as shown in Fig. 4. For non-convex curved surfaces, deriving closed form expressions for the curves corresponding to closest features is computationally expensive (Lin, Manocha and Canny, 1993).

Given two parametric Bézier surfaces,

$$\mathbf{F}(s,t) = (X(s,t), Y(s,t), Z(s,t), W(s,t))$$

and

$$\mathbf{G}(u,v) = (\overline{X}(u,v), \overline{Y}(u,v), \overline{Z}(u,v), \overline{W}(u,v)),$$

the contact between these surfaces can either be in terms of their boundary features (boundary curves in this case) or the two surfaces touching each other tangentially. The coefficients of these equations are changing with time (corresponding to the rigid motion undergone by the objects). The boundary intersections arise because we are allowing the surfaces to correspond to spline patches as opposed to only closed form objects like sphere, ellipsoid or torus. The problem of intersection determination reduces to finding solutions to algebraic equations. Let us analyze each case in detail:

- *Tangential Intersections :* The contact point lies in the interior of the two surfaces, the surface have a tangential intersection at that point (as shown in Fig. 3(a)). In other words, the cross product of the normal vectors at the point of contact is zero. The normal vector of a Bézier patch is given by: $\mathbf{F}_s(s,t) \times \mathbf{F}_t(s,t)$. The tangential intersection constraint is expressed in terms of the fact that the surfaces intersect at a point and their normal vectors are a scalar multiple of each other. These can be algebraically formulated as:

$$X(s,t)\overline{W}(u,v) - W(s,t)\overline{X}(u,v) = 0$$
$$Y(s,t)\overline{W}(u,v) - W(s,t)\overline{Y}(u,v) = 0 \tag{2}$$
$$Z(s,t)\overline{W}(u,v) - W(s,t)\overline{Z}(u,v) = 0.$$
$$(\mathbf{F}_s(s,t) \times \mathbf{F}_t(s,t)) = \alpha(\mathbf{G}_u(u,v) \times \mathbf{G}_v(u,v))$$

The last equation represented in terms of cross product corresponds to three scalar equations. We can eliminate α and represent them as solutions to two algebraic equations. Finally, we get five algebraic equations in four unknowns. This is an overconstrainted system and we solve it by applying the equation solving algorithms to compute the solutions of the first four equations and substituting them into the last equation.

- *Boundary Intersections :* They correspond to the intersection of the boundary curve of one of the surfaces with the other surface. Since the Bézier patches are defined in the domain, $(s,t) \in [0,1] \times [0,1]$, we obtain the boundary curves by substituting s or t to be 0 or 1. The resulting problem reduces to solving the equations:

$$X(s,1)\overline{W}(u,v) - W(s,1)\overline{X}(u,v) = 0$$
$$Y(s,1)\overline{W}(u,v) - W(s,1)\overline{Y}(u,v) = 0 \tag{3}$$
$$Z(s,1)\overline{W}(u,v) - W(s,1)\overline{Z}(u,v) = 0.$$

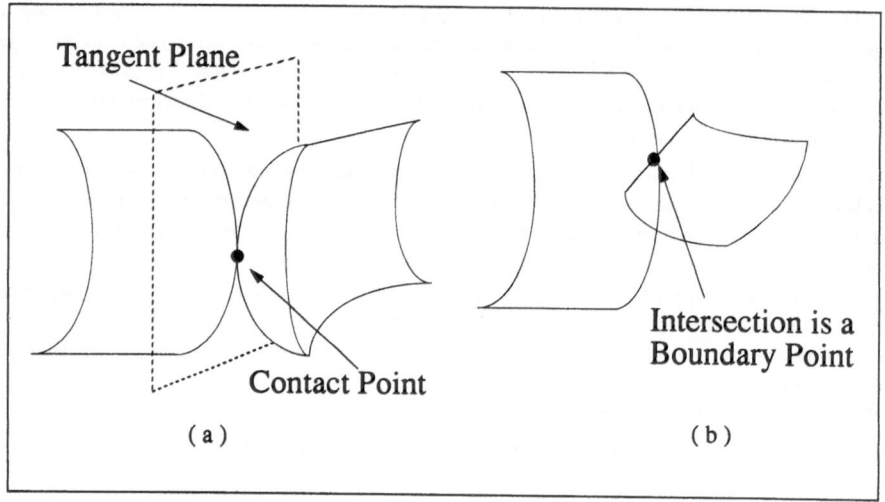

Figure 3: Tangential intersection and boundary intersection between two Bézier patches

Other possible boundary intersections can be computed in a similar manner. The intersection points can also be computed using geometric properties of control polytopes corresponding to Bézier curves and surfaces. An example has been shown in Fig. 3(b)

Two objects collide, if one of these sets of equations has a common solution in its domain, i.e. $(s,t) \in [0,1] \times [0,1]$ and $(u,v) \in [0,1] \times [0,1]$. A similar set of equations can be derived for surfaces represented algebraically. The tangency condition for two algebraic surfaces can be represented in terms of 4 equations in 3 unknowns.

The equations (2) and (3) can have more than one solution in the real domain. Given two objects in arbitrary configurations, it is difficult to find all solutions using local methods only. As a result, we use global methods highlighted in Section 2. However, finding all the solutions using global methods at each time instance can be slow. To speed up the algorithm, we compute the global solutions corresponding to the initial configuration. Furthermore, between successive time steps, the coefficients of the equations (2) and (3), corresponding to the new position change slightly. As a result we can compute their roots using the solutions at the previous time instance as starting points for the local methods. For most instances the local methods converge, unless the objects undergo abrupt motion and in such cases we can use the global solver.

When the two objects do not have a geometric contact, the system of equations (2) and (3) may have no real solutions. For example, consider two tori, represented algebraically, not touching each other in real space. All the solutions (if any) to the equations corresponding to the tangential intersection are therefore, complex. The fact that there is no real solution implies that there is no collision in the real space. However, as the two tori move towards each other, we update these complex solutions using local methods. As they come closer, the imaginary component of at least one root of the given system of equations is decreasing.

In a few degenerate cases, it is possible that the system of equations (2) and (3) have an infinite number of solutions. One such example is shown for two cylinders in Fig. 4. In such cases, the system of equations have infinite solutions. These cases can be easily detected using resultant methods.

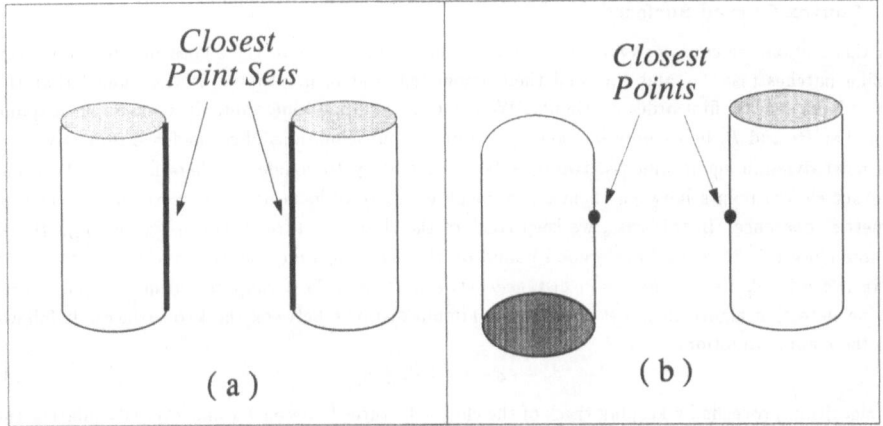

Figure 4: Closest features between two different orientations of a cylinder

5 Coherence for collision detection between curved objects

In this section we present an improved algorithm which combines the geometric coherence highlighted in Section 3 with the algebraic formulation given in Section 4 for an efficient collision detection between curved objects. An additional advantage of this approach lies in the fact that at each stage of the algorithm we have a good bound on the actual distance between the two geometric models, for choosing the appropriate time steps (see Lin, et. all 1993). The overall algorithm works very well for convex curved objects or those objects that can be expressed as a union of finite number of convex curved objects.

5.1 Approximate Representation of Curved Objects

We approximate each physical objects with curved boundary by a polyhedral model. These polyhedral models are used for collision detection, based on the fast algorithm utilizing local features. After the polyhedral objects collide, we use techniques based on equation solving to determine possible contact points. To compute the appropriate polyhedral approximations, we use ϵ-polytope approximations. In particular, an *ϵ-polytope* approximation of a surface is defined as:

Definition: Let S be a surface and P an ϵ-polytope approximation. For each point $\mathbf{p}$ on the boundary of polytope P, there is a point $\mathbf{s}$ on S such that $\| \mathbf{s} - \mathbf{p} \| \leq \epsilon$. Similarly for each point $\mathbf{s}$ on S, there is a point $\mathbf{p}$ on the boundary of P such that $\| \mathbf{p} - \mathbf{s} \| \leq \epsilon$.

The polyhedral model can be obtained by either a simple mesh generation or an adaptive polygonalization of surfaces. Algorithms for generating such meshes are highlighted for parametric patches in (Filip et. al. 1986) and for algebraic surfaces in (Hall and Warren 1990). Both simple polyhedral approximation and adaptive refinement inevitably introduce some modeling errors which, however, can be eliminated by defining a safety threshold to indicate a possible interference before two objects collide.

For some non-convex objects, it is possible to represent them as unions of convex objects. Otherwise it is always possible to decompose a concave polytope into a union of convex polytopes. Given concave objects as unions of convex subparts, we use hierarchical representations with each leaf node corresponding to each convex piece (and its ϵ-polytope approximation) and the root of the tree corresponding to the convex hull of the union of leaf nodes. More on hierarchical representations and their applications to large environments of several objects is given in (Lin, et. al. 1993).

5.2   Convex Curved Surfaces

In this section, we consider two convex spline models. The input to the algorithm are two convex B-spline patches (say S_A and S_B) and their associated control polytopes. It is assumed that the patches have at least first order continuity. We compute an ϵ-polytope approximation for each spline patch. Let P_A and P_b be ϵ_A-polytope and ϵ_B-polytope approximations of S_A and S_B, respectively.

In most dynamic environments, two objects are not likely to collide, so there is no need to find the exact closest points between them but a rough estimate of location to preserve the property of geometric coherence. In this case, we keep track of the closest features between P_A and P_B. Based on those closest features we have a good bound on the actual distance between the two surfaces. At any instance let d_p be the minimum distance between P_A and P_B (computed using our polyhedral collision detection algorithm). Let d_s be the minimum distance between the two surfaces. It follows from the ϵ-approximation:

$$d_p - \epsilon_A - \epsilon_B \leq d_s \leq d_p. \tag{4}$$

The algorithm proceeds by keeping track of the closest features between P_A and P_B and updating the bounds on d_s based on d_p. The closest features between the polyhedral approximation of two spheres are shown in Fig. 5. Whenever $d_p \leq \epsilon_A + \epsilon_B$, we use optimization routines to find the closest points between the two surfaces. However, we only use local optimization routines for computing the closest features and for a reasonably small ϵ_A and ϵ_B, the local method converge to a point. In case, the local methods fail to converge to a solution or at least one of the closest features corresponds to a line on the surface, we use the algorithm highlighted in the previous section based on global and local methods to solve equations.

The convergence of the optimization routines to the closest points is a function of ϵ_A and ϵ_B. In fact, the choice of ϵ in the ϵ-polytope approximation is important to the overall performance of the algorithm. Ideally, as $\epsilon \to 0$, we get a finer approximation of the curved surface and better the convergence of the optimization routines. However, a smaller ϵ increases the combinatorial complexity of the resulting polytope (i.e. number of vertices, edges, faces). Though polyhedral collision detection is an expected constant time algorithm at each step, the overall performance of algorithm is governed by the total number of feature pairs traversed by the algorithm, which is slightly dependent on motion and the resolution of the approximation. Consequently, a very small ϵ can slow down the overall algorithm. In our applications, we have chosen ϵ as a function of the dimension of a simple bounding box used to bound S_A. In particular, let l be dimension of the smallest cube, enclosing S_A. We have chosen $\epsilon = \delta l$, where $.01 \leq \delta \leq .05$. This has worked well in the examples we have applied the algorithm to.

If a given model can be decomposed into a union of convex objects, we use the above algorithm on the leaf nodes of object pairs along with the scheduling scheme for hierarchical models presented in (Lin, Manocha and Canny, 1993).

5.3   Concave Curved Objects

In this section we outline the algorithm for concave surfaces, which cannot be represented as a union of convex patches. A common example is a torus; a model of a teapot described by B-spline patches also comes in this category. The approach highlighted for convex patches in the previous section cannot be extended to a concave surface. In particular, given a concave surface, S, its ϵ-polytope is no longer a convex polytope, for a small ϵ. It is still possible to approximate a concave curved object by a union of convex polytopes (or polygonal meshes) and each of them is an ϵ-polytope. However, in general that requires at least $O(1/\epsilon)$ such polytopes. This can significantly slow down the algorithm for hierarchical models for a small ϵ (Lin, Manocha and Canny, 1993).

Given a B-spline surface, the algorithm decomposes into a series of Bézier patches. It uses a hierarchical representation for the resulting model and the leaf nodes correspond to the Bézier patches. At the intermediate level the representation consists of the convex hull of the control point of each

Figure 5: Closest features between polyhedral approximation of two spheres

resulting Bézier patch and the root of the tree corresponds to the convex hull of the control points of the B-spline surface.

Given such representations of two surfaces, the algorithm uses the almost constant time collision detection algorithm on the roots of the tree. In case, there is a collision between the polytopes at the root of the tree, the algorithm is applied to each pair of polytopes at the intermediate level along with the scheduling scheme for multiple object pairs (Lin, Manocha and Canny, 1993). Finally the algebraic algorithm for contact determination highlighted in Section 4 is used for contact determination between the Bézier patches.

5.4 Implementation and Performance

We have implemented the above algorithm and tested its performance on many cases. The collision detection routines give us an almost constant time performance for convex curved object. Besides spheres, cylinders and ellipsoids we have tried the algorithm on convex biquadric and bicubic patches as well.

In Fig. 6 and Fig. 7 we have illustrate the performance of the algorithm on a pair of tori. Each torus is represented as an algebraic surface of degree 4. Its equation is obtained by squaring the expressions in

$$F(x, y, z) = (\sqrt{x^2 + y^2} - k)^2 + z^2 - r = 0.$$

Each torus can be represented as a union of four Bézier patches. A hierarchical representation using the parametric as well as the implicit formulation of the torus is highlighted in (Lin, Manocha and Canny, 1993). The collision algorithm proceeds by running the constant time algorithm on the convex bounding polytope for each torus. After the two such polytopes intersect, the algorithm proceeds down the tree. Finally, the problem reduces to solving for equations corresponding to the tangential intersection between the two surfaces. The global solutions to these equations corresponds to computing all the solutions to three algebraic equations of degrees $4, 4$ and 6. The resulting system has 96 solutions and the problem reduces to finding the eigendecomposition of a 96×96 matrix (Manocha 1992). The eigendecomposition takes slightly more than a second on the IBM RS/6000 and all the solutions to the equations corresponding to tangential intersection are complex. We only keep track of a few solutions, whose imaginary parts are relatively small and decrease as the two tori move towards each other. Corresponding to the collision, the imaginary part of the solution is exactly zero.

6 Conclusion

A fast collision detection algorithm for curved objects in dynamic environments has been proposed here. It utilizes the expected *constant* time algorithm for polyhedra to locate the proximity of the closest points between two curved surfaces. Since the polyhedral collision detection algorithm is independent of the combinatorial complexity due to polygonalization, refining the polyhedral approximation will no longer have a detrimental side effect in run time using collision detection.

In many dynamic simulations, the assumption of rigid motion does not hold. For example, when we simulate deformable objects, the geometric coherence is quite difficult to capture between successive collision checks. We need to consider other approaches to animate flexible objects.

Acknowledgement: We would like to thank Prof. John Canny for useful discussions and Brian Mirtich for proof reading the manuscript. We are grateful to Anselmo Lastra's assistance in generating the color photos.

References

[1] D. Baraff (1990). Curved surfaces and coherence for non-penetrating rigid body simula tion. *ACM Computer Graphics*, 24(4):19–28.

[2] R. Barzel and A. Barr (1988). A modeling system based on dynamic constraints. *ACM Computer Graphics*, 22(4):31–39.

[3] J. W. Boyse (1979). Interference detection among solids and surfaces. *Comm. ACM*, 22(1):3–9.

[4] S. A. Cameron and R. K. Culley (1986). Determining the minimum translational distance between two convex polyhedra. *Proc. IEEE ICRA*, pages pp. 591–596.

[5] J. F. Canny (1986). Collision detection for moving polyhedra. *IEEE Trans. PAMI*, 8:pp. 200–209.

[6] B. R. Donald (1984). Motion planning with six degrees of freedom. Master's thesis, MIT Artificial Intelligence Lab. AI-TR-791.

[7] Tom Duff (1992). Interval arithmetic and recursive subdivision for implicit functions and constructive solid geometry. *ACM Computer Graphics*, 26(2):131–139.

[8] G. Farin (1990). *Curves and Surfaces for Computer Aided Geometric Design: A Practical Guide.* ACADEMIC PRESS INC., 1990.

[9] D. Filip, R. Magedson, and R. Markot (1986). Surface algorithms using bounds on derivatives. *GAGD*, 3:295–311.

[10] E. G. Gilbert and S. M. Hong (1989). A new algorithm for detecting the collision of moving objects. *IEEE Conference on Robotics and Automation*, pages pp. 8–14.

[11] E. G. Gilbert, D. W. Johnson, and S. S. Keerthi (1988). A fast procedure for computing the distance between objects in three-dimensional space. *IEEE J. Robotics and Automation*, vol RA-4:pp. 193–203.

[12] J. K. Hahn (1988). Realistic animation of rigid bodies. *Computer Graphics*, 22(4):pp. 299–308.

[13] M. Hall and J. Warren (1990). Adaptive polygonalization of implicitly defined surfaces. *IEEE Computer Graphics and Applications*.

[14] B. V. Herzen, A. H. Barr, and H. R. Zatz (1990). Geometric collisions for time-dependent parametric surfaces. *Computer Graphics*, 24(4):39–48.

[15] C. M. Hoffmann (1989). *Geometric and Solid Modeling*. Morgan Kaufmann, San Mateo, California.

[16] Ming C. Lin and John F. Canny (1991). Efficient algorithms for incremental distance computation. In *IEEE Conference on Robotics and Automation*.

[17] M. C. Lin, D. Manocha, and J. Canny (1993). Fast collision detection between geometric models. Technical report TR93-004. Departement of Computer Science, University of North Carolina.

[18] T. Lozano-Pérez and M. Wesley (1979). An algorithm for planning collision-free paths among polyhedral obstacles. *Comm. ACM*, 22(10):pp. 560–570.

[19] D. Manocha (1992). *Algebraic and Numeric Techniques for Modeling and Robotics*. PhD thesis, Computer Science Division, Department of Electrical Engineering and Computer Science, University of California, Berkeley, May.

[20] D. Manocha and J.F. Canny (1991). A new approach for surface intersection. *International Journal of Computational Geometry and Applications*, 1(4):491–516. Special issue on Solid Modeling.

[21] N. Megiddo (1983). Linear-time algorithms for linear programming in r^3 and related problems. *SIAM J. Computing*, 12:pp. 759–776.

[22] M. Moore and J. Wilhelms (1988). Collision detection and response for computer animation. *Computer Graphics*, 22(4):289–298.

[23] A. P. Morgan (1992). Polynomial continuation and its relationship to the symbolic reduction of polynomial systems. In *Symbolic and Numerical Computation for Artificial Intelligence*, pages 23–45.

[24] A. Pentland (1990). Computational complexity versus simulated environment. *Computer Graphics*, 22(2):185–192.

[25] A. Pentland nd J. Williams (1990). Good vibrations: Modal dynamics for graphics and animation. *Computer Graphics*, 23(3):185–192.

[26] F.P. Preparata and M. I. Shamos (1985). *Computational Geometru*. Springer-Verlag, New York.

[27] R. Seidel (1990). Linear programming and convex hulls made easy. In *Proc. 6th Ann. ACM Conf. on Computational Geometry*, pages 211–215, Berkeley, California.

[28] D. Sturman (1987). A discussion on the development of motion control systems. In *SigGraph Course Notes: Computer Animation: 3-D Motion Specification and Control*, number 10.

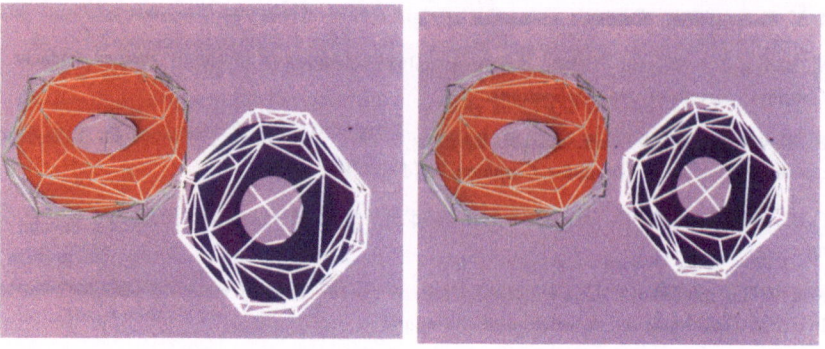

Figure 6: Constant time algorithm applied to the convex polytopes bounding the tori

Figure 7: Contact determination between the two tori

Ming C. Lin is currently pursuing her doctorate degree in electrical engineering and computer science at University of California, Berkeley. Lin received her B.S. and M.S. in electrical engineering and computer science from University of California, Berkeley in 1988 and 1991 respectively. Her research interests includes robot motion planning, computer animation, computational geometry, modeling, and software engineering. She is a member of IEEE and ACM.

Address: Department of Electrical Engineering and Computer Science, 211 Cory Hall, Box #79, University of California, Berkeley, CA. 94720, U.S.A.. E-mail: mlin@robotics.berkeley.edu.

Dinesh Manocha is currently an assistant professor in computer science at University of North Carolina at Chapel Hill. He received his B.Tech. degree in computer science from Indian Institute of Technology, Delhi in 1987; M.S. and Ph.D. in computer science at the University of California at Berkeley in 1990 and 1992, respectively. During the summers of 1988 and 1989, he was a visiting researcher at the Olivetti Research Lab and General Motors Research Lab, respectively. He received Alfred and Chella D. Moore Fellowship and IBM Graduate Fellowship in 1988 and 1991, respectively, and a Junior Faculty Award in 1992. He is a member of ACM, SIAM and IEEE. His research interests include geometric and solid modeling, virtual environments, physical based modeling, symbolic computation, and scientific computation.

Address: Department of Computer Science, Sitterson Hall, CB #3175, University of North Carolina, Chapel Hill, NC 27599-3175, U.S.A. E-mail: manocha@cs.unc.edu

An Integrated Computer Animation Environment

MINAKO M. HAYASHI, KEIJI NEMOTO, and YOSUKE TAKASHIMA

For those who are not familiar with computers and animation, there are three problems in making animation easily, i.e. making actors' shapes, defining actors' actions and directing animation. This paper introduces generating actors model, which consists of the shape module and the action module, and camera work model. We realized an integrated animation environment based on these models. The environment consists of three subsystems, making actors' shape, defining actors' actions, and directing animation (Fig. 1). Because three subsystems are tightly connected, user can browse among the subsystems.

An actors' shape is collections of solids. Each solid has a surface shape, a bone (or bones) and joints. Individual solids are connected to each other through joints. By combining solids with joints, users can define actors' shapes (Fig. 2). A motion is defined by a joint angle variation. When the motion is propagated to the next bone, the bone position changes. By compounding simple joint rotations, users can define more complex actions like "dance" and "walk". Users edit these complicated actions on time charts (Fig. 3). Because a scenario is sequences of actions of actors, the scenario is shown as a set of the time charts each of which corresponds to the sequence of the actor. Directing animation consists of positioning of actors, setting stage properties, camera-works, and so on. Camera-work plays an important role among them. Introducing a virtual camera object and camera control functions, such as zooming, panning, and so on, enables defining camera-work. Combining with plural camera control functions, users can create more complicated camera-works. Since a camera is defined as an actor without a shape, user can control camera-works on time charts as well as defining actors' actions.

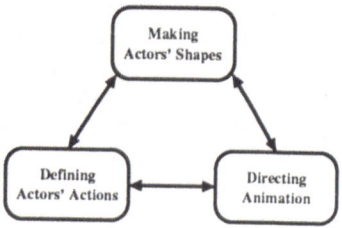

Fig. 1 : Construction of the environment

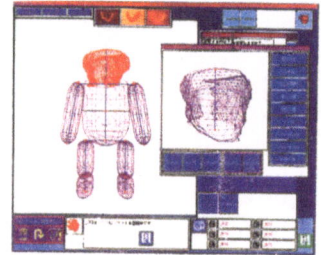

Fig. 2 : Making Actors' Shapes

Actor's data is defined in the form of tree structure and managed on a frame by frame basis. By adopting this data structure, users can define actors' simple actions, compound actions and camera-works in the same manner.

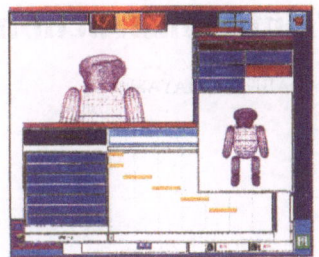

Fig. 3 : Defining Actors' Actions

Address: NEC Corporation, C&C Information Technology Res. Labs., 4-1-1 Miyasaki Miyamaeku, Kawasaki Kanagawa 216, Japan

Virtual Walker and Its Application for Plant Construction

MANABU KOBAYASHI

1. Introduction

The paper presents a overall description of the "Virtual Walker" which dynamically visualizes and simulates the interior of the buildings using the advanced computer graphics technique. The paper also describes its application for the scheduling and the timely progress control of the plant construcion.

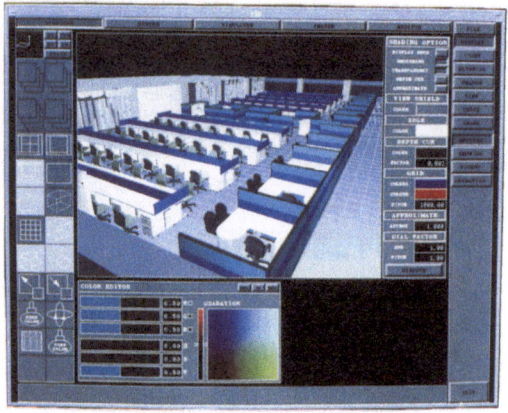

2. System Functions

VW consists of five major funcions, ;Modelling, Model Display, Walking Route Definition, Virtual Walking and Motion Analysis.

2.1 Modelling

In advance, each office furniture (desk, chair, partition, wall, etc.) has been created as CATIA or AUTOCAD surface or solid model, and stored in the furniture library.

2.2 Model Display

For the Model Display, view point and viewing pyramid are specified. Light type and position (up to 8) are also specified. Then Flat or Gouraud shading images of the given model are dynamically generated. These indications are all performed using OSF/MOTIF with Japanese letters. Morever, several advanced images which include the shadow calculation, texture mapping, background synthesis which is ispecially useful through transparent glasses are also prepared using RENDERMAN.

2.3 Walking route definition

Walking route is specified using two projection drawings. The body is projected on the XY and XZ plane, and on these drawings, walking route is defined as the discrete dots using mouse.

2.4 Virtual Walking

Virtual Walking can be carried out on the specified route. Surrounding scenery dynamically changes according to the walking. At the arbitrary point walking can be stopped and the eye can be changed into the upper, lower, left and right direction, and then walking can be restarted. Near and far clipping can be considered at the same time.

2.5 Motion Analysis

VW also makes it possible to define the motion of each object in the model, then the motion in the surroundings can be simulated. Moreover, the dimensions which show the distance between the two objects can be displayed dynamically. The interference of the objects can be also checked by changing the color.

3 .Application to the Plant Construction

In the plant construction process,   schedule planning and progress management have been carried out using the PMS (project management system) so far.   But in such PMS system, only the uninteresting figures and graphs are given,   then the understanding of the status or result has been so tiresome. The request to intellectually visualize the output of the PMS by connecting it to the real 3D plant model has been so enthusiastic and urgent. So, for the first time we have realized this strong request by applying VW to the PMS,   and also virtual walking on the inspection route where human being is not really able to approach owing to the danger, has become possible.   Descrinination of finished and unfinished parts by color and the simulation of machine motion are especially useful to the users.

Address: Techno. System Center,NK-EXA Co, Ltd, NKK Keihin Computer Blgd, 1-1, Minamiwatarida-cho, Kawasaki-ku, Kawasaki 210, Japan

Part II

Visualization and Applications

Navigation and Animation in a Volume Visualization System

Arie E. Kaufman, Lisa M. Sobierajski, Ricardo S. Avila, and Taosong He

ABSTRACT

The VolVis system for volume visualization supports numerous visualization algorithms and methods within a consistent and well-organized framework. Navigation and Animation components have been incorporated into VolVis which allow interactive object manipulation and quick specification of complex animation sequences. Navigation is controlled by a variety of 2D and 3D input devices. VolVis includes a unified protocol for communicating with these input devices, allowing for input device independent development.

Keywords: Volume Rendering, VolVis, 3D Input Devices, Volumetric Ray Tracing

1. INTRODUCTION

Volume visualization is becoming an integral part of many scientific fields (Kaufman 1990). Visualization techniques are used in applications as diverse as aiding physicians in surgical and radiation treatment planning (Herman and Udupa 1983), helping meteorologists understand weather patterns (Hibbard and Santek 1989), and assisting geologists in identifying potential oil reservoirs (Wolfe and Liu 1988). In the past, new visualization systems have been developed for each visualization application. In each system, assumptions are made about the type of data, the rendering algorithm, or the input device employed, creating a software package with limited applicability.

A few visualization systems have been developed which achieve some degree of independence. For example, a procedural interface was developed (Montine 1991) which provides a library of C routines for data visualization. A more complete system, ANALYZE (Robb 1990), provides the scientist with a rich set of tools for the manipulation, analysis, and display of 3D biomedical data. Another commercial system is VoxelView of Vital Images (Senft, Argiro, and Van Zandt 1990, Van Zandt and Argiro 1989), which has been developed for Silicon Graphics graphics engines. The ability to interactively manipulate data in a simple, intuitive way is an important part of a visualization system. Yet many systems provide only primitive tools for this purpose. For example, interaction in ANALYZE is achieved through keyboard and mouse input only, which does not always provide an intuitive method for performing 3D data manipulation and analysis.

In this paper we describe a comprehensive volume visualization system called *VolVis*, and focus on its Navigation and Animation component (also called the Navigator and Animator). The goal of the *VolVis* system is to create a powerful, yet consistent and well organized, volume visualization environment. To achieve this goal, the user is given control of many aspects of the visualization process. For example, when creating an image, the user can select between several rendering algorithms spanning the speed versus accuracy continuum. A brief discussion of the system functionality and rendering algorithms is given in Section 2. Positioning objects within a scene and selecting a view point can be a time-consuming process. For this reason, navigation facilities have been added to *VolVis*, which allow the user to interactively position objects and the view point using a variety of input devices. The user can interactively switch between different input devices for different tasks. For example, the user may wish to use the Spaceball to position the view, yet may prefer the DataGlove for manipulating objects. The Navigator and the use of input devices are described in detail in Sections 3-5. Since a better understanding of the 3D nature of a scene can be obtained from an animation sequence than from a single still image, facilities for generating animations are included in *VolVis*. The Animator is discussed further in Section 6.

2. SYSTEM FUNCTIONALITY

The *VolVis* system contains several primary components which are intended to meet the various needs of volume visualization users. These include File I/O, Filter, Object Control, Image Control, Rendering, Navigation, Animation, Quantitative Analysis, and Input Device. These components are described below.

The File I/O component handles all input and output of *VolVis*. This includes the ability to save and retrieve several volumetric data file types, geometric data files, multi-dimensional texture files, 24-bit image and animation files, world environment files, and interaction log files. It is often desirable to apply a filter to a volumetric data set during or after input in order to enhance features, smooth data, or reduce noise. For this purpose several standard filters are provided within the Filter component of *VolVis*.

Every object within *VolVis* contains properties which can be modified within the Object Control component. The *VolVis* system contains several basic object types, including *View*, *Volume*, *Light*, and *World*. The number and types of properties vary depending on the object in question. For example, some of the more relevant properties of a *Volume* are position and orientation, segmentation, color, texture, local shading model, cut geometries, and flags indicating whether this object is currently visible and/or modifiable. Modifiability allows the user to apply transformations to several *Volumes* and *Lights* simultaneously in order to perform complex object manipulations easily. Visibility simply determines whether a *Volume* is visible or a *Light* is active. The *View* specifies the current viewing properties. Viewing parameters such as eye position, field of view, and image size can be modified using the Object Control component. The global properties stored within the *World* such as ambient lighting, light attenuation factor, background color, and global cut geometries may also be modified in this component. The Object Control component provides a window-based method for modifying these properties. However, some properties may be modified utilizing more interactive methods within the Navigation component.

The Rendering component of *VolVis* provides the user with a variety of rendering algorithms, each having its own unique set of advantages and disadvantages. Generally speaking, these algorithms span the continuum from fast and inaccurate to slow and accurate. When a user is manipulating an object in the scene, it is necessary to have as fast a projection rate as possible. For this purpose, a fast projection algorithm has been incorporated into *VolVis*. This technique, which is used in the Navigator, involves the use of a reduced resolution representation of the scene and the exploitation of the graphics hardware of the machine in order to provide interactive projection rates, typically about 10 frames per second. The Navigator is further described in Section 3. Another projection algorithm, called Polygon Assisted Ray Casting

(PARC), provides highly accurate projections with relatively fast projection times (Avila, Sobierajski, and Kaufman 1992). Finally, a powerful volumetric ray tracer is included within the Rendering component to provide high quality projections using a global illumination model, similar to (Yagel, Cohen, and Kaufman 1992). This is particularly useful when global effects such as shadows and reflections can provide more clues about the structure of the data (Yagel, Kaufman, and Zhang 1991).

The Navigator is an interactive volumetric navigation aid which allows the user to specify complex flight paths through volumetric data sets as well as directly manipulate all objects defined within the *World*. The Navigator is the focus of Sections 3 and 5. One can create complex animations within the *VolVis* system through the use of the Animator. The Animator and the process of creating animations are discussed in Section 6.

The Quantitative Analysis component extracts quantitative measurements from volumetric data. Measurement capabilities include 2D and 3D distance, histogram, surface area, and volume measurements. These measurements are performed either on an entire volume or on a subregion selected within the Navigator component.

The Input Device component allows the user to choose the input devices currently in use within the *VolVis* system. The user may choose from among a standard mouse, a flying mouse, buttons and dials, an Isotrak, a Spaceball, or even a DataGlove. The Input Device component is described in more detail in Section 4.

3. THE NAVIGATOR

The Navigation component of *VolVis* (the Navigator) is responsible for the interactive manipulation and display of objects within the *VolVis* environment. This is accomplished through the use of the satellite window, the manual control window, and the projection window. The satellite window provides a quick projection from afar to convey the over all layout of the many objects within the scene. In addition, the satellite window may be used to interactively manipulate objects. The manual control window provides the ability to apply precise transformations to selected objects, while the projection window enables the user to interactively manipulate objects from the *View*'s eye position. For instance, the *View*'s position and orientation can be modified by either specifying a numeric transformation in the manual control window or by interactively moving the *View* through the scene in the projection window. The interactive manipulation of the *View* in the projection window is designed so that the user can fly through the scene by pointing the input device in the desired direction. In addition, the user may increase or decrease flight speed and stop at desired locations. The trajectory of the *View* during the flight is stored for possible use in an animation (see Section 6).

The interactive demands of the projection window require a quick rendering algorithm capable of providing a rough estimate of the actual image. A *VolVis* scene may contain numerous types of objects, ranging from simple geometric data to volumetric data. Fortunately, most current day workstations provide dedicated graphics hardware for the display of geometric primitives. This allows the quick projection of geometric data without much effort. The projection of volumetric data also makes use of standard graphics hardware by projecting a rough polygonal representation of the outer surface of each volumetric data set. The polygonal representation of a volume is constructed by subdividing the volume into small equal-sized subvolumes and checking each subvolume for the presence of a surface. All subvolumes containing a surface are then stored in a list for Navigator projections.

4. INPUT DEVICES

Input devices play a central role in the natural and interactive control of the Navigator. There are numerous types of input devices, ranging from the standard mouse to the relatively complex DataGlove. Each input device provides different information and is suitable for different applications. The purpose of the Input Device component is to create a unified and expandable protocol for controlling and communicating with each input device so that input devices can be utilized in a device independent manner.

To achieve this goal it is useful to observe that most applications need essentially similar information from the different types of input devices. For example, nearly all applications request 2D position information, while others may require 3D position and orientation data. Our goal is to provide the information to the application using a generalized input device protocol. This is accomplished by creating a *virtual input device* which effectively hides the details of the real input device and simplifies the coding.

The Input Device component is based on a client-server model. The physical input device is seen as the server while the application is treated as the client. A server can provide any of the following information to a client: 2D positions, 3D positions, 3D orientations, and selections. For example, a server may recognize both a right button press of the mouse and a "thumb's up" posture of the DataGlove. The server passes either of these events to the client as a "Confirm" selection, therefore the client does not need to know which input device was used to make the selection. A virtual input device may be created by combining information from two or more input devices, thereby creating a virtual server. For example, we can create a virtual input device whose position is provided by an Isotrak while orientation information is provided by a Spaceball.

Input devices are classified into four classes according to their dimensionality: primitive devices (0D or 1D; e.g., keyboard and dial), 2D devices (e.g., mouse), 3D devices (e.g., Isotrak, Spaceball, DataGlove), and special devices (e.g., eye-tracker, voice). In order to achieve true device independence, each device should be able to simulate any other device. This is fairly easy when handling buttons or selections since a keyboard is always available. In addition, particular event sequences from an input device can be implemented as selections. For example, a DataGlove "ok" gesture can be implemented as a selection. Input device simulation becomes much more complicated when an input device attempts to simulate another input device with a higher degree of freedom. One example of this is the simulation of an Isotrak, which is a six-degree-of-freedom device, with a mouse which has only two degrees of freedom. Therefore it is sometimes useful for the application to inquire the class of the current input device in order to provide more intuitive interaction methods.

The most important advantage of using a virtual input device is input device independence. A user need not be concerned with the initialization and the operation of the physical input devices, but can interactively control them through the user interface. Also, the addition of an input device is simply performed by adding a low level device driver and simulation programs. A user can interactively decide what combination of input devices is suitable for a specific application by changing the virtual input device configuration without affecting the application program.

5. NAVIGATION CONTROL

The Navigation component of *VolVis* achieves interactive control by accessing input devices using the device independent protocol described above. One of the more useful examples of this process is the ability to navigate the *View* through the *VolVis* scene. In order to perform this task while maintaining a high degree of device independence, it is necessary to make allowances for the several different classes of input devices.

Maneuvering the location of the *View* through the scene requires movement in 3D. In addition to the three degrees of freedom required to specify the location of the *View*, an additional three degrees of freedom are necessary to fully specify the *View*'s orientation. Provided that a six-degree-of-freedom input device is available, *VolVis* directly utilizes the position and orientation information from the input device to modify the *View*. Unfortunately, most workstations come equipped with a standard mouse, which only provides two degrees of freedom. The Navigator solves this problem by inquiring the class of the current input device, and utilizing interaction techniques appropriate for that class of input device. Navigation with a standard mouse is done by modifying the position and orientation of the *View* incrementally with the specification of a 3D vector. We consider the *View* as an object with a velocity and the 3D vector as a force being applied to the *View*. This gives the interactive control of the *View* the feel of a simple flight simulator. Given this paradigm, we only need three degrees of freedom from the input device in order to modify the *View*.

The most obvious solution to the problem of providing interactive control of the *View* using a mouse is to simulate a three-degree-of-freedom input device using a triad mouse paradigm (Nielson and Olsen Jr. 1986). The 3D position of the mouse is then translated into a 3D vector and applied to the *View*. However, it is quite difficult to get accustomed to this technique, and continuous movement is not provided in all directions. The solution used in the Navigator is to request only two degrees of freedom from the mouse and map these two degrees of freedom to 3D vector space. More specifically, navigation is performed by requesting the X and Y position of the mouse using the center of the Navigator projection window as our origin. We then map the X and Y position to some X and Y component of the 3D vector and assume a constant Z component. Finally, additional selections are provided for making changes to the Z component. With a suitable mapping we are able to intuitively maneuver the *View* through the scene by pointing in the desired direction.

6. THE ANIMATOR

The main goal of the Animation component of *VolVis* (the Animator) is to provide a method for quickly specifying complex animation sequences. Included in the Animator is the ability to preview the animation sequence using a reduced resolution projection, such as that provided by the Navigator. The user can then specify the desired rendering parameters and generate the images of the final animation sequence.

One method of specifying an animation sequence is to specify "key frames" of the animation, and interpolate to determine the parameters for the frames lying between key frames. A problem with this method is that if the key frames differ significantly, interpolation between the key frames becomes difficult. Yet specifying enough key frames for a long, complex animation can become quite tedious. To solve this problem, specification of an animation sequence in *VolVis* is accomplished through the use of the Navigator.

As described in the previous sections, the Navigator can be used to manipulate any object in the scene, including the *View*. If, for example, an animation is desired in which only the *View* moves, this can be specified easily using the Navigator. The user simply flies through the scene, and the trajectory taken is saved as a specification of the animation. Since video rates are typically 30 frames per second, and the Navigator generally updates at about 10 frames per second, some interpolation may be required to generate frames between the specified frames. This does not create the same interpolation problem as found in key frame specification, since consecutive frames of the Navigator flight path do not differ greatly.

More complex animations requiring several moving objects can also be specified using the Navigator. If an animation is required in which two objects move, as well as the *View*, this can be specified in three steps. First, one of the objects is interactively manipulated using the Navigator, with the path of the object saved as the current animation. This object is not necessarily always in the *View*, and therefore it may not be possible to specify its path using only the Navigator projection window. If this is the case, the user can utilize the Navigator satellite window to specify the trajectory. Next, the second object is manipulated, while the animation of the first object is played back. That is, while manipulating the second object, the user sees the motion of the first object. Finally, the user flies through the scene to specify the motion of the *View*, while the two objects are in motion.

The Navigation method of animation specification is quite simple to use. Investigating volumetric data through the use of animation typically requires that only the *View* be in motion. The time required to specify such an animation is approximately equal to the running time of the final animation, since the final animation matches the length of the sequence specified using the Navigator. For multiple objects in motion, the specification time is approximately the number of moving objects multiplied by the running length of the final animation.

One possible way to speed up the specification of an animation sequence even further is to add an "auto-pilot" feature to the Navigator. With this feature, the user specifies some parameters such as speed, region of interest, length of flight, etc., and the Navigator will fly on auto-pilot, creating a trajectory fitting the specified parameters. For example, the user can specify a two-minute-long animation at slow speed, focusing on areas of high intensity.

7. RESULTS

VolVis is currently running under X/Motif on HP and Silicon Graphics platforms, and under X/Openwindows on the Sun platform, taking advantage of the graphics hardware as available on HP, SGI, and Sun Workstations. Interactive control of *VolVis* is accomplished through either a standard mouse, buttons and dials, an Isotrack, a Spaceball, or a VPL DataGlove. Figure 1 shows the *VolVis* system running on a Silicon Graphics Indigo Elan. The Navigator projection window displays a rough approximation of the two volumetric data sets while the adjacent window shows the corresponding ray traced image. The *VolVis* top-level window, Navigator manual control window, rendering window, and image control window are also shown.

The *VolVis* system has been used extensively to visualize data from several disciplines. Collaborating with neurobiologists we have visualized nerve cell data scanned with a confocal laser microscope. Figure 2 shows two frame pairs from an animation which follows the axon of a bullfrog sympathetic ganglion nerve cell until it reaches the cell body. In both frame pairs the left image shows the frame computed by the Navigator while the right image shows the frame rendered with the *VolVis* ray tracer. The animation was created by first specifying a flight path within the Navigator projection window using a standard mouse as an input device. Then various lighting and shading parameters were modified to enhance the surface features of the nerve cell. Finally, a ray traced animation was computed, resulting in the final animation sequence.

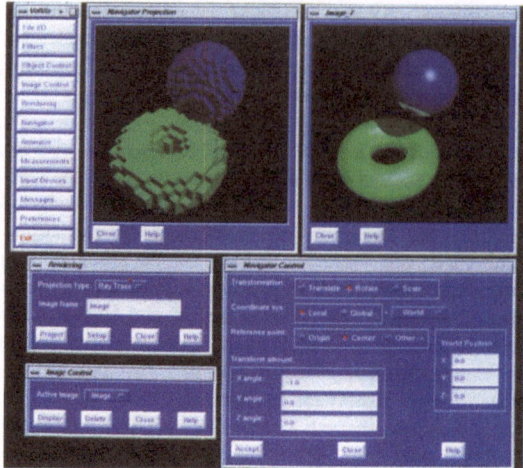

Figure 1: The X/Motif version of *VolVis* running on a Silicon Graphics Indigo Elan.

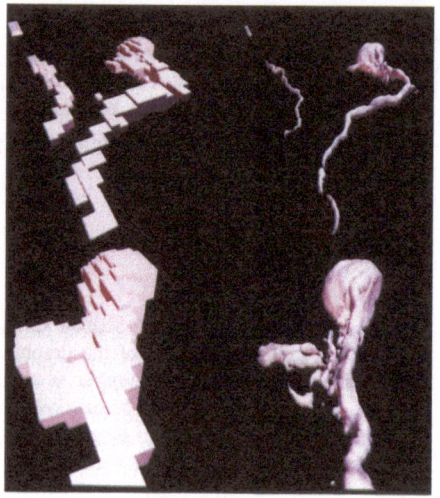

Figure 2: Two frame pairs from an animation which follows the axon of a bullfrog sympathetic ganglion nerve cell.

71

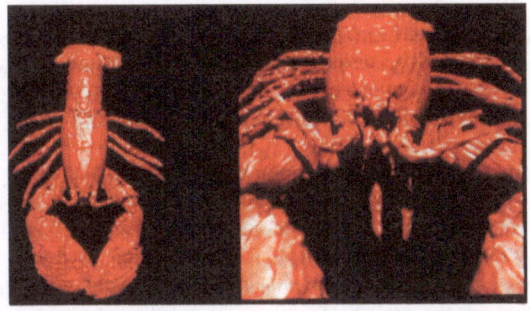

Figure 3: Two frames from an animation sequence of a flight through a lobster's claws rendered with the *VolVis* ray tracer.

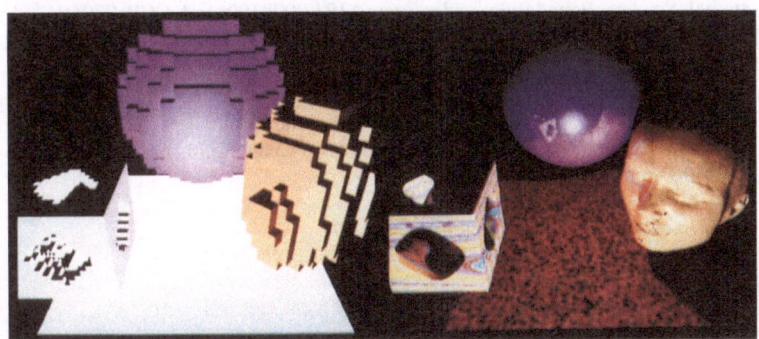

Figure 4: A frame pair from an animation which contains multiple geometric and volumetric objects. The left image was generated using the Navigator, while the right image was rendered using the *VolVis* ray tracer.

Figure 3 shows two frames from an animation sequence of a flight through the claws of a lobster. The data set was obtained from a CT scanner at a resolution of 320×320×34 voxels. The lobster was loaded into the *VolVis* system and s volumetric texture map was applied. A flight path was selected using the Navigator, and the final animation frames were computed using the *VolVis* ray tracer. The image resolution for this animation is 512×512 pixels.

Figure 4 shows a frame pair from an animation through a complex scene. The scene contains three volumetric objects and one geometric object. The volumetric objects include an MRI scanned human head (256×256×109 voxels), a volumetric sphere (120×120×120 voxels), and a minimal periodic function (100×100×100 voxels). The polygon used as a floor is a geometric object. The left image shows the Navigator projection of the scene. The Navigator was used to specify a flight path through the periodic function, around the sphere, then past the nose of the MRI head. The final animation frames were computed with the *VolVis* ray tracer at a resolution of 512×512 pixels. The right image shows the ray traced frame corresponding to the Navigator frame shown on the left.

8. ACKNOWLEDGMENTS

This project has been supported in part by a grant from the Center for Biotechnology, SUNY at Stony Brook, which is sponsored by the New York State Science and Technology Foundation, by the National Science Foundation under grants IRI-9008109 and CCR-9205047, by Howard Hughes Medical Institute, by a grant from the Department of Energy, and by a grant from the Hewlett-Packard Company. The confocal microscopy is courtesy of Paul R. Adams, Barry J. Burbach, and David Printzenhoff of the Howard Hughes Medical Institute at Stony Brook, New York. The CT lobster data set is courtesy of AVS and the minimal periodic function data set is courtesy of Ames Laboratory, Iowa. Special thanks to Sean Smith and Richard Calmbach for their help with the implementation of *VolVis*.

9. REFERENCES

Avila, R. S., Sobierajski, L. M., and Kaufman, A. E., (1992), "Towards a Comprehensive Volume Visualiztion System ", *Proceedings Visualization '92*, Boston, MA, pp 13-20.

Herman, G. T. and Udupa, J. K., (1983), "Display of 3D Digital Images: Computational Foundations and Medical Applications", *IEEE Computer Graphics and Applications*, **3**, 5, pp 39-46.

Hibbard, W. and Santek, D., (1989), "Visualizing Large Data Sets in the Earth Sciences", *IEEE Computer*, **22**, 8, pp 53-57.

Montine, J. L., (1991), "A Procedural Interface for Volume Rendering", *Proceedings Visualization '90*, San Diego, CA, pp 36-44 .

Nielson, G. M. and Olsen Jr., D. R., (1986), "Direct Manipulation Techniques for 3D Objects Using 2D Locator Devices", *Proceedings ACM Workshop on Interactive 3D Graphics*, Chapel Hill, NC, pp 175-182.

Robb, R. A., (1990), "A Software System for Interactive and Quantitative Analysis of Biomedical Images", in *3D Imaging in Medicine: Algorithms, Systems, Applications*, K. H. Hoehne, H. Fuchs, and S. M. Pizer, (eds), Springer-Verlag, Berlin, , pp 333-361.

Senft, S. L., Argiro, V. J., and Van Zandt, W. L., (1990), "Volume Microscopy of Biological Specimens Based on Non-Confocal Imaging Techniques", *Proceedings Visualization '90*, San Francisco, CA, pp 424-428.

Van Zandt, W. and Argiro, V., (1989), "A New 'Inlook' on Life", *Unix Review*, **7**, 3, pp 52-57.

Wolfe, R. H. and Liu, C. N., (1988), "Interactive Visualization of 3D Seismic Data: A Volumetric Method", *IEEE Computer Graphics and Applications*, **8**, 7, pp 24-30.

Yagel, R., Kaufman, A., and Zhang, Q., (1991), "Realistic Volume Imaging", *Proceedings Visualization '90*, San Diego, CA, pp 226-231.

Yagel, R., Cohen, D., and Kaufman, A., (1992), "Discrete Ray Tracing", *IEEE Computer Graphics and Applications*, pp 19-28.

Arie Kaufman is a Professor of Computer Science at the State University of New York at Stony Brook. He is also the director of the Cube project for volume visualization supported by the National Science Foundation, Department of Energy, Hughes Aircraft Company, Hewlett-Packard Company, Silicon Graphics Company, and the State of New York. He has conducted research in computer graphics for over 20 years specializing in volume visualization, computer graphics architectures and algorithms, user interfaces, and multimedia. He is currently the chairman of the IEEE Computer Society Technical Committee on Computer Graphics, has been the Papers or Program co-Chair for Visualization '90-93 Conferences, and co-Chair for several Eurographics Graphics Hardware Workshops. He received a BS in Mathematics and Physics from the Hebrew University of Jerusalem in 1969, an MS in Computer Science from the Weizmann Institute of Science (Rehovot) in 1973, and a PhD in Computer Science from the Ben-Gurion University in 1977.

Address: Department of Computer Science, State University of New York at Stony Brook, Stony Brook, NY 11794-4400, USA.

Email: ari@cs.sunysb.edu.

Lisa Sobierajski is currently a PhD student at the State University of New York at Stony Brook. Her research interests include global illumination models and rendering algorithms for voxel-based data, animation, and visualization systems. She is currently working on a visualization system which incorporates several data types into a single, consistent global illumination model. She received her BS Cum Laude (1989) and MS (1990) from the Department of Computer Science at the State University of New York at Stony Brook.
Address: Department of Computer Science, State University of New York at Stony Brook, Stony Brook, NY 11794-4400, USA.
Email: lisa@cs.sunysb.edu.

Ricardo S. Avila is a Senior Programmer at the Howard Hughes Medical Institute in the Department of Neurobiology and Behavior located at the State University of New York at Stony Brook. His research interests include voxel-based rendering algorithms, scientific visualization, animation, and input devices. He is currently working on the development of visualization tools for biological research. He received his BS and MS from the Department of Computer Science at the State University of New York at Stony Brook in 1989 and 1992, respectively.
Address: Howard Hughes Medical Institute, Department of Neurobiology & Behavior, State University of New York at Stony Brook, Stony Brook, NY 11794-5230, USA.
Email: avila@adamsgw.bio.sunysb.edu

Taosong He is a PhD candidate in computer science at the State University of New York at Stony Brook. He graduated from the Department of Computer Science at Fudan University in 1991, where he was also a research assistant. His current research interests focus on 3D input device applications and multimedia systems, which include input device independent 3D user interface design, direct manipulation with 3D input devices in volume visualization systems, input techniques for virtual reality, and device integration in multimedia environments.
Address: Department of Computer Science, State University of New York at Stony Brook, Stony Brook, NY 11794-4400, USA.
Email: taosong@cs.sunysb.edu.

Smooth Interpolation of Orientations

GREGORY M. NIELSON

ABSTRACT

The problem of smoothly interpolating between a given sequence of orientations is discussed. Methods of representing orientations are described and some of the more interesting and useful properties of orientation matrices, SO(3), are covered. It is shown how quaternions relate to this problem and several methods of smoothly interpolating quaternions are presented.

KEYWORDS

Animation, Interpolation, Orientations, Rotations, Quaternions

1. INTRODUCTION

It is a fundamental problem of computer animation and other computer simulations involving the dynamics of rigid bodies to be able to smoothly interpolate between a sequence of positions and orientations. In the past, traditional animation required animators to produce a large number of frame sequences to simulate a moving scene. In key frame animation, only a relatively small number of key frames have to be specified and a computer algorithm can compute the frames in between. A fly-through consisting of the path and orientation of a camera through a scene can be specified as a relatively sparse sequence of positions and orientations and then an interpolation technique can be used to compute intermediate position and orientations which are used to render the scene. The path of rigid bodies animated through space can be handled is much the same manner. Often, techniques for solving these problems separate the position and orientation. Whether or not this is a wise move, we do not discuss here. Interpolating smoothly to positions in space is relatively easy to accomplish with any number of the rich variety of curve techniques that are available today. Interpolating smoothly to a sequence of orientations is currently a much more interesting problem. What makes it interesting is the mathematics behind the problem and the fact that many commercial systems don't work very well. This is most likely due to the fact the these systems use simple techniques which are basically flawed for this application. In this paper we discuss a variety of methods for solving the problem of smoothly interpolating a sequence of orientations. In the remaining portion of this section, we discuss two methods for representing orientations: Eulerian angles and orientation matrices. We elaborate on orientation matrices and establish some useful and interesting properties about them. In the next section, we move to the actual problem of developing a method for smoothly interpolating orientation matrices. This requires some means of parameterizing orientation matrices. Quaternions are introduced and several methods based upon quaternions are described and compared. At the end of this section we discuss "knot spacing" which is an often overlooked and important aspect of this problem.

1.1 The Representation of Orientations

In order to obtain a solution to the problem we have described, we need some mathematical means of representing orientations. One method which has a long history with flight control and aerospace is the use of Eulerian angles. For this method, three angles of rotation, a, b and g are specified. These angles are often called pitch, roll and yaw. A point, P, is mapped to a point, P', by the successive application of these rotations about the coordinate axes;

75

$P' = P R_x(\alpha)R_y(\beta)R_z(\gamma)$

$$= P \begin{pmatrix} 1 & 0 & 0 \\ 0 & \cos(\alpha) & \sin(\alpha) \\ 0 & -\sin(\alpha) & \cos(\alpha) \end{pmatrix} \begin{pmatrix} \cos(\beta) & 0 & -\sin(\beta) \\ 0 & 1 & 0 \\ \sin(\beta) & 0 & \cos(\beta) \end{pmatrix} \begin{pmatrix} \cos(\gamma) & \sin(\gamma) & 0 \\ -\sin(\gamma) & \cos(\gamma) & 0 \\ 0 & 0 & 1 \end{pmatrix}. \tag{1}$$

In any system, there are two places where this representation may be used. First it may be used as a means of specifying the orientation and secondly, it may be used to represent the orientation and serve as a basis for the interpolation scheme. In the first use, it serves to establishes a certain model of interaction whereby the user places an object into a certain orientation by "rotating" it into position. The rotation being about the successive coordinate axes and applied in a predetermined order. Without modifications, this method of specifying orientations can have some problems. We will discuss one such potential problem. Usually when Eulerian angles are used in the interactive specification of orientation, they are applied in a "relative" manner. First a rotation about one of the coordinate axes is applied. This establishes a new coordinate system and subsequent rotation are performed relative to this new coordinate system. In terms of rotations about the original coordinate axes, we have the three relative rotations

$R_x(\alpha)$

$R_{y'}(\beta) = R_x(-\alpha)R_y(\beta)R_x(\alpha)$

$R_{z''}(\gamma) = R_x(-\alpha)R_y(-\beta)R_z(\gamma)R_y(\beta)R_x(\alpha)$

The composite operation of these three relative operators is just the same as the operators about the original coordinate axis, but in reverse order; i.e. $R_x(\alpha)R_{y'}(\beta)R_{z''}(\gamma) = R_z(\gamma)R_y(\beta)R_x(\alpha)$ This is no surprise since we are simply rotating the axes rather than the object. Even though the final composite form is rich enough to represent any orientation, because of the manner in which they are applied, there is a problem. An example will serve to point this out. Let $\alpha = \pi/2 = b$ then

$$R_{z''}(\gamma) = \begin{pmatrix} 0 & 0 & 1 \\ 1 & 0 & 0 \\ 0 & 1 & 0 \end{pmatrix} \begin{pmatrix} \cos(\beta) & 0 & -\sin(\beta) \\ 0 & 1 & 0 \\ \sin(\beta) & 0 & \cos(\beta) \end{pmatrix} \begin{pmatrix} 0 & 1 & 0 \\ 0 & 0 & 1 \\ 1 & 0 & 0 \end{pmatrix}$$

$$= \begin{pmatrix} 1 & 0 & 0 \\ 0 & \cos(\gamma) & \sin(\gamma) \\ 0 & -\sin(\gamma) & \cos(\gamma) \end{pmatrix}$$

which is the same as $R_x(\gamma)$ and so we have "lost one degree of rotation". This is sometimes caled "gimbal lock".

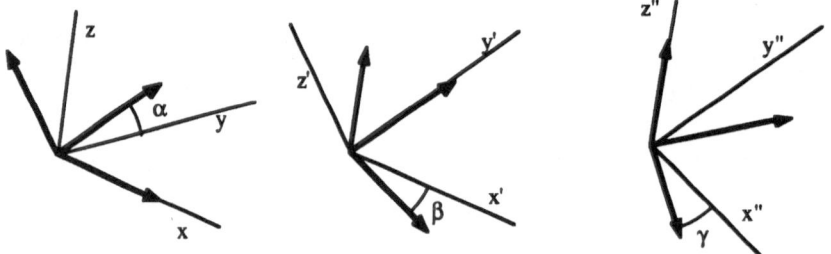

Fig. 1 Successive application of Eulerian angles

Problems can also arise in the second use of Eulerian angles. For example some orientations do not lead to uniquely determined representations. A specific example is given by an orientation where the x-axis is oriented in the direction (0, 0, -1), the y-axis is oriented in the direction (s, c, 0) and z-axis is oriented in the direction (c, -s, 0). For this example, the values c and s are arbitrary except that $c^2 + s^2 = 1$. Factoring this orientation into Eulerian angles leads to the conditions

$$\begin{pmatrix} 0 & 0 & -1 \\ s & c & 0 \\ c & -s & 0 \end{pmatrix} = R_x(\alpha)R_y(\beta)R_z(\gamma).$$

Multiplying both sides of this equation by $R_x(-\alpha)$ from the left and $R_z(-\gamma)$ from the right and comparing elements we are lead to the requirement that b must be $\pi/2$. The remaining constraints are

$$\begin{pmatrix} 0 & 0 & -1 \\ \sin(\alpha-\gamma) & \cos(\alpha-\gamma) & 0 \\ \cos(\alpha-\gamma) & -\sin(\alpha-\gamma) & 0 \end{pmatrix} = \begin{pmatrix} 0 & 0 & -1 \\ s & c & 0 \\ c & -s & 0 \end{pmatrix}$$

which are not sufficient to uniquely determine a and g and this is the problem.

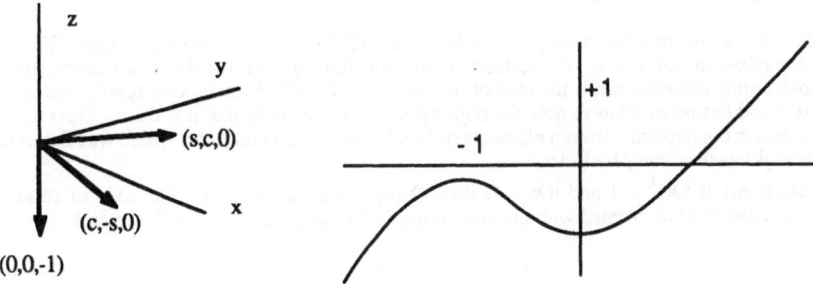

Fig. 2 Problem example   Fig. 3 Characteristic polynomial

A great many systems (in fact, most of the commercial animation systems we are aware of) use the Eulerian angle type of representation of orientations. Of course, there are a number of variations in the way they are implemented, but they all suffer from problems which can often be traced back to the flaws we have just identified. Also, there is the problem of how to interpolate in between. A large postive angle is close (or the same as) a small negative angle and also close to a small postive angle and so it is mandatory to have some type of "periodic" interpolation scheme which computes the intermediate values independently of how they are represented. Conventional interpolation methods applied in a straightforward manner to a, b and g simply do not work.

Another method of representation is to simply write the new coordinate of the oriented object in terms of a global coordinate system. We let $O_1 = (o_{11}, o_{12}, o_{13})$ be the new orientation of the x-axis, $O_2 = (o_{21}, o_{22}, o_{23})$ be the new orientation of the y-axis and $O_3 = (o_{31}, o_{32}, o_{33})$ the new orientation of the z-axis. If P is a point on the object in the original coordinate system, and P' is a point on the new oriented object then

$$P' = PO$$

and

$$O = \begin{pmatrix} o_{11} & o_{12} & o_{13} \\ o_{21} & o_{22} & o_{23} \\ o_{31} & o_{32} & o_{33} \end{pmatrix}. \tag{2}$$

The image of the original axes provides a frame which is also an orthonormal basis and so $(O_i, O_j) = \delta_{ij}$ which is the same as writing

$$OO^t = I$$

where I is the 3 by 3 identity matrix. In general a matrix with this property is called orthogonal. Let $|A|$ denote the determinant of A and recall that $|AB| = |A| |B|$ and $|A^t| = |A|$. From this, we can deduce that if Q is orthogonal then $|QQ^t| = |Q|^2 = 1$ and so the determinant of an othogonal matrix is either +1 or -1. Since the coordinate system remains right handed after orientation, we have that $O_3 = O_1 \times O_2$. Using this along with the fact that $|O| = (O_1 \times O_2, O_3)$ allows the conclusion that $|O| = 1$. Both of the properties of being orthogonal and having a unit derterminant are preserved under matrix multiplication. This group of orientation matrices (orthogonal matrices with determinate 1) has received a great deal of attention in the past. One of the main reasons, of course, is due to its ability to represent orientations of rigid bodies as we have established here. In the mathematical literature, this collection of matrices is often denoted by SO(3) which is a Lie group and as such has the structure of both a differential manifold and an algebraic group.

1.2 Properties of Orientation Matrices (SO(3))

There are some very interesting properties about SO(3) which are worthy of note. The first is the connection to rotations. Embedded in the terminology of the Eulerian angle approach to representing orientations, is the idea of rotations, but the SO(3) method of representation is simply direct and has no mind as to how the object got where it is, only that it is there. Nevertheless there is a strong connection between elements of SO(3) and rotation matrices which was first noted in the late eighteenth century by Euler.

Theorem: If $OO^t = I$ and $|O| = 1$, then O represents a rotation. The axis of rotation is the eigenvector of O associated with the eigenvalue 1. The angle of rotation, θ, satisfies

$$1 + 2\cos(\theta) = tr(O) \tag{3}$$

where $tr(O)$ denotes the trace (sum of diagonal elements).

In less formal terms, this theorem states that no matter how we arrive at a particular orientation, whether it be by a sequence of rotations (however long) or even by a sequence (even number) of reflections across arbitrary planes, we can at arrive at this very same orientation by one single rotation. It is interesting and instructive to go through some of the steps of the proof of this theorem. We want to first show that O has 1 as an eigenvalue. The first thing to note in this regard is that

$$(\lambda u, \lambda u) = |\lambda|^2 (u,u) = (uO, uO) = uO(uO)^t = uOO^t u^t = (u,u)$$

and so any eigenvalue must satisfy $|\lambda| = 1$. A direct computation will show that the characteristic polynomial can be written as

$$p(\lambda) = |\lambda I - O| = \lambda^3 - (tr(O)\lambda^2 + k(O)\lambda - 1 \tag{4}$$

where

$$k(O) = o_{22}o_{33} + o_{11}o_{33} + o_{11}o_{22} - o_{31}o_{13} - o_{21}o_{12} - o_{32}o_{23}.$$

Since $P(0) = -1$ and the coefficient of the leading term λ^3 is positive, we know that P must have at least one positive root and since this root must satisfy $|\lambda| = 1$, we know that $\lambda = 1$ must be an eigenvalue. See Fig. 3 above. The remaining two roots must be complex conjugates which have magnitude 1.

Let u denote an eigenvalue associated with the eigenvalue 1 so that u = uO. Let P be an arbitrary point and P' = PO. We want to show that P' remains in the plane which contains P and has u as a normal. P can be factored into the sum of a component along u and one perpendicular to u; namely P = (u,P)u + [P - (u,P)u]. See Fig. 4 below. Now P' = PO = (u,P)u + [P - (u,P)u]O and so P' is in this same plane since the second term in this sum is a vector that is perpendicular to u. This is because $([P - (u,P)u]O,u) = POu^t - Pu^tOu^t = 0$. Also, it is not difficult to show that the angle, q, between [P - (u,P)u]O and [P-(u,P)u] is independent of P and must satisfy tr(O) = 1 + 2 cos(θ).

As we noted earlier, all orthogonal matrices have a determinate that is either +1 or -1. If it is +1, then it is an orientation matrix and can be viewed as a single rotation about its eigenvector which associates with the eigenvalue 1. If the determinant of the orthogonal matrix Q is -1 then an argument similar to the one above involving the characteristic polynomial can be used to show that Q has -1 as an eigenvalue. If v, of length one, is an associate eigenvector then we can factor Q as

$$Q = R[I - 2v^tv] \quad \text{or} \quad Q = [I - 2v^tv]S$$

where $R = Q[I-2v^tv]$ is now orthogonal with determinant +1 and with associate eigenvector v. S has the same properties and so both R and S represent rotations about v. In general, the matrix

$$I - 2w^tw,$$

where ‖w‖ = 1, is rather interesting. It is called a Householder reflection and is frequently used in numerical analysis to compute singular value decompositions. In E^3 it represents the transformation of reflecting across the plane through the origin with normal w. It is symmetric, othogonal and so it is its own inverse. The product of two reflections $I-2u^tu$ and $I-2v^tv$ is an orientation matrix and can be viewed geometrically as a rotation about the axis perpendicular to both u and v. This is easy to verify since $[u \times v] u^tu = 0 = [u \times v] v^tv$. The angle of rotation is twice the angle between u and v. This is a direct result of the fact that $tr([I-2u^tu][I-2v^tv]) = 4(u,v)^2 - 1$ and equation (3) above.

We now summarize much of what we have said about orientation matrices into two inverse algorithmic procedures.

Given the rotation axis and angle, find the orientation matrix:

Let u be the vector representing the axis of rotation, θ the angle of rotation and P be an arbitrary point that is to be rotated. We can first decompose P into the sum of a component along u and one perpendicular to u. See Fig. 4 below. The image, P', is to be in plane containing P and perpendicular to u. The vectors P-(u,P)P and [P x u] are two vectors in this plane which are perpendicular and so they can be used as a local two-dimensional basis for elements in this plane. We can also note that ‖P-(u,P)P‖ = ‖P x u‖. The rotated image of the vector P-(u,P)P in this plane is now seen to be cos(θ)[P-(P,u)u] + sin(θ)[P x u] and so we have

$$P' = (P,u)u + \cos(\theta)[P - (P,u)u] + \sin(\theta)[P \times u]$$

We would like to represent this dependence of P' on P as a matrix multiplication. The first thing we can note is that forming the cross product can be viewed as multiplying by the matrix

$$U = \begin{pmatrix} 0 & -u_3 & +u_2 \\ +u_3 & 0 & -u_1 \\ -u_2 & +u_1 & 0 \end{pmatrix}$$

If we combine this with the fact that (P,u)u is the same as Pu^tu we have

$$P' = Pu^tu + \cos(\theta)P - \cos(\theta)Pu^tu + \sin(\theta)PU$$

which is the same as

$$P' = PR$$

where

$$R = u^tu + \cos(\theta)[I - u^tu] + \sin(\theta)U,$$

which can be written in the form

$$R = \begin{pmatrix} u_1^2 + \cos(\theta)(1-u_1^2) & (1-\cos(\theta))u_1u_2 - \sin(\theta)u_3 & (1-\cos(\theta))u_3u_1 + \sin(\theta)u_2 \\ (1-\cos(\theta))u_1u_2 + \sin(\theta)u_3 & u_2^2 + \cos(\theta)(1-u_2^2) & (1-\cos(\theta))u_2u_3 - \sin(\theta)u_1 \\ (1-\cos(\theta))u_3u_1 - \sin(\theta)u_2 & (1-\cos(\theta))u_2u_3 + \sin(\theta)u_1 & u_3^2 + \cos(\theta)(1-u_3^2) \end{pmatrix}$$

(5)

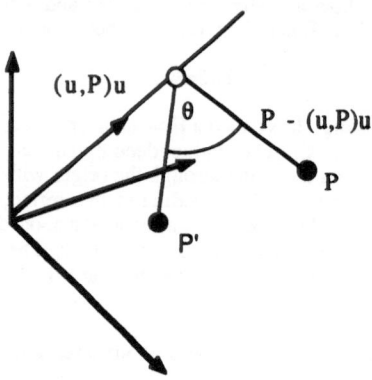

Fig. 4 Rotation of orientation matrix

A quite different approach (see Fillmore 1984) to this same result is a consequence of the following facts which hold for an arbitrary antisymmetric matrix

$$S = \begin{pmatrix} 0 & -s_3 & +s_2 \\ +s_3 & 0 & -s_1 \\ -s_2 & +s_1 & 0 \end{pmatrix}.$$

1) $e^S = I + S + \dfrac{S^2}{2} + \dfrac{S^3}{3!} +$ is orthogonal, since $S^t = -S$.

2) $|e^S| = 1$, since $|e^A| = e^{tr(A)}$ for any matrix and $tr(S) = 0$

3) $s = (s_1, s_2, s_3)$ is an eigenvector of e^S since $sS = 0$.

4) $tr(e^S) = 1 + 2\cos\|s\|$, since $tr(S^2) = -\|s\|^2$.

Using the identities $S^{2n} = (-1)^{n-1}\|s\|^{2n-1}S^2$, $S^{2n+1} = (-1)^n\|s\|^{2n}S$, the infinite exponential expansion reduces to

$$e^S = I + \frac{\sin\|s\|}{\|s\|}S + \frac{1-\cos\|s\|}{\|s\|^2}S^2.$$

Combining this, we have the alternate representation of a rotation about u an angle θ,

$$R = I + \sin(\theta)U + (1-\cos(\theta))U^2 \qquad (6)$$

Given an orientation matrix, find rotation axis and angle:

There are several ways to obtain the eigenvector which is the axis of rotation. For example, it can be taken as a multiple of any row of

$$R + R^t - (tr(R) -1)I.$$

The angle of rotation, q, can be computed from the identity

$$tr(R) = 1 + 2\cos(\theta). \qquad (7)$$

We should mention that this process of computing the axis and angle of rotation from the orientation matrix is very closely related to the conversion algorithm for quaternions covered below.

2. SMOOTH INTERPOLATION OF ORIENTATION MATRICES

We now discuss the problem of interpolating a sequence of orientation matrices. We assume we have a sequence of orientation matrices, R_i, $i = 1, \ldots, n$ and an associated sequence of parameter (time) values t_i, $i = 1, \ldots, n$. We wish to construct a smooth matrix valued function $R(t)$ such that $R(t)$ is an orientation matrix for all t and $R(t_i) = R_i$, $i = 1, \ldots, n$. An orientation matrix has 9 entries and we could easily compute a scalar valued interpolant for each of these nine entries, but this will clearly not work for there is nothing to guarantee that the intermediate matrices would continue to be an orientation matrix. The columns and rows must remain of unit length and they must be mutually orthogonal. So, what can we use for the interpolation so that we are guaranteed to always get an orientation matrix? What we need is to know how many degrees of freedom or free parameters there are involved in an arbitrary orientation matrix. In other words, we need some type of parameterization of orientation matrices. The results from above (see equation (5)) on the relationship to rotation matrices gives us some indications. Roughly speaking, it appears that they are three independent free parameters: two for the axis of rotation (it is normalized) and one for the angle of rotation. But the situation is more complicated and subtle than that. It is true that SO(3) is locally equivalent to E^3; that is, it is a three dimensional manifold. Euler established this in the late 18th century. But SO(3) is not the same as E^3, it is a different 3D manifold. Just as the sphere or the torus are two dimensional manifolds which are not equivalent to E^2, SO(3) is a 3D manifold different from E^3. While it is easy for us to comprehend what a torus or a sphere "looks like" when they are in E^3, it is very difficult to imagine what SO(3) "looks like" in E^4. In fact, it turns out that SO(3) can not be embedded in E^4. Hopf (1940) has shown the if we wish to embed SO(3) in E^k, then k must be greater than or equal to 5. (Whitney's embedding theorem gives an upper bound on k to be 2(3)+1 = 7.) Even though SO(3) can not be embedded in E^4, there is a mapping between SO(3) and the sphere in E^4 which is 1 to 2. That is, two points on the unit sphere in E^4 correspond to one point in SO(3). This association is the quaternion mapping and has proven to be very useful in this context. The fact that it is not an embedding (1 to 1) presents some special problems that must be dealt with carefully.

2.1 Quaternions

Based upon the same notation as in equation (5), we make the associations

$$q_x = u_1 \sin(\tfrac{\theta}{2}), \; q_y = u_2 \sin(\tfrac{\theta}{2}), \; q_z = u_3 \sin(\tfrac{\theta}{2}), \text{ and } q_w = \cos(\tfrac{\theta}{2}) \qquad (8)$$

then R takes the form

$$R = \begin{pmatrix} 1-2q_y^2-2q_z^2 & 2q_xq_y+2q_wq_z & 2q_xq_z-2q_wq_y \\ 2q_xq_y-2q_wq_z & 1-2q_x^2-2q_z^2 & 2q_yq_z+2q_wq_x \\ 2q_xq_z+2q_wq_y & 2q_yq_z-2q_wq_x & 1-2q_x^2-2q_y^2 \end{pmatrix} = R(q) \ . \tag{9}$$

The four-tuple, $q = (q_x, q_y, q_z, q_w)$ is a quaternion which has the property that

$$q_x^2 + q_y^2 + q_z^2 + q_w^2 = 1.$$

The rule for multiplying two quaternions is

$$\begin{aligned} qr = (&q_wr_x - q_zr_y + q_yr_z + q_xr_w, \\ &q_zr_x + q_wr_y - q_xr_z + q_yr_w, \\ &-q_yr_x + q_xr_y + q_wr_z + q_zr_w, \\ &-q_xr_x - q_yr_y + q_zr_z + q_wr_w \ ) \end{aligned}$$

so that $R(qr) = R(q)R(r)$. The multiplicative inverse of q is denoted by q^{-1} and is given by

$$q^{-1} = (-q_x, -q_y, -q_z, q_w)$$

The use of quaternions in the representation of rigid body motion has been discussed by many authors. Hamilton (1843) introduced quaternions and soon after Cayley (1845) noted the connection to rotation matrices. More recent discussion on this topic as it relates to practical issues for the computer generation and control of rigid bodies has been given by Brady (1982), Brekke (1978), Goldstein (1980), Schut (1960), Thompson (1958, 1959), Wittenburg (1977), Horn (1987), Ickes (1970), Kane, Likins and Levinson (1983), Robinson (1958), Sunkel (1976), Stuelpnagle (1964), Taylor (1982) and Wertz (1978).

The use of quaternions gives rise to a general approach to animating orientations which has three steps:

1) The quaternions

$$q_i = q(R_i) \ , \quad i = 1, \ldots, n$$

associated with each orientation are computed.
2) A curve $q(t)$, which lies on the four dimensional unit sphere, is constructed so that
$$q(t_i) = q_i \ , \quad i = 1, \ldots, n.$$

3) The inverse mapping, $R = R(q)$ which takes a quaternion back to an associated rotation matrix is then used to define the animation function,

$$R(t) = R(q)(t),$$

which has the required interpolation properties $R(t_i) = R(q)(t_i) = q(t_i) = q_i, i = 1, \ldots, n$.

Previously (see Nielson and Heiland (1992)) we used a certain conversion algorithm which has been proposed in the literature, but we now prefer the following:

Algorithm($q \leftarrow q(R)$

Solve for the largest in magnitude of q_x, q_y, q_z, and q_w from one of the equations

$$4q_w^2 = 1 + r_{11} + r_{22} + r_{33}$$

$$4q_x^2 = 1 + r_{11} - r_{22} - r_{33}$$

$$4q_y^2 = 1 - r_{11} + r_{22} - r_{33}$$

$$4q_z^2 = 1 - r_{11} - r_{22} + r_{33}$$

then solve for the remaining three values from three of the following equations:

$$4q_w q_x = r_{23} - r_{32}, \qquad 4q_w q_y = r_{31} - r_{13}$$
$$4q_w q_z = r_{12} - r_{21}, \qquad 4q_x q_y = r_{12} + r_{21}$$
$$4q_y q_z = r_{23} + r_{32}, \qquad 4q_z q_x = r_{31} + r_{13} .$$

As was mentioned earlier, the mapping from SO(3) to the quaternions is 1 to 2 which shows up here in the choice of positive or negative square root. In general, choosing the proper branch of this mapping could present a problem, but for our application we have the context of a sequence of values to aid us in our choice. For the first matrix, we take the quaternion produced by the above algorithm using the positive square root, then for subsequent orientations, we take either q or -q depending upon which one is closer (in geodesic distance on the unit 4D sphere) to the previously chosen quaternion.

We would like to point out an interesting property of quaternions. In some since the quaternions are richer than the elements of SO(3) as far as representing rotations. For example, elements of SO(3) can not distinguish between an orientation which results from zero rotation about an axis and one which results from a 360 degree rotation about the same axis, but the quaternions can make this distinction. The element of SO(3) which represents zero rotation is the identity matrix and the rotation of 360 degrees is the same matrix. For quaternions, $(0, 0, 0, 1)$ represents rotation of zero degrees and $(0, 0, 0, -1)$ represent rotation of 360 degrees. Now if we want to interpolate in between these two values we can do it with quaternions. (Interpolating between two identical orientation matrices does nothing.) Say the axis of rotation is (a,b,c) then

$$q(t) = (a\sqrt{2t-4t^2}, \, b\sqrt{2t-4t^2}, \, c\sqrt{2t-4t^2}, \, 2t-1), \quad 0 \pounds t \pounds 1$$

will spin entirely around this axis. Repeating this will give any number of spins around a specified axis.

2.2 Methods for Smoothly Interpolating Quaternions

In this section, we discuss several methods for determining a curve, $c(t)$, which interpolates to a given sequence of quaternions, q_i, $i = 1, \ldots, n$. We assume that knot values t_i, $i = 1, \ldots, n$ have been specified so we have the interpolation requirements

$$c(t_i) = q_i, \, i = 1, \ldots, n$$

From the discussion above, we know that it is important that $c(t)$ have the property that $\|c(t)\| = 1$ for all values of t. It is this constraint that makes this whole problem interesting. Geometrically, this constraint is equivalent to restricting $c(t)$ to be on a unit sphere and the figures of this section might give the impression that the curve methods we are describing are only for a two dimensional sphere in E^3, but the figures are only a guide and it should be kept in mind that the curve schemes are being defined for the space of quaternions.

Normalized Cubic Spline and Related Methods: A very simple approach it to choose $c(t)$ to be a cubic interpolating spline in E^4. The basic problem is that there is nothing to guarantee that the spline will remain on the unit sphere inbetween interpolation points. If we assume that $\|c(t)\| \pi 0$, we can force this condition by simply using the normalized spline,

$$C(t) = \frac{c(t)}{\|c(t)\|}.$$

This is really a rather inelegant way to solve the problem, but it does have the potential to give a C^2 curve which interpolates the data and remains on the unit sphere. The basic drawback to this approach is the potential occurrence of cusps or tight kinks which result form the normalization. This possibility is illustrate in the case of E^3 in Fig. 5.

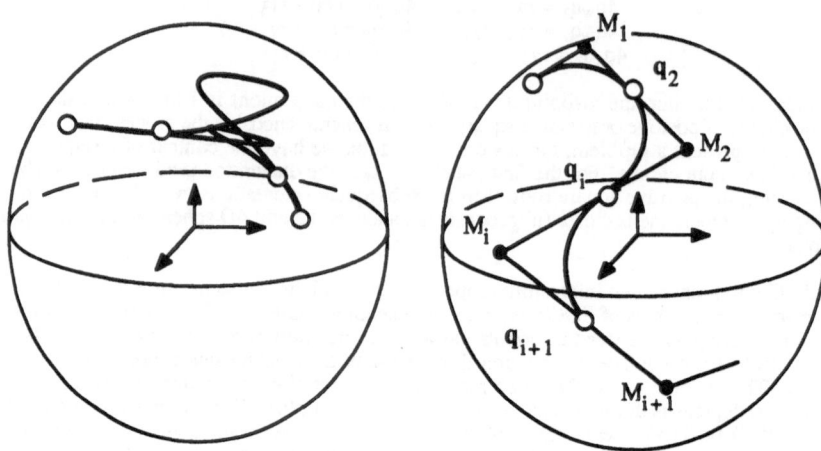

Fig. 5 Kinks and loops   Fig. 6 Nielson/Shieh Circle Spline

One way to pull out the kinks is to use the 4D version of the n-spline (see Nielson 1986). Similar to the normal cubic spline, the n-spline is a composite curve made up of cubic segments. In addition there is associated with each interpolation point a tension parameter, n_i, which can be used to tighten the curve in order to remove any unwanted inflection points, loops or kinks. If all tension values are zero, then the n-spline simply reduces to the standard cubic spline. It is very easy to compute a n-spline; only a tridiagonal system of equations must be solved. While it is true for non zero tension values that the n-spline is not C^2 at the joining points, it is G^2. The definition of a G^2 curve means that it can be reparameterized so as to be C^2 without changing the shape of the curve. In some respects this means that the curve is as smooth as a C^2 to begin with. Not only do the tension values add the ability to pull the kinks out of the interpolating curve, they also add some interesting and useful parameters to affect the "shape" and "speed" of the animation. The main drawback is the lack of any algorithm for automatically selecting the tension values. Of course this is not a drawback if one has the ability and inclination to interactively edit and "design" the interpolating curve. As usual, there are trade-offs.

The Nielson/Shieh Circle Method: The interpolation curve used for this method consists of a collection of rational quadratic curves constrained to lie on the unit sphere in E^4 and joined so as to have C^1 continuity. See Fig. 6 above. It is easy to verify that if

$$(M_i-q_i, q_i) = 0, \quad (M_i-q_{i+1}, q_{i+1}) = 0, \tag{10}$$

and

$$w_i = \sqrt{\frac{1-(q_i,q_{i+1})}{2(\|M_i\|^2-1)}},$$

then

$$c_i(t) = \frac{q_i(1-t)^2 + w_iM_i2(1-t)t + q_{i+1}t^2}{(1-t)^2 + w_i2(1-t)t + t^2}$$

has the properties

$$c_i(0) = q_i, \quad c_i(1)= q_{i+1},$$

$$c'_i(0) = 2w_i(M_i-q_i), \quad c'_i(1) = 2w_i(q_{i+1}-M_i) \tag{11}$$

and

$$\|c_i(t)\| = 1 .$$

In order to have a composite curve with C^1 continuity, it must be the case the q_i lies on the line segment joining M_i and M_{i+1}, $i = 1, \ldots , n$. This condition along with (10) uniquely determines all the M_i's once M_1 has been selected.

for $i = 2, \ldots , n-1$

$$M_i = \frac{q_i[1-(q_{i+1},M_{i-1})] + M_{i-1}[(q_i, q_{i+1})-1]}{(q_{i+1}, q_i-M_{i-1})} \tag{12}$$

The only conditions on M_1 are that $(q_1, M_1) = 1 = (q_2, M_1)$. The value of M_1 can have considerable effect on the overall shape of the composite curve and it is not easy to select an overall "good" value for M_1. We have found that a rather reasonable criterion is to select M_1 so as to minimize the overall length of the NURB polygon which defines the curve or some other similar quantity. That is, M_1 is selected so that

$$P(M_1) = \|M_1-q_1\| + \sum_{i=1}^{n-2}\|M_{i+1}-M_i\| + \|M_{n-1} - q_n\| \tag{13}$$

or, for example,

$$P(M_1) = \sum_{i=1}^{n-1} \|c_i(1/2) - M_i\|^2 \tag{14}$$

is a minimum.

We should point out that the composite curve is not really C^1 at this point. It is G^1. The tangents from the left and right at q_i are in the same direction, but they do not match in magnitude. It is possible to reparameterze each segment with a rational linear function of the form

$$t = \frac{s}{a_i +(1-a_i)s} \tag{15}$$

so that each curve segment remains a rational quadratic and the overall curve is C^1. This reparameterization does not change the shape (graph) of the composite curve, but it does change the "speed" with which it is spanned out by the parameter and so if we use this method for animating orientations, the reparameterization does not affect the orientations that are visited between key frames, but it does affect the speed at which these orientations are visited. In our view this reparameterization improves the "smoothness" of the animation.

Another method based upon circles is the method of Kim and Nam (1992) which uses a "hypercircle" (the intersection of a hyperplane and a sphere in E^4) to interpolate three quaternions

q_{i-1}, q_i and q_{i+1}. These circles are then blended together in a manner similar to Overhauser curves to yield an overall C^1 method.

Spherical Bernstein/Bezier Methods: There are a number of methods that are based upon a spherical analog of the the the de Casteljau algorithm for defining a Bernstein/Bezier curve. Usually low order curves analogous to quadratics or cubics are joined together so as to obtain an composite interpolating curve that is C^1. The de Casteljau algorithm for computing points on a Bernstein/Bezier curve is based upon successive use of the simple and basic operation of linear interpolation. In the cubic case, the B/B curve with control points b_0, b_1, b_2 and b_3 is evaluated at the argument t by performing the following sequence of linear interpolations. The last value $b_3^3(t)$ is the value on the curve for the parameter value t.

$$b_1^1(t) = (1-t)b_0 + tb_1, \quad b_2^1(t) = (1-t)b_1 + tb_2, \quad b_3^1(t) = (1-t)b_2 + tb_3$$
$$b_2^2(t) = (1-t)b_1^1(t) + tb_2^1(t), \quad b_3^2(t) = (1-t)b_1^1(t) + tb_3^1(t)$$
$$b_3^3(t) = (1-t)b_2^2(t) + tb_3^2(t)$$

There is a direct analog of this algorithm to case where the control points are on a unit sphere. Rather than linear interpolation, geodesic interpolation on the sphere is used. Given two points P_0, P_1, the parametric representation of the geodesic joining them is given by

$$G[P_0,P_1](t) = \frac{P_0\sin(1-t)\theta + P_1\sin(t\theta)}{\sin(\theta)} \tag{16}$$

where $\cos(\theta) = (P_0, P_1)$. We should point out that this formula also holds for the geodesic on the 3D sphere in E^4. The geometric version of the de Casteljau algorirhtm in the case of four points on a sphere is illustrated in Fig. 7.

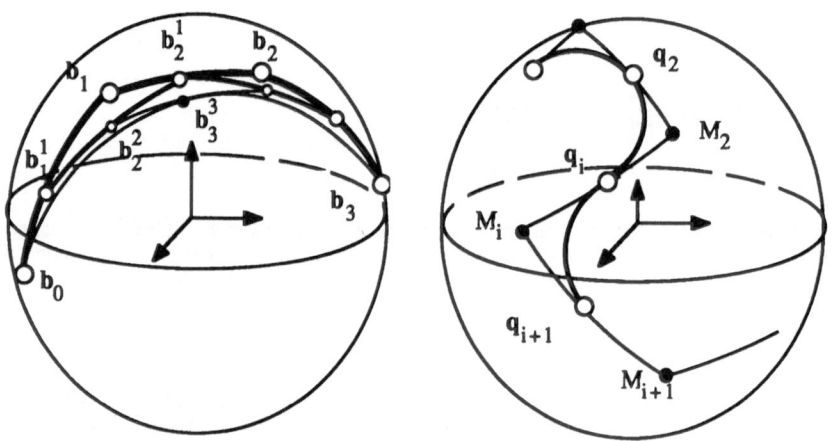

Fig. 7 Spherical de Casteljau   Fig. 8 Spherical Quad. B-Spline

In a more general situation, a formal definition of a spherical B/B curve with control point s_i, $i = 1, \ldots, n$ is taken to be

$$s_n^n = B[s_0, s_1, \ldots, s_n](t) \tag{17}$$

where

$$s_i^k(t) = G[s_{i-1}^{k-1}, s_i^{k-1}](t)$$

and $s_i^0 = s_i$, $i = 1, \ldots, n$.

It is not difficult to verify that $s_n^n(0) = s_0$, $s_n^n(1) = s_n$,

$$\frac{ds_n^n}{dt}(0) = n\cos^{-1}(s_0, s_1)\frac{s_0 \times s_1 \times s_0}{\|s_0 \times s_1 \times s_0\|}$$

and

$$\frac{ds_n^n}{dt}(1) = n\cos^{-1}(s_n, s_{n-1})\frac{s_n \times s_{n-1} \times s_n}{\|s_n \times s_{n-1} \times s_n\|}$$

The Spherical Quadratic B-spline Method: This method is similar in many respects to the Nielson/Shieh circle method. See Fig. 8 above. Between q_i and q_{i+1} the curve is defined by a second order spherical B/B curve

$$B[q_i, M_i, q_{i+1}](t) = B_i(t) . \tag{18}$$

In this case, the shoulder points, M_i, are on the sphere and given M_1 we can compute the remaining ones by

$$M_{i+1} = G[M_i, q_{i+1}](2), i = 1, \ldots, n \tag{19}$$

Similar to the Nielson/Shieh circle method, the overall shape of the curve is affected considerably by the choice of the first shoulder point M_1. Again, a reasonable choice is to select M_1 so that

$$P(M_1) = (M_1, q_1) + \sum_{i=1}^{n-1}(M_{i+1}, M_i) + (M_{n-1}, q_n) \tag{20}$$

or

$$P(M_1) = \sum_{i=1}^{n-1}|(B_i(1/2), M_i)|^2 \tag{21}$$

is a minimum. Regardless of how M_1 is chosen, this method is global in the sense that changing any of the orientations will effect the animation everywhere. From some points of view, this could be a desirable property depending upon the extent of the influence. One way to avoid having a global interpolating curve and to still have C^1 continuity is to use a "higher order" curve segments based upon four control points. These are the analogs of cubic curves given by

$$B[q_i, R_i, L_{i+1}, q_{i+1}](t), \quad 0 \pounds t \pounds 1, \quad i = 1, \ldots, n-1 \tag{22}$$

where we denote the inner Bezier points between q_{i-1} and q_i as R_{i-1} and L_i. See Fig. 9 below. As long as we choose the L's and R's so that

$$G[L_i, R_i](1/2) = q_i$$

then we will be guaranteed to have a C^1 curve. One approach is to take

$$R_i = G[G[q_{i-1}, q_i](2), q_{i+1}](1/2)$$

$$L_i = G[R_i, q_i](2)$$

Shoemake (1985) states "For the numerically knowledgeable, this construction approximates the derivative at points of a sampled function by averaging the central difference of the sample sequence". The Catmull/Rom spline is also based upon estimates of derivatives based upon central differences. These ideas can be mapped to the present context by the following choice of inner Bezier points

$$R_i = G(q_i, q_{i+1}q_{i-1}^{-1}q_i)(1/6)$$

$$L_i = G[q_{i+1}, q_i q_{i+2}^{-1} q_{i+1}](1/6) .$$

Hanson (private communication) has shown that this choice is the same as that of Schlag (1992).

The Nielson/Heiland Spherical B-spline Method: One the smoothest methods of this type that we have observed is a method proposed by Nielson and Heiland (1992) which is based upon "spherical B-splines". There is a well known geometric construction of cubic B-splines that is based solely upon linear interpolation. This construction is illustrated in Fig. 9, where the D_i's are the given control points. The inner Bezier points of the cubic segment are computed at 1/3 and 2/3 of the distance between the B-spline control points. Nielson and Heiland adapt this construction to a sphere by replacing linear interpolation with geodesic interpolation. B-splines do not interpolate to their data, they only approximate it. For the application of animating orientations, it is important to be able to construct a curve that interpolates the data. In much the same way that B-splines can be used as a basis for constructing a cubic **interpolating** spline, Nielson and Heiland use the spherical B-spline to find an interpolating curve which is composed of joining together segments of third order spherical B/B curves. In the conventional case, a tridiagonal, linear system of equations must be solved. In the spherical case, a system with the same sparsity (each equation has only three unknowns) must be solved, but it is no longer linear. They use an iterative method to solve it:

Choose an initial approximation to the spherical B-spline control points, $D_i^{(0)}$, $i = 1, \ldots, n$. Then iterate until convergence with:

$$D_1 = q_1$$
$$D_i = \frac{\beta_i q_i - \alpha_{i-1}(\frac{1}{3})D_{i-1} - \alpha_i(\frac{1}{3})D_{i+1}}{\alpha_{i-1}(\frac{2}{3}) + \alpha_i(\frac{2}{3})} \quad , i = 2, \ldots, n-1 \qquad (22)$$
$$D_n = q_n$$

where

$$\beta_i = \frac{\sin(\varphi_i)}{\sin(\frac{\varphi_i}{2})} , \qquad \cos(\varphi_i) = (L_i, R_i),$$

$$\alpha_i(t) = \frac{\sin(t\theta_i)}{\sin(\frac{\theta_i}{2})} , \qquad \cos(\theta_i) = (D_{i-1}, D_i) .$$

$$L_i = G[D_{i-1}, D_i](2/3) \qquad R_i = G[D_i, D_{i+1}](1/3)$$

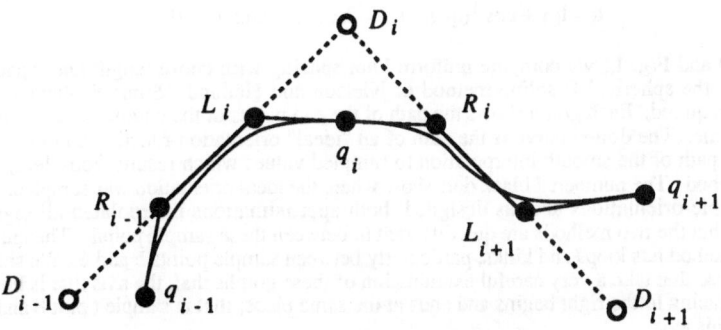

Fig. 9 Geometric construction of cubic B-spline

The Minimum Tangential Acceleration Method: Many of the methods of interpolating quaternions are based upon the ideas embedded in spline theory. The basic cubic spline is characterized as minimizing, subject to interpolation requirements, the quantity $\int |c''(t)|^2 dt$ which is a linear approximation to curvature. (It is equal to curvatureif the curve is parameterized by arc length.) For the quaternion problem we would have to add the additional condition that $\|c(t)\| = 1$. Barr et al (1992) argue that the curvature due to the this constraint can not be avoided and so the minimization process ought to concentrate on the "in sphere" curvature. They formulate the problem

$$\text{Minimize} \int \|c \times c'' \times c\|^2$$

subject to $\|c(t)\| = 1$ and the interpolation requirements. They discretize the problem and use canned software to produce the results for some examples. They use geodesic interpolation between computed values. One of the drawbacks to this method is the difficulty with implementing it and trusting the canned software to actually compute a true minimum.

2.3 Knot Spacing

One important aspect we have yet to discuss is knot spacing. By this we mean the choice of the parameter (time) values t_i, $i = 1, \ldots, n$. It is well known in the area of curve design that the selection of these values can have a dramatic affect on the overall shape of the curve. Often, either for convenience, ease of implementation or efficiency, the knots are chosen to be uniformly spaced. That is $t_i = t_{i-1} + h$, $i = 2, 3, \ldots, n$. For most methods, the choice of h and t_1 have no affect on the overall shape of the final curve. But chosing the knots to be uniformly spaced can have a very adverse affect on the interpolating curve; particularly if the points to which the curve is to interpolate are distributed in certain ways. Consider the case where the "distance" from q_{i-2} to q_{i-1} is about the same as the distance from q_i to q_{i+1}, but say the distance from q_{i-1} to q_i is very small compared to this other distance. If we use uniform knot spacing, then most curve interpolation schemes will produce a curve that has a loop or kink between q_{i-1} and q_i. Foley and Nielson (1989) and Nielson and Foley (1989) survey the general topic of knot spacing for conventional curve design. We have experimented with a number of knot spacing schemes in the case of quaternion interpolation and compared the results. We hope to report on these results and the results of this same study (see Chen 1990) which compare different end conditions in the near future. While it is not the case that a single one of these methods is clearly superior to all others, probably the overall best single choice is what we call chord length knot spacing. Here, a "chord" is taken to be a geodesic arc and we have that

$$t_i = t_{i-1} + \cos^{-1}(q_i, q_{i-1}), i = 2, \ldots, n \text{ and } t_1 = 0. \tag{23}$$

In Fig. 10 and Fig. 11 we compare uniform knot spacing with chord length knot spacing. The method is the spherical B-spline method of Nielson and Heiland. Some explanation of these graphs is required. Each graph shows the path of the end points of the coordinate axes spanned out through time. The dotted curve is the path of an "ideal" orientation function and the solid curve traces the path of the smooth interpolation to sampled values which results from the spherical B-spline method The numbered black dots show where the ideal orientation was sampled. There are eight sample orientations and, as designed, both approximations interpolated all eight sample locations, but the two methods are quit different in between these sample points. The uniform knot spacing method has loops and kinks, particularly between sample points 5 and 6. We should point out for those that take a very careful examination of these graphs that, the axis that is lined up in a direction facing to the right begins and ends at the same place; that is sample point 8 and 1 are the same for this axis.

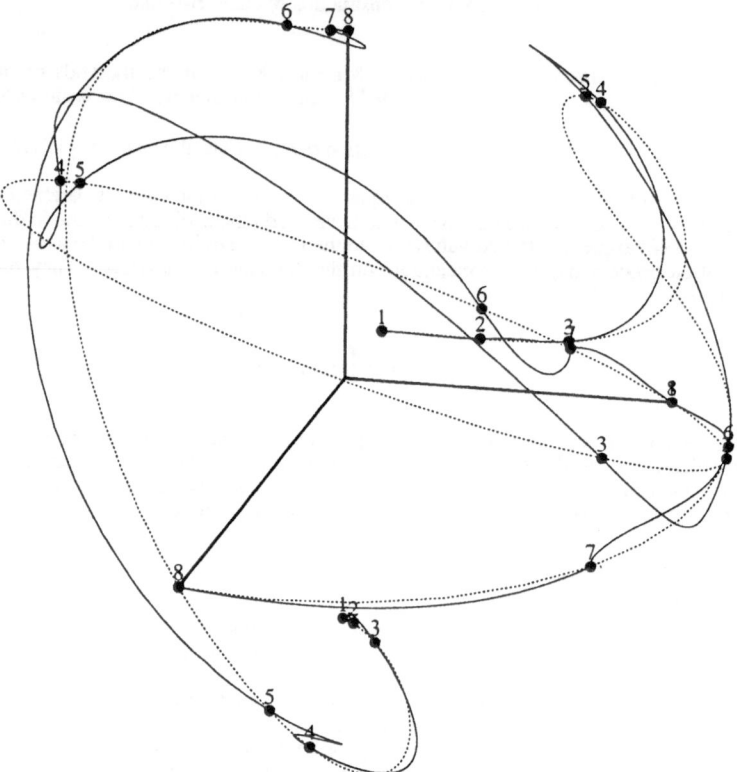

Fig. 10. Uniform knot spacing

3. REMARKS

When one is trying to assess the quality of some animation technique, it is very helpful to observe or experience the animation. Conventional publication media do not presently allow this. Possibly some of the new multimedia publications will remove this problem in the future. Also, future standards may allow us to ftp demonstration programs to each other. Still, it is a challenging problem to come up with some static means of showing the results of a method of smoothly interpolating orientations which you can publish in a standard paper. Sequential snapshots of a tumbling object leave much to be desired. We have found the "triad tracing graphs" of Fig. 10 and Fig. 11 to work quite well for making some types of qualitative assessments, but we are waiting for something better. In general there needs to be some standard methods of assessing the quality of a proposed technique for animation. Some standard set of test cases and some standard methods of comparing techniques would be very welcome to this area of research.

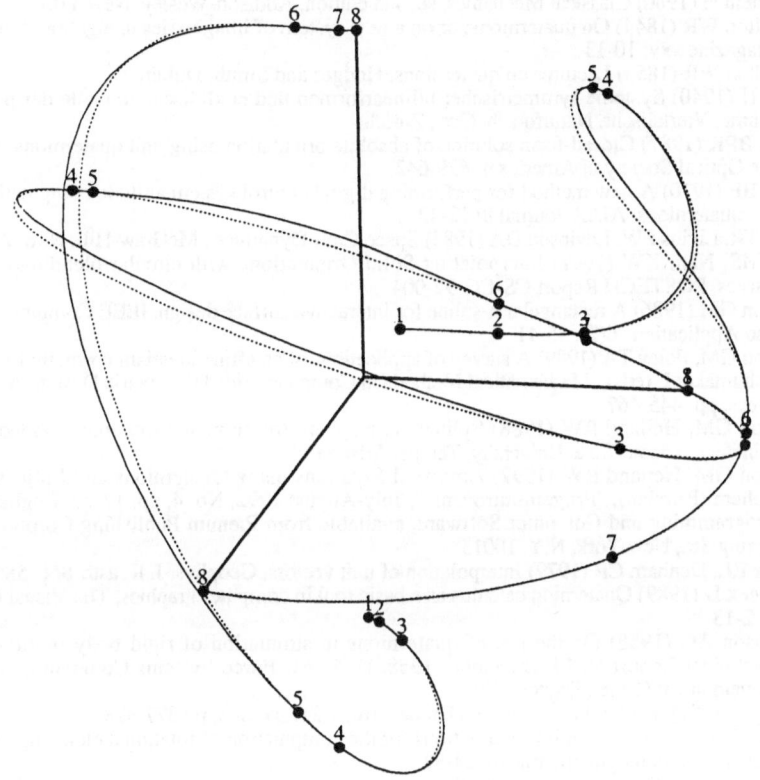

Fig. 11. Chord-length knot spacing

ACKNOWLEDGMENTS

This work was supported by the North Atlantic Treaty Organization under grant NATO RG. 0097/88. Many people have contributed to this work. Thanks to Randy Heiland and Charles Chen for writing some very nice demonstration programs. As always, many colleagues and students at ASU were very generous with their time and help. We appreciate this.

REFERENCES

Barr AH, Currin B, Gabriel S, Hughes JF (1992) Smooth interpolation of orientations with angular velocity constraints using quaternions, Computer Graphics 26(2): 313-320

Brady M (1982) Trajectory planning, in: Brady M, Hollerbach JM, Johnson JM, Lozano-Perez T (eds), Robot Motion: Planning and Control, The MIT Press, Cambridge

Brekke M (1978) Quaternions supplemental workbook, NASA Lyndon B Johnson Space Center Report QUAT-S2102

Cayley A (1845) On certain results relating to quaternions, Philosophical Magazine xxvi: 141-145.

Chen D (1990) Interpolation of orientation matrices using sphere splines in computer animation, MS Thesis, ASU, Tempe, AZ

Fillmore JP (1984) A note on rotation matrices, IEEE Computer Graphics and Applications 4: 30-33

Foley T, Nielson GM (1989) Knot selection for parametric spline interpolation, in Mathematical Methods in: Lyche T, Schumaker L (eds), Computer Aided Geometric Design, Academic Press, pp. 261-271

Goldstein H (1980) Classical Mechanics, second edition, Addison-Wesley, New York

Hamilton WR (1844) On quaternions; or on a new system of imaginaries in algebra, Philosophical Magazine xxv: 10-13

Hamilton WR (1853) Lectures on quaternions, Hodges and Smith, Dublin

Hopf H (1940) Systeme symmetrischer bilinearformen und euklidische modelle der projektiven raume, Vierteljschr. Naturforsch. Ges., Zurich

Horn, BPK (1987) Closed-form solution of absolute orientation using unit quaternions, Journal of the Optical Society of America 4: 629-642

Ickes BP (1970) A new method for performing digital control system attitude computations using quaternions, AIAA Journal 8: 12-42

Kane TR, Likins PW, Levinson DA (1983) Space Craft Dynamics , McGraw-Hill, New York

Kim MS, Nam KW (1992) Interpolating Solid Orientations with circular blending quaternion curves, POSTECH Report CS-CG-92-004

Nielson GM (1986) A rectangular n-spline for interactive surface design, IEEE Computer Graphics and Applications 6(2): 35-41

Nielson GM, Foley TA (1989) A survey of applications of an affine invariant norm, in: Lyche T, Schumaker L (eds), Mathematical Methods in Computer Aided Geometric Design, Academic Press, pp. 445-467

Nielson GM, Heiland RW (1988) Splines on a sphere for animated rotations, Video (VHS, 7 minutes), Arizona State University, Tempe, Arizona

Nielson GM, Heiland RW (1992) Animated Rotations using Quaternions and Splines on a 4D Sphere (Russian), "Programmirovanie", July-August 1992, No. 4, pp. 17-27. English edition, Programming and Computer Software, available from Plenum Publishing Corporation, 233 Spring Str., New York, N.Y. 10013

Parker RL, Denham CR (1979) Interpolation of unit vectors, Geophys. J. R. astr. Soc. 58: 685-687

Pletinckx D (1989) Quaternion calculus as a basic tool in computer graphics, The Visual Computer 5: 2-13

Robinson AC (1958) On the use of quaternions in simulation of rigid body motion, WADC Technical Report 58-17, December 1958, U. S. Air Force Systems Command, Wright Air Development Center, Dayton, Ohio.

Schlag J (1992) in: Graphics Gems II, Harcourt Brace Javanovich, pp 377-378

Schut GH (1960) On exact linear equations for the computation of rotational elements of absolute orientation, Photogrammetria 16: 34-37

Shoemake, K (1985) Animating rotation with quaternion curves, ACM Computer Graphics 19: 245-254

Stuelpnagle, JH (1964) On the parameterization of the three-dimensional rotation group, SIAM Rev. 6: 422-430

Sunkel JW(1976) Quaternions for control of the space shuttle, Johnson Space Center Internal Note

Taylor, RH (1982) Planning and execution of straight line manipulator trajectories, in: M. Brady M, Hollerbach JM, Hohnson TL, and Lozano-Perez T (eds.) Robot Motion: Planning and Control. The MIT Press, Cambridge, pp 69-73

Thompson EH (1958) A method for the construction of orthogonal matrices, Photogramm. Record 14: 55-59

93

Thompson EH (1959) On exact linear solution of the porblem of absolute orientaton, Photogrammetria 15: 163-179

Wertz JR 1978) Spacecraft attitude determination and control, Reidel, Dordrecht

Wittenburg J (1977) Dynamics of systems of rigid bodies, Teubner, Stuttgart

Gregory M. Nielson is a professor of computer science and adjunct professor of mathematics at Arizona State University where he teaches and does research in the areas of Computer Graphics, Computer Aided Geometric Design and Scientific Visualization. He has lectured and published widely on the topics of curve and surface representation and design; interactive computer graphics; scattered data interpolation; and the analysis and visualization of multivariate data He has collaborated with several institutions including NASA, Xerox, and General Motors. He is a participatory guest scientist at Lawrence Livermore National Laboratory.

Professor Nielson is on the editorial board of ACM's *Transactions on Graphics*, the *Rocky Mountain Journal of Mathematics, Computer Aided Geometric Design, Visualization and Computer Animation Journal, Computer Graphics* (Russian) and IEEE *Computer Graphics and Applications.*

He is one of the founders and members of the steering committee of the IEEE sponsored conference series on *Visualization* and he is currently a director of the IEEE Computer Society Technical Committee on Computer Graphics.

Professor Nielson received his Ph.D. from the University of Utah in 1970.

Address: Computer Science, Arizona State University, Tempe, Arizona, USA 85287-5406

An Animated Graphics Program for Solving Star-Sensor-Based Satellite Attitude Problems

MARK D. PRITT

ABSTRACT

Practical problems in satellite attitude determination can be
difficult to solve. An effective tool for solving these problems
is an animated computer graphics program. This program simulates
the motions of a satellite in an interactive and visual manner.
It displays the sky from the point of view of the satellite along
with the fields of view of the satellite's star sensors. It
allows the user to vary interactively the parameters governing the
motions of the satellite until the attitude problem is solved. The
present paper describes this graphics program and how it is used to
solve the problem of star-sensor-based satellite attitude
acquisition.

Keywords: satellite, attitude, star sensor, star tracker,
interactive graphics

INTRODUCTION

The attitude of a satellite is its orientation in space. The
determination and control of attitude are necessary for orienting
rockets for orbital maneuvers, pointing solar panels at the sun,
and aiming telescopes at the stars. Many satellites use star
sensors for attitude determination. Stars are identified by
comparing their positions in the sensor with known positions
obtained from a star catalog. The positions of the identified
stars in the fields of view of the star sensors determine the
attitude of the satellite. In this way the attitude can be
determined with a very high degree of accuracy.

For example the ROSAT x-ray astronomy satellite uses two star
sensors to determine its attitude for pointing its large telescope.
These star sensors have a field of view measuring 5.9x4.4 degrees,
and they identify stars from a 17,000-star catalog (Rupp and
Schneiders 1992).

As another example the Space Shuttle has two sensors, which are
housed in its nose. These sensors have a 10-degree square field
of view, and they identify stars from a 50-star catalog. The stars
they sight are selected before the mission based on the planned
orbital positions of the Shuttle at the scheduled times for star
sightings. The crew maneuvers the Shuttle to an attitude that
places a selected star in a star sensor field of view, and the
onboard software then attempts to locate and identify the star
(Smith et. al. 1983).

Other examples of satellites which use star sensors for attitude determination include Landsat (Saxena 1978), TOPEX Poseidon (Cassidy and Abreu 1990), and the Hubble Space Telescope (Sherrill 1982). Star sensors are also used by planetary exploration spacecraft (Jahanshahi 1982), and they are planned for use aboard the Space Station Freedom (Jones 1990).

This paper describes a common star-sensor-based satellite attitude problem called stellar acquisition. An animated graphics program is presented as an effective way to solve this problem. This program simulates the motions of the satellite in an interactive and visual manner, allowing the user to vary the problem parameters until a solution is found. After a description of the graphics display and animation of the program, the paper presents a brief exposition of how satellite attitude and star sensor positions are calculated. Finally several enhancements which broaden the program's usefulness and applicability to other problems are described.

STELLAR ACQUISITION

Stellar acquisition, or star-sensor-based satellite attitude acquisition, is the process of identifying the first few stars in the star sensors. It is necessary not only after separation from the launch vehicle, but also after a software or hardware error when the attitude of the satellite must be determined using little or no prior attitude information. There are a number of star identification algorithms, the simplest of which searches the star catalog for the star closest to the unidentified star (Kosik 1991; Sheela et. al. 1991; Gottlieb 1978). This and other algorithms require that an initial attitude estimate be derived from coarse attitude sensors such as magnetometers or sun sensors before beginning the star identification. Due to the coarseness of this initial estimate, which may be accurate to within only a few degrees, the onboard software may easily confuse one star with another. For this reason the onboard software uses a small star catalog consisting of bright and widely separated acquisition stars. Because there are usually no more than twenty or thirty acquisition stars, they are easily missed by the star sensors.

The problem of stellar acquisition consists in planning attitude maneuvers to position the star sensors so they will detect acquisition stars. The sensors must not be pointed too closely to the sun, moon or Earth, as they are easily damaged when pointed too closely (within twenty or thirty degrees) to a bright object. They also should not be pointed near planets, which may be mistaken for stars. To complicate matters, the Earth occludes different portions of the sky as the satellite orbits.

While star identification is usually performed by the satellite's onboard software, stellar acquisition maneuvers are planned by ground-based human analysts who uplink attitude commands to the satellite. This allows the onboard software to be as simple as possible, while allowing for human intervention during unforeseen contingencies. The planning of stellar acquisition maneuvers has proven to be a difficult and time-consuming task even for highly skilled analysts. Since there is no easy solution to the stellar acquisition problem, the following approach is typically adopted. A computer program is executed with the satellite's estimated attitude as an input parameter. The program determines where the star sensors will be pointing and whether or not any acquisition stars will be detected. If not, the program is run again with a different attitude "guess" as the input parameter. This trial-and-error approach, which may take hours, is repeated until a suitable attitude is found.

ANIMATED GRAPHICS APPROACH

A much better approach to solving the stellar acquisition problem is an animated graphics program that simulates the motions of the satellite in an interactive and visual manner. This graphics program, shown in Fig. 1, displays the sky from the point of view of the satellite. In addition to stars **1**, it shows the region of sky occluded by the Earth **2**; the "interference regions" around the moon **3**, sun **4** and planets **5** in which the star sensors should not point; and the fields of view of the star sensors **6,7**. Enlarged fields of view of the star sensors **8,9** are also displayed. The attitude of the satellite is adjusted by means of graphical slider bars **10**. As the slider bars are adjusted, the star sensors move across the sky, and stars pass through their fields of view. It is

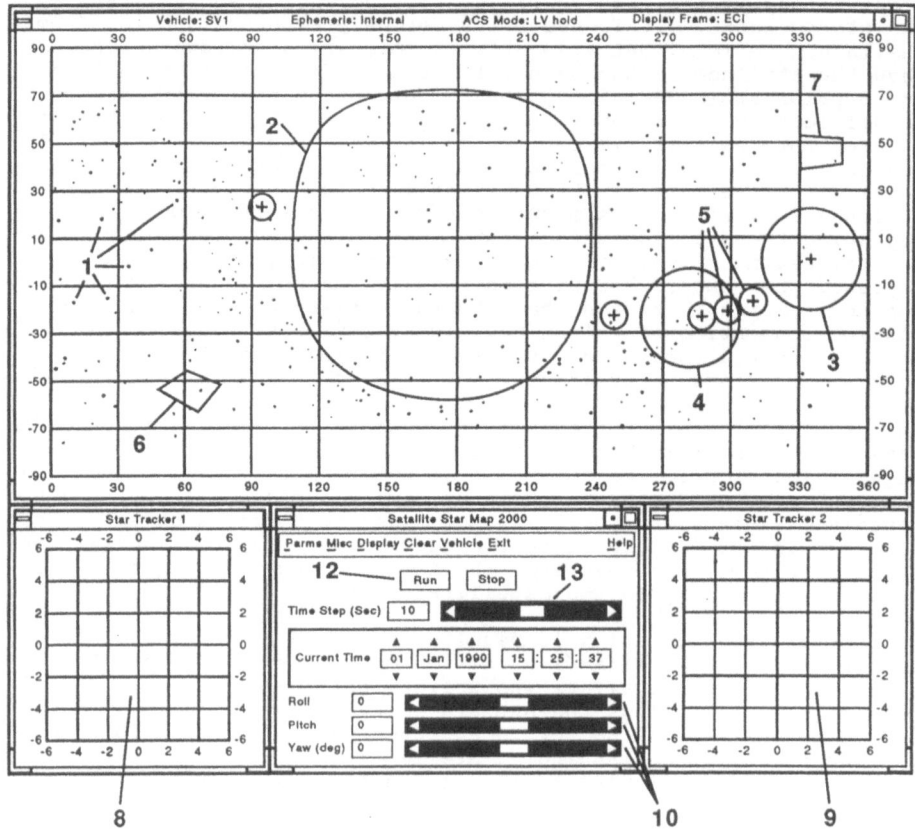

Fig. 1. The graphics display

immediately obvious where the star sensors are pointing, whether or not they will detect acquisition stars, and whether or not they will point too closely to the Earth, moon, sun or planets. The orbital position of the satellite is controlled by varying the date and time **11**. A simulation of the orbit can also be executed by depressing a push button **12** and controlling the speed and direction (forwards or backwards in time) by means of a slider bar **13**.

The stars and planets are identified by pointing at them with the mouse cursor. Star catalogs, star sensor coordinates, satellite ephemeris tables and other data are stored in user-definable files. Pop-up windows allow the entry of other data parameters. The program, named Satellite Star Map 2000*, was developed by the IBM Federal Systems Company as part of the Command and Control System 2000* family of satellite ground-control software. It runs on a workstation computer and uses X Windows** to manage the graphics, windows and slider bars. The graphics draws are performed using the Xlib functions, and the animation is accomplished using color table double buffering, a technique which has been described by Stroyan (1990). On an IBM RISC System/6000* workstation, the animation is performed at the rate of about 10 frames per second.

This graphics program reduces significantly the time and skill-level required to plan stellar acquisition maneuvers. Satellite analysts use it as follows. They first enter the estimated position and attitude of the satellite and see where the star sensors are pointing in the sky and where the acquisition stars are located. They then adjust the satellite attitude using the slider bars to bring the star sensors closer to these stars. When they have found an attitude where the star sensors will be able to detect several of these stars, and where there will be no interference from the Earth, moon, sun or planets, they have solved the stellar acquisition problem. The attitude commands are then uplinked to the satellite, which executes the commands and identifies the acquisition stars which appear in the star sensor fields of view.

The initial attitude uncertainty can be ignored if it is not too large and if the graphics program shows that the acquisition stars will fall close enough to the centers of the star sensor fields of view. For example, if the star sensors have 8x8-degree fields of view and if the initial attitude estimate is known to be accurate to within two degrees, then the acquisition stars must fall within two degrees of the center of the fields of view as shown by the graphics program, to ensure that they will in fact be detected by the star sensors.

DISPLAY AND ANIMATION

The Earth Centered Inertial (ECI) frame is a common coordinate frame for astronomical work. It is centered at the Earth's center

---

*Trademark or registered trademark of International Business Machines Corporation.

**Registered trademark of Massachusetts Institute of Technology.

and its Z-axis points toward the north pole as illustrated in
Fig. 2. Its X-axis points toward the vernal equinox, which is a
point of intersection of the equatorial plane and the ecliptic (the
plane defined by the Earth's orbit about the sun). The sky is
regarded as a sphere of infinite radius, the so-called <u>celestial
sphere</u>, on which the stars and planets are projected. Positions on
this sphere are given in terms of <u>right ascension</u> and <u>declination</u>
angles, which are analogous to longitude and latitude angles on the
Earth, as shown in Fig. 3. The equations for projecting a
normalized position vector $(x,y,z)^T$ to right ascension and
declination angles (a,d) are   a = arctan(y/x)   and   d = arcsin(z).
By centering the ECI frame at the satellite rather than the Earth,

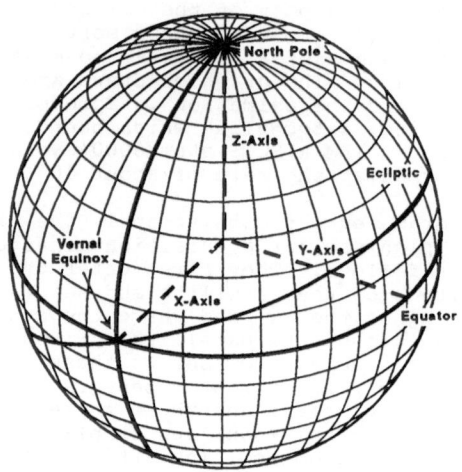

Fig. 2. The Earth Centered Inertial (ECI) coordinate frame.

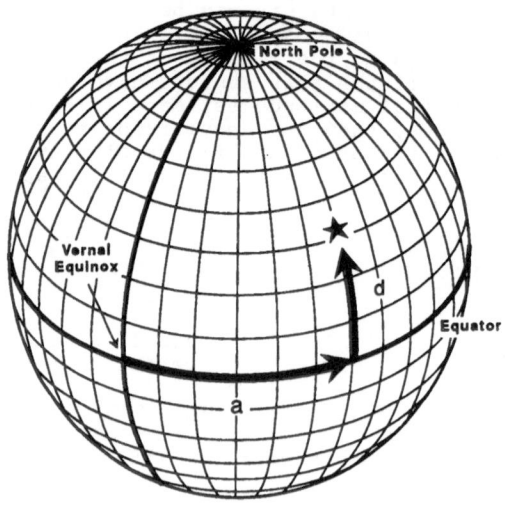

Fig. 3. Right ascension and declination angles.

the star sensor fields of view and the Earth itself can be projected onto the celestial sphere, as shown in Fig. 4.

The celestial sphere is projected onto the flat graphics display using the above equations. The horizontal axis of the display measures the right ascension angle, and the vertical axis measures the declination. Due to the distortion at the poles caused by this projection, the star sensors follow twisting, sinusoidal paths as the attitude of the satellite is varied (Figs. 5a and 5b). The region of the sky occluded by the Earth, the interference regions of the sun and moon, and the star sensor fields of view also become distorted near the poles and split into pieces at the edges of the

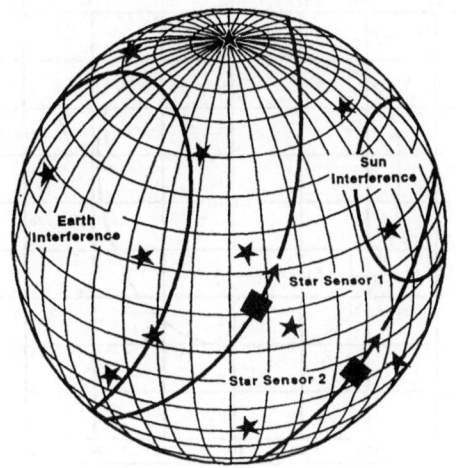

Fig. 4. The celestial sphere centered at the satellite.

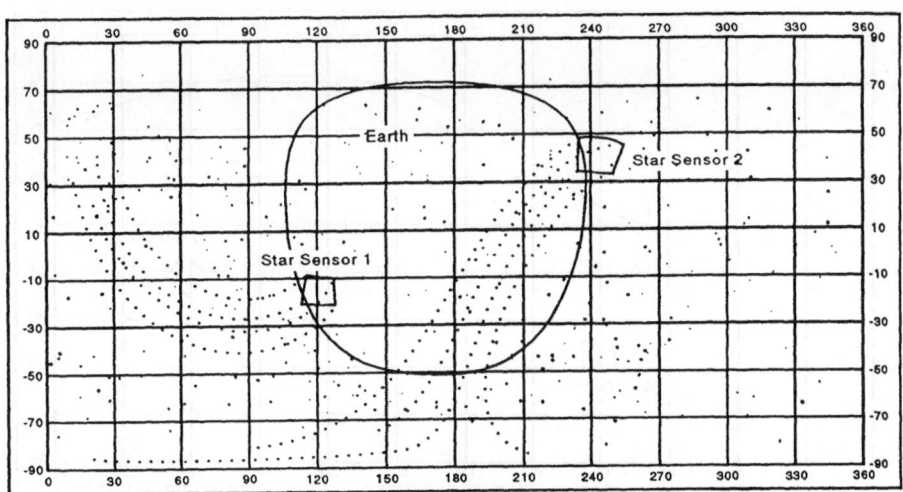

Fig. 5a. The paths of the star sensors as the attitude is varied.

display (Figs. 6a and 6b). These regions must be drawn by taking evenly-spaced points along their boundary in the ECI frame and projecting to right ascension and declination angles. Lines are then drawn to connect the points, with special attention paid near the poles and edges of the display.

Since the graphics program uses X Windows to manage its graphics, it is event-driven. Rather than consisting of statements to be executed sequentially as in conventional programming, it consists of functions that are executed when certain events occur. The events are stored on an event queue and processed by the X Windows

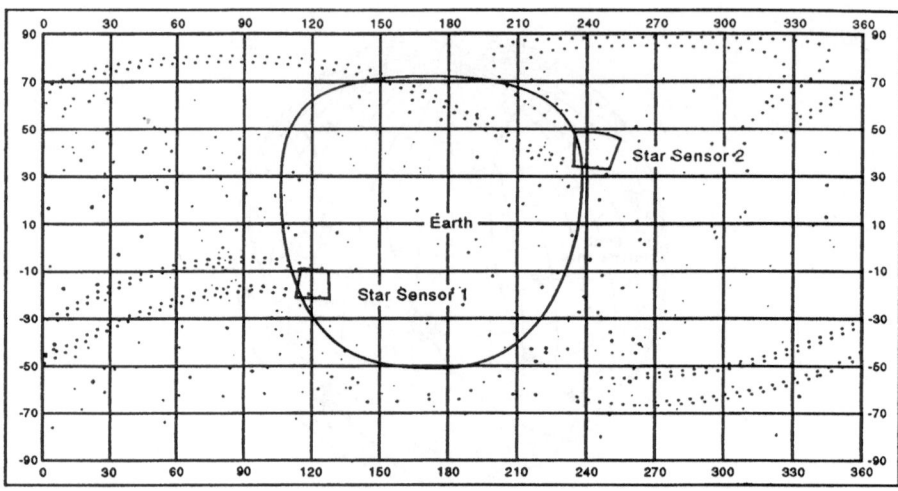

Fig. 5b. The paths of the star sensors as the attitude is varied.

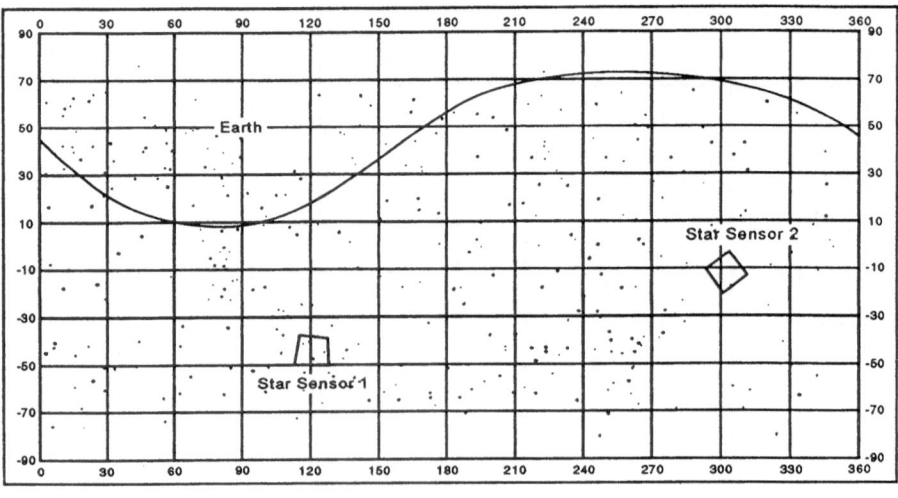

Fig. 6a. The distortion of the Earth near the poles.

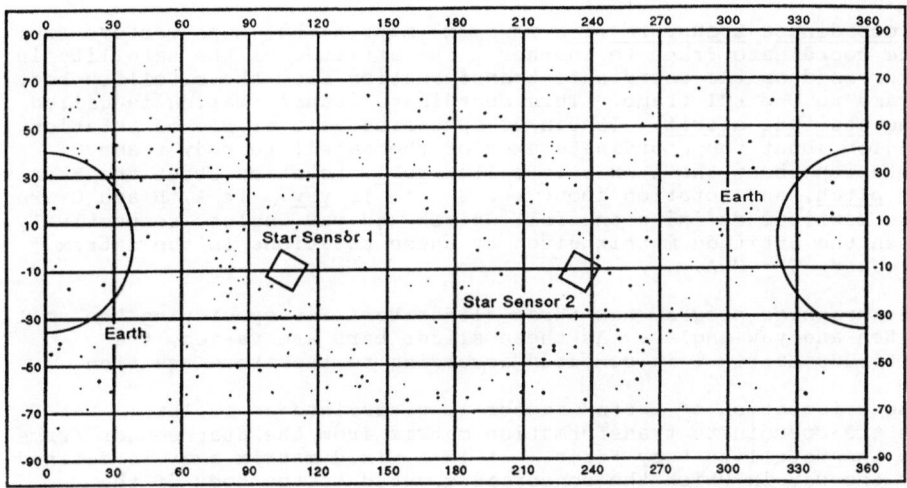

Fig. 6b. The Earth splits in two parts at the edges of the display.

software. Moving a slider bar is an event that triggers the
execution of functions which determine the attitude of the
satellite, calculate the orientations of the star sensors, and
perform the graphics draws. Depressing a push button to begin the
orbital simulation triggers the execution of these functions in
addition to the functions which compute the orbital positions of
the satellite, planets, sun and moon. (Orbital positions can be
calculated quickly from previously-generated orbital ephemeris
files. Fast algorithms such as the one described by Markley and
Jeletic (1991) may be used when high accuracy is not required.)
Between the frames of the animation the X Windows software can
process other events which occur, such as the re-sizing of a window
or the changing of the satellite attitude. This is accomplished by
issuing an X Windows WorkProc (Young 1990) after each frame, which
schedules the next frame. WorkProcs are not processed until the
event queue is empty.

SATELLITE ATTITUDE AND STAR SENSOR ORIENTATIONS

This section explains how the attitude of the satellite is
determined from the settings of the graphical slider bars. It also
describes how the orientations of the star sensors are determined
and how the positions of the stars in the star sensors are
calculated.

Three coordinate frames are required for the calculation of
satellite attitude and star sensor orientation:

1. The ECI frame, which is fixed relative to the stars.

2. The satellite body frame, which is fixed relative to the
satellite.

3. The star sensor frame (one frame for each sensor), which is
fixed relative to the sensor.

A <u>coordinate</u> <u>transformation</u> is a 3x3 matrix that maps vectors from one coordinate frame to another. The attitude of the satellite is expressed as the coordinate transformation from the satellite body frame to the ECI frame. This coordinate transformation is called the <u>attitude</u> <u>matrix</u>. It can be specified as a triple of rotation angles about the coordinate axes of the satellite body frame. Rotation about the X-axis is called <u>roll</u>, rotation about the Y-axis is <u>pitch</u>, and rotation about the Z-axis is <u>yaw</u>. If A, B and C are the matrices defining the roll, pitch and yaw angles, respectively, then the attitude matrix given by these rotations is the matrix product $T = CBA$.

The graphics program has three slider bars for specifying the roll, pitch and yaw angles. As these slider bars are varied, the attitude matrix T is computed according to the above equation.

The orientation of a star sensor is determined as follows. Let S be the coordinate transformation matrix from the star sensor frame to the satellite body frame. It is a fixed matrix that is defined by the way in which the sensor is mounted to the body of the satellite. The orientation of the sensor in the ECI frame is defined by the matrix product $U = TS$, where T is the attitude matrix of the satellite. The matrix U maps vectors from the star sensor frame to the ECI frame.

Star positions in the star sensor field of view are calculated as follows. Let (a,d) be the right ascension and declination angles of a star in the ECI frame. (Star positions in star catalogs are usually given in this form.) The ECI vector corresponding to this position is $\mathbf{v} = (\cos(a)\cos(d),\ \sin(a)\cos(d),\ \sin(d))^T$. This vector is converted to the star sensor frame by applying the inverse of the star sensor orientation matrix U defined above. The vector $\mathbf{u} = U^{-1}\mathbf{v}$ is converted to star sensor field of view coordinates (x,y) by the equations $x = \arctan(u1/u2)$ and $y = \arcsin(u3)$, where $\mathbf{u} = (u1,u2,u3)^T$, and where it has been assumed that the line-of-sight vector of the sensor is the Y-axis, and the horizontal and vertical axes of the field of view are the X-axis and Z-axis, respectively, in the star sensor frame.

ENHANCEMENTS

This section describes several features of the graphics program which enhance its usability.

During stellar acquisition the satellite's attitude is often held fixed relative to the <u>Local</u> <u>Vertical</u> (<u>LV</u>) frame rather than the ECI frame. The LV frame (Fig. 7) is centered at the satellite, and its Z-axis always points away from the center of the Earth. (The X-axis points roughly in the direction of the velocity vector.) It rotates with respect to the ECI frame at the rate of one rotation per orbit. The importance of the LV frame arises from the fact that the star sensors scan the sky as the satellite orbits, thereby increasing the probability of detecting acquisition stars. The sensors follow twisting, sinusoidal paths on the graphics display, similar to those illustrated in Figs. 5a and 5b. It may be difficult for the user to become accustomed to these paths. However, if the ECI frame is rotated so that its XY-plane matches the orbital plane of the satellite, the star sensors will move across the display in horizontal lines, making it immediately clear

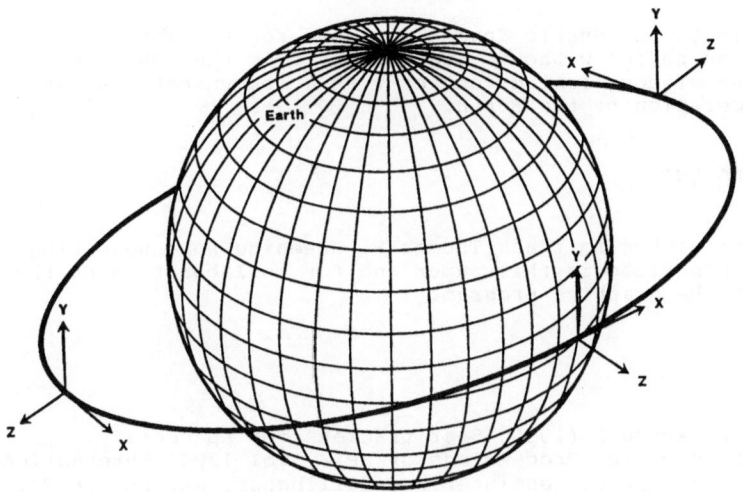

Fig. 7. The Local Vertical (LV) coordinate frame.

which stars will be detected in the course of an orbit. The
graphics program allows the user to rotate the ECI frame to any
desired orientation through the use of slider bars. Any rotation
of the satellite, including roll, pitch, yaw and LV rotations, can
become a simple horizontal motion on the display.

In addition to stars and planets, the graphics program can
propagate and display other Earth satellites. This feature allows
the user to determine contact times with a communications satellite
when the Earth will not block communication. The program also
allows the user to design and simulate complicated sequences of
slews (controlled rotations) and other maneuvers through the use of
slider bars. Finally, the program can be interfaced with telemetry
data to provide a visual representation of the satellite's current
attitude state.

CONCLUSION

This paper has described an animated graphics program for solving
star-sensor-based satellite attitude problems. The program
simulates the motions of a satellite using interactive slider bars
and animated graphics, and allows the user to vary the problem
parameters until a solution is found. This reduces the time and
skill-level required to solve the problem. Stellar acquisition has
been presented as a common attitude determination problem for which
this animated graphics approach is particularly effective.
Demonstrations have shown that users require only a few minutes to
get the "feel" of the satellite motions and to solve the stellar
acquisition problem. Although this particular problem could in
principle be solved automatically using sophisticated algorithms
such as those planned for the Space Station Freedom (Jones 1990),
the animated graphics approach is immediately applicable to a wide
variety of star sensor and attitude problems. For example, it
could be used to determine when a particular celestial object would

be visible to the Hubble Space Telescope for a sixty-minute
observation period without interference from the sun, moon or
Earth, and without losing contact with a communications satellite
due to occlusion by the Earth.

ACKNOWLEDGMENT

The author wishes to thank Thomas B. Greening for suggesting the
approach described in this paper and for collaborating on the
design of the graphics program.

REFERENCES

Cassidy LW, Abreu R (1990) Star trackers for spacecraft
    applications. In: Proceedings of SPIE, Vol 1304. International
    society for optical engineering, Bellingham, WA, pp. 58-74.
Gottlieb DM (1978) Star identification techniques. In: Wertz JR
    (ed) Spacecraft attitude determination and control. D Reidel,
    Boston, MA, pp. 259-266.
Jahanshahi MH (1982) Simultaneous calibrations of Voyager celestial
    and inertial attitude control systems in flight. IEEE Trans
    Aerospace & Electronic Sys AES-18(1):21-28.
Jones B (1990) Attitude determination concepts for the space
    station Freedom. In: IEEE Plans '90--Position, location and
    navigation symposium. IEEE, Piscataway, NJ, pp. 94-101.
Kosik JC (1991) Star pattern identification aboard an inertially
    stabilized spacecraft. J Guidance & Control 14(2):230-235.
Markley FL, Jeletic JF (1991) Fast orbit propagator for graphical
    display. J Guidance & Control 14(2):473-475.
Rupp T, Schneiders G (1992) High accuracy attitude determination
    for the x-ray satellite ROSAT. J Guidance, Control & Dynamics
    15(3):554-561.
Saxena AK (1978) Spacecraft attitude determination and control
    systems. In: Wertz JR (ed) Spacecraft attitude determination and
    control. D Reidel, Boston, MA, pp. 787-797.
Sheela BV, Shekhar C, Padmanabhan P, Chandrasekhar MG (1991) New
    star identification technique for attitude control. J Guidance &
    Control 14(2):477-480.
Sherrill TJ (1982) Space telescope orbital viewing constraints. J
    Spacecraft & Rockets 19(2):118-124.
Smith FE, Campbell ME, Blucker TJ, Manry CF, Saulietis I (1983)
    Shuttle orbiter stellar-inertial reference system. J Guidance &
    Control 6(6):424-431.
Stroyan M (1990) Three-dimensional graphics using the X Window
    system. Dr Dobb's Journal 15(2):28-35.
Young DA (1990) The X Window system: programming and applications
    with Xt, OSF/Motif edition. Prentice-Hall, Englewood Cliffs, NJ,
    pp. 151-155.

Mark D. Pritt received his BA and MA in mathematics from The Johns Hopkins University in 1985, and his MS and PhD in mathematics from Yale University in 1987 and 1989. He is currently a Staff Engineer/Scientist with the IBM Federal Systems Company in Gaithersburg, Maryland. His interests include image processing and computer graphics.
Address: IBM Federal Systems Company, 181/2D44, 800 N. Frederick Ave., Gaithersburg, MD 20879 USA.

A Tool for Graphically Animating the Execution of Office Tasks

N. Dachouffe

a. Graphical Animation.

In an organization, the information system (briefly, I.S.) design, and in particular the office information system (briefly, O.I.S.) design, is a long progressive process (Nolan 1979). The duration and the success of this process, doubtlessly, depend on the progress of technology. Meanwhile, it now appears that it is also strongly bound on one hand to the **learning capacity** of the computer workers and the future system users (Keen 1980), and on the other hand to the **adaptability to change** of the organization itself, and thus of its diverse members (Keen 1981).

In course of time, diverse **methods** and techniques have been developed for increasing these capacities :
- analysis or design methods for globally increasing the computer worker's work efficiency (in connection with the methods proposed for the O.I.S. design, see (Bracchi 1986));
- participative methods for improving the organizations adaptability (see a.o. (Hirschheim 1985; Mumford 1979)).

Recently, these methods have been improved upon by tools, called **prototyping tools** (for a complete review with regard to the prototyping, see a.o. (Budde 1984)). These tools have a common property (Alavi 1984) : they **concretely show**, wholly or partially, the principal features of a future I.S., before its definitive implementation. Thus, for example, some prototyping tools allow simulation of the end-user interface of an I.S., before its realization.

Our project aims in designing and realizing a tool particularly adapted to the O.I.S. design. This tool allows one to **animate graphically the working of office tasks**. Thus, the future user an **see** what exactly his future work in the O.I.S. will be, at the time of designing. Thanks to this visual "language", the users will be now able to help, to a greater extent, the computer workers to build an automated or a semi-automated O.I.S.

The realization of this tool is based on a specification language whose definition itself is based on an O.I.S. model. The animation method is based on the concept of scenario, by analogy with the production of a film (Claude 1959).

A prototype of this tool has been implemented in Smalltalk-80 on Macintosh II.

b. References.

Alavi M (1984) An Assessment of the Prototyping Approach to Information Systems Development. Communications of the ACM, Vol. 27, Nr 6.
Bracchi G, Pernici (1986) Trends in office Modeling. In : Verrijn-Stuart AA, Hirschheim RA (ed) Office Systems. Elsevier Science Publishers B.V. (North-Holland), IFIP.
Budde R and al (1984) Approaches to prototyping. Springer-Verlag, New York.
Claude RC, Bachy V, Taufour B (1959) Panoramique sur le Septième Art. Editions Universitaires, Paris.
Hirschheim RA (1985) Office Automation : a Social and Organizational Perspective. John WILEY - Information Systems Series.

Keen PGW (1980) Decision Support Systems : a research perspective. In : Fick G, Sprague RH Jr Decision Support Systems : Issues and Challenges. Proceedings of an International Task Force Meeting, Pergamon Press.

Keen PGW (1981) Information Systems and organizational Change. Communications of the ACM, Vol. 24, Nr 1.

Nolan RL (1979) Managing the Crisis in Data Processing. Harvard Business Review.

Address: Facultés Universitaires Notre Dame de la Paix, Institut d'Informatique, 21, rue Grandgagnage, B-5000 Namur, Belgium

Part III
Human Modelling and Animation

Constraint-Based Hand Animation

Jintae Lee and Tosiyasu L. Kunii

ABSTRACT

Simulation of hand motions is a complicated task since its articulation makes complex movements with at least 27 degrees of freedom involving various constraints. A new approach to hand modeling, reflecting constraints of human hands, is presented. The validity of the presented model is verified through experiments to automatically recognize complex hand motions based on the model.

Keywords: hand animation, constraints, modeling, perception

1. INTRODUCTION

The human hand is a remarkable instrument which is capable of performing countless actions. It is not surprising that so many scientists have been interested in modeling and simulation of human hands with variety of objectives. In spite of much interest and need, however, generation and perception of hand motions have always been difficult because of the following two problems :

- *Deformation of the skin*
  The skin around the joints and on the palm deform with the movement of joints. Special care is required for realistic animation.

- *Constrained articulation of joints*
  The articulation of human hand involves more than 27 bones, and its movement has approximately 27 degrees of freedom (DOF) even if we omit DOF of the palm. Furthermore the movements of finger joints are beautifully coordinated by constraints. These constraints exclude infeasible hand configurations in the hand configuration space.

The first problem has been dealt with by Thalmanns and their group in computer animation [3, 8]. However, the second problem has not been fully explored. This problem is also related to the *degrees of freedom problem* [15] which refers to the sheer volume of control information necessary for coordinating the motion of an articulated figure when the number of links is large, as in a human figure. Conventional models of the human hand lacking in constraints are limited in their usefulness in computer animation and vision. The main emphasis of this paper is on hand modeling with constraints and on application of modeling to simulation of hand motions.

The lack of constraints leads to models that do not behave naturally. Without incorporating the laws that govern and constrain the behavior of human hands, we cannot simulate or predict hand motions. This is a serious limitation for graphics, and it is becoming painfully evident when we attempt to produce computer animation of hand movements. To make realistic keyframes, models need to be guided by our own knowledge of constraints or by video images. When we attempt to bend a finger, it is likely to rotate around an incorrect axis of rotation if we move it manually. To have the segments appear as linked by a joint, we have to ensure

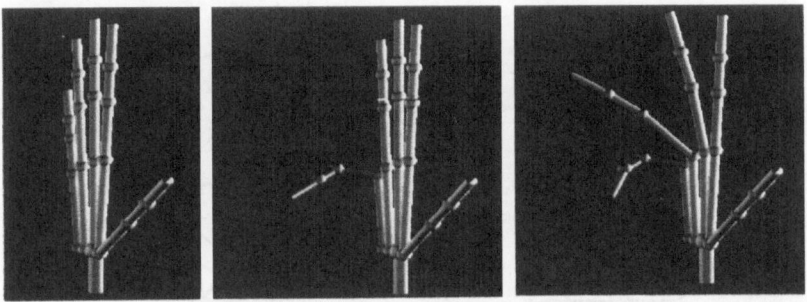

Figure 1: Some pitfalls of simple models. From left to right: (a) a simple hand skeleton (b) unnatural configuration resulting from overlooking the constraints (c) normal configuration

manually that they stay joined, which is quite tiresome if we handle each segment separately. Getting them to move plausibly is very difficult; we cannot foresee the effect of the motion of a finger on the other fingers.

By way of illustration, Fig. 1 (a) shows a simple model of a hand skeleton. When we attempt to move a finger (the little finger) to a new configuration, overlooking the constraints in repositioning the other fingers, leads to the ridiculous image shown in Fig. 1 (b). The right configuration is shown in Fig. 1 (c). The model itself contains nothing to indicate that configuration (b) is wrong.

Recognition of these difficulties led us to formulate a new approach to hand model building. We build and manipulate a hand model which reflects constraints of human hands. The constraints are obtained from anatomical analysis of human hands. As we are interested in the movement of the hand rather than the delicate changes of surface, the skeletal structure rather than the topography is important in this study. Fig. 2 illustrates the hand skeleton as seen from the palmar side ("Pernkopf Anatomy" [11]). The terminology in this figure will be used frequently when we discuss modeling and constraints in later sections.

I: Thumb II: Index III: Middle IV: Ring V: Little

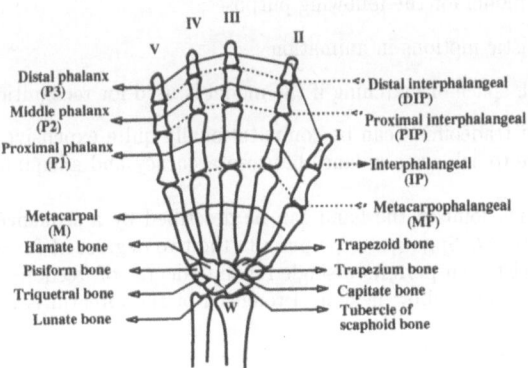

Fig. 2 The skeleton of the hand as seen from the palmar side.

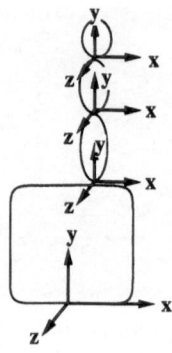 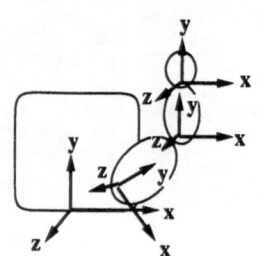

(a) Object coordinate systems of a finger   (b) Object coordinate systems of the thumb

Fig. 3 Object coordinate systems of the hand.

The hand is opened with a palm oriented toward the front in standard position, and the object coordinate system of each segment is established along the segment as in Fig. 3. Rotation around a coordinate axis of each segment will be expressed by the joint angles indexed by the name of the coordinate axis illustrated in this figure in later sections.

The discussion in this paper is organized as follows. The next section investigates the main constraints of human hands. In Sections 3 and 4, we solve the problem of fitting hand models to hand images which is a typical example that illustrates the importance of constraints in the model. Finally, in Section 5, we conclude this paper.

2. CONSTRAINTS ON HAND MOTIONS

As Badler [9] noted, a more accurate model is essential to further reality of human motion. The movements of the fingers are inter-dependent in the human hand, and constraints must be incorporated in the model for the following purposes:

1. to avoid unrealistic motions in animation

2. to reduce search space of matching if the model is used for recognition

Inevitably, there is a tradeoff. It can be computationally quite expensive to impose too many constraints. We have to achieve a balance between accuracy and adequate performance.

The movement of each joint in the hand can be described by a sequence of movement types *flexion, spherical* or *twist*. Spherical type permits the two degrees of freedom of spherical motion. Flexion and twist each permits a single revolute degree of freedom. A flexion movement is exemplified by knee and elbow flexion. Pronation of the forearm is an example of a twist movement.

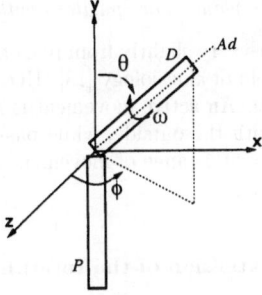

Fig. 4 Spherical Joint. Two variables determine the direction of the proximal segment, and the third determines its twist.

A schematic representation of a spherical movement is shown in Fig. 4. Let the proximal segment P be fixed in a coordinate system originating at the joint, and let the axis Ad of distal segment D be some line through the origin. The position of D is described by three variables. Two of the variables (ϕ, θ) are required to describe the direction of the axis Ad. The third variable (ω) describes the rotation of D about Ad. The motion permitted by variation of the first two joint variables (ϕ and θ) is called a *spherical movement*. The motion permitted by variation of the third variable is called a *twist*. The twist movement of the wrist is added because the hand is considered separately from the lower arm in the model.

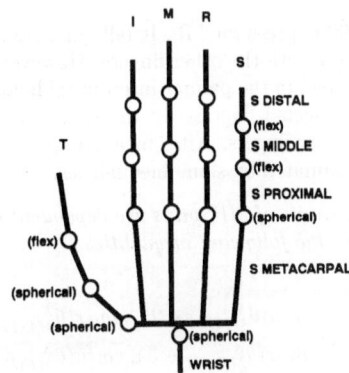

Fig. 4 Joints of the hand and their movement types.

Normally, the movements of the finger joints are beautifully coordinated by constraints, and some configurations are not feasible due to some constraints. We will see some of the prominent constraints on finger movements along with the anatomical mechanisms involved in this section. Specific constraints will be numbered for reference in later sections. The joint angle limit constraints are *static constraints* which are calculated unrelated to the values of the other joint variables, and the others are *dynamic constraints* that are calculated related to the values of the other joint variables.

2.1 Joint Angle Limits and Movement Types

From Fig. 4, we note that the possible movements of the joints of the four fingers are bending movements in the same direction or side-movements on the first joint.

Constraint 1 *The four fingers are planar manipulators with the exception of the MP joint.*

The allowable ranges of these angles vary slightly from person to person. The general ranges of these angles can be found in the field of kinesiology [13]. Here, we have to distinguish a *passive movement* and an *active movement.* An active movement is activated by tendons and muscles of the hand without interaction with the outside, while passive movement is forced from the outside. In general, joints have a greater range of movement in a passive movement than in an active.

2.2 Constraints on Flexion/Extension of the Interphalangeal Joints

A human finger has the property that it is almost impossible to move the joint of the last link (DIP) without moving the joint immediately next to it (PIP) and vice-versa, without forcing one of the two not to move in some unnatural way. That is, there is a dependancy between these two joints in an *active movement.* Some anatomical studies have been done on this phenomena by physiologists [4, 5, 6]. An empirical study by Girard and Rijpkema [12] reveals that there is an almost linear relationship between the DIP and PIP.

Constraint 2 *The joint angles of DIP and PIP have a dependency represented by the following equation:*

$$\theta_{DIP} = \frac{2}{3}\theta_{PIP}$$

2.3 Constraints on Extension/Flexion of the Metacarpophalangeal Joints

Flexion has a range of about 90 degrees for MP. It falls just short of 90 degrees for the index finger, but increases progressively with the other fingers. However, isolated flexion of the finger is checked by the tension developed in the palmar interdigital ligament. Thus flexion of a finger may bring about flexion of (adjacent) fingers. In the same way, the extension of a finger is hindered by the flexion of the other fingers. After measuring several human subjects, we found this could be reasonably approximated by some inequalities.

Constraint 3 *The joint angle limits of MP joints are dependent on the MP joint angles of the neighboring fingers according to the following inequalities:*

$$
\begin{aligned}
dmax(\theta^X_{MP(I)}) &= min(\theta^X_{MP(M)} + 25, smax(\theta^X_{MP(I)})) \\
dmin(\theta^X_{MP(I)}) &= max(\theta^X_{MP(M)} - 54, smin(\theta^X_{MP(I)})) \\
dmax(\theta^X_{MP(M)}) &= min(\theta^X_{MP(I)} + 54, \theta^X_{MP(R)} + 20, smax(\theta^X_{MP(M)})) \\
dmin(\theta^X_{MP(M)}) &= max(\theta^X_{MP(I)} - 25, \theta^X_{MP(R)} - 45, smin(\theta^X_{MP(M)})) \\
dmax(\theta^X_{MP(R)}) &= min(\theta^X_{MP(M)} + 45, \theta^X_{MP(L)} + 48, smax(\theta^X_{MP(R)})) \\
dmin(\theta^X_{MP(R)}) &= max(\theta^X_{MP(M)} - 20, \theta^X_{MP(L)} - 44, smin(\theta^X_{MP(R)})) \\
dmax(\theta^X_{MP(L)}) &= min(\theta^X_{MP(R)} + 44, smax(\theta^X_{MP(L)})) \\
dmin(\theta^X_{MP(L)}) &= max(\theta^X_{MP(R)} - 48, smin(\theta^X_{MP(L)}))
\end{aligned}
$$

2.4 Constraints on Adduction/Abduction of the Metacarpophalangeal Joints

In adduction and abduction, the movements of the fingers are referred not to the plane of symmetry of the body as a whole but to the axis of the hand which runs through M(III), the third metacarpal bone, and the middle finger. The first observation in adduction or abduction of the fingers is that the middle finger does not move appreciably during these movements.

Constraint 4 *There is little adduction/abduction of the MP joint of the middle finger.*

When the fingers are in their natural position, they can carry out approximation (adduction) or separation (abduction) freely. This is what we can expect since we have classified MP joints as "spherical". However, when the fist is clenched with the distal interphalangeal joints extended, the axes of the two distal phalanges of the four fingers and the axis of the thumb (excluding its terminal phalanx) converge to a point corresponding to the 'radial pulse'. In other words, abduction/adduction angles decrease continuously as flexion angles of the MP joints increase. At first sight, this seems to avoid collision between the fingers. However, careful observation revealed that this convergence takes place independently of other fingers.

Constraint 5 *Define*

$$\theta^Z_{MP} = abduction/adduction\ angle\ of\ a\ MP\ joint$$
$$\theta^X_{MP} = flexion\ angle\ of\ a\ MP\ joint$$
$$smax : maximum\ joint\ angle\ of\ static\ constraint$$
$$dmax : maximum\ joint\ angle\ of\ dynamic\ constraint$$

Then

$$dmax(\theta^Z_{MP}) = k \cdot smax(\theta^Z_{MP})$$

where $k = (1 - \frac{1}{smax(\theta^X_{MP})})\theta^X_{MP}$

There are some miscellaneous constraints besides those described above. They are not implemented in our system, for they increase the complexity of the system by far without meaningful gain.

2.5 Hand Tree

The data structure to represent the articulate structure typically consists of a "tree" of segments. The hand model used in our study also uses a hierarchical tree where each node represents a segment. However, the segments may have interdependency in our hand tree (Fig. 6).

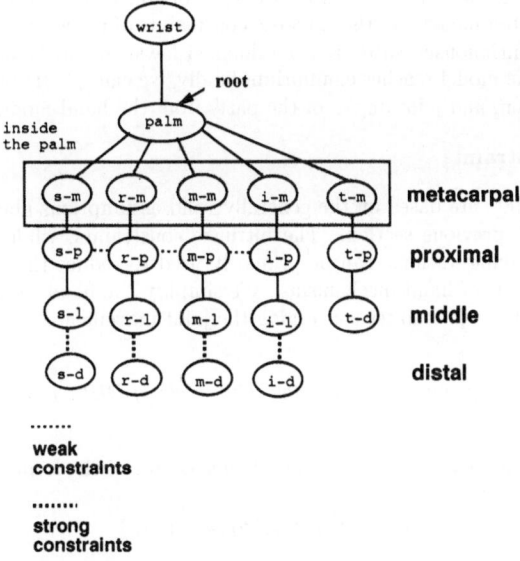

Fig. 6 Hand tree. The constraint-relations are represented by dotted lines.

3. IMAGE-DRIVEN HAND ANIMATION

The importance of constraints in models is more definite in computer vision than in computer graphics. For example, to manipulate unconstrained models in hand animation, the exact angles of each segment have to be specified manually in detail. Even if this is a big job, it is possible. However, in computer vision, we are given only a sequence of picture frames and need to derive a hand model in an automatic way. Inevitably, the constraints in the model have to fill in the missing information.

In this section, a way to infer the 3D structure of the human hand from images using an animated hand model will be presented. Inferring hand structure from images is an important technique in hand animation because it is tedious to specify 20 to 30 interacting parameters in order to specify a hand posture. However, this invloves quite difficult problems, given the fact that:

1. As the human hand is an articulated structure with about 27 degrees of freedom, it moves and changes shape due to forces and torques applied to the joints. Thus hand images change by moving the fingers as well as the hand as a whole.

2. As the four fingers remain side by side and the joints bend extremely, occlusion of the fingers occurs frequently (even more than in the case of the human body). And many tiny wrinkles on the skin make it difficult to detect meaningful edges in images: The conventional strategy [10] to segment the objects into parts by edge extraction and to align the parts sequentially along the central axes is not usable.

3. As the segments of the fingers are comparatively short and the surfaces deform with movement, it is very difficult to calculate accurate joint positions. Furthermore, MP joints are almost hidden inside the palm. The method to align segments between the joints one by one will fail as soon as it encounters a miscalculated joint position.

We propose an animated model with constraints framework to infer the hand structures from their images. In this framework, there are two types of constraints: the intrinsic constraints internal to the animated model and the extrinsic constraints of images driving the hand model. The model moves continuously, subject to mechanical laws, to satisfy intrinsic and extrinsic constraints. When the model reaches equilibrium finally, we can get 3D metric properties such as location, orientation, and joint angles of the parts from the hand model.

3.1 Intrinsic Constraints

The intrinsic constraints are based on the generally valid assumptions about human hand motion described in the previous section. The intrinsic constraints, while providing necessary conditions for hand configurations, can be primarily used to reduce the number of degrees of freedom for the analysis of hand mechanisms. We simplify the hand manipulator mechanism based on some reasonable postulates concerning the joint movements.

Postulate 1 *There is dependency between the joint angle of DIP and that of PIP for the four fingers (Constraint 2).*

The joint vector for the inverse kinematics of a finger is now of the form:

$$q_f = (\theta_{MP}^x, \theta_{MP}^z, \theta_{PIP}, \frac{2}{3}\theta_{PIP}) \tag{1}$$

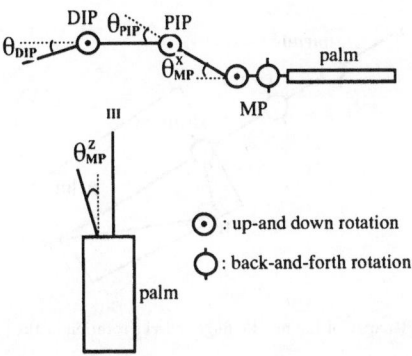

Fig. 7 Hand mechanisms represented by symbols of joints.

A second way to simplify the problem is based on the observation that the middle finger does not move in adduction or abduction of the fingers. As the other fingers are planar manipulators with the exception of the first joint, it follows that θ_{MP}^z can be calculated from the displacement of the fingertip in the object coordination frame of the middle finger (Fig. 7).

Postulate 2 *The middle finger does not make side movements in natural movements (Constraint 4).*

Now, the joint vector becomes

$$q_f = (\theta_{MP}^x, \delta_{MP}^z, \theta_{PIP}, \frac{2}{3}\theta_{PIP}) \tag{2}$$

where δ_{MP}^z is the angle of θ_{MP}^z measured relative to $\theta_{MP(III)}^z$. Now, the fingers other than the thumb have become a non-redundant manipulator, since the number of joint freedoms (DOF = 2) equals the number of freedoms associated with the end-effector task. In order that the fingers reach arbitrary points, there is an unique solution.

However, when we include the palm into the chain of a finger, it becomes a redundant manipulator. In other words, it has more degrees of freedom (on the palm) than the minimum number required to perform reaching a position.

$$q_h = (q_p, q_f) \tag{3}$$

where q_p is the joint vector of the palm. Here, we make a final hypothesis on palm movement.

Postulate 3 *The palm is assumed not to become hollow in a non-prehensile motion.*

In general, three points are necessary to align the palm with the images. However, if we assume that the palm does not become hollow, it is impossible to move the palm when the wrist, fingertips, and an extra MP joint in the palm are fixed. This can be explained by the fact that the middle finger is a planar manipulator (Fig. 8). The rotation of the *MP(III)* around the axis through W and *MP'* is checked to ensure planarity of the middle finger(*III*).

Postulate 4 *Under the previous postulates, the posture of the hand can be identified by determining the positions of five fingertips, the wrist, and a point on the palm.*

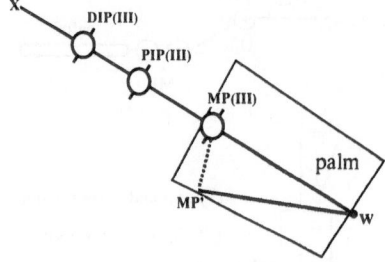

Fig. 8 Planarity of the middle finger checks rotation of the palm.

The thumb is a more complicated manipulator, because a large part of the thumb is part of the palm and the joints are moving along non-trivial axes. However, it is known that the inverse kinematics of the thumb can be calculated almost uniquely by experimental observations [12]:

$$\theta^x_{MP}(I) = 2 * (\theta^x_M(I) - \frac{1}{6} * \pi)$$
(4)

$$\theta^z_{MP}(I) = \theta^z_M(I) * \frac{7}{5}$$
(5)

3.2 Extrinsic Constraints

Some constraints are derived from the information content of images. These extrinsic constraints couple the model to the external image data. Although, in principle, we can exploit within our framework a variety of image-based cues, including profiles (also known as occluding contour), edges, shading and texture, they have been proved to be inefficient even to classify 3D hand shapes [14]. We exclusively use information about some selected points of the hand, called *characteristic points*, such as on the fingertips and the wrist. A pair of color-coded gloves is developed to foster the identification of these seven characteristic points.

For each characteristic region in the image, we attach a virtual spring pulling the corresponding segment toward the goal in the image (Fig. 9). Each such spring has an individualized spring constant. These virtual springs act on the model and change its posture to resolve the model fitting problem. Since the connectivity and joint constraints are conserved, the changes induced by the springs are reflected by translating, rotating, or twisting of the model.

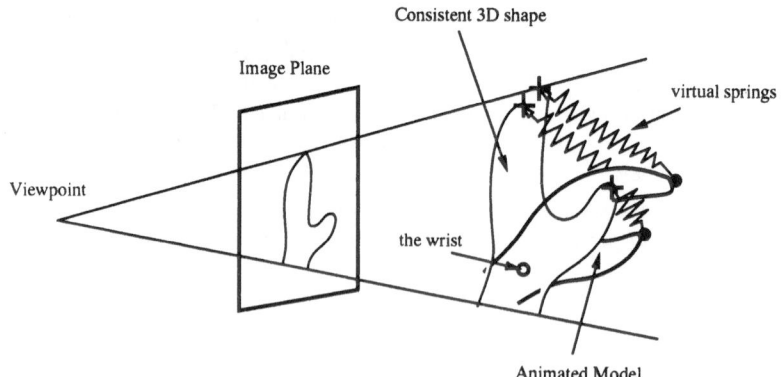

Fig. 9 Model fitting scenario. The arrows depict extrinsic forces in space which act on the animated model.

In general, it is not possible to deduce the spatial geometry of an unknown scene from a single image [1]. Even if the physical structure of the object under study is known beforehand, a single view is not sufficient for 3D reconstruction of a human body in general [7] because of what is called *the joint positional ambiguity*. Therefore we integrate information from multiple views. Each information source makes a contribution to the net force acting on the model. The extrinsic mechanical force submodel that governs our hand model provides a conceptually simple device for integrating information from multiple views.

3.3 Overview of Model Fitting

When we concentrate on the characteristic points, the model fitting problem reduces to the "reaching problem" or the "constraints satisfaction problem" of 3D model. Badler and his group [2] presented an elegant multiple-constraints satisfaction algorithm of an articulated body. However, it is not applicable to our model fitting since it did not consider joint angle limits and constraints as the authors also admitted in the paper. When the action of a node is induced simply by subtree weighted displacement by their algorithm, the segments always translate and do not turn. We extended their algorithm to use it for our constrained hand model.

The model fitting process is divided into two distinct phases: (1) a *hand guidance phase* and (2) a *fitting execution phase*. The hand guidance phase consists of a sequence of actions which guide the modeled hand from an arbitrary position and orientation to the vicinity of the image of the real hand. During this phase, the wrist of the modeled hand is positioned to the location of the image of the real wrist. The orientation of the model is preshaped to the central axis of the image of the real hand. An example explains how the model-fitting process works as shown in Fig. 10. When a characteristic point is viewed from more than one direction, we calculate the goal position in the 3D space by calibration. The front view has priority over the side views in calibration. When a characteristic point appears in only one direction, we estimate the unknown coordinate values by choosing the closest point among the possible points. If a finger is not seen from any direction even though this seldom occurs in multiple views, the finger is considered to be bent completely. After calculating every goal positions in the 3D space from the images, the model begins to move guided by the goal positions.

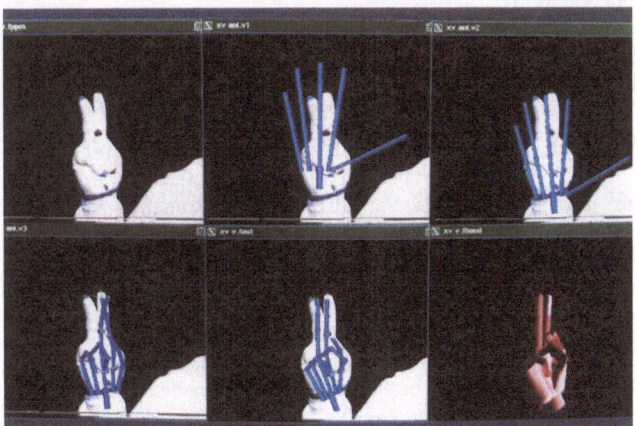

Fig. 10 Movement of the hand model (Front view). From top to bottom, left to right: (1) Original video picture (2) Initial state of the model (3) The hand guidance phase (4),(5) Fitting execution phase (6) Final result.

The fitting execution phase will be explained below. The model fitting algorithm has to be constructed considering a few characteristics of our model fitting task.

1. The goal positions of the characteristic points we achieved from the images are approximated values, and they contain errors inevitably. We also have to admit that there may be small inconsistency between the size of the model and the size of the object. Therefore, we cannot solve the problem analytically by a series of single alignments, because we do not know the positions of the goals exactly.

2. The best solution is selected out of the candidates which satisfy many goals for different points of the hand model simultaneously. Each goal is given a weight, which is interpreted as its "importance". The algorithm uses the weight values to decide which points must be closer to the goal and which can be permitted to remain farther away.

3. The position of the palm (the parent in the hand tree) can be decided based on the displacements of the fingers (the sons in the hand tree). The fingers are moved whenever the palm moves. Therefore, the fitting process has to traverse the hand tree bottom-up and top-down recursively.

We put heavy weight on the wrist (10) and the middle fingertip (3) because their alignment gives much influence to the posture of the whole hand. An iterative algorithm is designed that traverses the parent and the sons of the hand tree recursively.

3.4 Model Fitting Algorithm

The first step in the fitting execution phase is the construction of a reach tree having a part of the hand tree nodes, where each node either has an active goal or is linked with or more subtrees that contain nodes with active goals (Fig. 12). By constructing the reach tree, we can simplify the model fitting algorithm by identifying branches in the hand tree or identifying the node variables lwd, stwd, stwt or stweight in Fig. 11. The endpoints of the branches can be moved toward the goals by solving inverse kinematics. A node of the reach tree is shown in Fig. 11. The node information of the associated hand tree is available through a pointer htseg as explained in Fig. 11.

```
RTnode {/* reach tree node */
        RTnode *parent;
        RTnode *sons[];
        Segment *htseg; /* htseg is a pointer to */
                        /* associated hand tree segment */
        Vector lwd;     /* node variable lwd represents */
                        /* local weighted displacement */
        Vector stwd;    /* node variable stwd represents */
                        /* subtree weighted displacement */
        Vector stwt;    /* node variable stwt represents */
                        /* subtree weighted torque */
        float stweight; /* total subtree weight */
```

Fig. 11 Definition of a node of the reach tree.

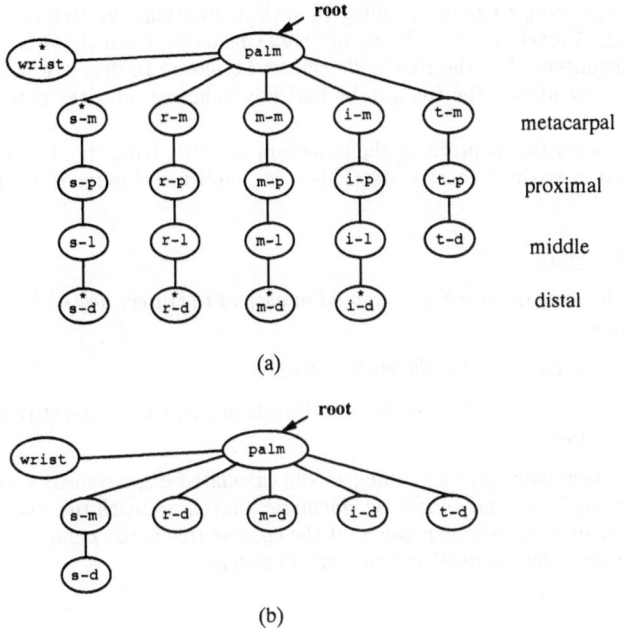

(a)

(b)

Fig. 12 Hand tree with goals(a) and reach tree (b). In (a), the nodes with asterisks are those with goals.

Associated with each node in the reach tree are two weighted displacements and a weighted torque. The local weighted displacement lwd is the displacement of the characteristic point of the current segment from its goal, scaled by the goal weight. This weighted displacement acts like attractive force since we assumed that there is a virtual spring between a characteristic point of the hand model and its goal position:

$$F = w(v_{goal} - v_{cur})$$

where F is the force and w is the goal weight. stwd is the sum of the subtree-weighted displacements for all of the nodes in the subtree rooted at the current node, including the displacement of the current node itself. stwd indicates the direction in which to move the current node to bring it closer to its goal and the goals of its children, considering the differences in importance between the goals. In a similar way, the subtree-weighted torque or stwt is the sum of the subtree-weighted torques for all of the nodes in the subtree rooted at the current node *around the current link*. One thing to note is that we use a slightly different concept of torque here. Qualitatively, our torque is a "twist" like the general concept of torque in physics. However, to derive a torque that minimizes the displacements between the goals and points on the model, we define torque quantitatively by

$$\tau = \frac{d \times F}{|d|}$$

where F is the force and d is the distance between the force and a given axis. This arrangement of the definition diminishes the effect of the distance of the force (displacement). stwt indicates the direction in which to rotate the current node to orient it toward the goals of its children.

With the notion of reach tree weight explained above, we define a *balanced tree* as a tree in which not only stwd of the root but also stwt of the root has zero magnitude. This is different from the definition of Badler (Page 35 of [2]). This occurs when the distance of each node from its goal is balanced with the others and the orientation of each node toward its goal is balanced with the others according to given weights. In such a situation, the tree is considered to be *perfectly* balanced. A reach tree can also be *optimally* balanced, when the subtree displacement has a nonzero magnitude, but the root node cannot be moved to decrease it without moving its parent. In this, eventually the tree can be perfectly balanced after the parent is moved.

The model fitting algorithm is precisely the process of perfectly balancing the reach tree associated with the current extrinsic constraints. This is accomplished through the following iterative algorithm:

Algorithm FITTING

1. *Recursively balance the reach trees rooted at each of the direct descendants of the current reach tree root.*

2. *Determine* **stwd** *and* **stwt** *for the current tree.*

3. *If torque has a smaller magnitude than the threshold value or the iterative limit is reached, then quit; else continue.*

4. *Determine a new movement according to the calculated displacement and torque: If the current tree is a finger, call an inverse kinematic solution to reach the characteristic points toward the goals as closely as possible; if the current tree is the palm, rotate it to reduce the torque caused by the displacements of the fingers.*

5. *Repeat.*

The movement of the fingers is stretching toward the goals by inverse kinematics. The movement of the palm is more complicated. A force exercised on the palm makes it turn or translate. The palm turns until the torque caused by the fingers disappears. When the torque becomes small enough, it begins to move linearly. The difficulty lies in deciding in what direction and how much to turn to decrease the torque. It is hard to solve this problem analytically because the torque depends on the force and the positions of the limbs that change dynamically. Therefore, we have chosen to make the model oscillate on a plane, damping out until it reaches equilibrium by controling the sign and size of the rotation using Fibonacci search. Let us choose the three rotation axes so that the orientation of the palm at a given time is directed toward one of them: x-axis, z-axis, and c-axis. c-axis is the central axis of the palm (Fig. 13).

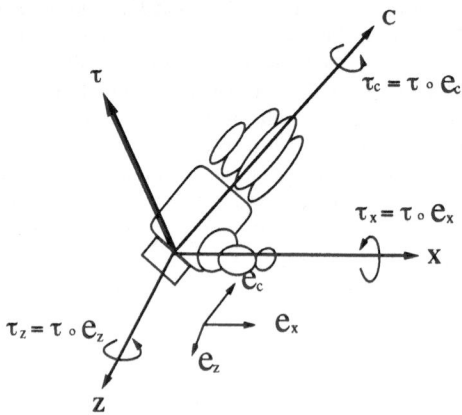

Fig. 13 Rotation axes of the model.

Let us choose The orientation of the palm is decided by the composition of three transformations, each of which arises from a rotation around one of the three rotation axes.

$$T_{palm.ori} = T_x * T_z * T_c$$

We calculate the torques of the palm around the three rotation axes, and choose an axis with the largest torque. It turns guided by the sign of the torque until the torque around the chosen axis becomes smaller than the threshold value (Fig. 14). Then, the palm choose another rotation axis by recalculating the torques around the three axes and repeats in a similar way.

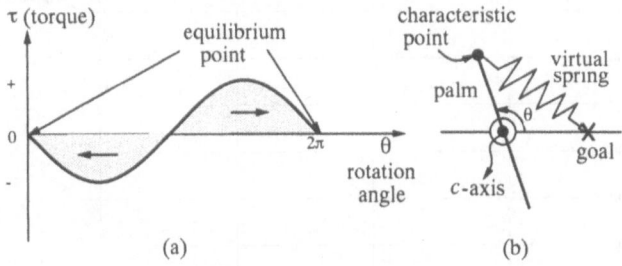

(a) (b)

Fig. 14 Rotation of the palm. In a simple example in which a characteristic point of the palm is connected to the goal position by a spring as (b), the torque of the palm changes like (a) as the palm turns around the c-axis. At a given time, we rotate the palm in the direction represented by the arrows to reach the equilibrium point.

4. EXPERIMENTS

The algorithm described in the previous section is based on the basic assumption that the displacement of the model from the image of the real hands becomes minimum when the torque of the total tree caused by the displacements becomes zero. The model fitting problem is a *nonlinear optimization* problem. Given the continuous torque function $\tau : V \to R$, the problem is to find

$$min\{\tau(v) : v \in R^3\}$$

and the vector $v \in R^3$ of three rotation angles in which the minimum is achieved. We need to verify whether the method converges to the solution. The result of experiments of 16 hand shapes randomly selected from the manual alphabets of American Sign Language (ASLM) show that the torque of the whole tree decreases continuously in general as the number of rotations increases. Fig. 14 is a typical example of convergence.

The iterative searching used to solve the inverse kinematics of the fingers is not a very efficient method, and it becomes the bottleneck of the algorithm : The examples illustrated in this paper execute in 40 to 80 minutes on an IRIS 70GT/40 workstation, and about 99.2% of the processing time is spent in solving the inverse kinematics of the fingers.

Defining the error rate after i rotations by

$$ER(i) = \frac{D(i)}{L(i)} = \frac{\sum_n \text{displacement of node } n \text{ from its goal}}{\sum_n \text{length of chain from root to node } n} \qquad (6)$$

where n is a node with goal in the reach tree, measures how closely the hand model has approached its characteristic points to the goals after the i-th rotation. The experimental results illustrated in this paper are achieved after the 5-th to 8-th rotation, and the average of $ER(7)$ for random samples is 0.023.

Change

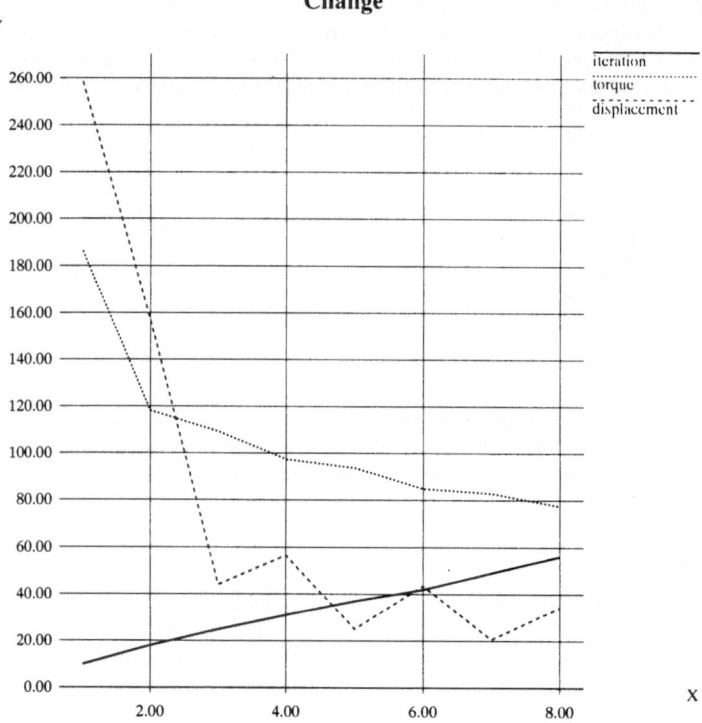

Fig. 14 Convergence of torque. The torque and the displacement of the reach tree decrease as the number of rotations increases.

5. CONCLUSION

Inferring the 3D structure of an articulated bodies from images - a routine work for a human visual system - is a difficult yet basic problem in computer animation and computer vision. A way to infer the 3D structure of human hands from multiple views has been investigated in this paper. A new animated model of the human hand with five main constraints has been proposed and tested. The modeled hand moves with reality according to the extrinsic forces derived from the image of the real hand maintaining the intrinsic constraints. The constraints in the model proved to be effective to avoid unrealistic motions and to reduce degrees of freedom in control.

Experiments of our model fitting method on 16 ASLMs (manual alphabets of American Sign Language) have produced reasonable results after 5 to 7 iterative rotations, and the error rate calculated was neglegibly small. The result shows that this model-based approach to hand image analysis can be applied to hand motion recognition or first-stage hand positioning for animation. Studies are under way to speed up processing and further reduce errors.

ACKNOWLEDGEMENTS

We thank Dr. Shinagawa and members of Kunii Lab for their support of this research. The comments from Dr. Michel Kuntz were valuable.

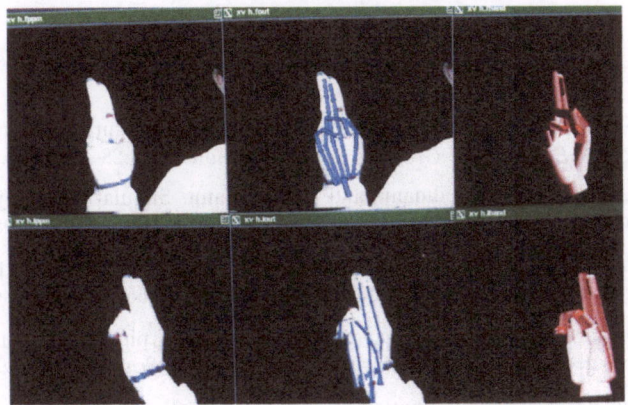

Fig. 15 Model fitting to ASLM-'h'[1].

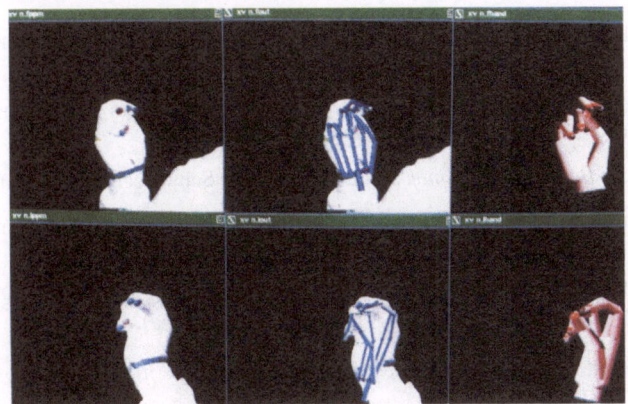

Fig. 16 Model fitting to ASLM-'n'.

---

[1] ASLM is the abbreviation of 'Manual alphabet of American Sign Language'.

References

[1] N. Ayache. *Artificial Vision for Mobile Robots: Stereo Vision and Multisensory Perception,* chapter 2. The MIT Press, 1991.

[2] N.I. Badler, K.H. Manoochehri, and G. Walters. Articulated figure positioning by multiple constraints. *IEEE Computer Graphics and Applications,* 7(6):28–38, 1987.

[3] J. Gourret, N. Magnenat-Thalmann, and D. Thalmann. Simulation of object and human skin deformations in a grasping task. *Computer Graphics,* 23(3):21–30, 1989.

[4] J.M.F. Landsmeer. Anatomical and functional investigations on the articulation of the human fingers. *Acta anatomica,* Supplementum 24:1–69, 1955.

[5] J.M.F. Landsmeer. A report on the co-ordination of the interphalangeal joints of the human finger and its disturbances. *Acta Morphologica Neerlando-Scandinavica,* 2:59–84, 1958.

[6] J.M.F. Landsmeer. The coordination of finger-joint motions. *The Journal of Bone and Joint Surgery,* 45-A(8):1654–1662, December 1963.

[7] H. Lee and Z. Chen. Determination of 3d human body postures from a single view. *Computer Vision, Graphics, and Image Processing,* 30:148–168, 1985.

[8] N. Magnenat-Thalmann, R. Laperriere, and D. Thalmann. Joint-dependent local deformations for hand animation and object grasping. In *Proc. Graphics Interface'88.* Edmonton, 1988.

[9] G. Monheit and N.I. Badler. A kinematic model of the human spine and torso. *IEEE Computer Graphics and Applications,* 11(2):29–38, March 1991.

[10] R. Nevatia. Structured descriptions of complex curved objects for recognition and visual memory. AIM-250, Stanford AI Lab, October 1974.

[11] E. Pernkopf. *Pernkopf Anatomy,* volume 2. Uran & Schwarzenberg, 3 edition, 1989.

[12] H. Rijpkema and M. Girard. Computer animation of knowledge-based human grasping. *Computer Graphics,* 25(4):339–347, 1991.

[13] Japan Orthopedics Society. A method of display and measuring joint angle limits. *Rehabilitation Medical Science,* 11(2):127–132, 1974(in Japanese).

[14] S. Tamura and S. Kawasaki. Recognition of sign language motion images. *Pattern Recognition,* 21(4):343–353, 1988.

[15] D. Zeltzer. Towards an integrated view of 3-d computer animation. *Visual Computer,* 1:249–259, 1985.

127

Jintae Lee is currently a doctoral course graduate student of the Department of Information Science at the University of Tokyo. His research interests include computer animation, computer graphics, computer vision, natural language processing and computer-aided translation. He received a B.S. in computer science and statistics from Seoul National University in 1981 and an M.S. in computer science from Korea Advanced Institute of Science and Technology in 1983. He will receive a PhD. in information science from the University of Tokyo in 1993. He is a member of IPSJ and KISS.

Address: Department of Information Science, Faculty of Science, the University of Tokyo, 7-3-1 Hongo, Bunkyo-ku, Tokyo, 113 Japan.

Tosiyasu L. Kunii is currently Professor of Information and Computer Science, the University of Tokyo.

He authored and edited more than 45 computer science books, and published more than 150 refereed academic/technical papers in computer science and applications areas.

Dr. Kunii is Honorary president of the Computer Graphics Society, Editor-in-Chief of *The Visual Computer: An International Journal of Computer Graphics* (Springer-Verlag), Associate Editor-in-Chief of *The Journal of Visualization and Computer Animation* (John Wiley & Sons) and on the Editorial Board of *IEEE Transactions on Knowledge and Data Engineering, VLDB Journal* and *IEEE Computer Graphics and Applications*. He is on the IFIP Modeling and Simulation Working Group, the IFIP Data Base Working Group and the IFIP Computer Graphics Working Group. He is on the board of directors of Japan Society of Sports Industry and also of Japan Society of Simulation and Gaming.

He received the B.Sc., M.Sc., and D.Sc. degrees in chemistry all from the University of Tokyo in 1962, 1964, and 1967, respectively. He is a fellow of IEEE and a member of ACM, BCS, IPSJ and IEICE.

Address: Department of Information Science, Faculty of Science, the University of Tokyo, 7-3-1 Hongo, Bunkyo-Ku,Tokyo, 113 Japan

Hair Animation with Collision Detection

TSUNEYA KURIHARA, KEN-ICHI ANJYO, and DANIEL THALMANN

ABSTRACT

We propose an efficient method for hair animation. The movement of hairs is modeled by simplified physical simulations. In particular the method can treat successfully collisions between hair and a human body or other objects, which provides realistic hair animation. The fast collision detection is achieved using cylindrical representation of the head and human body parts, despite a large number of hairs. The cylindrical representation allows collision detection to be performed by table look-up and interpolation, which assures that the computation time is independent of the complexity of the objects. A reaction constraint algorithm is also applied for the collision reaction to simulate inelastic contact. The efficiency of the method is well illustrated by the animation obtained.

Keywords: human character animation, hair, collision detection.

1. INTRODUCTION

Human character animation is one of the most challenging topics in computer graphics (Magnenat-Thalmann and Thalmann 1991). Human hair is important for the generation of natural human characters. However, many problems remain to be overcome for hair animation, because the number of hairs is very large (hundreds of thousands of strands).

Several techniques have been proposed relating to hair rendering. Miller (1988) successfully generated furry object by modeling each strand as long triangles. Kajiya and Kay (1988) used three dimensional texture mapping, *texel*, to generate images of a teddy bear. LeBlanc et al. (1992) used antialiasing and shadow buffer techniques to generate naturalistic images of human hair. Rosenblum et al. (1992) also used similar techniques. Watanabe and Suenaga (1992) proposed a 'trigonal prism and wisp model' to represent human hair.

These successful results of hair rendering have shown that more realistic human characters can be synthesized with modeling and animation techniques of hair. However, research of modeling and animation techniques is still an open field.

The movement of hair is governed by physical laws, so a physically based modeling approach (Terzopoulos and Fleischer 1988) may provide good results. Animating a single strand is not a difficult problem using the physically based approach. However, the large number of hairs makes it impossible or impractical to apply precise physical simulation of hair dynamics. Therefore, methods to animate hair assuming some simplification have been proposed. Rosenblum et al. (1992) proposed an animation method of hair using a mass spring model. This method neglects the effect of collision between hairs for simplicity. Anjyo et al. (1992) have proposed a method using one dimensional projective differential equations under a pseudo-force field. This method uses the pseudo-force field for roughly approximating the effect of collision between hairs. The collision of hair with other objects, such as the head, is simplified using a sphere or ellipsoid in both methods. The problem of self collision of hair is very difficult. However, the collision between hair and other objects is required to generate naturalistic movement of long hair.

Collision detection is an important issue in physically based approaches, and several methods have been proposed (Platt and Barr 1988; Moore and Wilhelm 1988; Lafleur et al. 1991). Again, precise treatment of collision detection between hairs and other objects cannot be performed because of the huge amount of hair strands. Ordinary methods of collision detection by polygon and line intersection algorithms are too time consuming to generate hair animation within the limitations of current computer technology. A simplified approach to collision detection is also required in addition to the simplified physical simulation of hair.

This paper presents a simplified and efficient method for hair animation with collision detection. Section 2 describes a dynamic model of hair based on simple differential equations of one-dimensional angular momenta. Section 3 introduces an efficient collision detection technique using cylindrical representation. Section 4 shows several examples of hair animation. Section 5 discusses the advantages and limitations of the method.

2. DYNAMIC MODEL OF HAIR

We follow the dynamic model of hair proposed in (Anjyo et al. 1992), introducing a hinge effect for wavy hair and a damping effect for obtaining more naturalistic movement. These effects are newly developed in this paper. A strand of hair is modeled as a series of line segments (Fig. 1). In this figure, s_i $(1 \leq i \leq k)$ is a segment, P_i $(0 \leq i \leq k)$ is a node, d is the length of each segment, and k is the number of segments in each strand. If the strand is not stretched, the shape of the hair is represented by the angles between segments. Taking the polar coordinate system as shown in Fig. 2, the behavior of the zenith angle θ_i and the azimuth ϕ_i of segment s_i are observed. This polar coordinate system is defined according to the coordinate system of the parent segment.

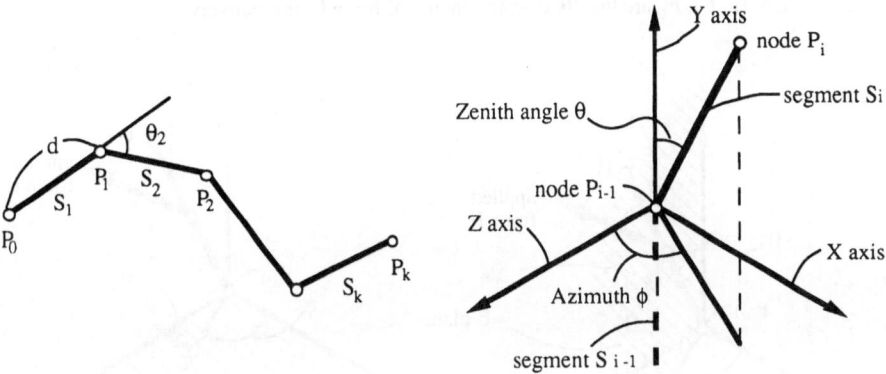

Fig. 1 Dynamic model of a single strand of hair.

Fig. 2 The polar coordinate system for a hair segment.

The variables $\theta_i(t)$ and $\phi_i(t)$ with the time parameter t are governed by ordinary differential equations:

$$I_i \frac{d^2\theta_i}{dt^2} + \gamma_i \frac{d\theta_i}{dt} = M_\theta$$

$$I_i \frac{d^2\phi_i}{dt^2} + \gamma_i \frac{d\phi_i}{dt} = M_\phi \qquad (1)$$

where I_i is the moment of inertia of the segment s_i, γ_i is the damping coefficient, M_θ and M_ϕ are the torque corresponding to the θ and ϕ components, respectively.

The inertial moment of segment s_i is defined as

$$I_i = \frac{1}{3} \frac{1}{i} \lambda k^4 d^3 \quad ,$$

(2)

where λ is the line density. The torque M_θ and M_ϕ applied to the segment s_i are derived from the hinge effect $M_{\theta spring}$, $M_{\phi spring}$ between two segments, and external moment $M_{\theta external}$, $M_{\phi external}$ from an external force, such as gravity, inertial force or wind:

$$M_\theta = M_{\theta\ spring} + M_{\theta\ external}$$
$$M_\phi = M_{\phi\ spring} + M_{\phi\ external} \quad .$$

(3)

$M_{\theta spring}$ and $M_{\phi spring}$ are defined as

$$M_{\theta\ spring} = -k_\theta(\theta - \theta_0)$$
$$M_{\phi\ spring} = -k_\phi(\phi - \phi_0) \quad ,$$

(4)

where k_θ and k_ϕ are spring constants, and θ_0 and ϕ_0 are the initial angles.
External moments are defined as

$$M_{\theta\ external} = u\ F_\theta$$
$$M_{\phi\ external} = v\ F_\phi \quad ,$$

(5)

where u is $(1/2)d$, and v is the half length of the segment that is the projection of s_i onto the ϕ plane (see Fig. 3 and 4). F_θ, F_ϕ are the "θ, ϕ -component" of force $\mathbf{F}$, respectively.

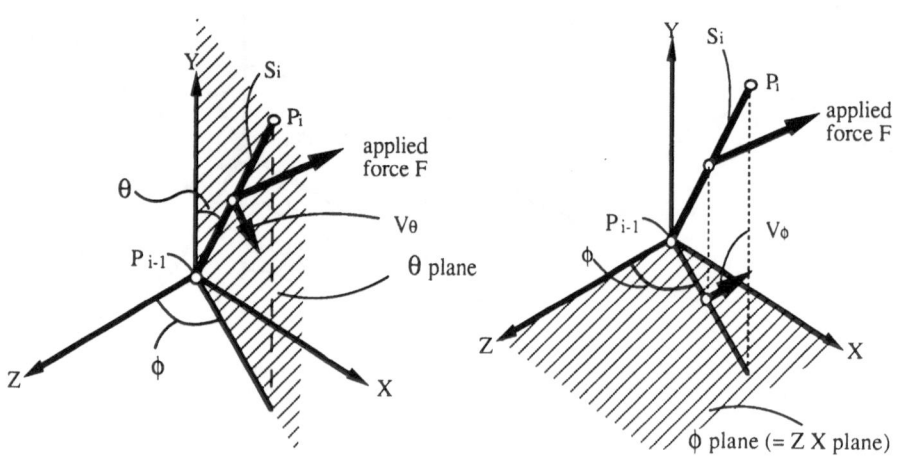

Fig. 3 Definition of the θ plane and V_θ.   Fig. 4 Definition of the ϕ plane and V_ϕ.

The above θ component F_θ of the applied force $\mathbf{F}$ is the scalar value defined by $F_\theta = (\mathbf{F}, \mathbf{V}_\theta)$, where $\mathbf{V}_\theta$ is the unit vector on the θ plane that is perpendicular to the segment s_i. Similarly, the ϕ component F_ϕ is defined by $F_\phi = (\mathbf{F}, \mathbf{V}_\phi)$, where $\mathbf{V}_\phi$ is the unit vector on the ϕ plane that is perpendicular to the projected segment of s_i onto the ϕ plane.

The external force **F** is defined as

$$\mathbf{F} = \rho d\ (\mathbf{g} + \mathbf{a}) + d\ \mathbf{f}, \tag{6}$$

where **g** is the acceleration due to gravity, **a** is the acceleration due to the movement of the head itself, and **f** is the density of the applied force, such as wind.

In the numerical simulation, Equation (1) is discretized as

$$
\begin{aligned}
I_i\ (\theta_i^{n+1} - 2\theta_i^n + \theta_i^{n-1}) + \gamma_i\ \Delta t\ (\theta_i^n - \theta_i^{n-1}) = (\Delta t)^2\ M_\theta \\
I_i\ (\phi_i^{n+1} - 2\phi_i^n + \phi_i^{n-1}) + \gamma_i\ \Delta t\ (\phi_i^n - \phi_i^{n-1}) = (\Delta t)^2\ M_\phi
\end{aligned} \tag{7}
$$

The calculation starts with segment s_1, and the new angle of s_i is successively determined using Equation (7).

3. COLLISION DETECTION AND RESPONSE

In order to generate naturalistic hair animation, collision between hair and other objects should be considered. An ordinary collision detection method finds intersections between polygons and points. However, this method is impractical because of the huge amount of data required for hairs and the polygons of the human body or other objects. In this section, we propose a simplified and efficient collision detection method for hair animation utilizing cylindrical representation, whose time complexity does not depend on the objects' complexity.

3.1 Collision Detection using Cylindrical Projection

Collision detection in our case entails determining whether each strand segment is within other objects or not. A correct test must consider line segments and objects. However, we consider only node point and objects test for simplicity. The problem is then to determine whether node **P** is inside of any objects or not.

First, we create a cylindrical representation of the human body or other objects. The human body is very irregular and cannot be described using one cylindrical representation. Therefore, we divide the human body or other objects into several parts, and each part is described by a cylindrical representation. For example, the human body is divided into the head, trunk, arms, and legs. Each part is described in a cylindrical coordinate system as (r, θ, y), where r is the radius, θ is the azimuth, and y is the height. We prepare an array of radius values on the discretized azimuth $i\Delta\theta$ and height $j\Delta y$ $(1 \le i \le m, 1 \le j \le n)$ by calculating the intersection between the line and object (Fig. 5). Along with the radius, we prepare the normal vector of each sample point for calculating collision response. Figure 6 shows examples of a cylindrical representation of the human body. Figure 6a is the original human body model with about 7000 polygons. Figure 6b shows the head and trunk model represented by a cylindrical coordinate system. These two models are defined with a [40 x 40] array of radius values.

When a cylindrical representation is created, a collision is easily detected. Let us consider a node **P** that is tested whether it is inside of an object or not. Then let **P** be (r_p, θ_p, y_p) in the cylindrical coordinate system. Next, we obtain the corresponding point **Q** of the object with the same azimuth θ_p and height y_p as point **P**. Assuming smoothness of the object surface, the position of **Q** can be approximated by linear interpolation as follows. We find index (i, j) which satisfies

$$
\begin{aligned}
i\,\Delta\theta \le \theta_p < (i+1)\Delta\theta \\
j\,\Delta y \le y_p < (j+1)\Delta y.
\end{aligned} \tag{8}
$$

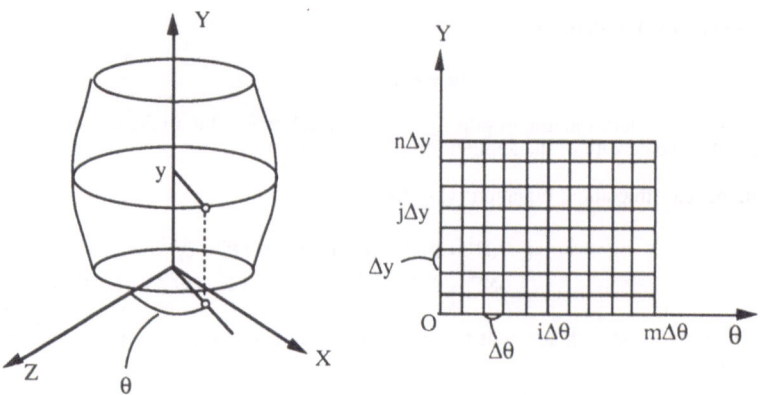

Fig. 5 Cylindrical representation of a three dimensional shape.

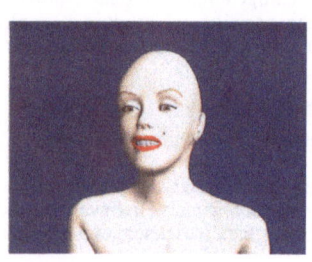
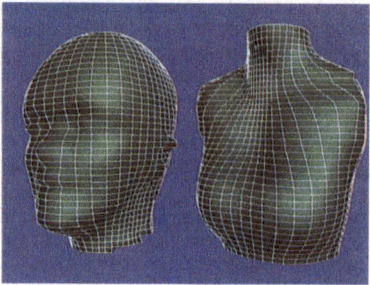

(a) The original human body.   (b) Cylindrical representation of the head and trunk.

Fig. 6   Examples of cylindrical representation.

The radius of point $\mathbf{Q}$ is then approximated as:

$$r_q = r(i,j) \cdot (1-s) \cdot (1-t) + r(i+1,j) \cdot s \cdot (1-t)$$
$$+ r(i,j+1) \cdot (1-s) \cdot t + r(i+1,j+1) \cdot s \cdot t \quad , \tag{9}$$

where

$$s = \frac{\theta_p - i\,\Delta\theta}{\Delta\theta}$$

$$t = \frac{y_p - j\,\Delta y}{\Delta y} \tag{10}$$

Collision detection is now reduced to comparing the radius part of point $\mathbf{P}$ and that of point $\mathbf{Q}$. If r_q is greater than r_p then point $\mathbf{P}$ is inside the object. Otherwise point $\mathbf{P}$ is outside of the object.

When point $\mathbf{P}$ is inside of the object, point $\mathbf{T}$ on the surface of object that is nearest to $\mathbf{P}$ is also required for collision response. $\mathbf{T}$ is approximated as follows (Fig. 7):

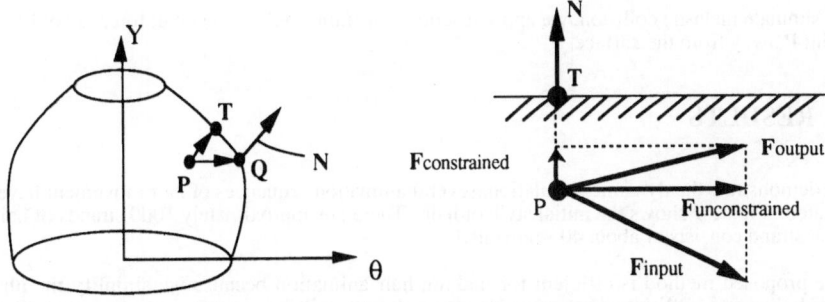

Fig. 7 Approximation of the nearest point **T**.   Fig. 8 Reaction constraint method
for collision response.

1. The normal vector **N** at point **Q** is the obtained using bi-linear interpolation. We use
   this normal vector as an approximation of the normal vector at point **T**.

2. Point **T** is on the surface of object and is nearest to point **P**. Thus, vector **PT** is
   parallel to normal vector **N**. Then point **T** is approximated as

$$\mathbf{PT} \approx (\mathbf{PQ} \cdot \mathbf{N})\, \mathbf{N}. \tag{11}$$

The proposed collision detection requires only table look-up and bi-linear interpolation. Therefore,
the computational cost is independent of the complexity of the objects.

3.2 Collision Response using Reaction Constraint

If a hair strand is detected to be inside of the body, the reaction constraint method (Platt and Barr
1988) is applied to keep hair outside of the body. Let $\mathbf{F}_{input}$ be the applied force to node point **P**.
Then the unconstrained component of $\mathbf{F}_{input}$ is

$$\mathbf{F}_{unconstrained} = \mathbf{F}_{input} - (\mathbf{F}_{input} \cdot \mathbf{N})\, \mathbf{N}, \tag{12}$$

where **N** is the normal vector at point **T** (see Fig. 8). This force $\mathbf{F}_{unconstrained}$ has no relationship
with the collision and is not changed.

The constrained force to avoid collision is

$$\mathbf{F}_{constrained} = -\,(k\, \mathbf{PT} + c\, \mathbf{V} \cdot \mathbf{N})\, \mathbf{N}, \tag{13}$$

where **V** is the velocity of point **P**, **T** is the nearest point on the surface from point **P**, k is the
strength of the constraint and c is the damping coefficient. Critical damped motion is obtained by
letting $c = \sqrt{2k}$.

The output force which is applied to point **P** is the summation of $\mathbf{F}_{unconstrained}$ and $\mathbf{F}_{constrained}$.

$$\mathbf{F}_{output} = \mathbf{F}_{unconstrained} + \mathbf{F}_{constrained}. \tag{14}$$

Using Equations (12), (13) and (14), the output force is written as

$$\mathbf{F}_{output} = \mathbf{F}_{input} - (\mathbf{F}_{input} \cdot \mathbf{N})\, \mathbf{N} - (k\, \mathbf{PT} + c\, \mathbf{V} \cdot \mathbf{N})\, \mathbf{N}. \tag{15}$$

To simulate inelastic collision, we apply reaction constraints only if the input force is not lifting the point **P** away from the surface.

4. RESULTS

To demonstrate the dynamic simulation, several animation sequences of hair movement have been created. Figure 9 shows the initial style of hair. There are approximately 1000 strands of hair, and each strand consists of about 40 segments.

The proposed method is efficient for making hair animation because we simplify the physical simulation and collision response. However, it may still be expensive to simulate all of the hundreds of thousand of strands of hair. When we observe real hairs, many neighboring strands move similarly. Thus, we simulate the movement of a cluster of strands, and not that of each strand, which reduces the computational cost significantly.

The cluster model of strands we have applied is very simple. We simulate the movement of typical strands and generate other strands by adding random numbers to the origin of the typical strands. Figure 10 shows the hair model generated by adding 20 strands for each typical strand of initial hair style, so the total number of strands is about 20,000.

Figure 11 shows four frames taken from a short film representing a windy scene. In this scene, only the force of wind and gravity are applied. The wind is blowing into the face. Note that the strands do not penetrate the head or shoulders because of the collision response.

Figure 12 shows four frames taken from a head shaking scene, where the head first moves left, then right, and finally left. A little wind is also applied blowing into the face.

Figure 13 illustrates the image rendered using a pixel blending and shadow buffer technique (LeBlanc et al. 1992). The number of strands in this image is about 40,000.

Animation software based on the presented method has been implemented on a Silicon Graphics Iris Series workstation (Iris PS25 TG). The wall clock time is typically 30 seconds per frame with collision response where the number of strands is about 1000, and each strand consists of about 40 segments. The clock time for the collision response alone is 3 seconds. This result shows the efficiency of the proposed collision detection method.

5. DISCUSSIONS

Ordinary collision detection methods calculate intersections between objects. Therefore, the complexity of the algorithm is $O(n^2)$ where n is the number of polygons. Space subdivision techniques, such as octree and voxel, reduce the computational cost. However, preparing these data structures is expensive when the object moves or deforms. The complexity of the proposed method is $O(n)$ because of the table look-up in the cylindrical coordinate system. In addition, preparing the cylindrical representation is not expensive. This is one of the advantages of the proposed method.

This collision detection method is a rough approximation of a precise one, such as line and triangle intersection checking. Therefore, it may fail to detect collisions when the resolution of the table is not high enough, or when the cylindrical representation is not sufficient to describe the objects. For example, the shoulders, the ears and the top of the head are not described precisely with cylindrical representation. However, the experiments show that this approximation can be sufficient for the purpose of animating hair.

Though this method utilizes a cylindrical coordinate system, other coordinate systems can also be used, such as a spherical coordinate system. The essential requirement is the mapping from a three-dimensional space to a two-dimensional space.

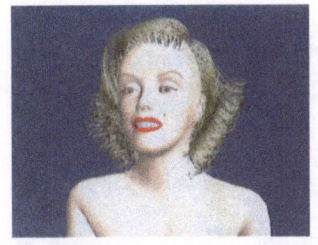

Fig. 9 Initial hair style.

Fig. 10 Hair using the cluster model.

Fig. 11 Blowing in the wind.

136

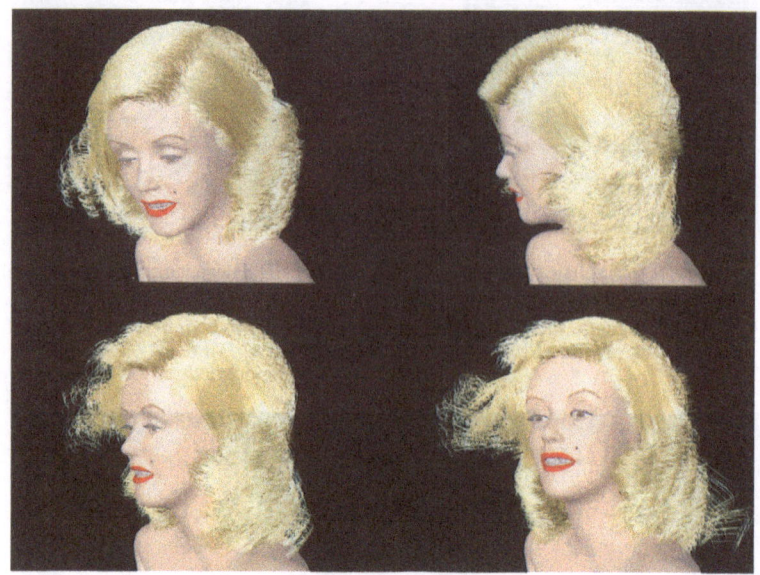

Fig. 12 Head shaking scene.

Fig. 13 Hair rendering by pixel blending and shadow buffer technique.

The proposed technique is simple and efficient for collision detection. Therefore, it can be applied to other applications as a rough approximation or efficient culling method for a more precise collision detection algorithm.

Unfortunately this method cannot be applied in treating self collision between the hairs, because it is difficult to represent the hair itself in a cylindrical coordinate system. Therefore, the self collision of hairs must be detected with other techniques, for obtaining more realistic hair movements.

6. CONCLUSIONS

We have presented an efficient method for animating hair. A simplified physical simulation and collision detection method make it possible to generate naturalistic motion of hair with reasonable computation cost. The collision detection algorithm for the hair and other objects is efficient and the computation time is independent of the complexity of the object.

The proposed method neglects strand-strand interaction for simplicity. However, realistic hair motion cannot be achieved without this effect, especially with a voluminous hair style. Precise treatment of strand-strand interaction will be too expensive within the limitation of current computational power. Therefore, some simplification of strand-strand interaction must be developed.

Acknowledgments

The authors would like to thank Agnes Daldegan for the design of the hair style, Guy Moreillon for hair rendering, and Geoff Wyvill and Russell Turner for valuable discussions. This research was performed at the Swiss Federal Institute of Technology during the first author's stay as a visiting researcher.

REFERENCES

Anjyo K., Usami Y. and Kurihara T. (1992) A Simple Method for Extracting the Natural Beauty of Hair, *Computer Graphics*, Vol. 26, No. 2, pp. 111-120.

Kajiya J.T. and Kay T.L. (1989) Rendering Fur with Three Dimensional Textures, *Computer Graphics*, Vol. 23, No. 3, pp. 271-280.

Lafleur B., Magnenat-Thalmann N. and Thalmann D. (1991) Cloth Animation with Self-Collision Detection, *Proceedings of IFIP WG5.10 - Modeling in Computer Graphics*, pp. 179-185.

LeBlanc A.M., Turner R. and Thalmann D. (1991) Rendering Hair using Pixel Blending and Shadow Buffers, *The Journal of Visualization and Computer Animation*, Vol. 2, No. 3, pp. 92-97.

Magnenat-Thalmann N. and Thalmann D. (1991) Complex Models for Animating Synthetic Actors, *IEEE Computer Graphics and applications*, Vol. 11, No. 5, pp. 32-44.

Miller G.S.P. (1988) From Wire-Frame to Furry Animals, *Proceedings of Graphics Interface '88* , pp. 138-146.

Moore M. and Wilhelms J. (1988) Collision Detection and Response for Computer Animation, *Computer Graphics*, Vol. 22, No. 4, pp. 289-298.

Platt J.C. and Barr A.H. (1988) Constraint Methods for Flexible Models, *Computer Graphics*, Vol. 22, No. 4, pp. 279-288.

Rosenblum R.E., Carlson W. E. and Tripp III. E. (1991) Simulating the Structure and Dynamics of Human Hair: Modelling, Rendering and Animation, *The Journal of Visualization and Computer Animation*, Vol. 2, No. 4, pp. 141-148.

Terzopoulos D. and Fleischer K. (1988) Deformable Models, *The Visual Computer*, Vol. 4, No. 6, pp. 306-331.

Watanabe Y. and Suenaga Y. (1992) A Trigonal Prism-Based Method for Hair Image Generation, *IEEE Computer Graphics and applications*, Vol. 12, No. 1 , pp. 47-53.

Tsuneya Kurihara is a researcher at the Central Research Laboratory, Hitachi, Ltd. He received the B.E. and M.E. degrees from the University of Tokyo, Tokyo, Japan, in 1981 and 1983, respectively. His research interests include computer animation, interactive sculpting and physically-based modeling. He is a member of ACM, IEEE CS and IPS of Japan.

Address: Central Research Laboratory, Hitachi, Ltd.,
1-280, Higashi-koigakubo, Kokubunji-shi,
Tokyo 185 Japan.
E-mail: kurihara@crl.hitachi.co.jp

Ken-ichi Anjyo joined Hitachi, Ltd. in 1982. He was a research scientist at the Hitachi Research Laboratory during 1982- 1992. Since Feb. 1992, he has been working for the Systems Engineering Division. His research interest focuses on geometric modeling, stochastic modeling and computer animation. He is a member of IPSJ, ACM Siggraph, and Eurographics.

Address: Systems Engineering Division, Hitachi, Ltd.,
4-6 Kanda-Surugadai, Chiyoda Tokyo 101 Japan.
E-mail: anjyo@hrl.hitachi.co.jp

Daniel Thalmann is currently full professor, head of computer science, and director of the Computer Graphics Laboratory at the Swiss Federal Institute of Technology in Lausanne, Switzerland. He also is an adjunct professor at the University of Montreal. Since 1977, he was Professor at the University of Montreal and director of the Computer Graphics laboratory. He received his diploma in nuclear physics and Ph.D in Computer Science from the University of Geneva. He was visiting Professor at the University of Nebraska and invited researcher in the Computer Graphics Group at CERN. He cochairs the EUROGRAPHICS Working Group on Computer Simulation and Animation. Daniel Thalmann's research interests include 3D computer animation, image synthesis, and virtual reality. He has published more than 150 papers in these areas and is coauthor of several books including: *Computer Animation: Theory and Practice* and *Image Synthesis: Theory and Practice*. He is also codirector of several computer-generated films *Dream Flight, Eglantine, Rendez-vous à Montréal, Galaxy Sweetheart, IAD, Flashback, Still Walking* and *Fashion Show*. He cochaired several conferences and workshops. He is also co-editor-in-chief of the *Journal of Visualization and Computer Animation* and editor of the *Visual Computer* and the *CADD journal*.

Address: Computer Graphics Lab,
Swiss Federal Institute of Technology,
CH-1015 Lausanne, Switzerland
E-mail: thalmann@eldi.epfl.ch

Modeling Coarticulation in Synthetic Visual Speech

MICHAEL M. COHEN and DOMINIC W. MASSARO

ABSTRACT

After describing the importance of visual information in speech perception and sketching the history of visual speech synthesis, we consider a number of theories of coarticulation in human speech. An implementation of Löfqvist's (1990) gestural theory of speech production is described for visual speech synthesis along with a description of the graphically controlled development system. We conclude with some plans for future work.

Keywords: facial animation, speech, coarticulation

1. INTRODUCTION

Our approach to the synthesis of visual speech starts with the study of speech perception. Much of what we know about speech perception has come from experimental studies using *auditory* synthetic speech. Synthetic speech gives the investigator control over the stimulus in a way that is not always possible using natural speech. Although the experimental validity of synthetic speech might be questioned, the phenomena uncovered using synthetic speech hold up when tested using natural speech. Synthetic speech also permits the implementation and test of various theoretical hypotheses, such as which cues are critical for various speech distinctions. The applied value of auditory synthetic speech is apparent in the multiple everyday uses for text-to-speech systems for both normal and hearing-impaired individuals. Its use is important for hearing-impaired individuals because it allows effective communication within speech — the universal language of the community. Finally, auditory synthetic speech provides an independent assessment of various models of speech production.

We believe that *visible* synthetic speech will prove to have the same value as audible synthetic speech. Synthetic visible speech will provide a more fine-grained assessment of psychophysical and psychological questions not possible with natural speech. Like audible synthetic speech, synthetic visible speech can have a valuable role to play in alleviating some of the communication disadvantages of the deaf and hearing-impaired. It is also a useful device for evaluation of theories of human speech production.

A guiding assumption for our research has been that humans use multiple sources of information in the perceptual recognition and understanding of spoken language. In this regard, speech perception resembles other forms of pattern recognition and categorization because integrating multiple sources of information appears to be a natural function of human endeavor. Integration appears to occur to some extent regardless of the goals and motivations of the perceiver. Brunswik (1955) acknowledged the multiple but ambiguous sources of influence on behavior. He stressed "the limited ecological validity or trustworthiness of cues . . . To improve its (the organism's) bet, it must accumulate and combine cues" (1955, p. 207).

There is valuable and effective information afforded by a view of the speaker's face in speech perception and recognition by humans. A perceiver's recognition of auditory-visual (bimodal) speech reflects the contribution of both sound and sight. Visible speech is particularly effective when the auditory speech is degraded, because of noise, bandwidth filtering, or hearing-impairment. As an example, the perception of short sentences that have been bandpass filtered improves from 23% to 79% correct when subjects are permitted a view of the speaker (Breeuwer & Plomp, 1985). This same type of improvement has been observed in hearing-impaired listeners and patients with cochlear implants (Massaro, 1987). The strong influence of visible speech is not limited to situations with degraded auditory input, however. If an auditory syllable /ba/ is dubbed onto a videotape of a speaker saying /da/, subjects often perceive the speaker to be saying /ða/ (Massaro & Cohen, 1990). The impact of visible speech is greater than what might be expected from a simple additive contribution. In a recent experiment (Massaro & Cohen, unpublished experiment), we tested subjects on 420 one-syllable English words given natural audible, visible, or bimodal speech. To degrade the input to produce errors, the speech was presented at three times normal speed on a video monitor. To accomplish this, a laser disk containing the stimuli (Bernstein & Eberhardt, 1986) was programmed to display only every third frame, resulting in no pitch shift for the auditory speech. Accuracy was 55% given audible speech, 4% given visible speech, and 72% given bimodal speech—a superadditive combination of the two sources of information.

2. SYNTHETIC VISIBLE SPEECH

Several investigators have used some form of simulated facial display for speech studies. Erber and De Filippo (1978) used relatively simple Lissajou's figures displayed on an oscilloscope to simulate lip movement. They varied the height and width of the simulated lips with analog control voltages. Montgomery (1980) developed a model for lip shape which allowed computation of coarticulatory effects for CVCVC segments (C=consonant; V=vowel). The lip shape display was done on a vector graphic device using about 130 vectors at a rate of about 4 times real time. Brooke and Summerfield (1983) implemented a real-time vector display system for displaying simple 2-dimensional faces. In contrast to these 2-dimensional models, our research utilizes 3-dimensional facial models (cued by lighting, shading, and in some cases texture). Visual scientists and artists have long stressed the importance of such 3-dimensional cues in the 2-dimensional representation.

Two general strategies for generating highly realistic full facial displays have been employed: parametrically controlled polygon topology and musculoskeletal models. Using the first strategy, Parke (1974, 1975, 1982, 1991) developed a fairly realistic animation by modeling the facial surface as a polyhedral object composed of about 900 small surfaces arranged in 3D, joined together at the edges. Although this model has teeth, the tongue has not been represented (nor has it been in other models). To achieve a natural appearance, the surface was smooth shaded using Gouraud's (1971) method. The face was animated by altering the location of various points in the grid under the control of 50 parameters, about 10 of which were used for speech animation. Parke (1974) selected and refined the control parameters used for several demonstration sentences by studying his own articulation frame by frame and estimating the control parameter values.

Parke's software and topology was given new speech and expression control software by Pearce, Wyvill, Wyvill, and Hill (1986). With this software, a user could type a string of phonemes which were then converted to control parameters which were changed over time to produce the desired animation sequence. Each phoneme was defined in a table according to values for segment duration, segment type (stop, vowel, liquid, etc) and 11 control parameters. The parameters used are jaw rotation, mouth width, mouth z (forward-back) offset relative to face, width of lips at mouth corner, mouth corner x (horizontal), y (vertical), z offsets (with respect to rest of mouth), tapered lower lip "f" tuck, tapered upper lip raise relative to lower lip, and teeth z and x offsets. The program made a transition between two phonemes by interpolating in a nonlinear fashion between the values for two adjacent phonemes. Different transition speeds were used depending on the type of segments involved.

A B-spline surface model has also been used to generate faces (Nahas, Huitric, & Saintourens, 1988). To derive the control points of the B-spline surface, Nahas et al used a scanning device to obtain 3D surface slices. B-spline control parameters were obtained to generate a facial shape for each phoneme. Images of these faces (held in a frame store) were then concatenated according to the sequence of phonemes desired.

Using the second strategy, human faces were made by constructing a computational model for the muscle and bone structures of the face (Platt & Badler, 1981; Terzopoulous & Waters, 1990, 1991; Waters, 1987, 1990; Waters & Terzopoulous, 1990, 1991). At the foundation of the model is an approximation of the skull and jaw including the jaw pivot. Muscle tissues and their insertions are placed over the skull. This requires complex elastic models for the compressible tissues. A covering surface layer changes according to the underlying structures. The driving information for such a model might be defined by a dynamically changing set of contraction-relaxation muscle commands. Platt and Badler (1981) use Eckman and Friesen's (1977) "Facial Action Coding System" to control the facial model. These codes are based on about 50 facial actions (action units or AU's) defined by combinations of facial muscle actions.

One drawback to this synthesis approach is that calculations needed for the tissue simulations take significantly longer to carry out than the calculations of the changing surface shapes in the polygon models. It also may be more difficult to achieve the desired articulations in terms of the constituent muscle actions as opposed to defining the desired shapes themselves. This difference in synthesis methods is parallel to the difference between articulatory (e.g. Flanagan, Ishizaka, & Shipley, 1975) and terminal-analogue formant (Klatt, 1980) synthesizers for auditory speech. As for visual speech, the auditory articulatory synthesizers required several orders more computation.

We have adopted the parametrically controlled polygon topology synthesis technique. Our current software is a direct descendant of Parke (1974) incorporating code developed by Pearce, Wyvill, Wyvill, and Hill (1986) and ourselves (Cohen & Massaro, 1990; Massaro & Cohen, 1990). Given the importance of the tongue in speech production and visual speech perception, a tongue was added to the facial model. Regardless of which type of facial model is used, the problem remains of how to best drive the face and tongue during speech. We now review some of what is known about the phenomenon of coarticulation in human speech production and how it may help us in animation.

3. COARTICULATION

Coarticulation refers to changes in the articulation of a speech segment depending on preceding (backward coarticulation) and upcoming segments (forward coarticulation). An example of backward coarticulation is a difference in articulation of a final consonant in a word depending on the preceding vowel, e.g. boot vs beet. An example of forward coarticulation is the anticipatory lip rounding at the beginning of the word "stew". Great improvement of more recent auditory speech synthesizers, such as MITtalk (Allen, Hunnicutt & Klatt, 1987) and DECtalk (1985), over the previous generation of synthesizers such as VOTRAX (1981), is partly due to the inclusion of rules specifying the coarticulation among neighboring phonemes.

An interesting question concerning the perception of visual speech is to what degree coarticulation is important. Benguerel and Pichora-Fuller (1982) examined coarticulation influences on lipreading by hearing-impaired and normal-hearing individuals. The test items were $/V_1CV_2/$ nonsense syllables. Coarticulation was assessed by contrasting consonant recognition in vowel contexts that produce large coarticulatory influences relative to those that produce small influences. Significant coarticulation influences on lipreading were noted for both groups. For example, the identity of V_2 had a significant effect on visible consonant recognition. Fewer consonants were recognized correctly when they were followed by $/u/$ than by $/i/$ or $/æ/$. By reversing the stimuli, and finding the same results, they demonstrated that the effect was due to articulation differences rather than the actual position in the stimulus as presented. Cathiard, Tiberghien, Cirot-Tseva, Lallouache, M.-T., and Escudier (1991) showed that observers can use the visual information produced by anticipatory rounding.

Although there have been many studies of coarticulation (e.g. Öhman, 1966; Benguerel & Cowan, 1974; Lubker & Gay, 1982; Bladon & Al-Bamerni, 1982; Recasens, 1984; Perkell, 1989), little consensus has been achieved toward a theoretical explanation of the phenomenon (Öhman 1967; Kent & Minifie, 1977; Bell-Berti & Harris 1979). Three main classes of models have been developed. Figure 1 illustrates these three model classes in two typical coarticulation situations. A VCV (top curves) or VCCV (bottom curves) is shown with the initial vowel unprotruded (i.e. $/i/$) and the final vowel protruded (e.g. $/u/$). In all three cases, the lip protrusion begins prior to onset (marked by the solid vertical line) of the protruded final vowel. What discriminates the models is the onset time and dynamics of the coarticulatory movement.

In the look-ahead model (Kozhevnikov & Chistovich, 1965, Henke, 1967; Öhman, 1967), illustrated in the left panel of Fig. 1, the movement toward protrusion starts (indicated by the solid vertical tick) as soon as possible following the unprotruded vowel V_1. Thus, the time relative to the V_2 onset differs depending on the number of intervening units. A variant of this model has been used by Pelachaud, Badler and Steedman (1991) for visual speech synthesis. In their system, phonemes are assigned high or low deformability rank. Forward and backward coarticulation rules are applied such that a phoneme takes the lip shape of a less

142

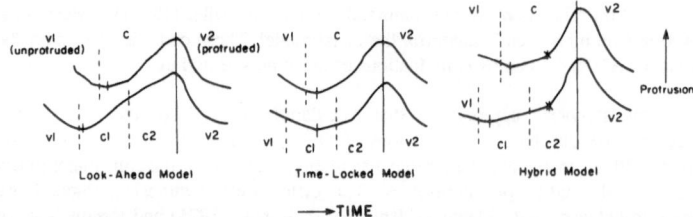

Fig. 1. Schematic representations of lip protrusion curves consistent with the look-ahead model (left panel), the time-locked model (center panel), and the hybrid model of coarticulation. From Perkell (1989). The solid vertical line is the onset of the protruded vowel V_2.

deformable phoneme forward or backwards. Their algorithm occurs in three passes. First one computes the ideal lip shapes, then in two additional passes, temporal and spatial muscle actions are computed based on certain constraints. For example, they take into account the contraction and relaxation time of the involved muscles. Conflicting muscle actions are then resolved through the use of a table of AU similarities.

In the time-locked model, also known as coproduction, (Bell-Berti & Harris, 1981, 1982) illustrated in the center panel of Fig. 1, the movement towards protrusion begins a fixed time prior to V_2 onset. This model assumes that gestures are independent entities which are combined in an approximately additive fashion.

The right panel of Fig. 1 illustrates a hybrid model typical of Bladon and Al-Bamerni (1982) and Perkell and Chiang (1986). In this type of model there are two phases of movement. The first phase begins gradually as early as possible as in the look-ahead model. A second phase begins at a fixed time prior to V_2, analogous to the time-locked model. During this second phase, more rapid movement occurs. In experimental data this model has been supported by an inflection point at the hypothetical phase transition point indicated by the X marks in the two curves (Perkell, 1989).

It should be pointed out that an important reason for the different theories of coarticulation comes from different empirical results, depending on a number of experimental (e.g. Gelfer, Bell-Berti, & Harris, 1989) and linguistic factors. In one recent study, Abry and Lallouache (1991) tested the three coarticulation models against physical measurements of lip rounding in French /ikstsky/ sequences. What they found was that none of the three models could account for the observed patterns of rounding anticipation, which instead may have depended on suprasegmental prosodic effects. In an example of the cross linguistic differences, Lupker and Gay (1982) compared speakers of American English and Swedish and found that the Swedish start anticipatory rounding earlier, perhaps to preserve contrasts among the vowels which are more numerous in that language. Similarly, Boyce (1990) describes differences between Turkish and American speakers in intervocalic protrusion. For the string /utu/ for example American speakers show a trough pattern (a decrease in protrusion between two peaks for /u/) versus a plateau pattern for the Turkish speakers (no decrease in protrusion for the /t/ between the vowels). She explained this in terms of the American speakers using a coproduction strategy while the Turkish speakers use a look-ahead strategy. Thus it may be that a single one of the three theories cannot account for coarticulation in all situations and perhaps a more flexible general framework is called for.

Such a framework is suggested by the articulatory gesture model of Löfqvist (1990). The central theme of the model is expressed in Fig. 2. In this figure we see that a speech segment has dominance over the vocal articulators which increases and then decreases over time during articulation. Adjacent segments will have overlapping dominance functions which leads to a blending over time of the articulatory commands related to these segments. In this regard the model shares the coproduction (Bell-Berti & Harris, 1982) view of gesture combination. It is also suggested that each segment has not a single dominance function but rather a set of such functions, one for each articulator. As can be seen in Fig. 3, different articulatory dominance

Dominance

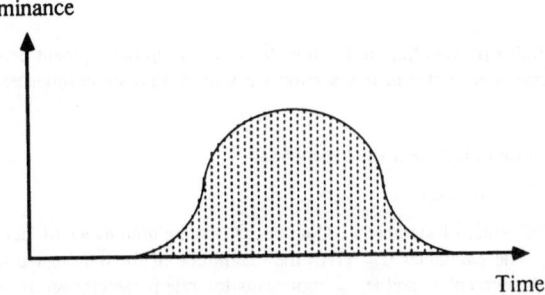

Time

Fig. 2. A representation of the speech segment over time in terms of its dominance on the articulators. From Löfqvist (1990).

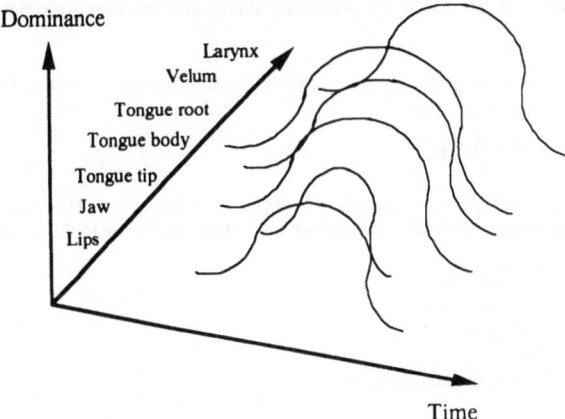

Time

Fig. 3. A representation of the speech segment over time in terms of its dominance on the articulators. Traces with differing characteristics are shown for different articulators. From Löfqvist (1990).

functions can differ in time offset, duration, and magnitude. Different time offsets, for example, between lip and glottal gestures could capture differences in voicing. The magnitude of each function can capture the relative importance of a characteristic for a segment. For example, a consonant could have a low dominance on lip rounding which would allow the intrusion of values of that characteristic from adjacent vowels.

The variable and varying degree of dominance in this approach is a nice feature which allows it to naturally capture the continuous nature of articulator positioning. It shares this characteristic with the idea of a numerical coefficient for "coarticulation resistance" associated with some phonetic features in the theory of Bladon and Al-Bamerni (1976) as contrasted to a number of other theories which assumed binary valued features (e.g. Benguerel & Cowan, 1974). We also note a similarity between this approach and Elson's (1990) use of Reynolds (1985) S-Dynamics animation control. In Elson's facial animation system, overlapping time-varying displacement magnitudes were used to interpolate between 10 possible phoneme shapes. This interpolation scheme was used in multiple layers to control all dynamic attributes of a whole body model.

We have adapted the Löfqvist gestural production model to drive our synthetic visual speech. Note that this model provides complete guidance of the facial articulators for speech rather than simply modulating some other algorithm to correct for coarticulation. To instantiate this model it is necessary to select particular dominance and blending functions. One general form for dominance is given by the negative exponential function,

$$D = e^{-\theta \tau^c} \quad .$$ (1)

In this function, dominance falls off according to the time distance τ from the segment center, to the power c modified by the rate parameter θ. Later in this section we will discuss some other general dominance functions that are possible.

In our algorithm, the general form of Equation 1 is expanded to

$$D_{sp} = \alpha_{sp}\, e^{-\theta_{\leftarrow sp}\,|\tau|^c}, \quad \text{if } \tau \geq 0 \quad .$$ (2)

for the case of time prior to the center of segment s. Quantity D_{sp} is the dominance of facial control parameter p of speech segment s. The parameter α_{sp} gives the magnitude of the dominance function of facial control parameter p of speech segment s, and $\theta_{\leftarrow sp}$ represents the rate parameter on the anticipatory side. Similarly, the dominance in the temporal range following the center of a unit is given by

$$D_{sp} = \alpha_{sp}\, e^{-\theta_{\rightarrow sp}\,|\tau|^c}, \quad \text{if } \tau < 0 \quad .$$ (3)

In both cases, the temporal distance τ from the peak of the dominance function is given by:

$$\tau = t_{c\ sp} + t_{o\ sp} - t$$ (4)

where t is the running time, $t_{o\ sp}$ gives the time offset from the center of segment s for the peak of dominance for facial control parameter p, and

$$t_{c\ sp} = t_{start\ s} + \frac{duration_s}{2}$$ (5)

gives the time of the center of segment s given its starting time and duration. Using these dominance functions, we can combine the target values T_{sp} for each unit over time according to the weighted average:

$$F_p(t) = \frac{\sum_{s=1}^{N} (D_{sp}(t) \times T_{sp})}{\sum_{s=1}^{N} D_{sp}(t)}$$ (6)

where N is the number of segments in an utterance.

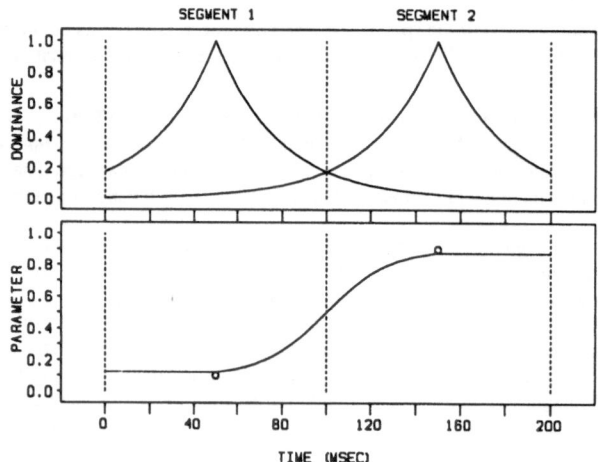

Fig. 4. Dominance of 2 speech segments over time (top panel) and the resulting control parameter function (bottom panel). Circles in the bottom panel indicate target control parameter values.

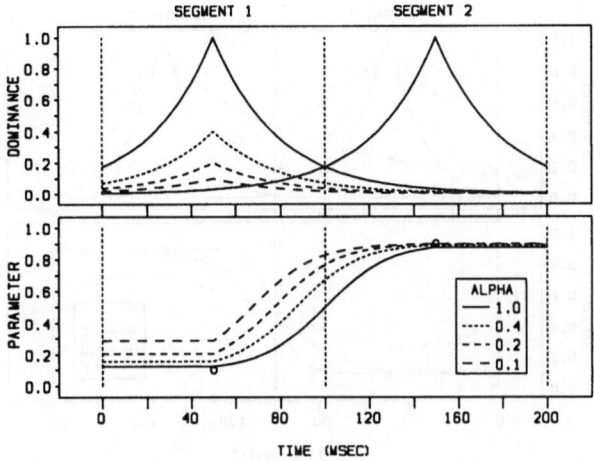

Fig. 5. Dominance of 2 speech segments over time (top panel) and the resulting control parameter function (bottom panel) with α of the first segment as a parameter.

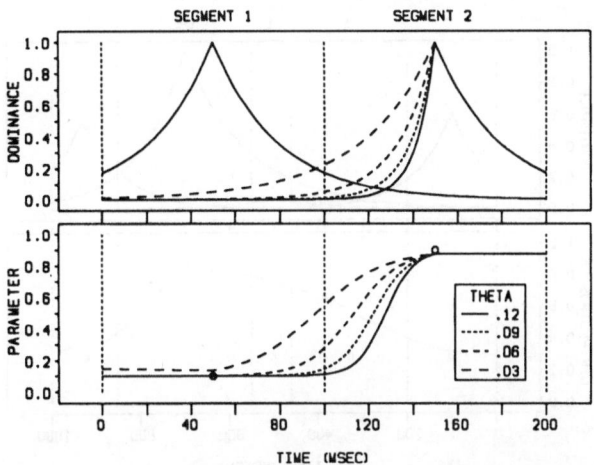

Fig. 6. Dominance of 2 speech segments over time (top panel) and the resulting control parameter function (bottom panel) with θ of the second segment as a parameter.

Figure 4 illustrates a simple case of how the algorithm functions. Dominance functions are shown for a single control parameter for 2 speech segments over time and the resulting control parameter function. For this example, $\theta_{\leftarrow sp} = \theta_{\rightarrow sp} = .035$, $c = 1$, *duration* = 100 msec for both segments, and the target values are .1 and .9. As can be seen, a gradual transition occurs between the two targets, although neither target is reached. Figure 5 illustrates how the control parameter function changes as the magnitude of the dominance function parameter α_{sp} decreases. As the value of α of segment 1 decreases, segment 1 increasingly allows the intrusion of the value from segment 2. Figure 6 illustrates how the anticipatory θ parameter of segment 2 controls the transition speed and location between the segments. As θ of segment 2 increases, the transition moves toward segment 2 and becomes steeper. Figure 7 illustrates how changes in the power c of the dominance function control the degree of transition and the transition duration between segments. As c increases, control functions come closer to the target values and the transitions become more abrupt, approaching a steplike change between segments. In practice we usually set $c = 1$.

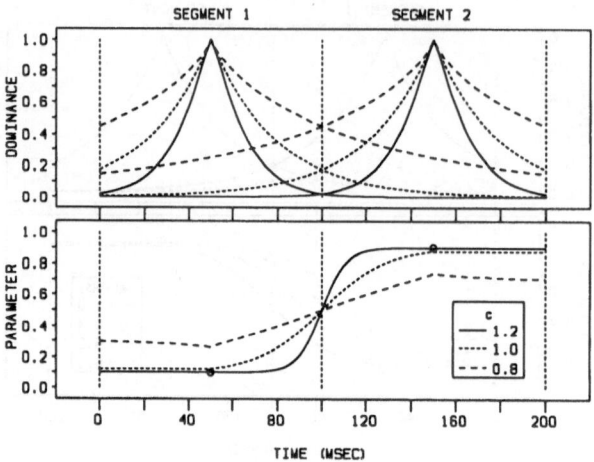

Fig. 7. Dominance of 2 speech segments over time (top panel) and the resulting control parameter function (bottom panel) with c as a parameter.

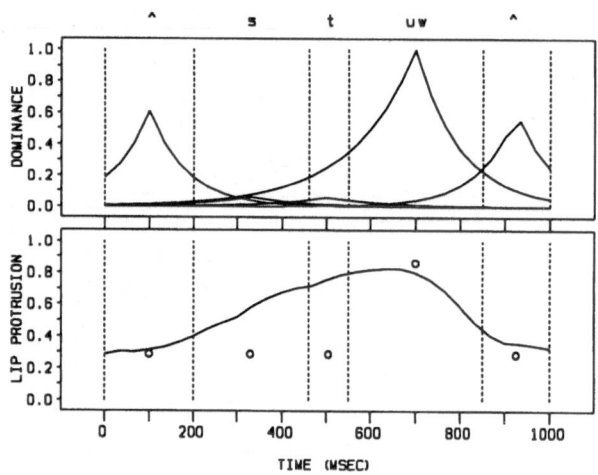

Fig. 8. Dominance functions (top panel) and parameter control functions (bottom panel) for lip protrusion for the word "stew".

Moving to an actual example of the system's operation, the top panel of Figure 8 illustrates the dominance functions for the word "stew". As can be seen, the /s/ and /t/ segments have very low dominance (α=.06) with respect to lip protrusion compared to /u/ (α=1). Also the low $\theta_{\leftarrow sp}$ value of /u/ (.07) causes its domination to extend far forward in time. The bottom panel gives the resulting lip protrusion trace. One can see how the lip protrusion extends forward in time from the vowel. Note that the figure only illustrates the dynamics for lip protrusion. For other control parameters, e.g. tongue angle, /t/ and /u/ have equal dominance (α=1). This allows the tongue to reach its proper location against the back of the upper teeth for /t/.

As noted above, other dominance functions are possible in the algorithm. For example,

$$D = e^{-\omega\tau}(1 + \omega\tau) \tag{7}$$

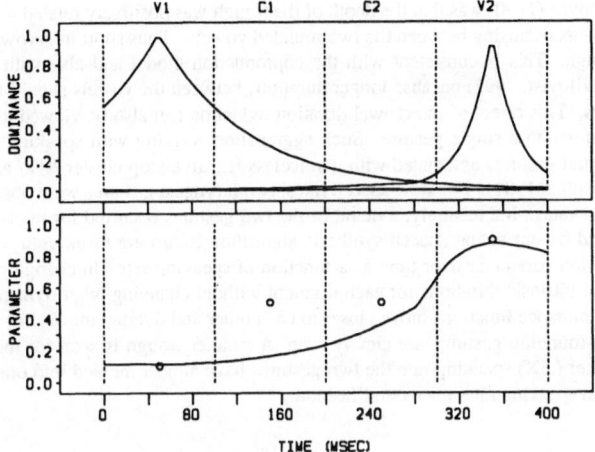

Fig. 9. Dominance and parameter control functions for a VCCV sequence using an inflected dominance function for V_2.

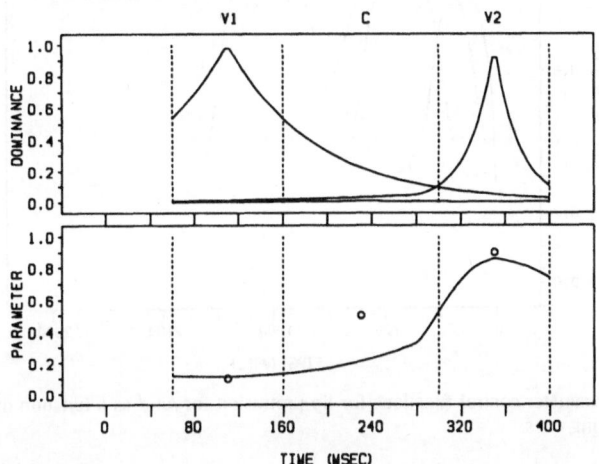

Fig. 10. Dominance and parameter control functions for for a VCV sequence using an inflected dominance function for V_2.

more closely approximates a physical transition process as an oscillation curve with critical damping. Experimentation with this version shows rather subtle differences from those produced with Equation 1. Figures 9 and 10 illustrate VCCV and VCV sequences with low dominance consonants when the dominance function contains a change in $\theta_{\leftarrow sp}$ 68 msec prior to the V_2 center. In this case both graphs show an acceleration at about 280 msec, in accord with Perkel's hybrid model, versus the more look-ahead-like behavior using Equation 1. Thus, the general scheme can be configured to account for a variety of production strategies. In addition, language specific differences can be captured in the segment definitions. For example, the trough vs plateau distinction reported by Boyce (1990) for the utterance /utu/ can be represented by a much lower α value for /t/ for Turkish versus English. If α is low enough, the high lip protrusion of the /u/ vowels will simply bridge across the /t/.

Another finding of Boyce (1990) was that the depth of the trough was positively related to the duration of the consonant or consonants occurring between the two rounded vowels. Thus short intervowel intervals led to a reduction in the trough. This is consistent with the coproduction model and also with Löfqvist's gesture model (Munhall & Löfqvist, 1992) because longer durations between the vowels should lead to less overlap of the vowel gestures. This effect of intervowel duration reduction can also be viewed as an aggregation of the two vowel gestures into a single gesture. Such aggregation, varying with speaking rate, has also been demonstrated for glottal gestures associated with a voiceless fricative-stop cluster /s#k/ across a word boundary (Löfqvist & Yoshika, 1981). For slow speech rates, two laryngeal gestures were observed versus only a single gesture for fast rates. Interestingly, a blend of the two gestures occurred for intermediate rates. This effect is also captured by our visual speech synthesis algorithm. Returning to the /utu/ example, Figure 11 shows the lip protrusion parameter over time as a function of speaking rate. In changing the speaking rate, we simply rescale the intrinsic durations for each segment without changing other dynamic parameters (e.g. $\theta_{\leftarrow sp}$). Thus, the dominance functions move closer to each other and overlap more. For a slow (2X) speaking rate, the two lip-rounding gestures are clearly seen. A smaller trough is seen for the normal (1X) rate speech, and for a faster (.5X) speaking rate the two gestures have almost merged into one. Thus, the model can handle changes in speaking rate in a natural fashion.

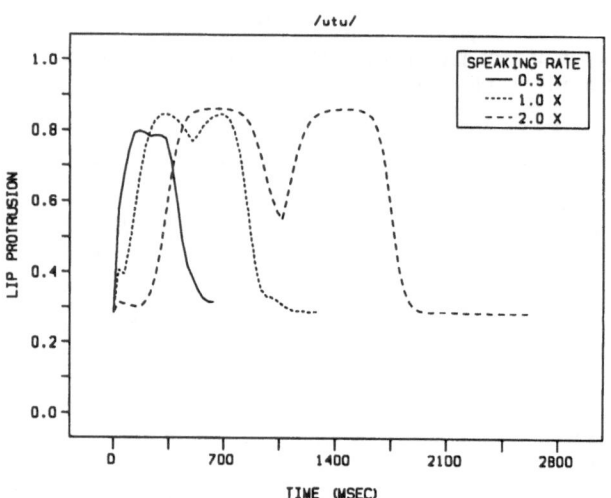

Fig. 11. Parameter control functions for lip protrusion for /utu/ as a function of time for three speaking rates.

4. DEVELOPMENT ENVIRONMENT

Our facial synthesis is being carried out on a Silicon Graphics 4D/CRIMSON-VGX workstation under the IRIX operating system. The software consists of roughly 12000 lines of C code and uses the SGI GL calls, and Overmars' (1990) Forms Library to construct the graphical user interface (GUI). A smaller version of the visual speech software with the same functionality but without the GUI is available for use under f77 main programs for perceptual experiments including the presentation of auditory speech and collection of responses from human participants.

Figure 12 shows the GUI for visual speech development. The master panel in the lower right of the screen has facial controls, facilities for editing speech segment definitions, sentence input, speaking rate, parameter tracking, call-ups for subsidiary control panels and other miscellaneous controls. The upper right panel is a text based interface which can control the face using files of commands. Also in the upper right of the screen is a menu panel for the selection of members of a set of tokens for synthesis. In this example, the menu is set to call one of 27 CV syllables whose definitions have been read in from a file. The lower left panel is the display output. This area can also be output in NTSC video using the SGI broadcast video output option. The upper left area contains the play controls with cursors for temporal zooming and displaying the face forward and backward in time, and plots of control parameters (bottom), dominance functions (middle) and derived facial measures (top). The displays in the first two of these displays shows the plots for the example "stew" also seen in Fig. 8.

Figure 13 shows a closeup from the display panel of a Gouraud shaded talker articulating /ða/. The tongue which is visible here is a new addition which has been implemented as a shaded surface made of a polygon mesh, controlled by several parameters: tongue length, angle, width, and thickness. This is a considerable simplification compared to a real tongue which has several more degrees of freedom, but it contributes a great deal to visual speech and can be computed very quickly (which allows 60 frames/second animation of the face). We have a more complex 13 parameter tongue model which is based on magnetic resonance imaging (MRI) scans but this runs at less than 30 frames/second for the tongue alone, and is not incorporated into the present face model.

Figure 14 shows a closeup of the GUI master panel. The yellow slides relate to speech control, blue slides relate to viewing, and pink slides control other facial characteristics. The buttons to the left of each column of slides select parameters for plotting and indicate the color used for each trace. The center row of buttons in each column is used to select which parameter's dominance function to plot. In addition to the tongue control parameters, a number of other new (relative to the earlier Parke models) parameters are used in speech control, including parameters to raise the lower lip, roll the lower lip, and translate the jaw forward and backward. Some parameters have more global effects than in the original Parke model. For example, as the lips are protruded the cheeks pull inward somewhat. Another example is that raising the upper lip also raises the some area of the face above.

Because some articulator positions (tongue positions) are obscured in normal viewing, one can cause the face to be displayed in a varying degree of transparency using one of the GUI control slides. This is illustrated in Fig. 15 with a side view of a transparent face.

English text entered into the interface can be automatically translated to phonemes using the Naval Research Laboratory letter-to-phoneme rule algorithm (Elovitz, Johnson, McHugh & Shore; 1976). Translation of an average sentence and the initiation of speech production takes a fraction of a second. Alternatively, phoneme strings in arpabet (one to two letter codes for phonetic symbols) can be entered.

Figure 16 shows one of the subsidiary panels called from the master panel which is responsible for materials and lighting editing and other display characteristics. Standard settings can be read in from files and new versions saved.

Figure 17 shows another subsidiary panel used for controlling a laser videodisk via a serial line. The Bernstein and Eberhardt (1986) lipreading corpus disks can be played to compare natural and synthetic visual speech side by side. The natural video is displayed on a monitor adjacent to the SGI console and the images can also be imported to the computer using a video I/O board under control of the panel. Figure 18 shows a typical frame from the videodisk. Using the controls on the panel one can cause the facial synthesis to play in synchrony with the videodisk in either real-time or one frame at a time forwards or backwards and with or without audio. Adjustments can be made and maintained in the delay between the synthetic and natural articulations to bring the two into close agreement. This process is also useful in refining the target values and temporal characteristics defining the synthetic speech segments which include 13 vowels, 25 consonants, and a resting state. There are also a number of segment slots for creating ambiguous tokens between any two segments. For example, seven intermediate articulations between /b/ and /w/ can be made. This synthesis is handled by another of the subsidiary panels.

An additional capability of the system is texture mapping. The left half of Fig. 19 shows a texture mapped face based on the laser disk image shown in Fig. 18. The right half of Fig. 19 shows a simulated Bill Clinton, with the texture taken from a video clip. For each texture, selectable from a menu in a texture control panel, information is stored regarding scaling and centering coefficients for the texture image, facial control parameter settings to adjust the face shape to conformity with the image, and materials settings. Once assignments have been made between facial vertices and points in the textures they are maintained as the

150

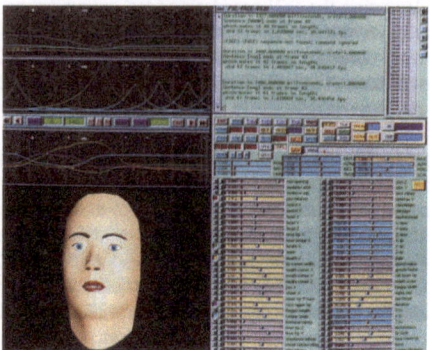

Fig. 12. Graphical user interface for face development. Master panel in lower right has facial controls, facilities for editing speech segment definitions, sentence input, speaking rate, parameter tracking, call-ups for subsidiary control panels and other miscellaneous controls. Upper right panel is text interface. Lower left panel is display output. Upper left is play control with cursors for zooming and moving face in time, and plots of control parameters (bottom), dominance functions (middle) and derived lip measures (top).

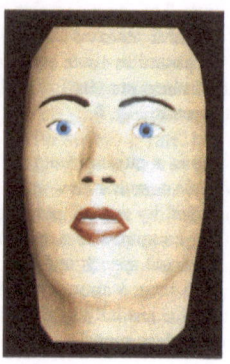

Fig. 13. Gouraud shaded face articulating /ða/.

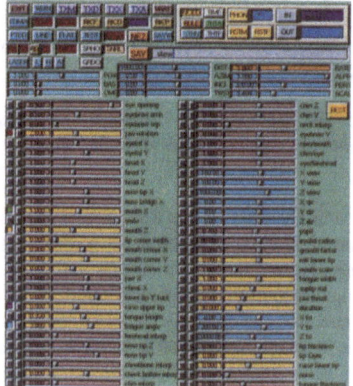

Fig. 14. Closeup of GUI master panel. Yellow slides relate to speech control, blue slides relate to viewing, and pink slides control other facial characteristics.

Fig. 15. Side view of a transparent face.

Fig. 16. Closeup of materials, lighting, and display edit control panel.

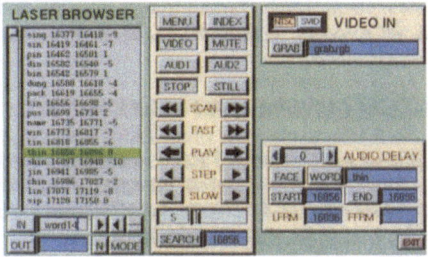

Fig. 17. Closeup of laser videodisk control panel.

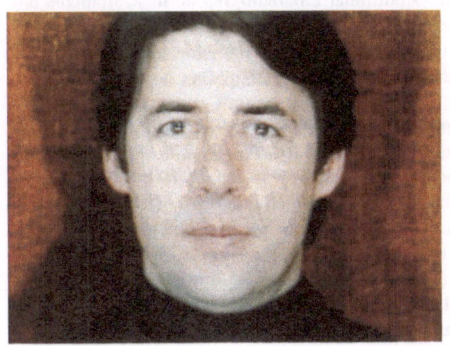

Fig. 18. Typical laser videodisk display.

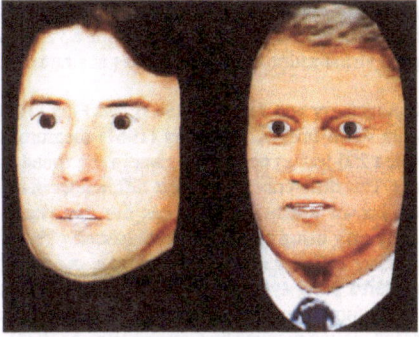

Fig. 19. Texture mapped facial displays which use the laserdisk image from Fig. 18 and video clip of Bill Clinton as the texture sources.

face is manipulated. Various texture mapping modes can be selected and for some faces, mapping of texture to the eyes can be enabled. In the texture mapped mode the maximum rendering rate is limited to 30 frames/second.

5. CONCLUSIONS AND FUTURE WORK

Löfqvist's gestural model seems to provide a good general framework for visual speech synthesis adaptable to a variety of coarticulation strategies. It operates in a simple and rapid manner, producing good quality visual speech. The development environment has proven useful for improvement of the facial animation and refinement of the segment definitions.

We are working on utilizing additional data to refine the specification of speech segments. There are many existing reports which give measurements of articulator position over time. For example, Perkell (1969) made careful measurements of many articulator movements by a single talker (e.g. lip protrusion) from cineradiographs (X-ray movies) for /hVCV/ segments. Cineradiographic measurements of articulator movements for a variety of VC, VCVC, CV, and CVCV utterances have been reported by Kuehn and Moll (1976). Several speakers at several speaking rates were observed. Additional cineradiographic measurements are given by Kent and Moll (1972). Especially useful parameter specification for our tongue model are a set of MRI scan videos we have recorded for a variety of VCV utterances. The recent flash-MRI technique allows good visualization of the soft tissues at a rate of several frames per second.

Montgomery and Jackson (1983) and Finn (1986) have made physical measurements of lip characteristics from video images. Fujimura (1961) measured the speed of lip opening for /b/, /p/, and /m/ using a high speed 200 frames per second camera. He found that the opening time was slowest for /b/, followed by /p/ and /m/. This difference may reflect differences in the maximum air pressure which builds up before release. It is not known whether subjects can use this visual difference, but an investigation of this question would be fairly easy using synthetic visual stimuli. There is some evidence that "cheek puffiness" resulting from the pressure differences can be used as a cue by observers (Scheinberg, 1980). This question will be further explored using synthetic stimuli by varying an existing cheek width control parameter. Additionally, valuable information on how labial consonant production changes with speaking rate was gathered using high-speed motion pictures by Gay and Hirose (1973).

Several additional characteristics of articulation not measured in previous studies might be informative including visibility of the teeth, changes in the jaw position and cheek surfaces, the visibility of facial fold lines. We are also using a motion analysis system to gather new articulation data by tracking points on a speakers face.

A number of improvements are planned. One concerns the addition of Klatt's context sensitive duration rules for segments (Klatt, 1976; Allen, Hunnicutt & Klatt, 1987). Although the system handles global rate effects in a reasonable fashion, there are many additional variables that should be taken into account. For example, segments should be lengthened at clause and phrase boundaries. Lexical information can also be used to determine when vowels are stressed or reduced and therefore lengthened or shortened, respectively.

We also plan to integrate the visual synthesis with a high level auditory speech synthesis system. Given the complexity of the high level linguistic and phonetic algorithms involved it would be a difficult task to simply attempt to synchronize the visual synthesis with a commercial product like DECtalk. One approach to this problem has been explored by Lewis and Parke (1987). In their system, spectral analysis of the auditory speech signal was used to determine the appropriate visual information to present. While this approach was fairly successful for a set of the nine vowels combined with three consonants, the generalization of this technique to unrestricted text is problematic, because it requires a solution to auditory speech recognition. In the restricted case where the phonetics are already known and the goal is just synchronization, Lewis and Parke's approach might be more easily used.

Our plan is use the same higher level software to translate English text into the required segment, stress, and duration information to drive both the visual and auditory synthesis modules. We have obtained the MITalk (Allen, Hunnicutt & Klatt, 1987) software for this higher level analysis.

Other improvements to the model include the addition of our more complex tongue model, and the visual presentation of higher-level linguistic cues such as punctuation and emphasis (Pelachaud, Badler, & Steedman, 1991).

Last but not least, experimental studies are underway to assess the quality of this synthetic speech versus natural speech. In one study we are presenting 414 single syllable English words using either natural auditory speech alone at -8 dB S/N ratio (combined with white noise), synthetic visual speech alone, or a combination of the two sources. A control condition uses natural visual speech. By comparing the overall proportion correct and analyzing the perceptual confusions made, we can determine how closely the synthetic visual speech matches the natural visual speech. We expect confusions for both the natural and synthetic visual speech. The question to be answered is how similar are the patterns of confusion for the two.

6. ACKNOWLEDGMENTS

The research reported in this paper and the writing of the paper were supported, in part, by a grant from the Public Health Service (PHS R01 NS 20314). The authors would like to thank Paula Smeele and Christian Benoit for their comments on the paper.

7. REFERENCES

Abry, C. & Lallouache, T. (1991) Audibility and Stability of Articulatory Movements: Deciphering two experiments on anticipatory rounding in French *Proc. of the 12th Int. Congress of Phonetic Sciences*, Aix-en-Provence, France, Vol.1, 220-225.

Allen, J., Hunnicutt, M. S., and Klatt, D. (1987) *From text to speech: The MITalk system* Cambridge, MA: Cambridge University Press.

Bell-Berti, F. & Harris K. S. (1979) Anticipatory coarticulation: Some implications from a study of lip rounding. *Journal of the Acoustical Society of America, 65,* 1268-1270.

Bell-Berti, F. & Harris K. S. (1982) Temporal patterns of coarticulation: Lip rounding. *Journal of the Acoustical Society of America, 71,* 449-459.

Benguerel, A. P. & Cowan, H. A. (1974) Coarticulation of upper lip protrusion in French. *Phonetica, 30,* 41-55.

Benguerel A. P. & Pichora-Fuller M. K. (1982) Coarticulation effects in lipreading. *Journal of Speech and Hearing Research, 25,* 600-607.

Bernstein, L.E. & Eberhardt, S. P. (1986) *Johns Hopkins lipreading corpus I-II: Disc I.* [Videodisc]. Baltimore: The Johns Hopkins University.

Bladon, R. A. & Al-Bamerni, A. (1976) Coarticulation resistance of English /l/. *Journal of Phonetics, 4,* 135-150.

Bladon, R. A. & Al-Bamerni, A. (1982) One stage and two-stage temporal patterns of velar coarticulation. *Journal of the Acoustical Society of America, 72,* S104(A).

Boyce, S. E. (1990) Coarticulatory organization for lip rounding in Turkish and English. *Journal of the Acoustical Society of America, 88,* 2584-2595.

Breeuwer, M., & Plomp, R. (1985) Speechreading supplemented with formant-frequency information for voiced speech. *Journal of the Acoustical Society of America, 77,* 314-317.

Brooke, N. M. & Summerfield, A. Q. (1983) Analysis, synthesis, and perception of visible articulatory movements. *Journal of Phonetics, 11,* 63-76.

Brunswik, E. (1955) Representative design and probabilistic theory in a functional psychology. *Psychological Review, 62,* 193-217.

Cathiard, M. A., Tiberghien, G., Cirot-Tseva, A., Lallouache, M.-T., & Escudier, P. (1991) Visual perception of anticipatory rounding during acoustic pauses: A cross-language study. *Proc. of the 12th Int. Congress of Phonetic Sciences*, Aix-en-Provence, France.

Cohen, M. M. & Massaro, D. W. (1990) Synthesis of visible speech. *Behavioral Research Methods and Instrumentation, 22,* 260-263.

DECtalk (1985) *Programmers Reference Manual* Maynard, MA: Digital Equipment Corporation.

Eckman, P. & Friesen, W. V. (1977) *Manual for the Facial Action Coding System* Palo Alto: Consulting Psychologists Press.

Elovitz, H. S., Johnson, R. W., McHugh, A., & Shore, J. E. (1976) Automatic translation of English text to phonetics by means of letter-to-sound rules. *NRL Report 7948*, document AD/A021 929. Washington, DC: NTIS.

Elson, M. (1990) Displacement facial animation techniques. *SIGGRAPH Facial Animation Course Notes*, 21-42.

Erber, N. P. & De Filippo, C. L. (1978) Voice-mouth synthesis of /pa, ba, ma/. *Journal of the Acoustical Society of America, 64*, 1015-1019.

Finn, K. E. (1986) *An Investigation of Visible Lip Information to be Used in Automated Speech Recognition* Ph.D. thesis, Georgetown University.

Flanagan, J. L., Ishizaka, K. & Shipley, K. L. (1975) Synthesis of speech from a dynamic model of the vocal cords and vocal tract. *Bell System Technology Journal, 54*, 485-506.

Fujimura, O. (1961) Bilabial stop and nasal consonants: A motion picture study and its acoustical implications. *Journal of Speech and Hearing Research, 4*, 232-247.

Gay, T. & Hirose, H. (1973) Effect of speaking rate on labial consonant production. *Phonetica, 27*, 44-56.

Gelfer, C. E., Bell-Berti, F. & Harris K. S. (1989) Determining the extent of coarticulation: Effects of experimental design. *Journal of the Acoustical Society of America, 86*, 2443-2445.

Gouraud, H. (1971) Computer display of curved surfaces, *IEEE transactions, C-20(6)*, 623.

Henke, W. L. (1967) Preliminaries to speech synthesis based on an articulatory model *Proceedings of the IEEE Speech Conference, Boston*, 170-171.

Hill, D. R., Pearce, A., & Wyvill, B. (1986) Animating speech: An automated approach using speech synthesized by rules. *The Visual Computer, 3*, 277-289.

Kent, R. D. (1970) *A Cinefluorographic-Spectrographic Investigation of the Consonant Gestures in Lingual Articulation*. Ph.D. thesis, University of Iowa.

Kent, R. D. (1972) Some considerations in the cinefluorographic analysis of tongue movements during speech. *Phonetica, 26*, 16-32.

Kent, R. D. (1983) The Segmental Organization of Speech. in P. F. MacNeilage (Ed.) *The Production of Speech*. New York: Springer-Verlag.

Kent, R. D. & Minifie, F. D. (1977) Coarticulation in recent speech production models. *Journal of Phonetics, 5*, 115-133.

Kent, R. D. & Moll, K. L. (1972) Tongue body articulation during vocal and diphthong gestures. *Folia Phoniatrica, 24*, 286-300.

Klatt, D. (1979) Synthesis by rule of segmental durations in English sentences. in B. Lindblom and S. Öhman (Eds.) *Frontiers of Speech Communication Research*. London: Academic Press.

Klatt, D. (1980) Software for a cascade/parallel formant synthesizer. *Journal of the Acoustical Society of America, 67*, 971-995.

Kozhevnikov, V. A. & Chistovich, L. A. (1965) *Rech: Artikulatsiya i Vospriatatie* (Moscow-Lenningrad). Trans. *Speech: Articulation and Perception*. Washington, DC: Joint Publication Research Service, No. 30, 543.

Kuehn, D. P. & Moll, K. L. (1976) A cineradiographic study of VC and CV articulatory velocities. *Journal of Phonetics, 4*, 303-320.

Lewis, J. P. & Parke, F. I. (1987) Automated lipsynch and speech synthesis for character animation. *Proceedings CHI+CG '87*, Toronto, 143-147.

Löfqvist, A. (1990) Speech as audible gestures. In W.J. Hardcastle and A. Marchal (Eds.) *Speech Production and Speech Modeling*. Dordrecht: Kluwer Academic Publishers, 289-322.

Löfqvist, A. & Yoshika, H. (1981) Laryngeal activity in Icelandic obstruent production. *Nordic Journal of Linguistics, 4*, 1-18.

Lubker, J. & Gay, T. (1982) Anticipatory labial coarticulation: Experimental, biological, and linguistic variables. *Journal of the Acoustical Society of America, 71*, 437-448.

Massaro, D. W. (1987) *Speech Perception by Ear and Eye: A Paradigm for Psychological Inquiry*, Hillsdale, NJ: Lawrence Erlbaum Associates.

Massaro, D. W. (1989) A precis of *Speech Perception by Ear and Eye: A Paradigm for Psychological Inquiry. Behavioral and Brain Sciences, 12*, 741-794.

Massaro, D. W. (1990) *A Fuzzy logical Model of Speech Perception Proceedings of the XXIV International Congress of Psychology*.

Massaro, D. W., & Cohen, M. M. (1983) Evaluation and integration of visual and auditory information in speech perception. *Journal of Experimental Psychology: Human Perception and Performance, 9*, 753-771.

Massaro, D. W. & Cohen, M. M. (1990) Perception of synthesized audible and visible speech. *Psychological Science, 1*, 55-63.

Montgomery, A. A. (1980) Development of a model for generating synthetic animated lip shapes. *Journal of the Acoustical Society of America, 68*, S58 (abstract)

Montgomery, A. A., & Jackson, P. L. (1983) Physical characteristics of the lips underlying vowel lipreading performance. *Journal of the Acoustical Society of America, 73*, 2134-2144.

Munhall, K. & Löfqvist, A. (1992) Gestural aggregation in speech: Laryngeal gestures. *Journal of Phonetics, 20*, 111-126.

Nahas, M., Huitric, H., & Saintourens, M. (1988) Animation of a B-spline figure. *The Visual Computer, 3*, 272-276.

Öhman, S. (1966) Coarticulation in VCV utterances: Spectrographic measurements. *Journal of the Acoustical Society of America, 39*, 151-168

Öhman, S. (1967) Numerical model of coarticulation. *Journal of the Acoustical Society of America, 41*, 310-320.

Overmars (1990) Forms Library. Dept. of Computer Science, Ultrecht University, Ultrecht, the Netherlands.

Parke, F. I. (1974) A parametric model for human faces, *Tech. Report UTEC-CSc-75-047* Salt Lake City: University of Utah

Parke, F. I. (1975) A model for human faces that allows speech synchronized animation. *Journal of Computers and Graphics, 1(1)*, 1-4.

Parke, F. I. (1982) Parameterized models for facial animation, *IEEE Computer Graphics, 2(9)*, 61-68.

Parke, F. I. (1991) Control Parameterization for facial animation, in N. M. Thalmann and D. Thalmann (Eds.) *Computer Animation '91* Tokyo: Springer-Verlag.

Pelachaud, C., Badler, N. I., & Steedman, M. (1991) Linguistic issues in facial animation. in N. M. Thalmann and D. Thalmann (Eds.) *Computer Animation '91* Tokyo: Springer-Verlag.

Pearce, A., Wyvill, B., Wyvill, G., & Hill, D. (1986) Speech and expression: A computer solution to face animation. *Graphics Interface '86.*

Perkell, J. S. (1969) *Physiology of Speech Production: Results and Implications of a Cineradiographic Study.* Cambridge, Massachusetts: MIT Press.

Perkell, J. S. (1990) Testing theories of speech production: Implications of some detailed analysis of variable articulation rate. In W.J. Hardcastle and A. Marchal (Eds.) *Speech Production and Speech Modeling.* Dordrecht: Kluwer Academic Publishers, 262-288.

Perkell, J. S. & Chiang, C. (1986) Preliminary support for a "hybrid model" of anticipatory coarticulation. *Proceedings of the 12th International Conference of Acoustics*, A3-6.

Platt, S.M. & Badler, N. I. (1981) Animating Facial Expressions. *Computer Graphics, 15(3)*, 245-252.

Recasens, D. (1984) Vowel-to-vowel coarticulation in Catalan VCV sequences. *Journal of the Acoustical Society of America, 76*, 1624-1635.

Reynolds, C. W. (1985) Description and control of time and dynamics in computer animation. *SIGGRAPH Advanced Computer Animation Course Notes*, 21-42.

Saltzman, E. L., Rubin, P. E., Goldstein, L. & Browman, C. P. (1987) Task-dynamic modeling of interarticulator coordination. *Journal of the Acoustical Society of America, 82*, S15.

Terzopoulous, D. & Waters K. (1990) Muscle parameter estimation from image sequences. *SIGGRAPH Facial Animation Course Notes*, 146-155.

Terzopoulous, D. & Waters K. (1991) Techniques for realistic facial modeling and animation. in N. M. Thalmann and D. Thalmann (Eds.) *Computer Animation '91* Tokyo: Springer-Verlag.

VOTRAX (1981) *User's Manual* Votrax, Div. of Federal Screw Works.

Waters, K. (1987) A muscle model for animating three-dimensional facial expression. *IEEE Computer Graphics, 21(4).*

Waters, K. (1990) Modeling 3D facial expressions. *SIGGRAPH Facial Animation Course Notes*, 109-129.

Waters, K. & Terzopoulous, D. (1990) A physical model of facial tissue and muscle articulation. *SIGGRAPH Facial Animation Course Notes*, 130-145.

Michael M. Cohen is a research associate in the Program in Experimental Psychology at the University of California - Santa Cruz. His research interests include speech perception and production, information integration, learning, and computer animation. He received a BS in Computer Science and Psychology (1975) and an MS in Psychology (1979) from UW-Madison, and a PhD in Experimental Psychology (1984) from UC-Santa Cruz.
Address: mmcohen@fuzzy.ucsc.edu. UC-Santa Cruz, 68 Clark Kerr Hall, Santa Cruz CA 96064, USA.

Dominic W. Massaro is a Professor of Psychology in the Program in Experimental Psychology at the University of California - Santa Cruz and is the book review editor of the American Journal of Psychology. His research interests include perception, memory, cognition, learning, and decision making. Massaro received a BA in Psychology (1965) from UCLA and an MA (1966) and a PhD (1968) in Psychology from UMass-Amherst.
Address: massaro@fuzzy.ucsc.edu. UC-Santa Cruz, 433 Clark Kerr Hall, Santa Cruz CA 96064, USA.

Facial Animation

MANJULA PATEL

Our faces serve two primary functions; those of identification and communication. The latter can be further broken down into verbal (speech) and non-verbal (expression) communication. The emphasis of the project has, so far, been on the form of the face and the non-verbal communication aspects. Computer synthesis of the face requires an interactive ability to create models of arbitrary faces and to generate and control simulated expressions. FACES, is an acronym for the *Facial Animation, Construction and Editing System* (Patel and Willis 1991). Major issues addressed as part of the project concern the modelling of a variety of faces and their subsequent animation. The problem of providing adequate and effective control for the user (Parke 1991) has also been considered.

FACES is an interactive, menu-driven system which helps with both the generation and animation of faces, while hiding the structural complexities of the face from the user. The software consists of four sub-systems named: CONSTRUCT, MODIFY, ANIMATE and RENDER. CONSTRUCT and MODIFY cater for modelling functionality to enable creation of distinct faces. The ANIMATE sub-system allows sequences which comprise facial movements to be generated. Control over facial colouration and motion evaluation are provided within the RENDER sub-system.

Several levels of control are available within both CONSTRUCT and MODIFY. Essentially, the CON-STRUCT sub-system deals with the bony structure of the head, while the MODIFY sub-system is concerned with skin, muscle and surface features. At a global level, changes can be made to overall proportions of the head and face. At a regional level, the head is considered in terms of three sections, so that modifications can be made to relative proportions. Local control facilitates amendments to individual bones, such as the *zygomatic* which is responsible for the prominence of the cheeks, as well as features such as the eyes, nose and lips.

The ANIMATE sub-system caters for motion specification and control. At a basic level, facial movement is generated through simulation of muscular contraction (Waters 1987). However, since generation of facial movement through manipulation of individual muscles would be a cumbersome task, the user is provided with two higher levels of control. Facial actions may be specified using a 'kit-of-parts' approach through selection from a repertoire of 31 *Action Units* which have been derived from the *Facial Action Coding System* (Ekman and Friesen 1978). These consist of actions such as 'raise-inner-eyebrow', 'jaw-drop' and 'wrinkle-nose'. At an even higher level, predefined expressions such as happiness, sadness, disgust, anger, surprise and fear, may also be used. Such expressions provide control at an "emotional" level, while Action Units provide flexibility for animators to create their own effects.

References

P. Ekman and W. Friesen (1978) Manual for the Facial Action Coding System. Consulting Psychologist Press, Palo Alto, California

F.I. Parke (1991) Control Parameterization for Facial Animation. Proceedings Computer Animation'91 pp3-31

M. Patel and P.J. Willis (1991) FACES—The Facial Animation, Construction and Editing System. Proceedings EUROGRAPHICS'91 pp33-45

K. Waters (1987) A Muscle Model for Animating Three-Dimensional Facial Expressions. Proceedings ACM SIGGRAPH 21(4):17-24

Address: Computing Group, School of Mathematical Sciences, University of Bath, Bath, Avon, U.K.

AnthroPI: A Dynamics-Based Modeller for Computer Animation

Stephania Loizidou and Gordon J. Clapworthy

SUMMARY

The main purpose of the project was to examine the motion control and motion coordination, of articulated bodies, in particular human models, through the use of dynamic analysis.

This paper has been concerned with the implementation details of the system AnthroPI (Anthropomorphic Programming Interface). AnthroPI, pronounced anthropee, is the plural, in Greek, of anthropos and means 'people'. This provided a convenient system for, first, specifying the motion required and initialising the dynamics equations of motion and, second, presenting the results graphically. The system is completely interactive and allows its user to specify the motion at any level of control he/she wishes.

The articulated body hierarchy is read from files which include information about the construction of local coordinate systems, inertia tensors, masses and orders of rotation for each link. The user can change these quantities interactively using the interface environment. This offers the facility of changing the root of the hierarchy on-line, which is very useful if an animated walking sequence is to be created. After the root of the structure is changed, the tree representation is redefined, i.e. the connectivity which is stored in a two-dimensional table is changed, so that the way the tree is traversed remains the same.

Joints have associated springs and/or dampers which act to exert internal forces or torques within that joint. Each joint has a certain range of angles that it is capable of moving through and angles outside this range will appear unnatural. For example, attempts to rotate the elbow beyond its physical limits will initiate an internal force in the opposite direction to keep the movement within the physically-possible bounds. The power functions have the functionality to achieve smooth blending and they offer rapid increase in the force as the joints limits are approached. However, the use of exponential springs for a small range of possible motions is in some cases satisfactory.

AnthroPI is sufficiently general to model any arbitrary articulated body capable of being represented as a tree structure. Figures used for dynamic analysis have generally been capable of 42 degrees of freedom or fewer, because of the high cost of dynamic analysis and the limited computer resources. Also, at this stage, we are more concerned with the correctness and realism of the movement, i.e. motion quality, whereas the geometric modelling of the static figure is beyond the purposes of this project.

AnthroPI is entirely written in the C programming language and uses the SunCore and SunView graphics packages. It runs under Berkeley Unix 4.2 and 4.3 BSD on a network of Sun 3/50-60 and Sparc workstations with Sun operating system 4.1.1, and it is totally interactive. It provides configuration files for initial estimates and menus for selecting and entering data and communicating with the environment as a whole. An on-line help facility is available.

The use of dynamics showed that such a system has the potential, with further development, to produce expected, realistic, natural and coordinated human motion. The results proved that it is feasible to create an animation system for articulated figures that offers an easy user interface, and it is independent of the configuration of the model. Such a system can be used as the basic platform where further investigations can take place so as to generate realistic and complex movement.

Address: P.O. Box 1589, Limassol, Cyprus

Part IV

Rendering and Natural Phenomena

An HDTV Animation System Using a Dedicated Graphics Computer SIGHT-2

Tokiichiro Takahashi, Masaharu Yoshida, Tadashi Naruse, and Kei Takikawa

Abstract

An HDTV animation system has been developed that produces photo-realistic images and animations with a ray tracing algorithm. The key component of the HDTV animation system is a dedicated multi-processor graphics system, SIGHT-2, which executes ray tracing at a high speed. SIGHT-2 consists of 16 processing elements (PEs) and an HDTV frame buffer. Since each PE of SIGHT-2 achieves 4.17 MFLOPS, a multi-processor system with 16 PEs results in a peak power of 66.72 MFLOPS. Two user interfaces have been developed to prepare rendering data for SIGHT-2: a PC-based polygon modeler and an image description language, IDL. The HDTV animation system has been utilized by NTT to create several technical presentation films since 1990.

Key words: Computer animation, HDTV image synthesis, image description language, graphics hardware, parallel processing, ray tracing.

1. Introduction

Ray tracing [Whitted] is a powerful yet simple approach for creating realistic images since it can simulate optical phenomena including reflection and refraction by tracing rays. The question is whether it can be employed to create HDTV, high definition television, images. Since the resolution of HDTV is, for example, 1920 X 1035 pixles, about 6 times more pixels than the conventional TV, one can observe the very fine structures and details of displayed objects. This capability is very attractive not only for graphics artists, but also for industrial designers to confirm and present their 3D design works visually. However, a significant problem lies in the enormous computation time HDTV ray traced image synthesis requires.

To accelerate the synthesis and animation HDTV images by using ray tracing, we have developed an HDTV animation system with a dedicated multi-processor graphics system, SIGHT2 [SIGHT89]. It consists of 16 processing elements (PEs) and an HDTV frame buffer. Each PE has an operation unit for parallel 3D vector calculations. It consists of three floating-point operation units, three register-files, and a simple interconnection network. SIGHT-2 embodies parallel processing at three levels in order to achieve the efficient execution of ray tracing: (1) multi-processor configuration, (2) operation unit for parallel execution of 3D vector calculations, and (3) functionally distributed parallel processing.

In ray tracing, parallel processing is possible at the pixel-level, since individual rays passing through pixels can be traced independently. This means that ray tracing can be efficiently conducted on a multi-processor system without communication between PEs. Several multi-processor systems have been developed for rapid ray tracing [for example, LINKS84] based on this property.

As the literature points out [LINKS85], however, a multi-processor system consisting of a large number of PEs does not always bring about high performance because the data transfer overhead between the host processor and the PEs increases with the number of PEs. Therefore, it is desirable to realize a fast image synthesis system in which each of the minimum practical number of PEs operates at very high speed.

One possible solution is to develop a PE which conducts the key operations of the ray tracing algorithm in parallel. By analyzing the algorithm in detail, we found out that most calculations are composed of three dimensional (3D) vector operations that are homogeneous along each of the three axes. This suggests the possibility of axiswise parallel operation using three ALUs. Based on the homogeneity of axiswise operations, there are several ways to build a graphics computer that achieves parallelism for the ray tracing algorithm, not only at the pixel-level, but also at the operation-level [SIGHT87a, 87b].

One PE of SIGHT-2 achieves 4.17 MFLOPS, therefore, a multi-processor system with 16 PEs results in a peak power of 66.72 MFLOPS. Experiments show that the efficiency of each PE is over 99% under static load balancing during ray tracing.

Since SIGHT-2 performs as a back-end image synthesis server, a PC-based modeler and an image description language, IDL, have been developed to provide good user interfaces that allow the animation system to be easily operated. The PC-based modeler is an interactive tool which can model, design and manipulate the shapes, optical properties, and motion of 3D polygonal objects. Modeling results are converted into IDL descriptions. Both hierarchical representations of 3D objects and constructive solid geometry (CSG) expressions are available in IDL, so one can easily describe complex scenes. All IDL descriptions are translated into binary files, then down loaded to SIGHT-2.

SIGHT-2 has been utilized by NTT to create technical presentation film sequences.

2. System Configuration

We have realized an HDTV animation system that consists of a host computer (VAX-4500), SIGHT-2, and an HDTV VTR unit as shown in Figure 1. The host computer runs the server program, controls both SIGHT-2 and the HDTV VTR unit, and responds to various client requests. All PCs connected via Ethernet can send requests to the host computer using the TCP/IP protocol.

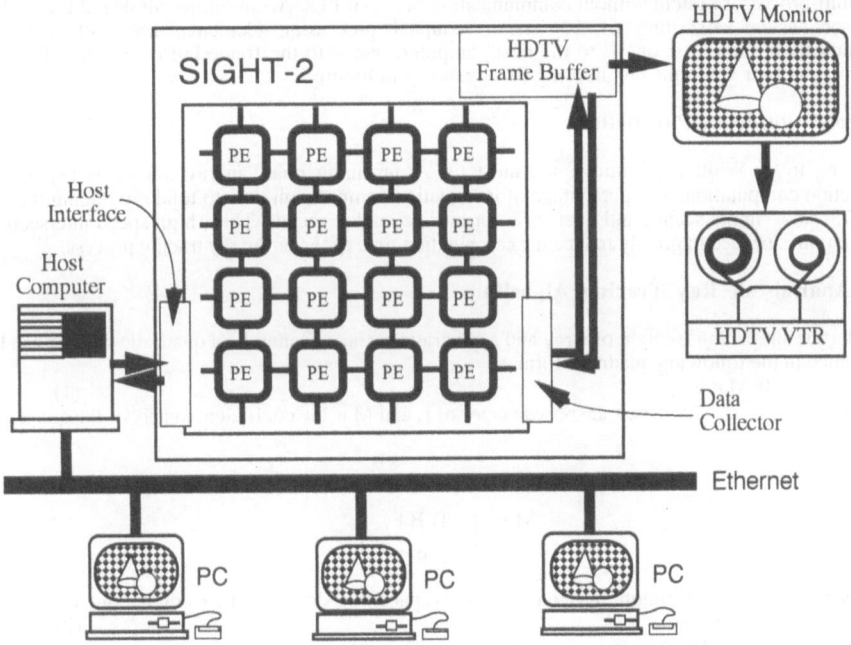

Figure 1. HDTV Animation System Configuration

In this configuration, SIGHT-2 is working as a back-end processor for fast image synthesis, and connected to the host computer via a Q-Bus. SIGHT-2 consists of 16 PEs, a host interface, a data collector, and a full color HDTV frame buffer. The resolution of the HDTV frame buffer is 1920 (horizonal) x 1035 (vertical) pixels, and the depth of each pixel has 24 bits.

The executable files of ray tracing programs and rendering data are supplied by the host computer. Each PE executes the ray tracing program by referring to loaded files and sends the calculated pixel values to the frame buffer through the data collector. Rendered images are displayed on an HDTV monitor, and are then recorded by the HDTV VTR unit frame by frame.
The details of SIGHT-2 architecture and configuration are described in the next section.

3. SIGHT-2

In this section, the architecture of SIGHT is reviewed since SIGHT-2 is the key component of the HDTV animation system.

3.1 Pixel-level Parallelism

The heart of the ray tracing algorithm consists of three steps:
    (1) Deciding the ray to be traced.
    (2) An intersection computation between the ray and the surfaces in the field of view. If the surface is transparent or a mirror, reflection and/or refraction computations are carried out, and the reflected and/or refracted ray(s) is(are) newly traced.
    (3) A shading computation on the surfaces that intersect the ray.
The above calculation steps are repeated until all pixel values of the screen have been determined. The calculation cost of ray tracing is proportional to the product of the number of pixels and objects. Therefore, ray tracing requires enormous computing costs to synthesize a photo realistic image.

In ray tracing, however, parallel processing is possible at the pixel-level, since rays passing through different pixels can be traced independently. This means that ray tracing can be efficiently conducted on a multi-processor system without communication between PEs. Accordingly, SIGHT-2 is a multi-processor system consisting of 16 loosely coupled processing elements. Each PE has six communication interfaces: one is to the host computer, one is to the frame buffer through the data collector, and four are to the neighboring PEs as shown in Figure 1.

3.2 Operation-level Parallelism

According to T. Whitted [Whitted], the most time consuming phase in ray tracing is ray-object intersection computation. The percentage of intersection computation time to total ray tracing time is about 75% for simple scenes and over 95% for more complex scenes. Thus, high speed intersection computation is needed to greatly reduce the computation time of the entire ray tracing process.

3.2.1 Analysis of Ray Tracing Algorithm

Consider the simple intersection of a ray and a quadratic surface. Generally a quadratic surface can be represented in the following quadratic form,

$$^{T}r \, M \, r = 1, \tag{1}$$

where $r = {}^{T}(x, y, z)$, ^{T}r is the transposed vector of r, and M is the coefficient matrix of the quadratic surface:

$$M = \begin{pmatrix} A\,D\,E \\ D\,B\,F \\ E\,F\,C \end{pmatrix}$$

A ray is represented by a straight line equation in 3D space. It is described by using parameter t as in

$$r = a\,t + v \tag{2}$$

where $r = {}^{T}(x, y, z)$ denotes a point on the ray, $a = {}^{T}(a_x, a_y, a_z)$ is a direction cosine vector, and $v = {}^{T}(v_x, v_y, v_z)$ is an eye-position vector. Substituting Eq.(1) into Eq.(2) yields the following quadratic equation with respect to t;

$$^{T}a \, M \, a \, t^2 + 2 \, {}^{T}a \, M \, v \, t + {}^{T}v \, M \, v = 1. \tag{3}$$

By solving Eq.(3) for t and from Eq.(1), the intersection point of the line and the surface is obtained. The major computations in the above equations are 3D vector operations such as vector-matrix multiplications, inner products and scaler and vector multiplications. Therefore, the key point for high-speed computation of ray tracing is the high-speed execution of 3-D vector operations.

Each coefficient of Eq. (3) can be expanded as follows :

$$^T\textbf{a M a} = A\, a_x^2 + B\, a_y^2 + C\, a_z^2 + 2D\, a_y\, a_z + 2E\, a_z\, a_x + 2F\, a_x\, a_y,$$
$$^T\textbf{a M v} = A\, a_x\, v_x + B\, a_y\, v_y + C\, a_z\, v_z + D\, a_y\, v_z$$
$$+ E\, a_z\, v_x + F\, a_y\, v_y + D\, a_z\, v_y + E\, a_x\, v_z + F\, a_y\, v_x,$$
$$^T\textbf{v M v} = A\, v_x^2 + B\, v_y^2 + C\, v_z^2 + 2D\, v_y\, v_z + 2E\, v_z\, v_x + 2\, F\, v_x\, v_y. \tag{4}$$

Eq.(4) has the following features, which are the basic properties of the 3D vector operations :

(1) Product terms in each line of the right hand side such as $A\, a_x^2$, $B\, a_y^2$ and $C\, a_z^2$ are symmetrical with respect to x, y, and z axis components and can be calculated independently.

(2) Cross product terms such as $a_y\, a_z$, $a_z\, a_x$ and $a_x\, a_y$ are in cyclic order with respect to the subscripts x, y, z.

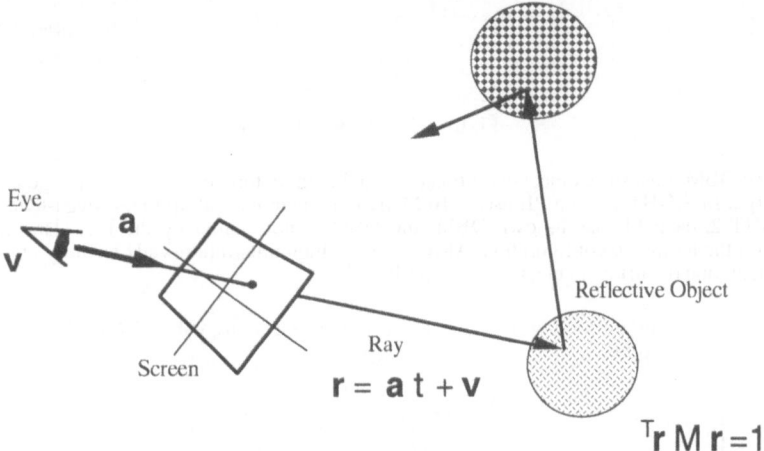

Figure 2. Operation-level Parallelism

3.2.2 PE Configuration

Considering parallel processing for 3D vector operations, we proposed a new PE architecture, in which operation level parallelism is embodied. The PE consists of an operation unit (TARAI), a control unit (master processor unit, MP), a memory manager (MM), and a main memory unit (data base memory unit, DBM) as shown in Figure 3. The TARAI and the MP are independently controlledby their own microprogram sequencers, so that they can work in parallel.

The TARAI configuration is the principle feature of the SIGHT architecture. TARAI consists of three floating-operation units (FOPUs) and register files interconnected by a simple network. The network connects each register files to the upward, the right-upward or the left-upward FOPU. The homogeneity of axiswise operations allows this simple network to conduct 3D vector operations. With TARAI, the 3D vector operations of the ray tracing algorithm can be efficiently executed in parallel. Thus, operation-level parallelism is realized by TARAI. TARAI cycle time is 720 nanoseconds, and TARAI can realizes up to 4.17 MFLOPS.

The MP controls all other units, conducts operations such as address computations of data in the DBM, and communicates with the host processor via the MM.

The register files are used as a working area for each operation unit, and as storage for image synthesis parameters such as the screen size and the current pixel location on the screen. The register files work as a cache memory for the DBM. MM controls data transfers between both DBM and TARAI and MP register files in DMA mode.

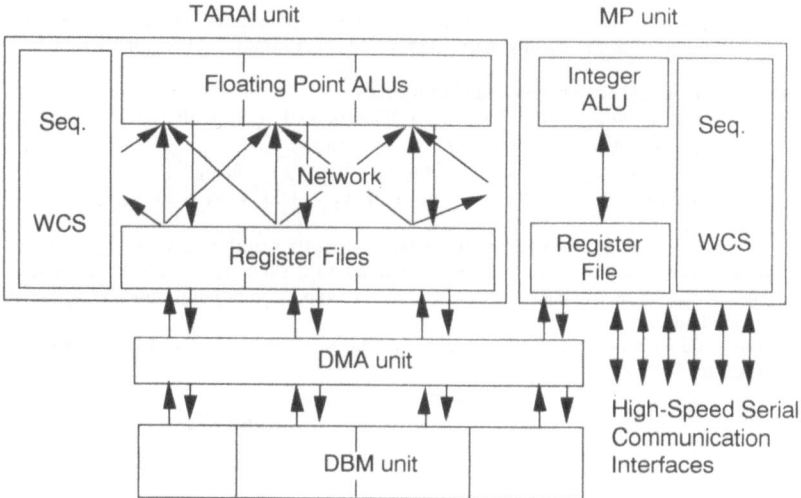

Figure 3. PE Configuration

Since the DBM must store object definition data, and both texture and bump mapping data, it must be very large. In SIGHT-2, each PE uses a 16 Mega-byte memory and up to 64 Mega-byte is possible. In SIGHT-2, each PE has its own DBM; the DBM is not shared by the PEs. This construction simplifies the hardware configuration. Also, low cost, high integration-scale memory chips allow the implementation of sufficient memory in each PE.

The hardware configuration of the PE is detailed in [SIGHT87b], [SIGHT89].

TARAI unit	MP unit	DMA unit
Intersection Calculation	Calculation of Stored Address	
	Invoke DMA	
		Data Transfer
	Receive Results	
	Invoke TARAI	
	Decision	
Intersection Calculation	Calculation of Stored Address	
	Invoke DMA	
	Receive Results	Data Transfer
	Invoke TARAI	

Figure 4. Unit-level Parallelism

3.3 Unit-level Parallelism

TARAI and MP are independently controlled by their own microprogram sequencers so that they can work in parallel. The ray tracing program as shown in Fig.4 was designed to make both TARAI and MP work concurrently, and at maximum capacity. That is, while TARAI carries out 3D vector operations in parallel, MP controls data flow and manages the data structure. During ray-object intersection computations, MM also transfers, in advance, the next data to be processed. Accordingly, DBM access overhead is eliminated due to the concurrent execution of TARAI instructions.

3.4 Performance Evaluation

Several experiments were conducted to evaluate the performance of SIGHT-2. The dynamic execution steps of ray tracing were analyzed as shown in Figure 5. TARAI reduces the execution time of vector operations by two-thirds by operating three FOPUs in parallel. MM reduces the time needed for data transfer between the DBM and register files by three-quarters. Consequently, one SIGHT-2 PE can execute ray tracing program 2.9 times faster than a single processor system. This confirms that TARAI is suitable for accelerating 3D vector operations which are the dominant operations in ray tracing. In addition, unit-level parallelism increases execution speed by a factor of 4.9. Therefore, both operation-level and unit-level parallelism have been verified.

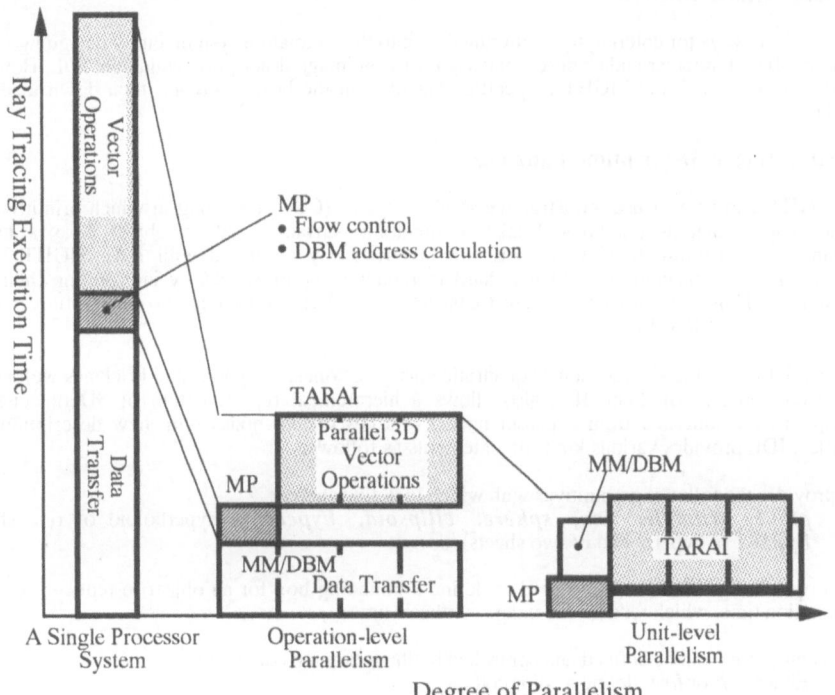

Figure 5. Effectiveness of Parallelism

The assignment of image generation areas to each PE is shown in Figure 6. Each PE is repeatedly assigned every 16th pixels along each horizontal scanline. The load balance of each PE is statically controlled. Furthermore, this static load balancing is easy to implement, and works well with increasing image complexity. Measured system performance of 16 PEs is 15.9 times faster than that of one PE. This means that pixel-level parallelism is highly efficient.

It can be concluded that SIGHT-2 utilizes an efficient dedicated architecture for quickly executing the ray tracing algorithm.

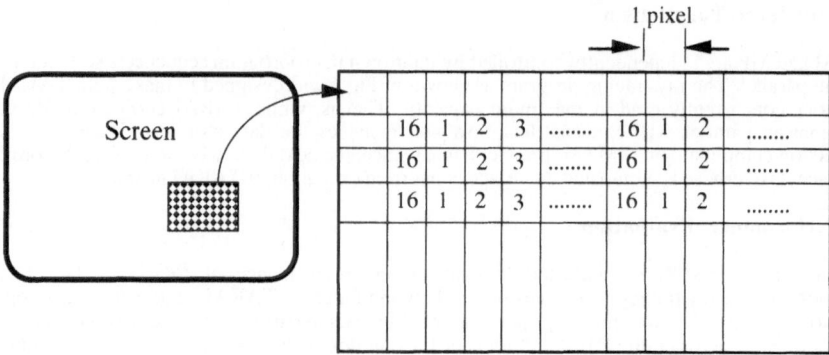

Figure 6. PE Assignment

4. User Environment

There are two ways for entering the rendering data into this animation system: either designing scenes by the PC-based modeler and/or describing scenes by an image description language, IDL. Both sets of data are translated into SIGHT-2 specific data files on the host computer, then down loaded to SIGHT-2.

4.1 IDL, Image Description Language

The SIGHT-2 ray tracer uses constructive solid geometry (CSG) modeling in which primitives are simple shapes such as polygons, bricks or quadratic surfaces, and an object is as a logical combination of primitives. CSG models can be efficiently described with IDL. SIGHT-2 is a microprogrammed machine so that it is hard to render complex scenes by interpreting their IDL descriptions. Thus, IDL descriptions are translated by an IDL Translator into binary files that are easily handled by SIGHT-2.

IDL can define simple shapes such as quadratic surfaces, cones, polygons and bricks as well as any logical combination of them. IDL also allows a hierarchical representation of 3D objects, and descriptions are inherited from a parent node to its descendant nodes until new descriptions are specified. IDL provides various kinds of statements as follows.

IDL provides the following primitives with which to define shapes:
> *plane, triangle, box, sphere, ellipsoid, hyper1* (a hyperboloid of one sheet), *hyper2* (a hyperboloid of two sheets), *cone*.

As an option, *b_volume* can be used to define a bounding box for an object to reduce ray-object computation time, which reduces the image synthesis time.

Optical properties can be defined and controlled by the following commands:
> Either *rgb* or *hsv* define a color code,
> *metal*   the color code of a specular reflection component,
> *refract*   an optical index,
> *ambient* ambient light reflection coefficient,
> *diffuse*   diffuse reflectance coefficient,
> *specular* specular reflectance coefficient, and
> *sharp*   the index of reflection.

To support texture and bump mapping, the following command sets are provided, where a command beginning with *c_* means a command for texture mapping, a *b_* indicates a bump mapping command.
> *c_map*   specifies the file name of a stored texture pattern,
> *c_cord*   defines the origin of the u-v coordinate system,

c_range   the mapping range of the u-v coordinate system and the number of mapping repetitions.
c_rot   defines how much the u-v coordinate system is rotated around its origin, and
c_cont   a blending ratio of the texture.

All these *c_* commands have bump mapping command equivalents.

b_map, *b_cord*, *b_range*, *b_rot*, and *b_cont*.

The following operators describe CSG operators:

+ (or), - (subtract), and * (and).

The following Affine transforms and laying-out statements are available.
mov   transforms an object to a point,
rot   rotates an object around three axes continuously, and
scale   enlarges or reduces an object.

Lighting environments can be designed with
point   for a point light source, and
para   for a parallel light source.

Spot light sources are not yet supported.

There are for camera parameters. The view direction is a straight line defined by *from* - *to* commands. The perspective view angle is defined by *angle* command. *up* defines the camera's top direction. In addition, the *aspect* command defines the aspect ratio precisely.

The following commands control special visual effects that are frequently used:
invisible defines whether an object is visible or invisible,
shadow   defines whether an object generates a shadow or not,
ref_con   controls the maximum number of reflections, and
trp_con   also controls the maximum number of refractions.

These features make IDL descriptions simple yet powerful.

Figure 7 shows an example of a scene description in IDL and Fig.8 its image. The grammar of IDL in Backus-Naur form is given in Appendix.

Figure 8. Synthesized Image of Figure 7.

```
/* declaration section */
/* No upper and lower case letters are
   distinguished in this file. */
#no_case

/* File "color.names" includes color
   names definitions. */
#include color.names

/* cluster declaration */
/* This scene consists of the following three
major objects: a bearing, a robot, & a round
table. All the parts of each major object are
described below. */

/* The bearing consists of four parts. */
bearing {
        shaft + rotary_cylinder + base
        + balls
}

    /* describe the shapes of all the parts
       consisting of the bearing */
    shaft { /* a shaft */
        { green {
            { mov -30.0 0.0 0.0
                shaftB }
        + { mov 7.5 0.0 0.0
                shaftV }
        + { mov -7.5 0.0 0.0
                shaftV } }
        }
        +
        silver {
                ellipsoid 10.0 10.0 1.0E38
            * box 200.0 10.0 10.0 }
        } /* small parts of the shaft */
        shaftB {
                { ellipsoid 15.0 15.0 1.0E38
                * box  40.0 15.0 15.0 }
                - ellipsoid 10.0 10.0 1.0E38
        }
        shaftV {
                { ellipsoid 27.5 27.5 1.0E38
                * box 10.0 27.5 27.5 }
                - ellipsoid 10.0 10.0 1.0E38
        }
......
/* The robot consists of five parts. */
robot {
        head + arm + link + leg + foot
}
......
```

```
/* A wooden texture pattern is mapped on the
round table. */
 /* make a round table */
table { desk * cutter }

    desk {
        /* texture file name */
        c_map wood.texture
        /* define the origin
           at the u-v coordinate system */
        c_coord 0.0 0.0 0.0
        /* define the mapping range
           at the u-v coordinates
           and the repetition number */
        c_range 0.0 1.0 1 /* v-axis */
               0.0 1.0 1 /* v-axis */
        /* define how much the u-v coordinate
           system is rotated around the origin. */
        c_rot 0.0 0.0 0.0
        c_cont 0.7
        /* a blending ratio of the texture */
        white { plane 0.0 1.0 0.0 0.0 } }
    }
......
/* procedure section */
main {          /* cluster labels */
    robot
    + bearing
    + { mov -128.0 -55.0 -128.0
        { table } }
} /* This scene consists of the above three major
objects. */


[File: color.names]
/* attribute bundle */
/* define color names */
silver {
            rgb 1., 1., 1. /* a white color */
            metal 1., 1., 1. /* highlight color */
            diffuse 0.6 /* diffuse reflectance */
            specular 1.0 /* specular reflectance */
            sharp 32 /* sharpness of highlight */
            }
white {
            rgb 1., 1., 1.
            metal .... }
green {
            rgb 0., 1., 0.
            metal .... }
......
```

Fig.7 Example of IDL.

4.2 Monolith, PC-based Interactive Polygon Modeler

It is a tedious task to describe a complex scene in IDL, or to give numerical expressions for defining 3D objects. Besides, IDL does not support animation yet; only still images. To improve the user interface, we adopted a commercial product, Monolith [SIG], as an interactive modeling tool, and have developed a conversion tool to change the modeling results output by Monolith into IDL descriptions.

PC-based modeling environments are often used for their ease of use. Monolith allows 3D shapes to be interactively generated and modified by (1) selecting basic primitives such as bricks, spheres, or cylinders from a menu, or (2) sweeping user-defined cross-sections along or around a straight line. Affine transformation can be used to modify the original 3D shape. Although Monolith is user-friendly and can import DXF files, there is some weakness in its linkage to SIGHT-2.

Monolith does not output data in the CSG format adopted by SIGHT-2. However, Monolith does provide some simple rendering tools that permit some simple shapes to be converted into CSG descriptions. The tools include BOX, CUBE, CONE, CYL(cylinder), and SPH(sphere). We have developed a conversion tool that interprets the operation history of a Monolith file and, where possible, creates CSG descriptions. Shapes which cannot be so treated, are tessellated and represented as sets of polygons. The conversion results are described as an IDL file.

Figures 9 and 10 show an animation sequence modeled by Monolith and sample images from the animation sequence.

A summary of the procedures used to operate SIGHT-2 are illustrated in Fig. 11.

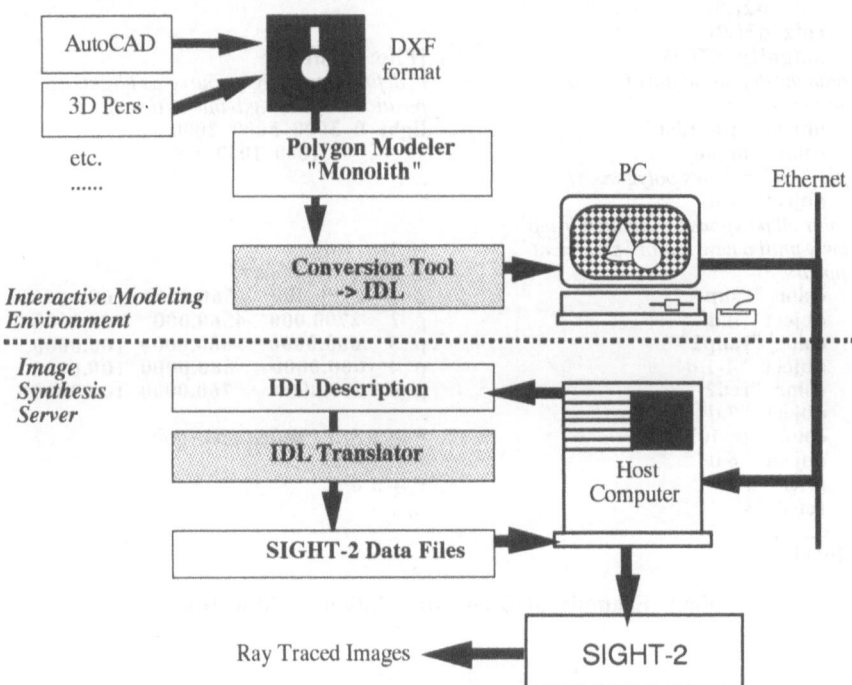

Figure 11. Procedure to Operate SIGHT-2

```
level "world"                              level "2"
    /* define the view angle and field */      outfile "2.sp1"
        fov 35 0.1 1000000                      infile "2.sp1"
    /* store key frame positions of             tran d4(,0) d5(,0) d6(,0)
      animation */                              rotx d1(,0)
        outfile "world.sp1"                     roty d2(,0)
        infile "world.sp1"                      rotz d3(,0)
    /* assign function keys to                  magnify d7(,1)
      Affine transformations functions */   color "red3"
        tran d4(,0) d5(,0) d6(,0)          object "2.d"
        rotx d1(,0)                        color "gun"
        roty d2(,0)                        object "2-1.d"
        rotz d3(,0)                        end_level
        magnify d7(,1)                     ........
    /* inherit all Affine transformations
      obtainedthis node to node "all" */
        refer "all"                        [File: color.lst]
    /* define color names */               ....
        object "color.lst"                 def_color "mono"
end_level                                      oc 57 76 57 /* color code */
                                               sp 255 255 255 0.1
level "all"                                    /* specular reflectance and its index */
        outfile "all.sp1"                      df 200 /* diffuse reflectance */
        infile "all.sp1"                       am 20 /* ambinent */
        tran d4(,0) d5(,0) d6(,0)              tr 0      /* transparency */
        rotx d1(,0)                        ....
        roty d2(,0)
        rotz d3(,0)
        magnify d7(,1)                     [File: light.lst]
    /* read the definition file of         /* define a point light source as #light, its
      light sources */                     position, and its r,g,b intensities */
        object "light.lst"                 light 0 3000 5000 2000
        color "mono"                               1000 1000 1000
    /* file "1.d" includes polygons. */    ....
        object "1.d"
    /* color all polygons hereinafter "ranp"
      newly until a new "color" statement   [File: 1.d]
      appears. */                          /* define 3D points */
        color "ranp"                       p 1 -2700.000 -4560.000 100.0000
        object "4.d"                       p 2  2700.000 -4560.000 100.0000
        color "ranp2"                      p 3   600.0000  -880.0000 100.0000
        object "4-1.d"                     p 4  -600.0000  -880.0000 100.0000
        color "red2"                       p 5  -600.0000   760.0000 100.0000
        object "7.d"                       ....
        color "body"                       P 1 2 3 ; /* define a polygon */
        object "8.d"                       P 1 3 4 ;
        refer "2"                          P 4 5 6 ;
        refer "3"                          ......
        ......
end_level
```

Fig.9 Example of Scene Description in Monolith.

(a)

(b)

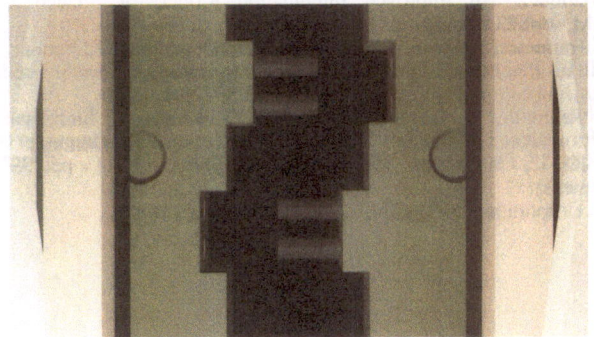

(c)

Fig.10 Example Images of Fig.9.

174

5. Concluding Remarks

We have described an HDTV animation system that consists of a host computer, the dedicated graphics multi-processor system SIGHT-2, and an HDTV VTR unit. SIGHT-2 works as a back-end processor to execute ray tracing at high speed and so synthesize photo-realistic images.

We adopted a commercial product software, Monolith, as an interactive modeling tool, and have developed a conversion tool to change Monolith output into IDL descriptions. Monolith can model and generate 3D shapes, define their optical properties, and design their motion. IDL specifies final data to be rendered by SIGHT-2. IDL can define simple shapes such as quadratic surfaces, cones, polygons and bricks as well as any logical combination of them. IDL also allows a hierarchical representation of 3D objects, and all descriptions are inherited from a parent node to its descendant nodes until new descriptions are specified. IDL descriptions are translated into the data files that SIGHT-2 can handle.

Several technical presentation films have been created by NTT, in which several animation sequences have been rendered by the HDTV animation system. SIGHT-2 is useful and efficient to accelerate the synthesis of HDTV images using the ray tracing program.

Acknowledgments
We would like to thank Dr. Takahiko Kamae, Dr. Rikuo Takano, Mr. Takashi Sakai and Dr. Kazuyoshi Tateishi for their continuous support. We would also like to thank all members of our research section for their advice and encouragement.

References

[SIGHT87a] T. Naruse, M. Yoshida, T. Takahashi, and S. Naito, "SIGHT - A Dedicated Computer Graphics Machine", Computer Graphics Forum, Vol.6, No.4, pp.327-334 (1987).
[SIGHT87b] T. Takahashi, T. Naruse, and M. Yoshida, "Architecture and Performance Evaluation of the Dedicated Graphics Computer: SIGHT", Proc. of IEEE MONTECH'87/Compint'87, pp.153-160 (1987).
[SIGHT89] M. Yoshida, T. Naruse, and T. Takahashi, "A Dedicated Graphics Processor SIGHT-2", Proc. of 4th Eurographics Workshop on Graphics Hardware, pp.151-169 (1989).
[Whitted] T. Whitted, "An Improved Illumination Model for Shaded Display", Comm. ACM, Vol.23, No.6, pp.343-349, (1980).
[LINKS84] H. Nishimura, H. Ohno, T. Kawata, I. Shirakawa, and K. Omura, "LINKS-1: A Parallel Pipelined Multimicrocomputer System for Image Creation", Proc. 10th Annu. Int'l Symp. on Comput. Arch., pp.387-394, (1984).
[LINKS85] H. Nishimura, H. Deguchi, T. Tatsumi, T. Kawata, I. Shirakawa, and K. Omura, "Performance Evaluation of Parallel Processing in Computer Graphics System LINKS-1", Trans. on IECEJ (D), Vol.J68-D, No.4, pp.733-740, (1985) (In Japanese).
[SIG] SIG Corporation, "Monolith Reference Manual", 1987.

Appendix: IDL in Backus-Naur Form

IDL in Backus-Naur form is shown below.

<description file>	::=	<declaration part> <procedure part>
<declaration part>	::=	(<NULL>	<directives>	<bundle declaration>| <cluster declaration>
<directives>	::=	<no_case statement>	<include statement>
<no_case statement>	::=	#no_case
<include statement>	::=	#include <string>
<bundle declaration>	::=	<bundle label> <bundle>
<bundle label>	::=	<string>
<bundle>	::=	{ <attribute> (<attribute>) }
<cluster declaration>	::=	<cluster label> <cluster>
<cluster label>	::=	<string>
<cluster>	::=	{ [<modifier>] <cluster core> }
<modifier>	::=	(<bundle label> | <attribute> | <location operator>)
<location operator>	::=	(<mov statement> | <rot statement> | <scale statement>)
<mov statement>	::=	mov <value> <value> <value>
<rot statement>	::=	rot <value> <value> <value> <rot operator>
<scale statement>	::=	scale <value>
<rot operator>	::=	[-]	(xyz | xzy | yzx | yxz | zxy | zyx)
<adding operator>	::=	+	-
<multiplying operator>	::=	*
<sign>	::=	+	-
<cluster core>	::=	<element>	<term>
<element>	::=	<primitive>	<cluster label>	{ <expression> }
<term>	::=	<element>	<term> <multiplying operator> <element>
<expression>	::=	<term>	<expression> <adding operator> <term>	<sign> <term>
<procedure part>	::=	main <cluster>
<string>	::=	<character> (<character>)
<attribute>	::=	<attribute identifier> [<parameter> (, <parameter>)]
<primitive>	::=	<primitive identifier> [<[parameter> (, <parameter>)]
<parameter>	::=	<value>	[-] <string>

Terminologies:
    < x >   x is a meta-variable
    < > definition of meta-variable (a meta-symbol)
    ::= definition of meta-statement (a meta-symbol)
    | or (a meta-symbol)
    [ ] options
    { } selection (select one)
    ( ) possible repetition zero or more times

Tokiichiro Takahashi* is currently a supervisor, senior research engineer of the Autonomous Robot Systems Laboratory, NTT Human Interface Laboratories. He received the B.E. degree in electronic engineering from Niigata University in 1977. After graduating, he joined NTT and has been doing research into Computer Graphics since 1984. He received the Best Papers Award of The Information Processing Society of Japan in 1992. His current research interests include both photorealistic and comprehensible rendering algorithms as well as their implementation on parallel processors. He is a member of IEEE, The Institute of Electronics, Information and Communication Engineers, The Institute of Image Electronics Engineers of Japan, and NICOGRAPH.
E-mail: toki@nttarm.ntt.jp (Internet)

Masaharu Yoshida* is currently a senior research engineer of the Autonomous Robot Systems Laboratory, NTT Human Interface Laboratories. He received the B.E. degree and M.E. degree in electrical engineering from Chiba University in 1976 and 1978, respectively. His current research interest includes computer architectures of parallel processing. He is a member of Eurographics, The Institute of Electronics, Information, and Communication Engineers, and The Information Processing Society of Japan.
E-Mail: hal@nuesun.ntt.jp (Internet)

Dr. Tadashi Naruse* is currently a senior research engineer, supervisor of the Autonomous Robot Systems Laboratory, NTT Human Interface Laboratories. He received a B.E. degree from Shinsyu University in 1975, and M.E. and Ph.D in Information Science from Nagoya University in 1977 and 1992, respectively. He joined NTT in 1977. His research interests include computer architecture, parallel processors, and processors for computer graphics. He received the 30th Anniversary Paper Award of The Information Processing Society of Japan (IPSJ) in 1990. He is a member of IPSJ, The Institute of Electronics, Information and Communication Engineers, and ACM.
E-mail: naruse@nttarm.ntt.jp (Internet)

Kei Takikawa** is currently a senior engineer and supervisor of the Video Communications Service Department, Visual Communications Sector, NTT. He received the B.E. degree from Tokyo Institute of Technology in 1972. He joined NTT in 1972, and his work involves development of a video telephone terminal, a video conference system, a videotex system, computer graphics and a multimedia database system. In 1981, he was with the Government of Canada, Communications Research Centre, Ottawa, Ont., as an exchange scientist, working on still picture coding for the Telidon videotex system. His interests include digital television, computer graphics and multimedia/hypermedia systems. He is a member of The Institute of Electronics, Information, and Communication Engineers, and The Institute of Television Engineers of Japan.

Address: *Autonomous Robot Systems Laboratory, NTT Human Interface Laboratories, NTT,
3-9-11, Midori-Cho, Musashino-Shi, Tokyo 180, Japan.
Telephone: (+81) 422-59-2406, Facsimile: (+81) 422-59-2245
**Video Communications Service Department, Visual Communications Sector, NTT,
1-1-6, Uchisaiwai-Cho, Chiyoda-Ku, Tokyo 100, Japan.

Animation of Water Droplets on a Glass Plate

KAZUFUMI KANEDA, TAKUSHI KAGAWA, and HIDEO YAMASHITA

ABSTRACT

This paper proposes a method for generating an animation of water droplets and their streams on a glass plate, such as a windowpane or windshield, taking into account the dynamics between fluid and solid. Water droplets run down an inclined glass plate if their masses are greater than a static critical weight. The streams from the droplets do not run straight down the glass plate but meander and some amount of water remains behind the flow due to the nature of the wetting phenomenon. Therefore, the mass of the water droplet decreases. When the mass becomes smaller than a dynamic critical weight, the flow stops. In this paper, a discrete model of a glass plate is developed to simulate the streams from the water droplets as described above. The glass plate is divided into small meshes. For rendering scenes through a glass plate upon which there are water droplets, we also develop a high-speed rendering method taking into account reflection and refraction of light. Instead of calculating the intersections between the ray and the objects, one of the most time-consuming processes in ray tracing, the proposed method determines pixel colors by using the intersection between the ray and a cuboid onto which objects in a scene are projected. Animations of rain droplets on a pane or windshield demonstrate the usefulness of the proposed method.

Keywords: Water Droplet, Flow, Discrete Model, Dynamics, Interfacial Tension

1. INTRODUCTION

A lot of methods have been developed for modeling and rendering fluid such as water in recent years. For rendering water surface such as the ocean, methods of modeling waves have been proposed (Max 1981; Mastin 1987; Peachey 1986; Fournier 1986; Ts'o 1987). To render more realistic images involving water, the color of water surfaces is calculated taking into account the radiative transfer of light in the water (Kaneda 1991a) and underwater glittering due to lens effect has also been rendered (Watt 1990). Methods of rendering fog (Nishita 1987; Kaneda 1991b) caused by vapor and wet road surfaces (Nakamae 1990) have also been proposed. In spite of these techniques, a lot of problems remain unaddressed because of the multiformity and the complex motion of water.

The animation of water droplets on a glass plate is vital for drive simulators and for displaying scenes through a windowpane on a rainy day. The shape and motion of droplets on a solid surface are under the sway of such factors as gravity, surface tension, interfacial tension, air resistance, and so on. Many efforts have been done to understand the phenomena between liquid and solid (de Gennes 1985; Janosi 1989). However, no computer graphics model considering these dynamics has previously been presented and water droplets and their streams down a pane have yet to be animated realistically.

Most of the water models developed for computer graphics (Max 1981; Mastin 1987) principally attempt to render large bodies of water without boundaries, such as the ocean. Therefore, they don't generate realistic scenes containing a seashore, where there is a boundary between liquid and solid. By taking into account the motion of water near boundaries, the realism of water animations has been improved (Peachy 1986; Fournier 1986; Ts'o 1987). However, these methods of modeling water cannot realistically animate the flow of very small amounts, because particles of water move in circular or ellipsoidal orbits around their initial positions in the models. To solve this problem, a method of

177

modeling shallow water taking into account fluid dynamics has been presented (Kass 1990), when an animation of rain falling on a concave surface was screened. However, it is difficult to animate the streams of water drops using this model because of the absence of interfacial dynamics.

This paper proposes a method for generating a realistic animation of water droplets and their streams on a glass plate taking into account interfacial dynamics. As mentioned above, the shape and motion of water droplets on a glass plate depend on gravity to droplets, the respective surface tensions of the glass plate and the water, and the interfacial tension between them. Water droplets whose masses are greater than a static critical weight run down an inclined glass plate. They also tend to meander because of the roughness of the surface, any microscopical impurities on the surface, etc. The mass of the droplet running down decreases, because some amount of water remains behind the flow due to the nature of the wetting phenomenon. Finally, the mass becomes smaller than the dynamic critical weight and the flow stops.

To simulate the streams of water droplets described above, this paper proposes a discrete surface model of a glass plate. In the model, water droplets move from one grid to the next on the discrete surface. It is quite difficult to simulate the flow of water droplets for the purpose of high-precision engineering, because such a flow is a complicated process, where many parameters play a role (de Gennes 1985). Our main purpose is to generate a realistic animation, taking into account the dominant parameters of dynamical systems: gravity to water droplets, interfacial tensions, and the merging of water.

For reducing the calculation cost of animations containing scenes through a rainy windowpane or windshield, we also propose a high-speed rendering method taking into account reflection and refraction of light. The proposed method is an extension of environment mapping (Greene 1986) to be able to render water droplets efficiently. That is, objects in a scene are projected onto the planes of a cuboid, whose center is on the glass plate. Instead of calculating the intersections between the ray and objects, one of the most time-consuming processes in ray tracing, the proposed method generates an image by using pixel colors at the intersection between the ray and the cuboid.

In the following sections, methods for modeling the flow and shape of a water droplet and for high-speed rendering are described. Animations of rain droplets on a pane or windshield demonstrate the usefulness of the proposed method.

2. THE FLOW AND SHAPE OF WATER DROPLETS

The sticking and flowing of water droplets on a solid surface are very complicated phenomena and we need a lot of unmeasured parameters for their accurate simulation. As our main purpose is the generating of realistic animations, the proposed method is based on dominant parameters within the dynamics.

2.1 The Flow of Water Droplets

A water droplet begins to run down an inclined glass plate if the mass exceeds a static critical weight. This depends mainly on interfacial tensions and slightly on the slope of the glass (Janosi 1989). The route of the stream as it meanders down the plate is determined by impurities on the surface or in the droplet itself. Some amount of water remains behind because of the nature of the wetting phenomena. Therefore, the mass of the droplet decreases and finally the flow stops.

In order to animate water droplets and their stream as described above, the surface of the glass plate is divided into small meshes, and water droplets travel from one mesh point to the next. Figure 1 shows a $n \times n$ lattice on the glass plate, and an affinity for water, $f_{i,j}$ $(0 \le f_{i,j} \le 1)$, is assigned in advance to each lattice point. Consider a water droplet on a lattice point (i, j) whose mass is $m_{i,j}$. The droplet runs down if the mass satisfies the following equation:

$$m_{i,j} > m_c^s(\varphi) ,$$

(1)

where $m_c^s(\varphi)$ is the static critical weight when the inclination angle of the surface is φ.

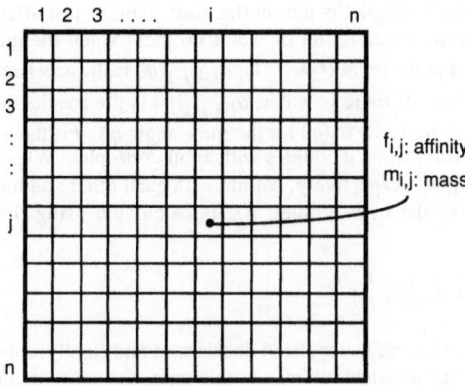

Fig. 1. Discrete surface model

A droplet at lattice point (i, j) moves to one of three points $(i-1, j+1)$, $(i, j+1)$, and $(i+1, j+1)$ to simulate the meandering. If no water exists at any of the three points, the droplet moves to the point where the following equation has the largest value.

$$d_{i+k,j+1} = w_1(\varphi, k)\, f_{i+k,j+1}, \quad (k = -1, 0, 1) \tag{2}$$

where $d_{i+k,j+1}$ is the tendency for a water droplet move in direction $(i+k, j+1)$, $w_1(\varphi, k)$ is a parameter depending on an angle of the plate's inclination, φ, and its range is $0 < w_1(\varphi, k) \le 1$. If water exists in one of these three directions, then the droplet moves in the direction in which the water exists. In the case of it existing in more than two directions, the highest priority is direction $(i, j+1)$. If there is no water at point $(i, j+1)$, the droplet moves in the direction in which the water mass is larger.

The mass of the remaining water, $m'_{i,j}$, that is, the mass of a water droplet at point (i, j) at the next step depends on the affinity for water, $f_{i,j}$, at point (i, j):

$$m'_{i,j} = \begin{cases} m_{i,j} & (\text{if } m_{i,j} < f_{i,j}\, m_{\min}) \\ w_2\, f_{i,j}\,(m_{i,j} - f_{i,j}\, m_{\min}) + f_{i,j}\, m_{\min} & (\text{if } f_{i,j}\, m_{\min} \le m_{i,j} \le f_{i,j}\, m_{\min} + \dfrac{m_{\max} - m_{\min}}{w_2}) \\ f_{i,j}\, m_{\max} & (\text{if } m_{i,j} > f_{i,j}\, m_{\min} + \dfrac{m_{\max} - m_{\min}}{w_2}) \end{cases}, \tag{3}$$

where $m_{\min}$ and $m_{\max}$ are the maximum and minimum mass of water, respectively, that a lattice point hold, and w_2 is the parameter for remaining water. Then, at the next step, the mass of water, $m'_{i+k,j+1}$, at point $(i+k, j+1)$ $(k = -1, 0, 1)$ which the water ran into is given by the following equation:

$$m'_{i+k,j+1} = m_{i+k,j+1} + m_{i,j} - m'_{i,j}. \tag{4}$$

The speed of a running water droplet, v, doesn't depend on the mass of the droplet. It depends on the wetness of the direction $(i+k, j+1)$ and the angle of inclination of the glass plate φ.

$$v = v_0 + a_{i+k,j+1}(\varphi)\, t, \tag{5}$$

where v_0 is the speed when the droplet is put on the glass plate or just after the droplet collides with another, and $a_{i+k,j+1}(\varphi)$ is the acceleration of water droplets when the glass plate is inclined at φ degrees. If there is no water at the point $(i+k, j+1)$, $a_{i+k,j+1}(\varphi)$ is the acceleration, $a_d(\varphi)$, when a water droplet runs on a dry surface. If there is water, $a_{i+k,j+1}(\varphi)$ is the acceleration, $a_w(\varphi)$, when a water droplet runs on a wet surface $(a_w(\varphi) > a_d(\varphi)$ for the same angle $\varphi)$. t is the time from when the droplet is put on the glass plate or from when it collides with another droplet. When two droplets whose mass and speed are m_1, m_2 and v_1, v_2, respectively, collide with each other and merge into one droplet with mass $m_1 + m_2$, the speed of the new droplet, v'_0, is calculated using the law of conservation of momentum:

$$v'_0 = \frac{m_1 v_1 + m_2 v_2}{m_1 + m_2} . \tag{6}$$

A running water droplet that has no water ahead decelerates and finally stops when the mass becomes smaller than the dynamic critical weight $m_c^d(\varphi)$. In this case, the speed of the droplet, v', is given by the following equation:

$$v' = v_0 - a'_d(\varphi) t , \tag{7}$$

where $a'_d(\varphi)$ is a deceleration of the droplet on the plate whose angle of inclination is φ, v_0 is the speed when the mass of the droplet becomes smaller than the dynamic critical weight, and t is the time from when the mass becomes smaller than the dynamic critical weight.

Using the algorithm described above, the positions and masses of all water droplets on an inclined glass plate are calculated for every frame of the animation.

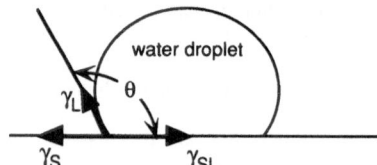

Fig. 2. Contact angle and interfacial tensions

2.2 The Shape of Water Droplets

Let's consider a water droplet on a horizontal glass plate. Interfacial tensions and the contact angle, θ, of water and the glass plate satisfy the following equation (de Gennes 1985) (see Fig. 2):

$$\gamma_{SL} - \gamma_S + \gamma_L \cos\theta = 0 , \tag{8}$$

where γ_{SL} is the interfacial tension between the glass and the water, and γ_S and γ_L are their respective surface tensions. Water spreads on the glass when $\gamma_S > \gamma_{SL} + \gamma_L$. In the case of this condition not being satisfied, a droplet on a plate in the stationary state has a shape, the contact angle of which θ satisfies Eq. 8.

In a dynamic state, that is, when a droplet is moving on the plate, the understanding of the shape of the droplet becomes more complicated than that in the stationary state. For example, a running droplet has different contact angles in its head and tail (advancing and receding contact angles, respectively) because of contact angle hysteresis (de Gennes 1985). This is because droplets have several contact angles which minimize its energy due to the roughness of the surface, uneven quality of the glass, and so on. Therefore, the contact angle changes from a locally stable angle to another as the droplet runs down. Furthermore, if the speed of the droplet is high, air resistance is no more a negligible factor with regard to the shape of the droplet. As mentioned above, the shape of a water droplet running down a plate depends on the roughness of the surface, the uneven quality of the solid, the speed of the droplet, and so on.

In this paper, our main purpose is not an accurate simulation but a realistic animation of water droplets and their streams. Moreover, the animation should be generated at a reasonable cost. For these reasons, we use a sphere to model a droplet on a plate. That is, a water droplet on a horizontal plate is modeled by the space which simultaneously satisfies the following two equations (see Fig. 3):

$$(x - x_0)^2 + (y - y_0)^2 + (z - z_0)^2 \leq r^2 \tag{9}$$

$$z \geq r \cos\theta + z_0 , \tag{10}$$

where x_0, y_0, and z_0 are coordinates of the droplet's center, r is a radius of the droplet, and θ is the contact angle. The radius r of a water droplet with mass m is given by the following equation:

$$r = \left(\frac{3m}{\pi (2 + \cos^3\theta - 3\cos\theta)} \right)^{\frac{1}{3}} \tag{11}$$

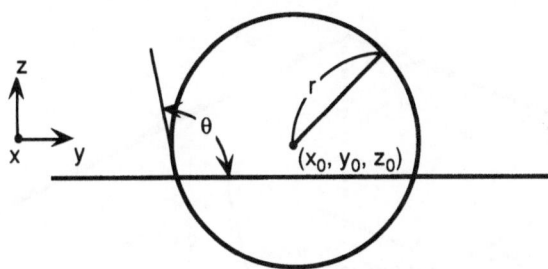

Fig. 3. Modeling a water droplet

2.3 Modeling of the Shape and Flow of Water Droplets

Using the method proposed in Section 2.1, the positions and masses of water droplets on an inclined glass plate are calculated for each frame of the animation. For each droplet with mass $m_{i,j}$, a radius $r_{i,j}$ is calculated by Eq. 11. Taking into account contact angle hysteresis, the contact angle of running droplets (i, j) with no water in front of them, i.e., $(i-1, j+1)$, $(i, j+1)$, or $(i+1, j+1)$, is set to the advancing contact angle θ_A, and the contact angle of droplets following the top droplet is set to the receding contact angle θ_R $(0 < \theta_R < \theta_A)$. If droplets overlap, their shape is modeled as a union of these regions.

3. RENDERING THE WATER DROPLETS

Ray tracing (Whitted 1980) is commonly used to render transparencies taking into account reflection and refraction of light. In spite of its many advantages, this method requires a lot of calculation time. To solve this problem, many improved methods have been proposed (Arvo 1989). However, in making an animation, a lot of calculation time is necessary, because thirty images per a second are required.

In this paper, we propose an extended method of environment mapping (Greene 1986) for rendering scenes through a glass plate with water droplets with a view to generating a realistic animation as cheaply as possible. Instead of calculating the intersections between rays and objects, the proposed method generates an image using background textures calculated in advance.

The proposed method can be outlined as follows:
(1) Background textures are calculated by projecting objects in the scene onto the faces of a cuboid whose center is on a glass plate.
(2) Calculating the direction of rays reflected or refracted by water droplets on a glass plate.
(3) Determining pixel colors by using background textures and the intersection of the ray and the cuboid.

3.1 Generating Background Textures

The cuboid used for generating background textures is set as follows. As shown in Fig. 4, the center of the cuboid is located at the center of the glass plate, and the front face, F_f, of the cuboid coincides with the projection plane. To generate the six background textures, the viewpoint is set at the center of the cuboid, and objects are projected onto its six faces. The resolution of the background texture on the front face is determined by that of the images in the animation. The resolution of the other background textures may be lower, because the number of rays reaching the other faces is fewer than the number reaching the front one.

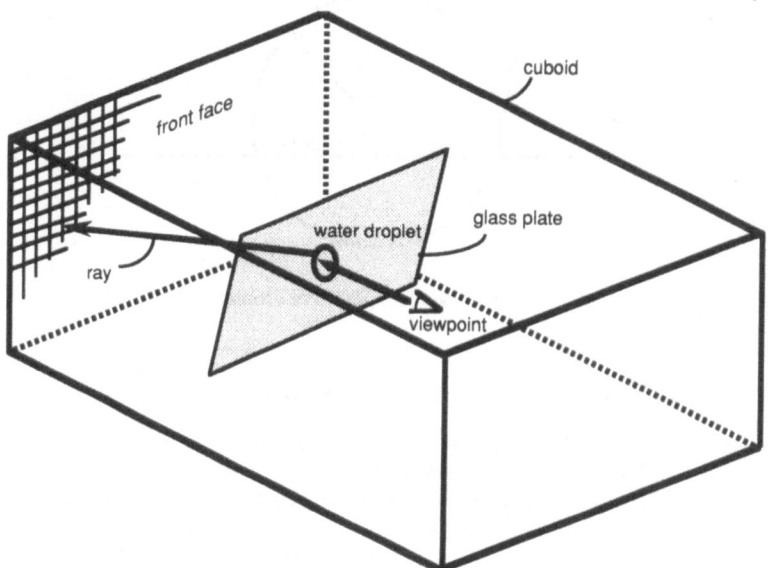

Fig. 4. A cuboid for generating background textures

3.2 Calculation of the Direction of a Ray

A ray of light incident on a transparent object such as water and glass splits into two directions; transmission and reflection. However, in the case of water and glass, the range of the incident angle that gives almost the same amount of light in these two directions of transmission and reflection is very narrow. For example, Fig. 5 shows a transmission coefficient obtained from the Fresnel equation (Hardy 1932) when light travels from water into the air. Most of the light is either just transmitted or reflected over a wide range of incident angles. Therefore, rays are traced in only one direction, that being the one in which the larger amount of light travels.

Fig. 5. Transmission coefficient when light travels from water to the air

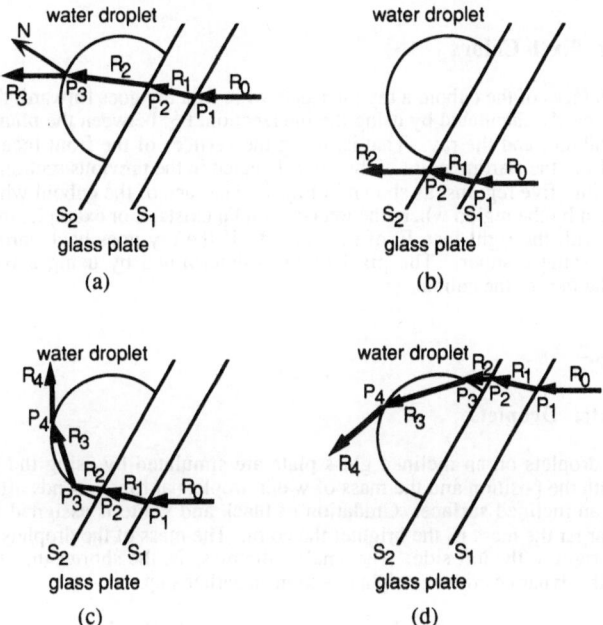

Fig. 6. Calculation of the direction of a ray

Let's consider a ray R_0 connecting the viewpoint and a point on the projection plane (see Fig. 6 (a)). First, the intersection, P_1, between the ray R_0 and the surface of the glass plate, S_1, is calculated. Using the normal of the surface S_1 and the index of refraction of glass, the direction of the refracted ray, R_1, is calculated. The intersection, P_2, between the ray R_1 and the other surface of the glass plate, S_2, is also calculated in the same manner. Next, using Eq. 9, it is checked whether the intersection P_2 is inside a water droplet or not. If it is, the intersection, P_3, between the ray R_2 and the surface of the droplet is calculated, and using the normal, N, of the surface and the index of refraction of water, the direction of the refracted ray, R_3, is calculated. If the intersection P_2 is outside a water droplet, the direction of the ray is calculated by using the normal of the surface S_2 (see Fig. 6 (b)).

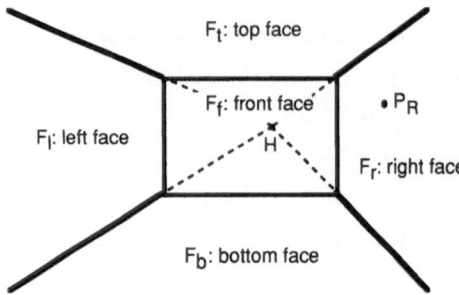

Fig. 7. Selecting a face of a cuboid

If the ray is reflected at the intersection P_3 (see Fig. 6 (c)) or the ray travels from the air into water (see Fig. 6 (d)), the direction of the ray away from a water droplet or the glass plate is calculated in the same manner described above.

3.3 Determining Pixel Colors

It is checked which faces of the cuboid a ray intersects with. If a ray goes forward, the face with which it intersects can be easily calculated by using the intersection, P_R, between the plane, F, including the front face of the cuboid, and the ray. That is, using the vertices of the front face F_f and a foot of a perpendicular, H, from the starting point of the ray calculated in the previous section to the plane F, the plane F is divided into five regions, as shown in Fig. 7. The face of the cuboid which intersects with the ray is determined by the region where the intersection P_R exists. For example, in the case of Fig. 7, the ray intersects with the right face F_r of the cuboid. If the ray goes backwards, the face can be determined in the same manner. The pixel color is determined by using a background texture corresponding to the face of the cuboid.

4. EXAMPLES

4.1 Flow of Water Droplets

Streams of water droplets on an inclined glass plate are simulated by using the proposed method. Figure 8 shows both the position and the mass of water droplets at four seconds after several droplets have been put on an inclined surface. Gradation of black and white is assigned to the mass of the droplets, and the larger the mass is, the brighter the color. The mass of the droplets put on the surface is larger from the right to the left side. The smaller the mass is, the shorter the stream, because the mass decreases to the dynamic critical weight due to in an earlier step.

Figure 9 shows the flow of water droplets every other second. Random amounts of water are fed every second from ten positions on the inclined surface. The figure shows that droplets follow the streams. In Fig. 10, random amounts of water are fed at random positions in advance. The droplets whose masses exceed the static critical weight start to run down, and a running droplet merges with another which is lying in its path. As time passes, the streams break, because droplets remaining behind gradually run down.

4.2 Animation of the Water Droplets

Figure 11 shows several frames of an animation rendered by using the proposed method described in Section 3. An outdoor scene is rendered through a windowpane on which water droplets are flowing. The angle of inclination of the windowpane is 90 degrees, and water is fed in the same way as in Fig.

9. Table 1 shows the parameters used in this animation. The boundary of the droplets is dark, because rays near the boundary are reflected by the surface of the droplet and do not go outside the room.

Figure 12 shows part of an animation on a rainy day. A street scene is rendered from the driver's seat of a car parked on a road. The inclination of the windshield is 35 degrees. Rain droplets are scattered in advance in the same way as in Fig. 10, and several droplets are fed every frame of the animation. Images containing a wet road surface (Nakamae 1990) are used as background textures. The resolution of the images is 512×395, and the rendering time per one frame is four minutes using a SiliconGraphics IRIS Indigo R4000.

Table 1. The parameters used in Fig. 11

φ	$m_c^s(\varphi)$	$m_c^d(\varphi)$	$w_1(\varphi, k)$		
90°	0.15	0.08	0.8 ($k = -1$)	1.0 ($k = 0$)	0.8 ($k = 1$)
m_{min}	m_{max}	w_2	$a_d(\varphi)$	$a'_d(\varphi)$	$a_w(\varphi)$
0.001	0.1	0.1	4.0	4.0	5.0
θ	θ_A	θ_R			
60°	70°	50°			

5. CONCLUSIONS

This paper proposes a method for generating an animation of water droplets and their streams on a glass plate taking into account interfacial dynamics. A discrete surface model is developed to simulate the stream of a water droplet running on a plane. This model makes it possible to animate water droplets meandering on an inclined glass plate.

Realistic images of water droplets can be generated taking into account the contact angles between water and solid. A simple method for rendering a scene through a wet windowpane is also proposed. Taking into account refraction and reflection of light, the proposed method generates an animation at a reasonable cost. Animations of rain droplets on a pane or windshield demonstrate the usefulness of the proposed method.

We need several parameters for modeling water droplets, and these parameters play an important role in creating a realistic animation. Some of the parameters are already measured, but some are not. To pursue a more realistic animation, research into these parameters should be undertaken.

A stream is modeled as a group of water droplets in the proposed method. It is suitable for an animation, because of its low calculation cost, but is not suitable for still, close-up images. A more sophisticated model of a stream, using mathematical surface patches such as Bezier and/or NURBS tensor products, is required for such a purpose.

REFERENCES

Arvo J, Kirk D (1989) A Survey of Ray Tracing Acceleration Techniques. In: Glassner AS (ed) An Introduction to Ray Tracing. Academic Press, London San Diego, pp 201-262

de Gennes PG (1985) Wetting: Statics and Dynamics. Rev. Mod. Phys. 57(3): 827-863

Fournier A (1986) A Simple Model of Ocean Waves. Computer Graphics 20(4): 75-84

Greene N (1986) Environment Mapping and Other Applications of World Projections. IEEE Computer Graphics & Applications 6(11): 21-29

Hardy AC, Perrin FH (1932) Principles of Optics. McGraw-Hill, New York

Janosi IM, Horvath VK (1989) Dynamics of Water Droplets on a Window Pane. Physical Review 40(9): 5232-5237

Kaneda K, Yuan G, Tomoda Y, Baba M, Nakamae E, Nishita T (1991a) Realistic Visual Simulation of Water Surfaces Taking into Account Radiative Transfer. Proc. Second International Conference Computer Aided Design & Computer Graphics: 25-30

Kaneda K, Okamoto T, Nakamae E, Nishita T (1991b) Photorealistic Image Synthesis for Outdoor Scenery under Various Atomospheric Conditions. The Visual Computer 7(5-6): 247-258

Kass M, Miller G (1990) Rapid, Stable Fluid Dynamics for Computer Graphics. Computer Graphics 24(4): 49-57

Mastin GA, Watterberg PA, Mareda JF (1987) Fourier Synthesis of Ocean Scenes. IEEE Computer Graphics & Applications 7(3): 16-23

Max NL (1981) Vectorized Procedural Models for Natural Terrain: Waves and Islands in the Sunset. Computer Graphics 15(3): 317-324

Nakamae E, Kaneda K, Okamoto T, Nishita T (1990) A Lighting Model Aiming at Drive Simulators. Computer Graphics 24(4): 395-404

Nishita T, Miyawaki Y, Nakamae E (1987) A Shading Model for Atmospheric Scattering Considering Luminous Intensity Distribution of Light Sources. Computer Graphics 21(4): 303-310

Peachey DR (1986) Modeling Waves and Surf. Computer Graphics 20(4): 65-74

Ts'o PY, Barsky BA (1987) Modeling and Rendering Waves: Wave-Tracing Using Beta-Splines and Reflective and Refractive Texture Mapping. ACM Transactions on Graphics 6(3): 191-214

Whitted T (1980) An Improved Illumination Model for Shaded Display. Comm. ACM 23(6): 343-349

Watt M (1990) Light-Water Interaction using Backward Beam Tracing. Computer Graphics 24(4): 377-385

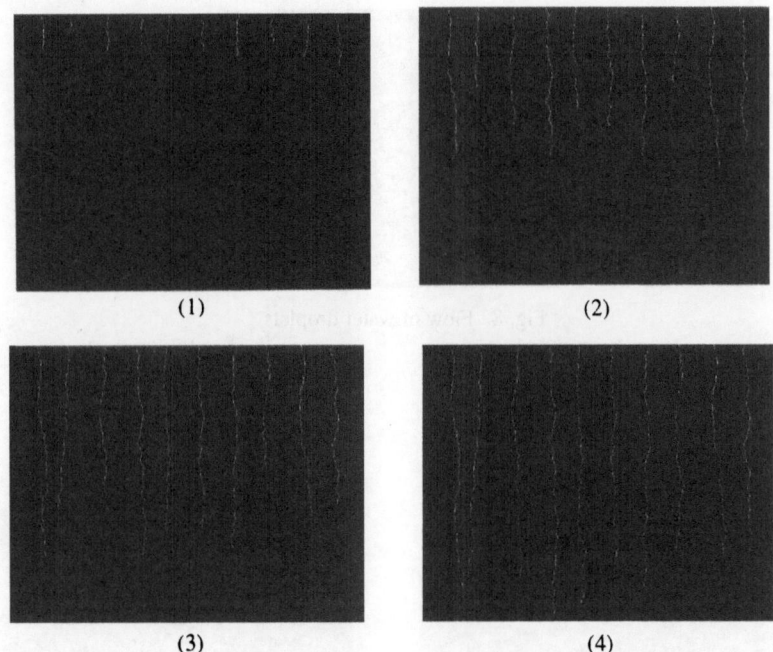

(1)　　　　　　　　　　(2)

(3)　　　　　　　　　　(4)

Fig. 9. Flow of water droplets

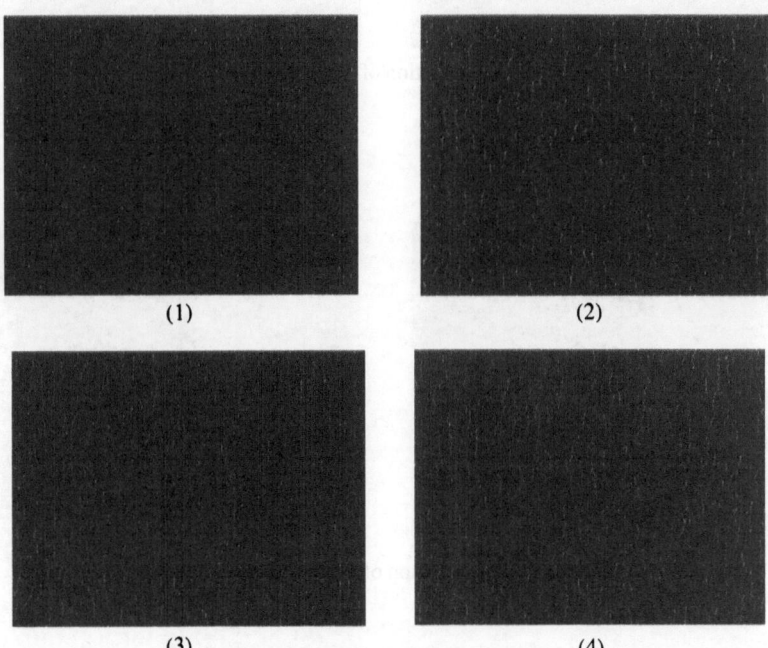

(1)　　　　　　　　　　(2)

(3)　　　　　　　　　　(4)

Fig. 10. Flow of water droplets

Fig. 8. Flow of water droplets

Fig. 11. Animation of water droplets

Fig. 12. Animation of water droplets

189

Kazufumi Kaneda is a research associate in Faculty of Engineering at Hiroshima University. He worked at the Chugoku Electric Power Company Ltd., Japan from 1984 to 1986. He joined Hiroshima University in 1986. He was a visiting scholarship at Brigham Young University from 1991 to 1992. His research interests include computer graphics and image processing. Kaneda received the BE, ME, and DE in 1982, 1984, and 1991, respectively, from Hiroshima University. He is a member of ACM, IEE of Japan, IPS of Japan, and IEICE of Japan.
Address: Faculty of Engineering, Hiroshima University, 1-4-1 Kagamiyama, Higashi-hiroshima, 724 Japan.
E-mail: kin@eml.hiroshima-u.ac.jp

Takushi Kagawa is currently a master course graduate student of Electric Machinery Lab. at Hiroshima University. His research interests include computer graphics and its applications. He received the B.E. degree in electric engineering from Hiroshima University in 1991. He is a member of IPSJ.
Address: Faculty of Engineering, Hiroshima University, 1-4-1 Kagamiyama, Higashi- hiroshima, 724 Japan

Hideo Yamashita was born in Hiroshima, Japan, in 1941. He received the B.E. and M.E. degrees in electrical engineering from Hiroshima University, Hiroshima, Japan, in 1964 and 1968, and Dr. of Engineering degree in 1977 from Waseda University, Tokyo, Japan. He was appointed as a Research Assistant in 1968 and Professor in 1992 of the Faculty of Engineering, Hiroshima University. He was an Associate Researcher at Clarkson University, Potsdam, N.Y. in 1981-1982. His research interests lie in the area of the visualization and field analyses by using the Finite Element Method and Boundary Element Method. He is a member of the IEEE, ACM, the IEE of Japan, the IECE of Japan, and the IPS of Japan.
Address: Faculty of Engineering, Hiroshima University, 1-4-1 Kagamiyama, Higashi-hiroshima, 724 Japan.
E-mail: yama@eml.hiroshima-u.ac.jp

Polyhedral Rendering for Motion Blur

KEITH M. GOSS

ABSTRACT

A simple and general rendering scheme for producing motion-blurred images for
moving polygons is described. It combines Korein and Badler's visible segment
determination approach with a 4-d paradigm in which moving polygons are
represented by polyhedra in 4-d space-time. Segment endpoints at each pixel
are determined by passing the polyhedra through a simple 4-d rendering
pipeline. The major part of this consists of scan-converting polygons with
interpolated t and z values. The segments are merged and ultimately resolved
for visibility within a segment buffer, a variation of the A-buffer. The
algorithm performs visibility calculations over time, produces α channel
output for compositing, and may be guaranteed to produce a smooth blur.

Keywords: motion blur, anti-aliasing, A-buffer, polygon rendering,
multi-dimensional graphics.

1.INTRODUCTION

Any animator who wishes to produce motion-blurred images of reasonable quality
within limited time constraints has two options, stochastic point-sampling
and post-processing. Since distributed ray tracing (Cook et al 1984, Cook 1986)
is computationally expensive, the former option reduces further to an approach
such as the Accumulation Buffer (Haeberli and Akeley 1990), in which a z-buffer
polygon renderer is applied at each sampled instant and the resulting images
combined. Point-sampling has the advantage of allowing motion blur to be
integrated with other effects such as depth of field. However, it does not
automatically produce a smooth blur; the greater an object's displacement
across the screen during one frame, the more samples are required if the result
is not to be unacceptable noisy.

Post-processing methods (Max and Lerner 1985, Max 1990, Potsemil and
Chakraverty 1983) blur a previously-rendered image of an object in the
direction of that object's motion on the screen. This blurring operation may
be very fast, and is guaranteed to give a smooth appearance. Moreover, α
channel output is naturally produced, which gives the animator the flexibility
of being able to composite the result with other images (Porter and Duff 1984).

The approach is too restricted to be generally applicable, however. As a
2-d technique, it cannot account for rotations or the changes in shading as an
object moves relative to the light sources. In addition, compositing an image
of one moving object with that of another moving object cannot account for the
interval of time one obscures the other. For example, a pathological case
would be a bi-plane viewed from above, where the lower wing would erroneously
contribute to the image through the upper wing (Cook et al 1984).

This paper presents a third option for the practical production of motion
blurred images which counters each of these disadvantages. In particular, it
has the following attributes:

- it may be guaranteed to produce a smooth blur;
- it performs visible surface determination over time;
- it can approximate any form of motion;
- it can accommodate changes in shading;
- it retains the additional flexibility of α channel output for
  compositing;
- it consists for the most part of simple variations on familiar
  polygon processing techniques.

The last attribute is the most signigicant. A paradigm of polyhedra in 4-d
space-time underpins much of this approach, and hence the details of the
algorithms are derived from the attributes of 4-d geometry and topology.
However, these details reduce in practice to simple polygon rendering
techniques, the polygons in question forming the boundary of the polyhedra.
For example, much of the visible surface algorithm consists of scan-converting
polygons with additional interpolated t and z co-ordinates. Hence this paper
shows in part how motion blur may be achieved by building on established
and well-understood techniques.

2.THE APPROACH

The core of the algorithm is a combination of two existing approaches, neither
of which has been considered practical as originally given. The first is
visible segment determination. In one of the earliest algorithms on motion
blur, Korein and Badler (1983) showed how the visible surface problem over
time could be dealt with by resolving segments in (t,z) space at each pixel
(Fig. 1). The colour of the pixel is found by integrating the colours of the
visible segments over a 1-d domain. Since segment comparisons are easily
performed to any chosen resolution this approach may be guaranteed to produce a
smooth blur.

This approach may be divided into two sub-tasks:
(1) Generating the segment endpoints;
(2) Resolving the segments for visibility.

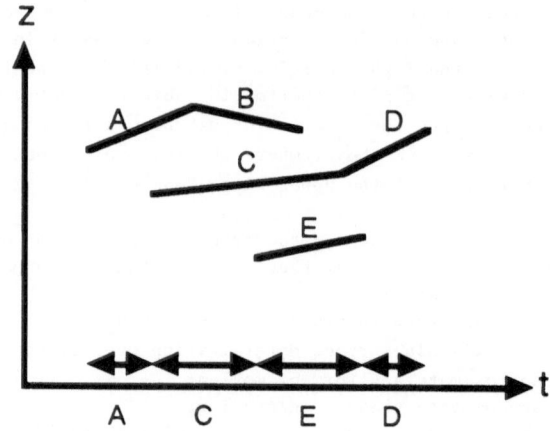

Fig. 1 Segments in tz space are resolved for visibility at each pixel.

For sub-task (1), Korein and Badler's example of moving disks requires the solution of quadratic equations at each pixel. Their suggested solution for polygons requires each edge of a polygon to be tested against a view ray for each pixel. To solve sub-task (1) more efficiently, this paper employs the second existing approach to motion blur, namely a 4-d metaphor. Grant (1985) and Dippe (1985) have each shown how polyhedra in 4-d space-time may represent moving polygons. However, those authors employ this paradigm in order to perform the complicated task of combining analytic and temporal antialiasing, achieved via lengthy clipping operations. By contrast, this work employs it for simplicity. In this framework, sub-task (1) is shown to consist of interpolating t and z values over the bounding polygons of each polyhedron in a scan-conversion procedure. Preliminary clipping and back-face removal operations are also described, giving a 4-d rendering pipeline. In this respect, this work also includes refinements and additions to the existing 4-d models, particularly with the notions of back-face removal and orientation.

For sub-task (2), Korein and Badler's original algorithm requires a (possibly large) segment list to be sorted by t at each pixel. Rather than repeat this, the algorithm presented here employs a segment buffer. This is adapted from the A-buffer (Carpenter 1984). Since the integral domain at each pixel is 1-d, however, the visibility calculations can easily be made exact, and it is this which automatically produces a smooth blur. The use of a buffer allows each polyhedron to be created and dealt with one at a time, thereby easing the large object data requirements normally found in multi-dimensional algorithms. Merging operations reduce the memory burden of the segment buffer itself, but introduce a level of approximation into the visible surface calculations. Like the A-buffer, the segment buffer generates α channel output naturally.

In the following, the camera shutter is assumed to open instantaneously and close instantaneously. All points on the image plane are thus exposed for the same interval of time, here referred to as the shutter interval.

3.OVERVIEW

Section 4 summarizes the 4-d model, in particular the form of the projection
from 4-d eye space to 4-d image space. Section 5 describes the conditions
that the polyhedra must satisfy if the rendering pipeline is to deal with them
consistently, and summarizes the geometric aspects of the polyhedral
representation upon which the rendering pipeline must be based. Simple
polyhedron construction algorithms, based on Grant's work, are then given in
section 6. Clipping and back-face removal procedures for polyhedra are then
described, followed by the scan-conversion procedure which completes sub-task
(1) for each polyhedron. The use of the segment buffer is described in section
10. Finally, sample images are presented, with a discussion on those areas in
which further work may be performed and refinements made.

4.THE 4-D SPACE-TIME MODEL

The polyhedra are constructed in the 4-d eye co-ordinate system. This system
has the eye as a straight line coincident with the t axis (at which x=y=z=0).
The field of view is assumed to be constant throughout the shutter interval,
with the direction of view parallel to the z axis in the direction of positive z.
The point (x',y',t') on the 3-d screen onto which a point (x,y,z,t) in eye
space projects is given by a perspective projection for the x and y dimensions,
that is

$$x' = \frac{S_x \cdot x}{z} + C_x \qquad (1)$$

$$y' = \frac{S_y \cdot y}{z} + C_y \qquad (2)$$

but by an orthographic projection for the t co-ordinate, i.e.

$$t' = S_t \cdot t \qquad (3)$$

A depth value Z', where

$$z' = S_z \cdot z \qquad (4)$$

is also retained with the projection, giving the notion of 4-d image space. To
distinguish between the polygons of a polyhedron in 4-d and the original moving
polygons, the latter are referred to as 3-space polygons.

5.A POLYHEDRAL REPRESENTATION

This section outlines the conditions which each polyhedron must satisfy in order
to be dealt with consistently by the rendering pipeline. These are that the
polyhedron must be linear in 4-d eye space, it must be oriented and it must be

convex.

5.1 Linearity in Eye Space

A polyhedron, and each of its bounding polygons and edges, must be linear in
4-d eye space. This is equivalent to stating that each edge, polygon and
polyhedron must lie in eye space on a 1-, 2- or 3-flat, respectively. The
equation of a 3-flat in 4-d may be written as

$$Ax + By + Cz + Dt + E = 0$$

where (A,B,C,D) is the normal to the 3-flat and E is the 4-d dot product of this
normal and the vector from any point on the 3-flat to the origin. This form
of a polyhedron's equation is the most convenient for describing the back-face
removal procedure.

The defining equations for the other components are best summarized in a form
which aids explanation of the scan-conversion procedure. In n-dimensional
space, a p-flat is defined by n-p linear equations; assigning an order to the
n co-ordinates allows these equations to be arranged such that co-ordinates
p+1 to n are each expressed in terms of co-ordinates 1 to p. Table 1 summarizes
the defining equation(s) of each component type in this form given the
co-ordinate ordering yxtz.

Table 1. The Form of Each Component's Defining Equation(s) in Eye Space.

Component	Equation(s)	no
polyhedron	$z = \lambda_{51}y + \lambda_{52}x + \lambda_{53}t + \lambda_{54}$	5
polygon	$t = \lambda_{61}y + \lambda_{62}x + \lambda_{63}$	6a
	$z = \lambda_{64}y + \lambda_{65}x + \lambda_{66}$	6b
edge	$x = \lambda_{71}y + \lambda_{72}$	7a
	$t = \lambda_{73}y + \lambda_{74}$	7b
	$z = \lambda_{75}y + \lambda_{76}$	7c

Linearity in eye space implies non-linearity in image space, however, due to
the different projection rules for x and y against t and z. Table 2 gives the
form of these equations in 4-d image space.

5.2 Orientation

The 3-flat of a polyhedron has two normals (A,B,C,D) and $(-A,-B,-C,-D)$. The
back-face removal calculations require the calculated normal to point outside
the extruded 4-d object, which in turn requires the polyhedron to be oriented.
This section limits itself to a description of how each polyhedron may be oriented
and how that orientation should be interpreted when calculating the 3-flat
equation; the correct orientation has to be derived from the orientation of the

input 3-space polygon as described in section 6.

Table 2. The Form of Each Component's Defining Equation(s) in Image Space.

Component	Equation(s)	no
polyhedron	$z' = \dfrac{\lambda_{81}t' + \lambda_{82}}{\lambda_{83}y' + \lambda_{84}x' + \lambda_{85}}$	8
polygon	$t' = \dfrac{\lambda_{91}y' + \lambda_{92}x' + \lambda_{93}}{\lambda_{94}y' + \lambda_{95}x' + \lambda_{96}}$	9a
	$z' = \dfrac{\lambda_{97}y' + \lambda_{98}x' + \lambda_{99}}{\lambda_{94}y' + \lambda_{95}x' + \lambda_{96}}$	9b
edge	$x' = \lambda_{101}y' + \lambda_{102}$	10a
	$t' = \dfrac{\lambda_{103}y' + \lambda_{104}}{\lambda_{105}y' + \lambda_{106}}$	10b
	$z' = \dfrac{\lambda_{107}y' + \lambda_{108}}{\lambda_{105}y' + \lambda_{106}}$	10c

To give a polyhedron an orientation, we give each of its polygons an
orientation such that all the edges obey Möbius's rule, i.e. each edge is
considered to be in a different direction by each of the two polygons which
share it (Fig. 2).

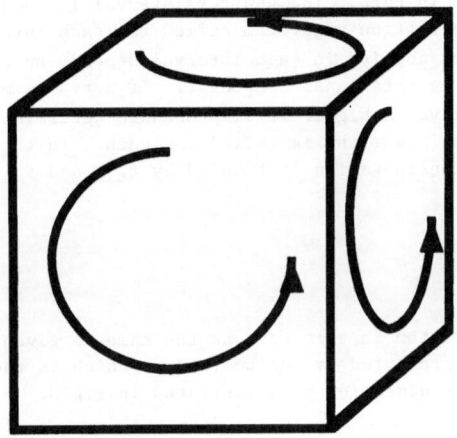

Fig. 2 An oriented polyhedron.

When calculating the polyhedron's equation, three vertices are chosen from any
polygon in the order given by that polygon's orientation; any vertex not on this
polygon is then chosen as a fourth vertex. These four points v_i ($i=1...4$) give
three vectors V_i ($i=1...3$), where $V_i = v_{i+1} - v_i$. The 4-space normal is then
derived according to the pseudo-determinant

$$\begin{vmatrix} i & j & k & 1 \\ v_{1x} & v_{1y} & v_{1z} & v_{1t} \\ v_{2x} & v_{2y} & v_{2z} & v_{2t} \\ v_{3x} & v_{3y} & v_{3z} & v_{3t} \end{vmatrix}$$

where i, j, k and 1 denote the unit vectors along the x, y, z and t axes, respectively. Thus, for example, $A = v_{1y}(v_{2z}v_{3t}-v_{3z}v_{2t})-v_{1z}(v_{2y}v_{3t}-v_{3y}v_{2t}) + v_{1t}(v_{2y} v_{3z}-v_{3y}v_{2z})$. Provided the column ordering is fixed and the polyhedron is convex, any four non-coplanar vertices selected in this manner will give the same normal.

5.3 Convexity

The polyhedron must be convex for the above procedure to always produce the same normal. Convexity also simplifies the scan-conversion process by ensuring that only one coverage segment is generated per polyhedron per pixel.

6.POLYHEDRA CONSTRUCTION

The rendering pipeline will deal with a polyhedron constructed in any manner if it conforms to the conditions of the previous section. The polyhedron construction strategy considered here is similar to that of Grant. Each 3-space polygon is considered in turn. The shutter interval is subdivided if necessary and a polyhedron construction algorithm called for each interval. The construction algorithm applied in each interval depends on whether the 3-space polygon moves with some rotational component. If not, its motion is assumed to be constant velocity. A higher-level procedure determines the sub-intervals and which construction algorithm is called for each. In the following, the time interval under consideration is bounded by t_{min} and t_{max}.

6.1. Constant Velocity

The construction algorithm in this case as the same as given by Grant. The 3-space polygon is represented by one polyhedron which is the extrusion of the 3-space ploygon in one dimension as illustrated in Fig.3.

The co-ordinates of each 3-space vertex are transformed to their location at t_{min} and assigned to the x, y and z co-ordinates of the corresponding 4-space vertex at t_{min}. The t co-ordinate in each case is assigned the value of t_{min}. 3-d vertex normals are also transformed and assigned; texture map co-ordinates are assigned unchanged. The equivalent process occurs at t_{max}.

The correct orientation is imparted by ensuring that the polygon at t_{min} has the same orientation as the 3-space polygon; Möbius's rule dictates the orientation of each of the remaining polygons. Given the vertex selection

scheme and particular column ordering of section 5.2, the polyhedron's normal
will point outside the extruded 4-d object.

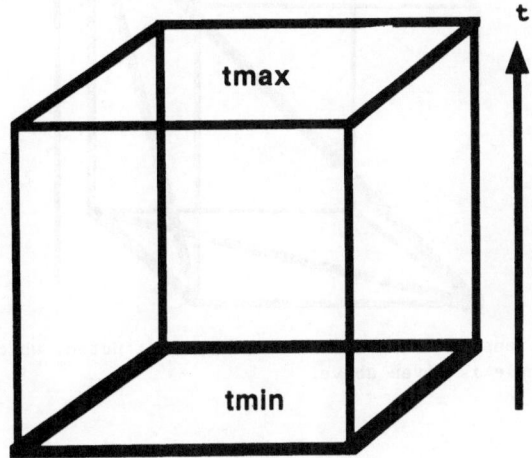

Fig. 3 For constant velocity the polyhedron is the extrusion of the 3-space
polygon in time.

6.2. Arbitrary Motion

For the case in which the 3-space polygon moves with some rotational component,
Grant overcomes the resulting non-linearity of each side polygon by splitting
it into two triangles, and deals with the non -linear polyhedron equation within
the visible surface algorithm. This scheme cannot be employed here, however,
for the simple reason that the crease formed between a pair of side triangles
can in some cases make the polyhedron concave.

Instead several tetrahedra are created to represent the 3-space polygon over
the given interval. These are best described in terms of the extruded
polyhedron of Fig.3. One vertex of this polyhedron is selected. All side
polygons except the two which impinge upon this chosen vertex are split into
triangles. Each of these triangles forms one face of a tetrahedron, with the
remaining three faces formed by extending each edge of the triangle to the
chosen vertex. Figure 4 illustrates one such tetrahedron. The orientation
of each tetrahedron follows from that of its base triangle, which is derived in
turn from that of the extruded polyhedron described in the previous section.
In practice, each tetrahedron is constructed and passed to the rendering
pipeline individually.

7. CLIPPING

The first stage of the rendering pipeline clips the current polyhedron to the
4-d eye space viewing volume. This is bounded by 3-flats with the following

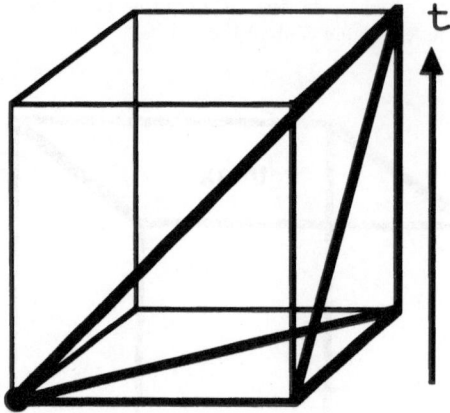

Fig. 4 For rotations, several tetrahedra are constructed, which share a common vertex. One example is given above.

equations

$$x = k_x \cdot z \qquad\qquad x = -k_x \cdot z$$
$$y = k_y \cdot z \qquad\qquad y = -k_y \cdot z$$
$$z = \text{hither} \qquad\qquad z = \text{yon}$$
$$t = \text{shutterstart} \qquad\qquad t = \text{shutterend}$$

where k_x and k_y equal the cotangent of half of the field of view in the x and y directions, respectively. The first six 3-flats listed above are the six clipping planes from the equivalent 3-d viewing volume extended orthogonally in time. Since all polyhedra are constructed to lie between shutterstart and shutterend, clipping need only be performed to these six 3-flats.

The polyhedron is clipped against each 3-flat in turn. Each of its polygons is clipped to the current 3-flat via a standard polygon clipping algorithm. If the polyhedron intersects the 3-flat, an additional polygon is created. This polygon has as its edges the set of all new edges created during the polygon clipping process. The orientation of each is reversed when it is assigned to the new polygon, to preserve Möbius's rule.

8. BACK-FACE REMOVAL

If the current polyhedron survives clipping, the coefficients of its defining equation in 4-d eye space are calculated as outlined in section 5.2. Since clipping preserved the orientation of the polyhedron, the half-space for which

$$Ax + By + Cz + Dt + E > 0$$

lies outside the extruded 4-d object. Since the eye is a line, it is possible that some eye points lie in this half-space and some in the other. In other words, a polyhedron may be both front-facing and back-facing. When the polyhedron represents a 3-space polygon moving with constant velocity, this has a simple intuitive explanation. At some point the projection of the moving polygon may reduce to a line on the screen. In Dippe's work the significance of this lies in the fact that it inverts the projection of the polyhedron in 3-d screen space. More importantly here, however, it also marks the point at which the moving polygon switches from beingfront-facing to being back-facing, or vice versa.

Intersecting the 3-flat of the polyhedron with the eye (i.e. the time axis) gives the point $(0,0,0,-E/D)$. $t=-E/D$ is the instant at which the polyhedron switches from being front-facing to being back-facing or vice versa. Of course, this instant may be outside the shutter interval, and it will never occur if the polyhedron represents a stationary 3-space polygon (in which case $D=0$). For those times satisfying $Dt+E<0$ the polyhedron is back-facing; back-face removal is effected by simply clipping the polyhedron against the 3-flat $Dt+E=0$, removing that portion lying in this negative half-space.

9.SCAN CONVERSION

We now consider the most important part of the rendering pipeline. Each vertex of the polyhedron is now transformed into image space as in section 4. The rendering pipeline now has the task of generating the segment formed by the polyhedron at each pixel onto which it projects. Confirmation that a polyhedron gives a linear segment at each pixel may be obtained from equation 8 in Table 2 which reduces to a linear relationship between z' and t' when y' and x' are both constant. Each segment endpoint is given by the t' and z' values of a polygon; two of these project onto each pixel. Determining the endpoints of each segment is thus a matter of scan-converting each polygon and interpolating t' and z' values.

From the polygon equations in Table 2 it may seen that the t' and z' values for a polygon are each given by the quotient of two expressions in y' and x', and both share a common denominator. Interpolating t' and z' values is therefore exactly the same as interpolating u and v when texture mapping polygons in perspective (Heckbert 1986). These values are thus found by incrementing the two numerators and one denominator down edges and between pixels, dividing at each pixel. Coefficients λ_{91} to λ_{98} (λ_{99} is set to 1.0) may be determined empirically by solving 8 simultaneous linear equations obtained from 4 points as with texture mapping. Alternatively, they may be derived from the constants in equations (1) to (4) and coefficients λ_{61} to λ_{66} from Table 1. Texture map co-ordinates, normals (Phong 1975) and colours (Gouraud 1971) can be interpolated as usual.

The polygons of the current polyhedron may be scan-converted concurrently, in which case the lateral sorting in y' and x' familiar from traditional scan-line algorithms is required, or they may be dealt with one at a time, in which case the first endpoint determined at each pixel must be stored. The latter solution is simpler and is easily incorporated into the segment buffer. The first endpoint generates a segment which is flagged as incomplete and inserted

at the head of the list for that pixel; the second endpoint completes the
segment which is removed from the head and dealt with as below.

As soon as both endpoints of a segment have been determined, the colour of that
segment is calculated. As Korein and Badler discuss, there are several options
for achieving this; each has a trade-off between accuracy and speed. Assuming
Phong shading with texturing for the diffuse coefficient, the current
implementation performs the following. The segment marks a line in the
texture map. A line drawing algorithm steps along this line, accumulating
the colour of each texture sample into an average diffuse coefficient value.
Accurate endpoint positioning is important, especially with low resolution
maps, since otherwise the effect of a smooth blur is diminished. The shading
model is then applied at the segment endpoints, and possibly at points
inbetween if the difference in endpoint normals is large. Once its colour has
been calculated, it is passed for inserting into the segment buffer.

10.THE SEGMENT BUFFER

The segment buffer stores a depth-sorted list of segments for each pixel. The
incoming segment is compared with those stored in the list for the appropriate
pixel. A segment in the list is merged into the incoming one if they both
belong to the same object and an endpoint of one is coincident with an endpoint
of the other. Back-face removal ensures that a coincident point is always
the left endpoint of one segment and the right of the other. Merging thus
means shifting one endpoint of the incoming segment. Its colour is recalculated
as follows:

$$C_{in} = \frac{C_{in} \cdot I_{in} + C_m \cdot I_m}{I_{in} + I_m}$$

where m denotes the segment to be merged and the I's denote the length of time
covered by each segment. An equivalent calculation gives the new α value. The
incoming segment should still be tested for merging with others in the list in
case in its original form it bridged the gap between two segments in the list.
Any segment merged into the incoming one is removed from the list and its
memory is freed. The incoming segment is then stored in the appropriate place
in the list.

Once all polyhedra have been passed through the rendering pipeline, a recursive
packing procedure is invoked for each pixel. Each call of the procedures
returns a colour C_{ret} and an α value α_{ret} given a segment list and the bounds t_1
t_2 of a time interval. At the bottom of the recursion, when the list is
empty, α_{ret} is set to $t_2 - t_1$ and C_{ret} is set to the background colour.
Otherwise, the head of the segment list defines at mose three sub-intervals:
the left, which is that part of the interval between t_1 and the left of the
segment, the right, equivalently defined, and the middle, which is that part of
the interval covered by the segment itself. Figure 5 illustrates.

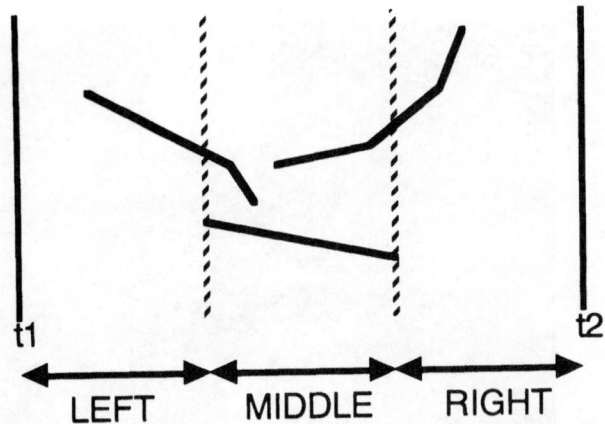

Fig. 5 The head of the segment list defines three sub-intervals.

If the left interval is non-zero, a recursive call with the remainder of the list returns C_{left} and α_{left}. The same applies for the right interval. If the middle interval is non-zero, then if the segment is opaque, C_{middle} is the colour of the segment and α_{middle} is the length of time it covers. Otherwise a recursive call gives the colour and α value behind the segment, which are combined with those of the segment. Then

$$\alpha_{ret} = \alpha_{left} + \alpha_{middle} + \alpha_{right}$$

$$C_{ret} = \frac{C_{left} \cdot \alpha_{left} + C_{middle} \cdot \alpha_{middle} + C_{right} \alpha_{right}}{\alpha_{ret}}$$

Intersections with the head segment are easily detected. These calculations can be carried out to arbitrary resolution, and hence a smooth blur is assured.

11.DISCUSSION AND FURTHER WORK

Figures 6 to 9 show some sample images produced by this algorithm. Figures 6 and 7 both depict balls on a green table viewed from directly above. In the first, the white ball is travelling towards the others. In the second, it has propelled the others forward and is veering rightwards. Figure 8 shows a collection of balls being tipped out of a bucket onto a checkered table. In Fig.9 the left ball has struck the box, causing it to rotate about an axis running through its bottom face. The other ball is on top of the box. In this case, the patterns on the balls and on the box are formed by texture mapping.

The algorithm works best when the objects move with constant velocity. As may be seen from Fig.9, the construction algorithm described here for arbitrary

Fig. 6   The white ball is approaching the others.

Fig. 7   The white ball has propelled the others forward.

Fig. 8 A collection of balls tipped out of a bucket onto a table.

Fig. 9 Two texture-mapped balls and a texture-mapped box.

motion shows the effect of rotation, but it is only a first solution. The
design of more rigorous construction algorithms constitutes the largest area
of future work. A rigorous approach to this problem requires some measure
of how well a given set of polyhedra approximate a 3-space polygon undergoing
a certain form of motion, and the design of algorithms which produce an
adequate approximation with the minimum number of polyhedra. These are
challenging exercises.

Variations on the details described here are possible. For example, instead of
the condition that polyhedra must be linear in eye space, an alternative
strategy would be to construct polyhedra which are linear in image space.
Simple linear interpolation could then be employed in the scan-conversion
procedure. However, the components would then be non-linear in eye space, and
the clipping and back-face removal procedures would hence have to be more
complicated than those presented here. Similarly, linearity may be forsaken
altogether and segment endpoints determined by bilinear interpolation. The
options are as wide as in 3-d rendering.

Spatial antialiasing has not been addressed in this paper. With the algorithm
employed here, the worst effects of spatial aliasing are noticeable only on
objects which are stationary during a frame; if an object moves at all,
the temporal antialiasing blurs its edges. Spatial aliasing effects may hence
be alleviated by moving each stationary object a small distance towards the eye,
constructing polyhedra to match. A better solution might lie in scaling
each stationary 3-space polygon individually in x' and y' by an amount dependant
on the radius of the spatial filter. The difficulties in this case lie in
finding suitable scaling and polyhedron construction algorithms which do not
produce cracks between adjacent polygons.

REFERENCES

Carpenter L (1984) The A-Buffer, an Antialiased Hidden Surface Method. Comput.
    Graph. 18(3):103-108
Cook RL, Porter T, Carpenter L (1984) Distributed Ray Tracing. Comput. Graph.
    18(3):137-145
Cook RL(1986) Stochastic Sampling in Computer Graphics.ACM Trans.Graph.5(1):51-72
Dippe M(1985) Antialiasing in Computer Graphics. PhD Thesis, Univ. of California
Gouraud H (1971) Continuous Shading of Curved Surfaces. IEEE Trans. Comput.
    C-20(6):623-629
Grant CW (1985) Integrated Analytic Spatial and Temporal Anti-Aliasing for
    Polyhedra in 4-Space. Comput. Graph. 19(3):79-84
Haeberli P, Akeley K (1990) The Accumulation Buffer. Comput.Graph.24(4):309-318
Heckbert P (1986) Survey of Texture Mapping. IEEE CG&A 6(11):56-67
Korein J, Badler N (1983) Temporal Anti-Aliasing in Computer Generated Animation.
    Comput. Graph. 17(3);377-388
Max NL, Lerner DM (1985) A Two-and-a-Half-D Motion Blur Algorithm. Comput.Graph.
    19(3):85-93
Max NL (1990) Polygon-Based Post-Process Motion Blur. Vis. Comput. 6:308-314
Phong B(1975)Illumination for Computer Generated Pictures.Commun.ACM 18(6):311-17
Porter T, Duff T (1984) Composing Digital Images. Comput. Graph. 18(3):253-259
Potsemil M, Chakravarty I (1983) Modelling Motion Blur in Computer-Generated
    Images. Comput. Graph. 17(3):389-399

205

Keith Goss is currently a lecturer in the Computer
Science Department of Brunel University, West London.
He received his BSc from Hull University in 1987, and
his PhD from Brunel University in 1991, the latter in
the area of multi-dimensional techniques for high-
quality rendering.
His current research interests include non-WIMP user
interfaces, multi-dimensional graphics, information
visualisation, and information systems. He is a
member of ACM SIGGRAPH.
Address: Computer Science Department, Brunel University, Uxbridge,
Middlesex UB8 3PH, UK. JANET: keith.goss@brunel.ac.uk

Reflections in a Spherical Cavity

Kevin G. Suffern, Scott Hopwood, and Iain Sinclair

ABSTRACT

Fractal images are produced by ray tracing spheres inside a hollow sphere. Since the resulting images can completely surround the camera position, a new ray tracing technique was developed for visualising the images that involves projecting the camera rays onto the surface of a sphere, instead of onto a flat projection plane. The technique can be applied not only to this situation, but to any situation where the scene surrounds the camera. Interesting fractal computer art images are also produced.

Keywords: *ray tracing, fractals, visualisation, computer art*

1. INTRODUCTION

Spheres have been a popular subject for ray tracing since Whitted's (1980) classic paper on recursive ray tracing. After 12 solid years of ray tracing spheres, it may have been thought that there was nothing new to discover about them. However, Korsch and Wagner (1991) recently pointed out that the inter-reflections of light between spheres is chaotic in nature, with the result that many of the images obtained by ray tracing them are fractals. The fractal nature of the images becomes apparent when high levels of recursion are used. While Korsch and Wagner used a simple colouring scheme (three or four colours) to ray trace small numbers of spheres in various configurations, Suffern and Sinclair (1992) and Suffern (1993) used the Whitted (1980) illumination model to produce full colour images of four spheres whose centres are at the vertices of a regular tetrahedron. Many interesting fractals can be obtained from this, and one is shown in Fig. 1. An animated fly through of these spheres has also been produced.

This paper is concerned with ray tracing a small number of spheres in a spherical cavity. Again, the reflections are chaotic, and many interesting images can be obtained. We have two reasons for examining this situation - one scientific, and the other artistic. The scientific reason is curiosity about the way things would look like inside such a cavity. Since the standard projection model used in computer graphics is inadequate for rendering some of the scenes that a viewer would see in such a cavity, we have developed a new ray tracing technique for visualising the scenes. When combined with animation, it provides an excellent visualisation tool, not only for this situation, but for other situations as well, where the scene to be rendered surrounds the camera. This new ray tracing technique is the main contribution of this paper.

The artistic reason is to explore the potential of spherical cavity reflections for producing computer art, for both still images and animation. By varying the parameters, a wide variety of fractal images can be obtained which have artistic merit, and are completely different from those obtained by reflecting light on the outside of spheres.

Inakage (1992) has also studied reflections in a spherical cavity, and other enclosures, with spheres and other shapes. His aims were purely artistic.

2. THE SCIENCE

The geometric situation is illustrated in Fig. 2, which shows the configuration of spheres that were ray traced for several of the illustrations presented in this paper. The outer circle is a hollow sphere with a reflective inner surface, and the smaller disk is an orange sphere inside the hollow sphere. There is also a single point light source and camera position inside the hollow sphere. As a single sphere is sufficient to illustrate the general nature of the reflections, most of the illustrations in this section use the sphere depicted in Fig. 2.

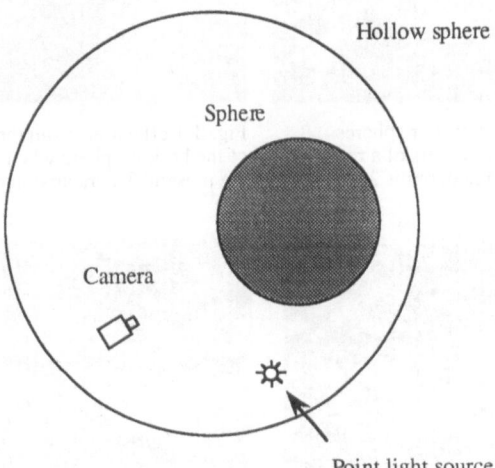

Fig. 2.   Example configuration of spheres for ray tracing in a spherical cavity.

The inside surface of the hollow sphere is black, so as not to contribute any colour of its own to the images, its Phong specular exponent is 400, and its coefficient of global reflection is 0.85. Figure 3 shows some of the reflections visible when there are no other spheres present. This image was ray traced to a recursion depth of 15. Figure 4, also ray traced to a depth of 15, shows the orange sphere (centre of the figure) surrounded by some of its reflections on the hollow sphere. Here the camera is looking directly at the orange sphere. The reflections pass outside the image, and in an attempt to show more of them, Fig. 5 is the same as Fig. 4, but rendered with the projection plane closer to the camera. Severe perspective distortion is apparent, and this figure actually gives no real idea of what a viewer would see. The reason for the perspective distortion is that the reflections for this particular orange sphere and camera configuration extend all around the hollow sphere (see below), and the projection plane in Fig. 5 is inside the sphere. The geometric situation appears in Fig. 6, and reflections from the hollow sphere suffer increasing amounts of perspective distortion as they approach the projection plane. Reflections on camera side of the projection plane are not rendered at all.

2.1 New Rendering Technique

Most ray traced scenes are rendered with the camera looking *into* the scene from a distance. This is particularly important when rendering spheres, because only spheres centred on the viewing direction have circular outlines when projected onto a flat projection plane. To provide an effective visualisation technique for situations such as we have here, where the scene to be rendered surrounds the camera, we use another sphere centred on the camera position as the projection surface, instead of a plane. We call this the *projection sphere*. The surfaces of spheres in this position are the only surfaces that can hold an undistorted projection of a scene from all directions. The problem then is how to render the resulting image on the surface of the projection sphere. We use ray tracing for this

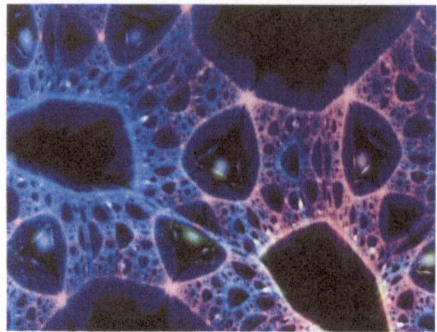

Fig. 1. Ray traced image of four spheres whose vertices are at the corners of a regular tetrahedron. The recursion depth is 20.

Fig. 3. Reflections from the inside surface of the hollow sphere when no other spheres are present. The recursion depth is 15.

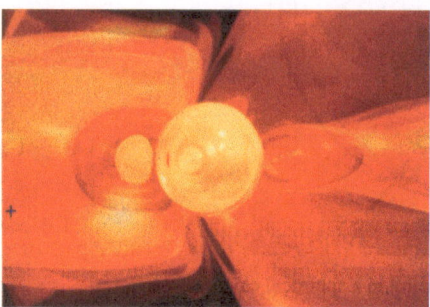

Fig. 4. Single orange sphere and its reflections on the inside surface of the hollow sphere.

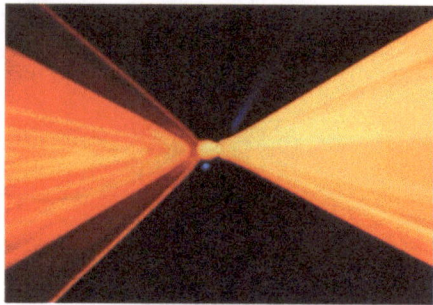

Fig. 5. Same as Fig. 4, but with the projection plane closer to the camera. Severe perspective distortion is present over most of the image.

Fig. 8. The reflections on the hollow sphere from Fig. 3, but ray traced from the outside.

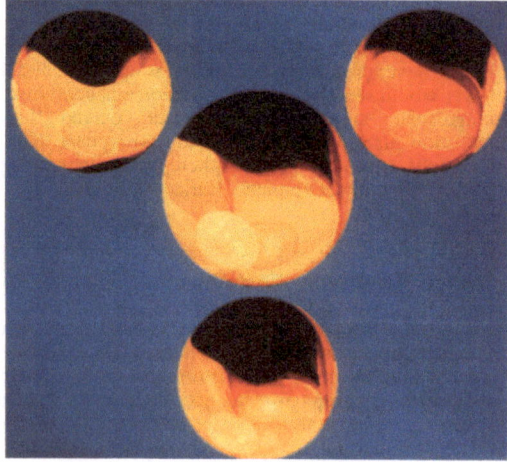

Fig. 9. The reflections on the hollow sphere from Figs. 4 and 5 ray traced from the outside.

by placing another camera outside the projection sphere and ray tracing it in the conventional manner, as depicted schematically in Fig. 7. For programming convenience, the radius of the projection sphere is large enough to contain the hollow sphere. The intersection of a ray and the projection sphere, and the inside camera position, define the initial ray direction for ray tracing inside the hollow sphere. As far as the external ray tracing is concerned, the resulting RGB colour is defined as a procedural texture on the projection sphere.

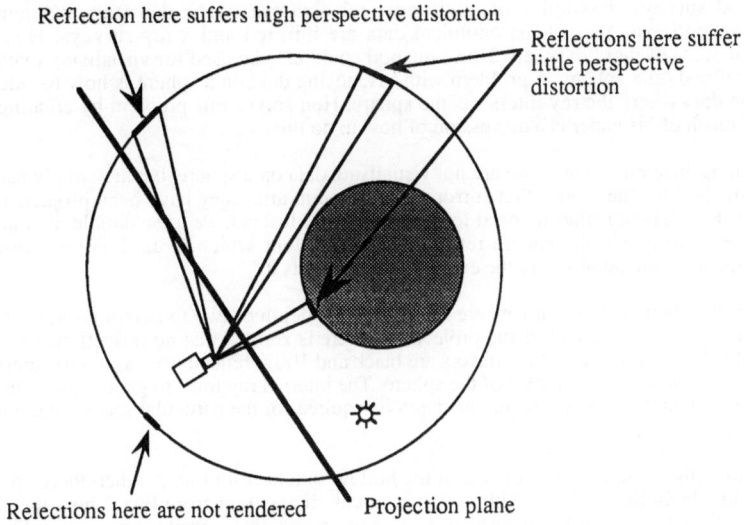

Fig. 6. Illustration of why perspective distortion occurs when projecting onto a flat projection surface.

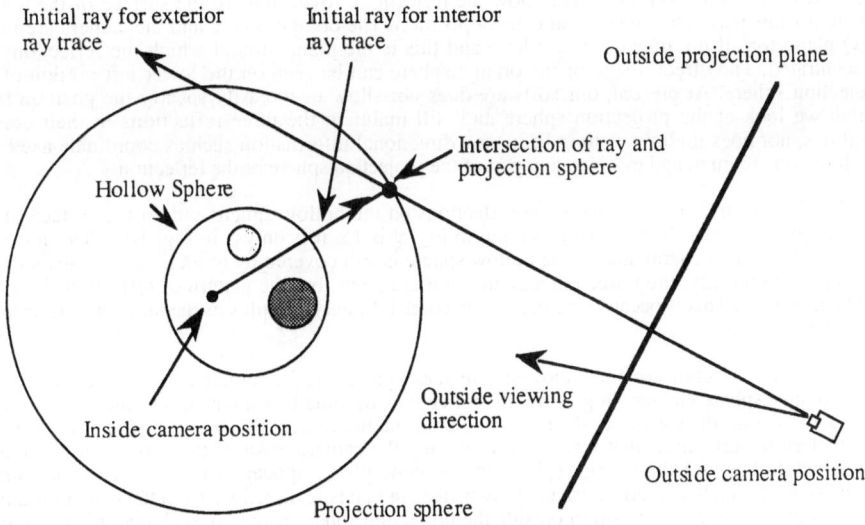

Fig. 7. The projection sphere and external viewing geometry.

2.2 Rendering the Projection Sphere

We could render the projection sphere with a first hit (ray casting) technique, but we would have to render the sphere from several directions to see the entire surface. To avoid having to do this we use a technique developed by Hon (1991) that renders the surface of a sphere together with its reflections in three mirrors in such a way that all parts of the surface are visible. Hon's work was concerned with visualising data on the surface of a sphere. Two important types of data in this category are environmental data gathered from satellites that cover the entire surface of the earth, and whole sky astronomical surveys. Examples of environmental data are ozone densities and temperature distributions, and examples of astronomical data are infrared and x-ray surveys. Hon presents examples of some of these data sets. Hon's method could also be used for visualising mathematical functions defined on a sphere. A problem with visualising data on a sphere is how to calculate the value of the data where the ray intersects the sphere. Hon solves this problem by creating look-up tables, and much of his paper is a discussion of how to do this.

Our problem is different because we are not visualising data on a sphere, but are simply using Hon's rendering method for the scenes that surround the camera, after they have been projected onto the projection sphere. There is thus no need for look-up tables. Instead, we use a double ray trace, where the ray trace from inside the sphere returns an RGB colour which is used as the colour of the projection sphere at the point where the external ray intersects it.

The projection sphere and the mirrors are ray traced to a depth of two to obtain the reflections, and the global reflection coefficient of the projection sphere is zero so that no reflections or any of the background colour appear on it. The mirrors are black and 100% reflective so as not to contribute any colour of their own to the reflections of the sphere. The internal ray trace to get the projection sphere texture is carried out to whatever recursion depth is required for the particular scene we are interested in visualising.

Figure 8 shows the pattern of reflections on the hollow sphere from Fig. 2, when there are no other spheres inside the hollow sphere. Although it is not at all apparent from Fig. 2 how the pattern of reflections is distributed over the surface of the hollow sphere, this is made very clear in Fig. 8. Here the central sphere is the projection sphere, and it can be seen that the pattern of reflections covers a significant part of the surface of the hollow sphere. There is a bright reflection in the opposite direction to the concentration of reflections shown in Fig. 2.

Figure 9 shows the pattern of reflections for the orange sphere and camera configuration in Figs. 4 and 5. It is apparent from this figure how the reflections cover most of the surface of the hollow sphere for this particular sphere and camera position. The orange sphere and the camera are in the (x,y) plane for all the images shown here and this is the plane around which the reflections are concentrated. The direct image of the orange sphere can be seen on the lower left portion of the projection sphere. At present, our software does not allow us to easily specify the position from which we look at the projection sphere and still maintain the three reflections in their correct positions, nor does it allow us to indicate any directional information such as coordinate axes. We can however, zoom in and examine any part of the projection sphere or the reflections.

The level of recursion used affects the reflections on the hollow sphere and on the surface of the orange sphere. While the level of recursion in Fig. 9 is 15, it is only 5 in Fig. 10, where it can be seen that the same general area of the hollow sphere is still covered by reflections. As the recursive depth goes to infinity, the reflection stay inside these areas, but the pattern of reflections becomes fractal in nature . This is because the patterns become infinitely complex as the number of reflections approaches infinity.

The pattern of reflections on the hollow sphere varies greatly as the camera position and the position of the orange sphere change. In general, the reflections become less spread out as the orange sphere moves away from the surface of the hollow sphere, and the camera position approaches the surface. The pattern of reflections that results from moving the camera towards the surface of the hollow sphere while keeping the orange sphere in the same place, appear in Fig. 11. They are not as extensive as in Fig. 9, and are restricted to two areas in opposite directions from the camera position. In this figure, the viewing position outside the projection sphere is not optimal, and it is not easy to see that the reflections are concentrated in two areas. For situations like this where reflections are concentrated over a small area, direct interior rendering is quite effective, as shown in Fig. 12.

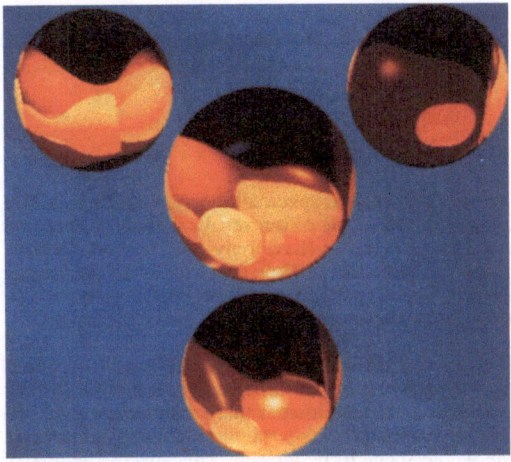

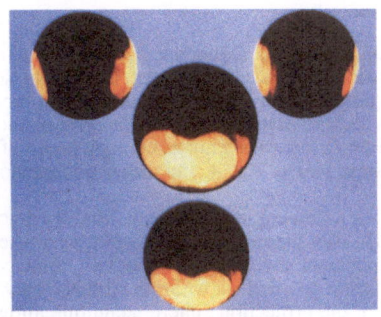

Fig. 10. Same as Fig. 9, but with the depth of recursion equal to 5 instead of 15.

Fig. 11. Same as Fig. 9, but with the camera closer to the surface of the hollow sphere.

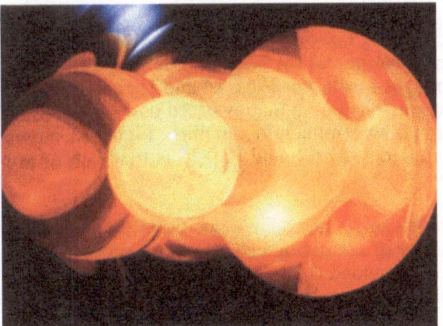

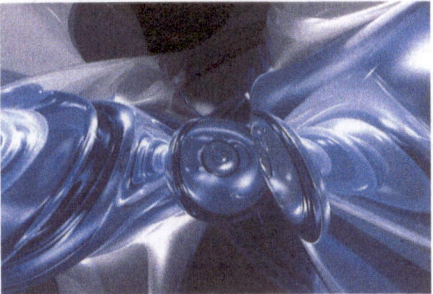

Fig. 12. Part of the reflections visible in Fig. 9 ray traced from inside the hollow sphere.

Fig. 13. Ray traced image of blue and gray spheres inside the hollow sphere.

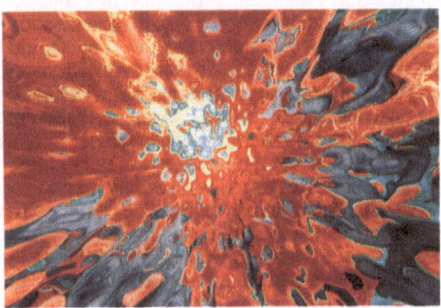

Fig. 14. Red and turquoise spheres with bump map.

Fig. 15. Brown sphere with bump map.

In general, animation combined with the projection sphere visualisation technique is the best method for visualising the way the reflections change as the positions of the camera and orange sphere change.

3. THE ART

As mentioned above, we also wanted to explore the potential of spherical cavity reflections for the production of computer art, and in this section we present some of our results. Although there are many methods that could be used to produce artistic effects, we have only explored two, both of which involve placing one or more reflective spheres inside the hollow sphere and then producing interior ray traced images to high levels of recursion. The first method produces images in exactly the same way as Fig. 4, and the second method uses a bump map on the surface of the hollow sphere.

The following images result from ray tracing the inside of the hollow sphere, as in Figs. 3, 4, 5, and 12. The external ray tracing is very useful in the planning of the images, because without this technique available, it can be very time consuming to search for images that are interesting from an artistic point of view. Some of these only appear in certain directions and under high magnification, but the projection sphere technique allows the whole scene to be viewed. This speeds the task of examining small areas on the surface of the hollow sphere.

The first configuration of spheres consists of a grey and blue sphere inside the hollow sphere. A portion of the reflections on the hollow sphere appears in Fig. 13, ray traced to a depth of 14. The blue sphere has a glass-like transparent appearance, although it is not transparent.

When a random bump map is applied to the surface of the hollow sphere, images of the interior spheres are completely destroyed by the random perturbations to the reflection angles after a few inter-reflections. However, very dynamic and fluid images result. For Figs. 14 and 15, a white noise random bump map was used to perturb the normal vector. The bump map is based on Perlin's vector noise function (Perlin, 1984), using linear interpolation between the lattice points. Figure 14 shows the results of ray tracing a red and turquoise sphere to a depth of 4, and Fig. 15 is the result of ray tracing a single brown sphere, also to a depth of 4.

When some of the parameters are animated, for example camera and sphere positions, the magnitude of the bumps, the depth of recursion, etc., a wide variety of animation effects can be produced. We have used the *Swish* animation language developed by Hopwood (Hopwood *et al*, 1992), because its ability to animate any aspect of a scene makes it ideally suited for this purpose.

4. CONCLUSIONS AND FUTURE WORK

We have developed a new ray tracing technique for effectively visualising and animating scenes that completely surround the camera position, and have applied it to visualising reflections in a spherical cavity. Much work remains to be done before our software is flexible tool for such visualisation purposes. For example, when the exterior camera position is changed, the software should automatically adjust the positions of the three planes so that, where possible, the three reflections of the projection sphere remain completely visible, as do all positions on its surface. This will not be possible for all viewing positions, and the constraints need to be determined. Also, we made the projection sphere large enough to enclose the hollow sphere for programming convenience; in this way the exterior rays only hit the projection sphere and the planes, and the interior rays only hit the hollow sphere and anything inside it. As this technique is applicable for visualising any scene that surrounds the camera, its flexibility should be improved so that the projection sphere does not have to surround the objects in the scene. For example, it should be possible to use the technique to ray trace scenes that extend outside the projection sphere. This will be easy to accomplish by allowing the external ray tracer to only ray trace the projection sphere and the three mirrors, and allowing the internal ray tracer ray trace everything in the scene, but not the projection sphere and mirrors. Work is proceeding on these extensions.

We have presented some images of the reflections inside a hollow sphere that contains a single orange sphere. The reflections become fractal in nature as the depth of recursion goes to infinity.

We have also explored the potential of reflections in a spherical cavity for producing computer art, and have achieved some interesting results. Much work remains to be done with this, as we have only explored a few of the many techniques that could be used.

REFERENCES

Bui-Tuong, Phong (1975) Illumination for Computer Generated Pictures, CACM, 18 (6), 311-317.

Hon D (1991) A new method for visualizing data on a sphere , Computers in Physics, Sep/Oct 1991, 505-513.

Hopwood S, Sinclair I, and Suffern K G (1992) A language for Animating Scene Descriptions, *Animating Virtual Worlds*, 249-257, (Proceedings of Computer Animation '92, Springer, New York).

Inakage M (1992) Infinite Reflection Models for the Visual Arts, The Journal of Visualization and Computer Animation, 3, 23-29.

Korsch H J and Wagner A (1991), Fractal Mirror Images and Chaotic Scattering, Computers in Physics, Sept/Oct 1991, 497-504.

Mandelbrot B B (1982) *The Fractal Geometry of Nature*, (W H Freeman and Co., New York).

Perlin K (1984) An Image Synthesizer, Computer Graphics, 19, (3), 287-296, (Proceedings of SIGGRAPH '84).

Suffern K G and Sinclair I (1992), Fractal Sphere Reflections and Sphere Fractals, presented at the Third International Symposium on Electronic Art, Sydney, Australia.

Suffern K G (1993) Fractal Sphere Reflections and Sphere Fractals: It's all done with mirrors. Proceedings of the Third International Symposium on Electronic Art. To be published.

Walker J (1988) The Amateur Scientist, Scientific American, 259 (12), 84-87.

Whitted J T (1980) An improved illumination model for shaded display. Comm. ACM, 23 (6), 343-349.

Kevin Suffern received an M Sc from Cornell University in Astronomy in 1973 and a Ph D in Applied Mathematics from the University of Sydney in 1978. From 1979 to 1981 he worked in the School of Mathematics and Physics at Macquarie University in Sydney, before joining the School of Computing Sciences at the University of Technology, Sydney, where he is currently a Senior Lecturer. In 1986 he was a Visiting Research Scientist in The Center for Interactive Computer Graphics, Rensselaer Polytechnic Institute, and in 1990 he was a Visiting Associate Professor in the Rensselaer Design Research Center, Rensselaer Polytechnic Institute. His main interests are computer graphics, computer aided geometric design, and computer art. He is a member of ACS, ACM, and SIGGRAPH.

Address: School of Computing Sciences, University of Technology, Sydney, PO Box 123, Broadway, NSW, AUSTRALIA.

E-mail: kevin@socs.uts.edu.au

Scott Hopwood is Masters student at the University of Technology, Sydney. His research interests include computer graphics, languages, and visualisation.

Address: School of Computing Sciences, University of Technology, Sydney, PO Box 123, Broadway, NSW, AUSTRALIA.

E-mail: @shopwood.socs.uts.edu.au

Iain Sinclair is an undergraduate student at the University of Technology, Sydney. His interests include computer animation, computer art, and human-computer interaction.

Address: School of Computing Sciences, University of Technology, Sydney, PO Box 123, Broadway, NSW, AUSTRALIA.

E-mail: axolotl@socs.uts.edu.au

Part V

Motion Control

Controlling Movement Using Parametric Frame Space Interpolation

SHANG GUO, JAMES ROBERGÉ, and THOM GRACE

ABSTRACT

In this paper, we introduce a technique for controlling movement, parametric frame space interpolation, that extends the artistic expressiveness of parametric keyframe animation to a higher level of movement control. An animator using this technique defines a range of movements, a frame space, in terms of a set of reference (key) movements. The animator then generates movements that interpolate between these reference movements by specifying paths within the frame space. The resulting animation process can be used as a freestanding animation technique or as a tool for editing movements produced using other animation methods.

Keywords: Animation, motion control, keyframe, frame space

1. INTRODUCTION

One of the continuing challenges in computer animation is the creation of motion control methodologies that are highly expressive, but that provide an animator with the ability to control movement on an artistic, visual level. In conventional parametric keyframe animation, an animator envisions a movement, and then defines the movement in terms of the position of a figure's limbs and joints at various points throughout the movement. Although defining movement at this level of detail requires significant, painstaking effort, keyframe animation allows an animator to control movement using familiar visual metaphors and constraints. Not only does the resulting creative process blend well with the animator's principal focus — the aesthetics (or "look") of the resulting movement — but the absence of physical constraints allows the animator to easily express stylized movements that are deliberately unnatural in appearance, exaggerated dance or non-human movements, for instance.

On the other hand, the fact that parametric keyframe animation describes movement at a very low level — rather than in terms of a physically-based motion model, movement algorithm, or movement script — makes it difficult for an animator to modify movements and to derive new movements from existing ones. Even minor modifications in the nature of a movement entail adjusting limb and joint parameters at the same highly-specific level of detail that was used in creating the movement initially.

Recent efforts in motion control have focused upon relieving the animator of this burden by providing mechanisms that control motion at higher levels of abstraction. In these efforts, a figure's motion

216

is modeled as a kinematic system (Zeltzer 1982; Korein and Badler 1982; Philips et al. 1990) or a dynamic system (Magnenat-Thalmann et al. 1985; Barzell and Barr 1988; Bruderlin and Calvert 1989). Different solutions to a given system yield different movements. Motion control is expressed through the application of a set of constraints to the solution process. These constraints may be kinematic (e.g., limb positions, joint angles, limits on degrees of freedom) or dynamic (e.g., forces, torques, physical laws).

While these kinematic and dynamic constraints may be specified directly by the animator, they are frequently the product of still higher-level control constraints. In Zeltzer (1982), for instance, a finite-state control is used to specify a goal-directed motion simulation from which a kinematically-constrained movement is produced. Witkin and Kass (1988) and Cohen (1992) define a movement in terms of an optimized solution over a set of goals and constraints in spacetime.

Still higher levels of control are possible. Bazault et al. (1992) use experimental data on human walking to derive a functional model of human locomotion that takes advantage of the intrinsic dynamics of walking to extend the model's application to movements in which the speed and direction of motion can be varied continuously. In a similar vein, Raibert et al. (1991) direct the movement of various multi-legged creatures using a set of control algorithms derived from their studies of movement. Badler et al. (1985) guide movement using a set of task-level constraints, while Bruderlin and Calvert (1992) use a hierarchical control process in which an animator controls an approximate dynamic movement model through a set of high-level walking parameters and a set of goal-directed constraints.

The movements produced using these models are extremely fluid and natural in appearance. Unfortunately, creating a movement using these methods requires considerable computation (Thalmann 1989). More importantly, it is not easy for an animator to use dynamic and higher-level constraints to guide the production of an envisioned movement. While the impact of kinematic constraints upon a movement are readily predicted, the impact of dynamic and higher-level constraints are often difficult to predict, both as absolute and relative (modified) values.

We have developed an animation technique, parametric frame space interpolation, that has its roots in parametric keyframe animation, but that supports a higher level of control. Using this technique, an animator defines a range of movements — a movement pattern or style — in terms of a set of reference movements. The animator then specifies an envisioned movement as an interpolation between these reference movements. The reference movements themselves may be the product of parametric keyframe animation or the product of more sophisticated motion models. The resulting animation process extends the efficiency and expressiveness of keyframe animation to include key-movements, as well as keyframes. In doing so, it provides an animator with the means for creating new movements by blending, composing, and fine-tuning movements from a variety of sources.

2. PARAMETRIC FRAME SPACE INTERPOLATION

If we denote the total number of degrees of freedom (DOF) in an articulated figure by m, then the relative position of the figure's joints and limbs at a given moment in time can be expressed as a point P in an m-dimensional space

$$P = (a_1, a_2, \ldots, a_m)^T$$

where each a_i is a parameter that describes the rotational or translational transformation associated with a particular DOF. Including the transformations associated with the figure's root as DOFs yields a point in m-D space that describes the absolute (world space) position of the figure's joints and limbs.

A path in m-D space represents the positional component of a continuous movement, that is, the positions taken by the figure's joints and limbs as they progress through the movement. Such a path can be described using an m-D vector function in parametric form

$$F(s) = (F_1(s), F_2(s), \ldots, F_m(s))^T \qquad (0 \leq s \leq 1)$$

where each $F_i(s)$ is a function that describes the variations in a particular DOF during the movement, and where the points $F(0)$ and $F(1)$ are the initial and final points in the movement.

Mapping the positional component of a movement onto time yields a complete movement in spacetime. By composing the m-D vector function $F(s)$ with a mapping of parameter s onto time $s=g(t)$ we produce an m-D vector function

$$F(g(t)) = (F_1(g(t)), F_2(g(t)), \ldots, F_m(g(t)))^T \qquad (t_0 \leq t \leq t_n, \; g(t_0)=0, \; g(t_n)=1)$$

that describes the spacetime characteristics of the movement. Note that the application of different time mappings to a given path in m-D space will produce movements that have very different motion qualities (uniform, jerky, accelerating, decelerating, and so forth), as will varying the path itself.

Using this notational framework, keyframe animation can be described as a process that begins with a sequence of points (keyframes) in m-D space $K_1, K_2, \ldots, K_n$. The path that is constructed through these keyframes can be described using an m-D vector interpolation function $F(s)$ for which there exists an ordered sequence of values of parameter s

$$s_1, s_2, \ldots, s_{n-2} \qquad (0 \leq s_i \leq 1 \text{ and } s_i \leq s_{i+1})$$

such that

$$F(0)=K_1, \quad F(s_1)=K_2, \quad \ldots \quad , \quad F(s_{n-2})=K_{n-1}, \quad F(1)=K_n.$$

Different paths may be produced depending upon the interpolation function that is used to construct the path.

Once completed, this path is mapped onto time by composing the interpolation function $F(s)$ with a temporal mapping $s=g(t)$ and the result sampled to produce a sequence of points (frames) $F_1, F_2, \ldots, F_w$.

The process of sampling to form frames can be described using an ordered sequence of values of parameter t

$$t_1, t_2, \ldots, t_w \quad (t_0 \leq t_i \leq t_n \text{ and } t_i \leq t_{i+1})$$

such that

$$F(g(t_1)) = F_1, \quad F(g(t_2)) = F_2, \quad \ldots, \quad F(g(t_w)) = F_w.$$

A movement produced by an algorithmic or script-based motion model can also be represented as a time-mapped path in m-D space. In this case, the m-D vector function $F(s)$ and the time mapping $s = g(t)$ are encoded within the motion model itself. Since this paper focuses upon the use of existing movements to construct new movements, we will be more concerned with the output of motion models, rather than the details of the models themselves. The output of a motion model is a sequence of points (frames) $F_1, F_2, \ldots, F_n$ that lie along on a path in m-D space. In this case, n is quite large and the points are quite close to one another.

2.1 Frame Spaces

The path formed by a sequence of points $P_1, P_2, \ldots, P_n$ and an m-D vector interpolation function $F(s)$ is a delimited one-dimensional space. We will refer to this delimited one-dimensional space as a **1-D frame space** (Fig. 1). Classic parametric keyframe animation has concentrated upon the use of these 1-D frame spaces to specify movements. This paper explores the use of these 1-D frame spaces as building blocks of higher dimensional frame spaces, and the use of these higher-dimensional frame spaces to generate and modify movements.

F

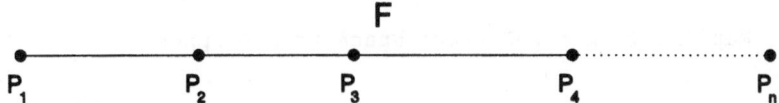

P_1 P_2 P_3 P_4 P_n

Fig. 1 A 1-D frame space

A 2-D frame space is a two-dimensional space that is delimited by a pair of 1-D frame spaces (Fig. 2b). Each point in a 2-D frame space represents an m-D vector. A point Q in a 2-D frame space can be mapped to a point P in m-D space through an interpolation F' between the m-D vector interpolation functions that are associated with the 1-D frame spaces that delimit the 2-D frame space. For example, F' might be a linear combination of the m-D vector interpolation functions F_1 and F_2 (Fig. 3)

$$P = F'(Q) = F'((x,y)) = (1-a)*F_1(x) + a*F_2(x)$$

where

$$a = (y - y_1)/(y_2 - y_1).$$

Note that we have adopted the convention used in keyframe animation and have substituted the dimensional parameter x for the parameter s used in the discussion above.

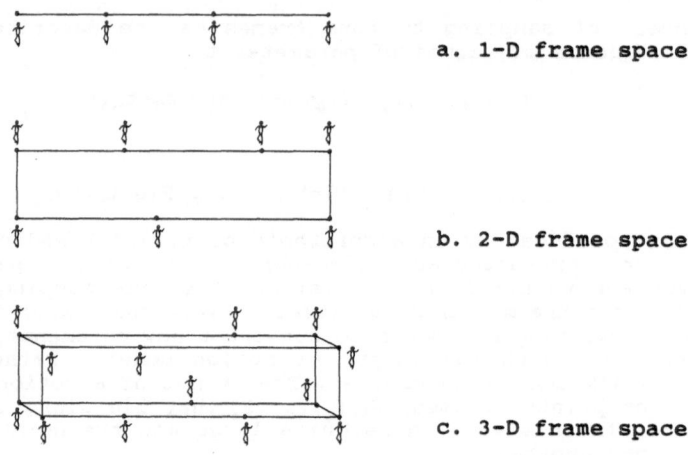

Fig. 2 Multidimensional frame spaces

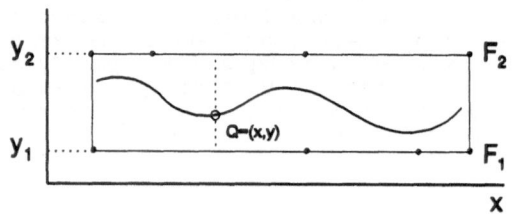

Fig. 3 Mapping from a 2-D frame space to m-D space

While the function F' shown in this example is a linear combination of m-D vector interpolation functions F_1 and F_2, F_1 and F_2 need not be (and likely, are not) linear themselves. In addition, F' need not be linear. Any of a variety of non-linear functions might be used in place of the linear interpolation function shown above.

On a conceptual level, a 2-D frame space represents a range of movements. The paths that can be drawn within a 2-D frame space represent those movements that can be produced by combining the movements represented by the 1-D frame spaces that delimit the 2-D frame space.

Continuing to three dimensions, a 3-D frame space is a three-dimensional space that is delimited by a pair of 2-D frame spaces, or equivalently, by four 1-D frame spaces (Fig. 2c). Each point Q in a 3-D frame space can be mapped to a point P in m-D space through an interpolation F' between the m-D vector interpolation functions that are associated with the 1-D frame spaces that delimit the 3-D frame space (Fig. 4). A linear combination is given below

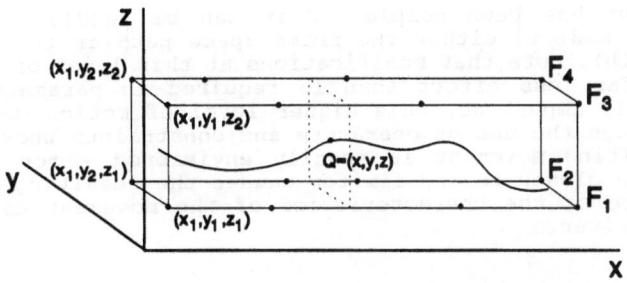

Fig. 4 Mapping from a 3-D frame space to m-D space

$$P = F'(Q)$$
$$= F'((x,y,z))$$
$$= (1-a)*(1-b)*F_1(x) + a*(1-b)*F_2(x) + (1-a)*b*F_3(x) + a*b*F_4(x)$$

where

$$a=(y-y_1)/(y_2-y_1) \text{ and } b=(z-z_1)/(z_2-z_1).$$

This process can be readily extended to include still higher-dimensional frame spaces. In general, an n-D frame space can be constructed from two $(n-1)$-D frame spaces or 2^{n-1} 1-D frame spaces. Including more than 2^{n-1} 1-D frame spaces in the definition of a given n-D frame space will allow an animator to include still finer levels of gradation between the movements that delimit the frame space (Fig. 5). In addition, these added 1-D frame spaces will support the use of more sophisticated frame interpolation functions (cubic, spline, and so forth) in place of the linear frame interpolation functions (F') outlined above.

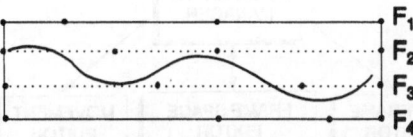

Fig. 5 An n-D frame space formed from more than 2^{n-1} 1-D frame spaces

If the interpolation functions of the 1-D frame spaces that delimit a given frame space incorporate temporal mappings, then the same interpolation methods used to map a point Q in the frame space to a point P in m-D space can also be used to map point Q to a point in time. In this case, the frame interpolation function F' includes an interpolation s' between the temporal mappings that are associated with the 1-D frame spaces. The interpolation function used in s' may be the same as that used in F' or it may be an interpolation function that is specifically designed to preserve (or restore) first- and/or second-derivative continuity in the resulting movement (Guo 1992). Alternatively, the animator may elect to define a new temporal mapping for the interpolated movement.

Once a movement has been completed, it can be readily modified. Changes can be made to either the frame space path or the temporal mapping (or both). Note that modifications at this level of abstraction require far less effort than is required in parametric keyframing. Equally important, this higher level of motion control is expressed through the use of operators and constraints whose impact upon the resulting movement is readily envisioned — for example, moving the path closer to a delimiter causes the resulting movement to take on more of the characteristics of the movement associated with that delimiter.

3. APPLICATIONS OF PARAMETRIC FRAME SPACE INTERPOLATION

In this section, we examine the use of parametric frame space interpolation in three somewhat different roles: as a freestanding animation tool, as a method for editing frame sequences that have been produced by physically-based or algorithmic motion models, and as a simple motion modeling tool.

3.1 Animation Tool

Figure 6 shows the functional components of an animation tool that is based upon parametric frame space interpolation. This tool, developed for the Silicon Graphics IRIS platform, supports the creation of movements using the interpolation process described above.

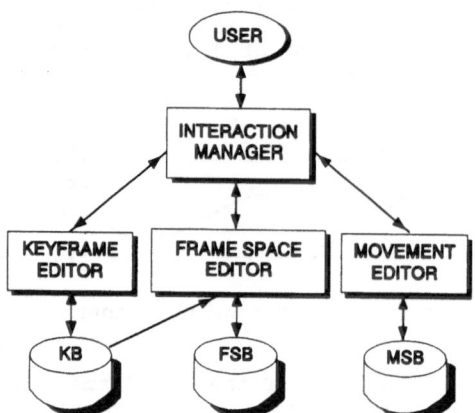

Fig. 6 Functional components of the animation tool

The Keyframe Editor allows an animator to create and edit individual parametric keyframes. The resulting keyframes are stored in the Keyframe Base (KB). The Frame Space Editor is used to construct frame spaces using either a sequence of keyframes from the Keyframe Base or a sequence of frames that have been output by another animation tool. The resulting frame spaces are stored in the Frame Space Base (FSB).

Using the Movement Editor, an animator can experiment within a given frame space, creating paths (Fig. 7) and observing the resulting movements (Fig. 8). Should an animator so desire, a temporal mapping can be defined dynamically by moving a cursor along a movement's frame space path in real-time while observing the resulting movement (Fig. 9). By varying the rate at which the path is traversed, a variety of different movement styles can be produced from a single path. This same process can also be used to fine-tune an interpolated temporal mapping — to correct a perceived defect in the fluidity of the movement or to deliberately introduce discontinuities into the movement, for instance. Completed movements are stored in the Movement Base (MB) for later retrieval and display.

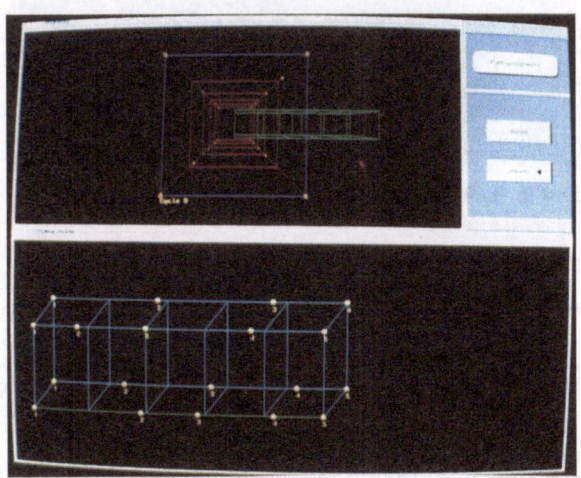

Fig. 7 Creating a path in a 3-D frame space

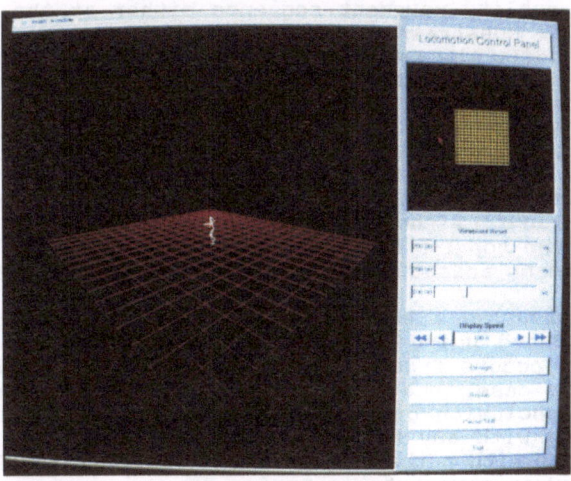

Fig. 8 Displaying a movement

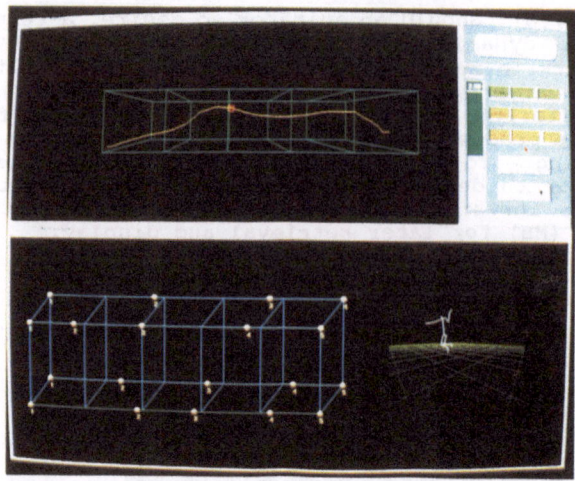

Fig. 9 Creating a temporal mapping

3.2 Movement Editor

Motion models that incorporate dynamic and task-oriented constraints
are capable of producing movements of extremely high quality.
Unfortunately, these models are computationally expensive to use and
are often difficult to control (Thalmann 1989). Having produced a
movement that is not quite what was envisioned, an animator is faced
with the challenge of modifying the movement model's constraints so
that the movement more exactly conforms to her/his mental image of
what the movement should look like. The costly process of generating
a movement must then be repeated.

Parametric frame space interpolation provides a potential means for
addressing this problem. Rather than being faced with choice of fine-
tuning a high-quality movement sequence either at the level of the
movement model's constraints or at the keyframe parameter level, an
animator can modify the sequence by constructing a frame space that
incorporates the movement along with a set of movements (either
keyframe-based or from another animation model) that address the
problems in the movement. The animator is then free to experiment
with paths within this frame space until the envisioned movement is
produced. This experimentation takes place within an environment that
is computationally efficient, visually oriented, and yet, quite
expressive. Figure 10 shows a frame sequence from a high-quality
motion model (the top 1-D frame space) being fine-tuned by combining
it with a keyframe animation sequence (the bottom 1-D frame space).

This same approach can also be used to blend together movements that
have been produced using different motion control techniques — a
situation that occurs frequently when generating animation produc-
tions. In this case, the animator constructs a frame space that
overlaps the conclusion of one movement with the start of the next
movement (along with any needed modifying movements). The animator
then experiments with paths within the frame space until the desired
transition between movements is produced.

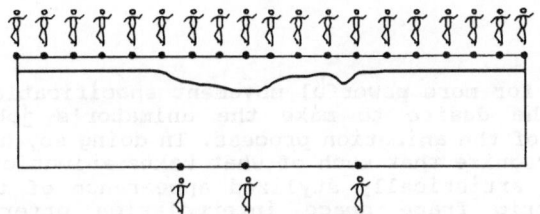

Fig. 10 Editing a sequence of frames that have been generating by a motion model

3.3 Simple Motion Modeling Tool

As we noted above, the frame space path interpolation function F' need not be a simple linear combination of the interpolation functions of the delimiting 1-D frame spaces. Figure 11 shows a 3-D frame space that defines a range of simple walking movements. The 1-D frame spaces that delimit this frame space correspond to the following variations in gait pattern:

- Short, low strides (SL)
- Long, low strides (LL)
- Short, high strides (SH)
- Long, high strides (LH)

The movements corresponding to each of the 1-D frame spaces differ in the length and height of the strides and in the body orientation during the strides.

The path interpolation function F' that combines these 1-D frame spaces incorporates both the kinematics and dynamics of the resulting movement, albeit at a relatively simple level. The movement described by the path shown in Fig. 11 (the demarcations divide the frame space into ten-stride intervals) begins with short, low strides (almost a shuffle); continues with short, higher strides (in the style of a drum major); progresses to long, high strides (a Monty Python-esque "silly walk") and concludes with long, low strides (a brisk walk).

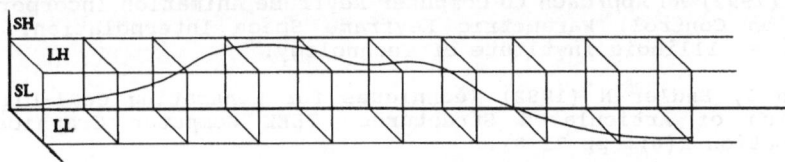

Fig. 11 Specifying a sequence of walking movements

4. CONCLUSION

The search for more powerful movement specification techniques is rooted in the desire to make the animator's job simpler by automating more of the animation process. In doing so, however, it is important to recognize that much of what makes animation unique (and popular) is the artistically stylized appearance of the resulting images. Parametric frame space interpolation offers a visual, flexible method for creating or modifying movements at the level of movements, rather than at the level of keyframes or scripts. As such, it establishes a middle ground between keyframe animation and algorithmic or script-based motion models.

5. ACKNOWLEDGEMENTS

The authors would like to thank Daniel Thalmann for his comments and suggestions on this work.

REFERENCES

Badler N, Korein JD, Korein JU, Radack G, Brotman L (1985) Positioning and Animating Human Figures in a Task-Oriented Environment. Visual Computer 1(4): pp 212-220.

Barzell R, Barr A (1988) A Modeling System Based on Dynamic Constraints. Proceedings of SIGGRAPH '88, Computer Graphics 22(3): pp 179-188.

Bazault L, Boulic R, Magnenat-Thalmann N, Thalmann D (1992) An Interactive Tool for the Design of Human Free-Walking Trajectories. SIGGRAPH '92 Course Notes: pp 181-188.

Bruderlin A, Calvert T (1989) Goal-Directed, Dynamic Animation of Human Walking. Proceedings of SIGGRAPH '89, Computer Graphics 23(3): pp 233-242.

Cohen M (1992) Interactive Spacetime Control for Animation. Proceedings of SIGGRAPH '92, Computer Graphics 26(3) pp 293-303.

Guo S (1992) An Approach to Computer Keyframe Animation Incorporating Motion Control: Parametric Keyframe Space Interpolation. Ph.D. Thesis, Illinois Institute of Technology.

Korein J, Badler N (1982) Techniques for Generating Goal-Directed Motion of Articulated Structures. IEEE Computer Graphics and Animation 2(6): pp 71-81.

Magnenat-Thalmann N, Thalmann D, Fortin M (1985) MIRANIM: An Extensible Director-Oriented System for the Animation of Realistic Images. IEEE Computer Graphics and Animation 5(3): pp 611-73.

Phillips C, Zhao J, Badler N (1990) Interactive Real-time Articulated Figure Manipulation Using Multiple Kinematic Constraints. Proceedings of SIGGRAPH '90, Computer Graphics 24(3): pp 245-250.

Raibert M, Hodgins K (1991) Animation of Legged Locomotion. Proceedings of SIGGRAPH '91, Computer Graphics 25(3): pp 349-358.

227

Thalmann D (1989) Motion Control: From Keyframe to Task-Level
Animation. In: Magnenat-Thalmann N, Thalmann D (eds) State of the
Art in Computer Animation, Springer, Tokyo Berlin Heidelberg New
York London Paris, pp 3-17.

Witkin A, Kass M (1988) Spacetime constraints. Proceedings of
SIGGRAPH '88, Computer Graphics 22(3): pp 159-168.

Zeltzer D (1982) Motor Control Techniques of Figure Animation. IEEE
Computer Graphics and Animation 2(9): pp 53-59.

Shang Guo is currently an Assistant Professor of
Computer Science at Vassar College. Her research
interests include animation, modeling, and image
synthesis. Guo received a B.S. in Mathematics in
1981 and an M.S. in Computer Science in 1984,
both from Zhejiang University, China. She was
awarded a Ph.D. in Computer Science in 1992 from
the Illinois Institute of Technology. Guo is a
member of the ACM. Guo's address is Department
of Computer Science, Vassar College, Pough-
keepsie, NY 12601.

James Robergé is an Assistant Professor of
Computer Science at the Illinois Institute of
Technology. His research interests focus upon
the expression of user control in computer
graphics, visualization, and image manipulation.
Robergé received his B.S., M.S., and Ph.D. in
Computer Science from Northwestern University.
He is a member of the ACM and the IEEE Computer
Society. Robergé's address is Department of
Computer Science, Illinois Institute of Technol-
ogy, Chicago, IL 60616.

Thom Grace was awarded the B.S., M.S., and Ph.D.
degrees in Mathematics from the University of
Illinois at Chicago. He has been on the faculty
of the Computer Science Department at the Illinois Institute of Technology since 1982, and is
a member of the Association for Computing Machinery (ACM), the ACM Special Interest Group in
Computer Graphics (SIGGRAPH), the IEEE Computer
Society, the American Mathematical Society, and
the Mathematical Association of America. His
interests include realistic image synthesis,
programming languages, and computational algebraic structures. Grace's address is Department
of Computer Science, Illinois Institute of
Technology, Chicago, IL 60616.

Adaptive Meta Control of Path Planning with HIP

Kim Trans

ABSTRACT

This paper describes a method for the inclusion of intentional game control in computer games. The main idea is to let the game progress due to a goal oriented control paradigm. The result is a more unpredictable game where the the underlying game control reacts more intelligently as if it were another human player. The applied control method is composed of a hierarchical temporal identification of the present situation and a corresponding hierarchical planner to generate the appropriate moves.

Keywords: computer games, expert systems, hierarchical structure, intentional control, planning

1. INTRODUCTION

This paper mainly deals with the program part of interactive computer games with one or more players. The aim of the paper is to describe an optimized edition of the common game nethack, and to define and describe the methods applied. This gives an optimization of the pleasure of playing as it uses methods from artificial intelligence to make the computer play a more intelligent game.

The problem in question is thus to implement some limited kind of intentionality (Dennett 1978) in a game and in this way make it react more goal oriented, i.e. as if the machine were another active player and not just a machine. This limited intentionality will make it more difficult to outplan the program, as it introduces goals with some fixed order of priority. This makes it possible for the program to switch the focus to another obtainable goal in cases where the main goal is not reachable anymore, or maybe just for the moment.

The solution applied in this paper is built on several artificial intelligence methods for movement control. These methods are used for the control of the movements of those parts which the game controls, in the same way as it is used in advanced robotic controls (Albus 1981). This motion control is implemented with goal directed planning, subsequent adaption to changing circumstances, and it uses meta-knowledge to guide the planning process in nontrivial situations.

This paper contains the results from applying these methods for movement control in the game nethack, which has been chosen as an example due to the fact that this is free software. The source code

written in ansi C (Kernigan 1988) is widely available and can be
compiled on most available machines of all sizes. The obtained result is that the reactions from the program are more human-like and
the enhanced game thus resembles more precisely the original Dungeons and Dragons game.

2. PROBLEM

The problem to be solved can be stated as: how to make computer
games more realistic in an intellectual way, not just by adding advanced sounds and graphics, but by really changing the functionality
of the game, such that it appears to be reacting more intelligently.
The game nethack has been chosen, as a working case and as a means
of illustrating the methods applied

The nethack game is a Dungeons and Dragons game, it has a very primitive user interface which is based on the ascii character set, and
the player moves in the same way as in the standard UNIX vi editor.
The game supports only limited graphics and the interface looks like
this:

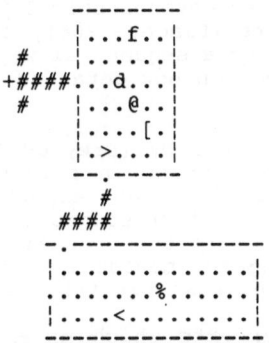

Fig. 1. The nethack game interface

where the player is represented by the character @, and the characters f and d represent hostile monsters trying to kill the player.
The game can functionally be defined as a *search and destroy* type of
game.

The goal of the human player is to escape the caves with some arti-
fact that is hidden deep inside a system of connected caves. For a
player to reach this goal he has to collect different items and kill
most of the mosters that he meets during the search. The primitivity
of the user interface is unimportant, the interesting point being
the control of the hostile monsters, as their actions are determining the complexity and realness of the game.

In this way the control problem of the game can be stated as the
generation of an intentionally specified sequence of movements directed against the human player. In any situation the problem is to
control the monsters and let them react intelligently, i.e. as if
they are acting upon some purpose and not just acting as a number of
primitive obstacles that must be defeated.

A corresponding possible solution of a problem stated in this way is: define and implement an intelligent monster movement control system in order to simulate intelligence in the same way as the human player is using his or hers own intelligence. The simulated intelligence is used to try to beat the opponent, which just means that the problem in the concepts of artificial intelligence can be stated: how to intentionally interpret the current state of the game, and how to create an appropriate primitive reaction, or for more complex states, how to create an entire reaction plan.

3. SOLUTION

The definition of a good solution is not difficult, as any solution where the human player feels that the game reacts intelligently is an acceptable solution. In this way the problem to be solved is how to make the program behave in the same way as any human player. This way of behaviour will introduce some indeterminancy (Wilensky 1983) into the game that will make the game less predictable, as human beings are mostly liable to react as usual, i.e. they are approximative rule governed.

To find a solution it is a good idea to look more generally at human behaviour, and according to psycholochical theories for normal human behavior including experts (Piaget 1968), human knowledge is structured in a hierarchical and a sequential way, and whether you are an expert or not only depends on how detailed your knowledge in a particular domain is.

This view is partly supported by (Dreyfus 1986), who describes the transition from novice to expert in five stages, novice, advanced beginner, competent, proficient, and expert. There is a qualitative difference between the first four stages and the fifth, as an expert at this fifth stage solves relevant domain problems in an easy intuitive way without using any mental energy. The operation at this stage has the structure of a simple table lookup.

This gives a model of experts which makes them no different from other persons, except that they have a more detailed mental model (Johnson-Laird 1983) of a specific domain. A real expert works in the following way. His more detailed representation of the domain makes it possible for him to classify the situation to a very high degree, and in this way to make a perfect and unique identification of the present situation. With this identification of the situation he kan choose appropriate procedural actions that will lead him to the wanted solution. For an expert, the corresponding mental model will be so differentiated that it usually gives only one possible action.

From the above charaterization of experts, a naive and premature solution to the problem of intentional game control can be derived. The main idea is to use identification as the basic step and then use planning to find the next action. The action found can then be seen as the next step in the sequenece of steps which eventually in the end will lead to the desired goal. If this primitive movement generator is enhanced with the possibility of replanning whenever the wanted action is impossible, a game in progress will be able to adapt to the changing circumstances only if the control of the program implements cyclic control, or some other method of checking the obtained result. In this way the effect of other interacting agents (Winograd 1986) can be handled effectively.

Planning is the construction of a sequence of movements that may lead to a desired goal (Rich 1991). For planning in any concrete case the result is a sequence of primitive directly executable actions. This kind of planning is most optimal in cases where the desired solution is directly obtainable and can be found by search in the corresponding problem space. Meta-planning is the use of heuristics in the actual planning process.

In fact meta-planning is defined as knowledge about planning (Wilensky 1983), so it can easily be applied to the generation of skeleton plans. These skeleton plans can then in the course of their execution be refined to fit to the actual data. In this way, meta-planning is a way to make high level planning. This skeleton plan can be made more detailed later as the found plan progresses, which means that highly detailed planning is only relevant for the next subplan element, and thus the need for computing power is substantially reduced. In this way meta-planning can be seen as an optimization principle, as it reduces the computing load.

Adaption is the fitting and detailed planning of a high level plan, and it can be very useful in cases where the actual sequence of movements and the corresponding data from a real execution are not available. In these cases it will suffice to classify the movement elements into high level classes and then construct a meta-plan where these classes are the elements of the plan. This of course means that the planning will be imprecise or even faulty. This again means that some initiative has to be taken to correct the actual execution in order to eliminate eventual emerging errors due to this sloppiness in the planning process.

Cyclic control is control using a simple read-eval-write loop (Abelson 1985) with an appropriate grain size (Lewis 1992). The interpretation cycle first identifies the present situation, then the current plan is checked for coherence with that identification. If this is the case, the next step of the current plan is executed, otherwise the rest of the plan is replanned with the present identification of the current situation as the starting point. The third and last step in the read-eval-write loop is to execute the chosen action, and thus creating new data as this execution itself will causally effect the situation, i.e. the plan will continue to make progress one way or the other.

This feedback effect will be mirrored in the data that will be used in the next cyclus of the interpretation loop. In this way the use of a read-eval-write loop with an appropriate grain size can control the execution of a game in progress, even in domains where no concrete knowledge exists. In these cases the planning will be at the error prone meta-level. The trumpet model (Rosenhead 1989)

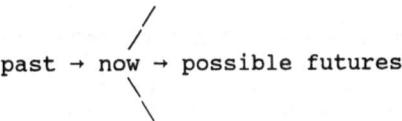

past → now → possible futures

Fig. 2. The future trumpet

which is implemented through the interpretation loop, works very well in ill-defined domains. This is due to the fact that it shows a very high degree of robustness, which just means that using this method gives a better probability for success. This again is due to the fact that the model maximizes the set of possibilities, i.e. it tries to push choice and commitment as far out in the future as possible.

3.1. Problem Related Solution

From the above characterization, a proper solution to the problem of intentional game control can be derived. The ideas defined in the previous section are used here to develop a solution applicable to the nethack game. Any reference to an actual game will refer to the game in progress shown on fig. 1.

Identification is used as the basic step to generate a description of the present situation in the game. This situation description is modified at every move, as it is important to know the states of all important variable values showing the progress gained together with eventual future opportunities. This identification is a description of the state of the game, and it implicitly defines the open possibilities which the set of possible actions have to use in the present situation at the starting point of a plan, in order to achieve any wanted goal.

The values being relevant in all situation descriptions are: the positions of the player @, the monsters d, f, all items $[$, %, and the layout of the cave with notification of the doors +, tunnels # and stairs < that lead to other connected caves (see fig. 1). These values can be used in the planning process to compute the steps, i.e. a sequence of movements, needed to intercept any plan that the machine can infer is used by the human player. In this way the program can create more obstacles or maybe even trap the player, thus preparing the ultimate demise of the player - i.e. the machine wins this game.

Planning is used to find the next action, in which case planning can be described as the generation of a sequence of concrete or meta-level moves to be executed by the machine, which can lead from the present situation to the desired goal state. The planning process schedules only the movements of the monsters, as the movements of the human player are dispelled by the adaptive control. This is done in situations where the movement of the human player interfer with the monster movement plan.

In the actual game, the goal will be to kill the player, and the meta-plan will be to let the two monsters attack. The actual plan is a sequence of moves for the two monsters, like three moves j for the monster f and one move n for the monster d. The most obvious move for the player will be to try to escape through the stair, which unfortunately cannot be avoided in the present case.

The planning process uses a small set of meta-plans for guidance and a small set of subplans that can be applied in most cases. The planner then generates an appropriate sequence of these meta-plans and subplans. Some of the meta-plans are for pursuing and attacking the player. These have the following structure,

$$find\text{-}player \rightarrow get\text{-}close \rightarrow attack$$

Other meta-plans like framing, set-ups and trap generation, contain creative ways for the machine to win the game. This is due to the fact that most traps cannot be foreseen in advance by the human player (Johnson-Laird 1983), but will emerge as true surprises. One way to construct such a trap is to let some gang of monsters sneak in from behind or through a hidden door.

Adaption means the fitting of a detailed planning of any generated meta-plan to the actual data and situation. This includes an eventual replanning whenever the fitted sequence of actions is not possible in the present situation. A game in progress can adapt to these changing circumstances if cyclic control is implemented. Adaption is used where the actual sequence of situations and the corresponding data of an actual execution are not available at planning time.

A trivial case of fitting is when an object or a monster is substituted by another. This occurs when a monster is killed, or when an object that is not vital for the outcome of the current plan is destroyed. A trivial case of detailed planning is when the actual layout of a specific cave cannot be computed in advance, and thus has to be represented by a meta-plan which will in time be substituted by the right subplan, depending on the actual situation. A trivial case of replanning - which in itself is never trivial - is when some vital monster gets killed and the attack plan under progress has to be abandonned, or when a vital object is destroyed and another goal has to be generated, as the original one does not exist anymore.

4. STRUCTURE OF THE HIP EXPERT SYSTEM SHELL

This above characterization of an expert has been used to design a new type of expert system shells (Trans 91), which support the way real experts work, as a *read-eval-write* loop with small step forward chaining. *Read* is a holistic identification of the situation, *eval* finds the corresponding action, and *write* executes it.

The use of a small step forward chaining read-eval-write loop means that the system just executes one operation and then does the loop again, and as a consequence it can follow moving targets as done in the real world with real time applications, or work where it only has partial or incomplete domain knowledge.

4.1. Problem Solving As Cyclic Planning

What is a problem and what is problem solving? A problem can be defined from the relations between a given initial state S and the wanted goal state S'. If the distance

$$\mu|S' - S| > 0$$

where μ is an abstract measure function, it is characterised as a problem. Problem solving is then to find or construct a function f so that

$$f(S) \rightarrow S'$$

The construction of the problem solving function f is called planning. There exists a special form of planning called cyclic planning, where the obtained result from the execution of each small step in the plan is compared with the wanted result of this step, and the step in question may then be modified, if it does not give the wanted result. Otherwise the next step in the ongoing plan is executed.

This kind of planning system is a TOTE (Test Operate Test Exit) system (Pribram 1971), where a plan step is executed (TO) until it satisfies the wanted goal, and then finished (TE). Each element in a plan, as well as the entire plan, can be characterized in this way.

Expert systems were originally intended to be automatic experts that could be used instead of human experts. Expert systems are usually (Rich 1991) structured as rule based systems with rules like

IF <state> THEN <action>

where <state> is the condition for the rule and <action> is the action to be executed if the condition is true. Taken as it is, this is a very primitive kind of system; but the concept may serve as a basic idea for a cyclic planner, if it is seen as

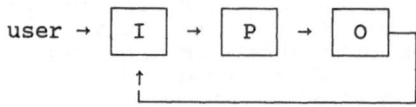

Fig. 3. Cyclic planner

where I is the input module, P is the cyclic planner, and O is the output module. The <state> from the previous model is now the two modules I and P, and <action> is now the O module.

The function of the I module is to make an identification of the data, and this is done hierarchicaly just like humans do (Piaget 1968), and an identification can be viewed as correct if it initiates the corresponding expected action (Kripke 1980). Hierarchical identification is a way of using the internal structure of the knowledge to find the highest and most abstract possible identification of the data. It is done one layer at the time, where the data at one level are classified by the concepts at the level above. The identification is total when one topmost symbol is reached, otherwise it is ambiguous. The hierarchical identification can be done in two modes, as a temporal or as a nontemporal identification, depending on the structure of the knowledge base, and on the stream of data to the input module.

The nontemporal identification is the basic step where the data is identified as a whole, and it has the structure of a tree

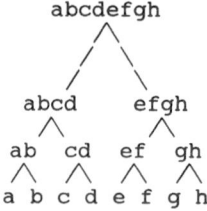

Fig. 4. Nontemporal identification

where the elements {a, b, c, d, e, f, g, h} are identified as the

structure *abcdefgh*. The value of the identification is the root symbol of the tree, and every permutation of the data elements will
give the same value.

The temporal identification is built upon the nontemporal identification, as the nontemporal value found is used as an element in the
temporal identification. This new value and the state of the ongoing
plan are identified at the hierarchical level above them. It has the
structure of a list

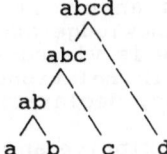

Fig. 5. Temporal identification

where the sequence of nontemporal elements {a, b, c, d} are identified as a temporal structure $a \to b \to c \to d$ under the symbol *abcd*.
This kind of identification corresponds to the understanding of a
sequence of elements as one symbol.

The function of the P module is to find a reaction to the identified
data from the input module I. This reaction is the main part of the
answer from the system, as it is a command to the output module O.
The main basis for the reaction is the state of the planner: it can
be in the middle of a plan, or it can be ready for new assignments.
This planning of an answer can be done in one of the following three
ways: 1. direct action, 2. initiate stored plan, or 3. construct a
new plan. The choice of a planning method is made in the same priority as the above mentioned three ways of planning.

The direct action is the most simple way to choose an action. It
works as a normal S-R (Stimulus Response) system (Pylyshyn 1984). If
the identified data fits in the ongoing plan, the next element of
that plan is executed.

$$\text{identification(data)} \to \text{continue(action)}$$

The second way to find an action is when there is no ongoing plan;
then the data initiate the corresponding response part to the identified situation, if it exits, as an action. This can be simple responses or the initialization and start of a stored plan. This is
what corresponds most to the traditional way of constructing expert
systems as rule based systems

$$\text{identification(data)} \to \text{initiate(action)}$$

The third and last way to find an action is to construct a plan to
solve the posed problem. This is no trivial problem, and there are
many types of solutions to it (Wilensky 1983). The problem is to try
to construct a path in the knowledge base from the symbol for the
actual state to the symbol for the wanted state, and then to modify
the found plan, if it becomes necessary in the course of the execution of the found plan.

$$\text{Identification(data)} \to \text{construct(plan)} \to \text{initiate(action)}$$

An expert system shell like this can be characterized as a state transition machine (Aho 1986), where the state consists of the current state and the actual data, and every executed action and any new data will change the state of the ongoing plan. Those new data serve two goals, firstly as general data about the starting state for the planner, secondly as corrections and feedback to the planner such that it can modify the ongoing plan.

Knowledge Representation

The above defined system is an expert system shell for knowledge based systems, but what is knowledge about, and what can it be used for? In this paper, knowledge is viewed as a symbolic representation of known structures and their relations (Holland 1986). Knowledge can be divided into two types, declarative and procedural.

Declarative knowledge is descriptive and shows the relations between the discrete elements of the knowledge base. The organization is typically networks (Sowa 1984) or frames (Minsky 1985), and it usually has a hierarchical structure.

Procedural knowledge is prescriptive and shows how actions are done and what consequenses they have. The organization is typical in sequences (Piaget 1968) or scripts (Schank & Abelson 1977) which may have a hierarchical structure

Higher orders of declarative knowledge are called meta-knowledge, and this is knowledge about knowledge. Higher orders of procedural knowledge are called plans, and this is knowledge about how to use or act upon knowledge. The distinction between the two kinds of knowledge is not total at the higher levels of knowledge, as an element can belong to both types, depending on the situation and what it is to be used for. An example could be the temporal identification tree above. This can be interpreted as both kinds of knowledge, as a sequence $a \rightarrow b \rightarrow c \rightarrow d$ to be identified as the execution of a plan, or as a hierarchical identification of the same structure $abcd$.

To represent knowledge in an expert system shell it is necessary to have some kind of syntactic structure, a formalism, in which the elements and their relations can be expressed. The HIP system uses a unitary representation that contains both kinds of knowledge, mainly because it is not always obvious to which type a particulair piece of knowledge belongs. The representation uses a five place object vector

    object = (name, supertypes, subtypes, antecedents, consequences)

and the elements of the vector can be defined

$$\begin{array}{c} \text{supertypes} \\ \uparrow \\ \text{antecedents} \rightarrow \text{name} \rightarrow \text{consequences} \\ \uparrow \\ \text{subtypes} \end{array}$$

Fig. 6. Knowledge representation vector

where supertypes and subtypes define the hierarchical structure of the declarative knowledge, and where antecedents and consequences define the position of name in the stored sequences of procedural knowledge. In this formalism most elements are defined as mixed structures. The structures can be used both as declarative knowledge in the identification phase, and as procedural knowledge in the planning phase.

In this representation formalism, meta-knowledge of a symbol is defined as the hierarchical knowledge above the symbol that can be reached by the use of upward inheritance (Rowe 1988). In this representation formalism a plan is defined as a sequence of symbols containing a unique connected chain of (name, consequence) pairs. This is an ordered list of symbols that describes how to get from the first symbol S to the last symbol S' on the list, and this sequence contributes a possible solution to the stated problem. An example of meta-knowledge can be general knowledge about animals, that they are alive, that they breathe, etc. This knowledge is meta-knowledge valid for any animal, and as an elephant is an animal, everything known for animals will hold for any elephant. An example of a plan can be a description of the steps to be done in order to assemble a new chair. It is just a description of the time ordering of the included steps.

4.3. Planning

Of the three kinds of planning which the planner can do, it is only the third - constructing a new plan - that is real planning (Wilensky 1983). The others are just simple control systems, and because these simple methods are always tried first, the real planning method can be seen as a superstructure upon the rest of the system. There are many ways to construct new plans, and this expert system shell uses one that is a generalization of the general problem solving theories in (Piaget 1968), which says that a new plan is always made by concatenating old plans.

A new plan is a path in the knowledge base from the current state to some wanted goal state, and using the current state as a beginning point, a new plan is constructed in three steps.

First, it is checked that the goal symbol is not in the subtype tree beneath the current state, or that it is not an immediate consequence of it. Secondly, the consequences are checked, i.e. whether they have the goal symbol somewhere in their subtrees or as a consequence. This vertical search is continued until the goal is found, or until this vertical level has been searched totally. Thirdly, if the plan has not yet been found, the planner moves one level up in the hierarchy above the starting point and tries whether the first, second or third step is successful from this level.

If this third recursive step does not find the goal symbol, no solution to the posed problem can be found in the current knowledge base. If the goal symbol is found and with this a plan, the planner executes the first element of it, checks the result and then due to the obtained result continues by the next interpretation cycle in one of the three ways of planning according to their priority.

5. HIP-SOLUTION TO THE INTENTIONAL GAME CONTROL PROBLEM

An implementation of the intentional game controller as a forward chaining rule based system (Rich 1991) has been programmed in the HIP expert system shell - not directly in C, like the original net-hack game. This section shows how the methods of identification, planning and adaption are applied in this implementation of the intentional game controller.

The intentional control goals are defined through a priority list that defines the implicit order of the goals. The priorities are: reach win position, set traps, save resources, attack, each priority level having its own set of meta-plans. All the meta-plans share a common set of subplans, as the actual layout and thus the possible set of movement are fairly restricted. The subplans and their over-types (the meta-plans) are represented in a hierarchy to support planning and adaption.

This hierarchy is part of the overall knowledge representation, as the HIP shell uses a uniform representation format. This hierarchy is structured due to the principles of genus and differentia (Sowa 1984) in order to optimize the identification. The basic represented knowledge is for the identification of the current situation and thus for the initiation of appropriate actions. These actions are the above described representations of subplans and meta-plans. This means that the identification supports both the planning and the a-daption aspect of the read-eval-write control loop.

To actually use the knowledge representation for identification pur-poses it is seen as a set of independent hierarchical rules, where each rule has the following structure

$$\text{IF} \bigwedge_{i=1}^{n} \text{subtypes}_i \text{ THEN name}$$

which means that if the entire set of subsymbols of a name is in working memory, then remove the subtypes subset and place name in working memory. All satisfied rules are executed in each cycle. When no more rules can be applied, the resulting interpretation is found as the remaining symbol in working memory. Any ambiguity can be re-solved as described in (Trans 1992).

The inference has to be forward, as it is not feasible to use back-ward chaining in the construction of a hierarchical interpretation. In the worst case all possible interpretations of the text have to be computed. This is due to the definition of the goal to be reached - a hierarchical interpretation - but this is still to be found with forward chaining in a finite search space.

Thus, the identification af a sequence of symbols is performed through one or more cycles of the inference engine. In each cycle all satisfied rules are executed, and when there are no more rules in the conflict set, the sequence is identified. The resulting iden-tification is done according to the possible options for actions that is available in this situation, i.e. whether any standard trap is possible or whether the default plan of plain headless attack has to be used.

The process of planning has been implemented through three different sets of rules, one for each method of planning, and a small set of meta-rules to specify which of the three basic planning rules to apply, and how to define the application domain of the rules. To ac-tually use the knowledge representation for planning purposes, it is seen as a set of independent causal rules, where each rule has the following structure

$$\text{IF name THEN } \bigwedge_{i=1}^{n} \text{consequences}_i$$

Again the inference has to be forward, as any plan is severely constrained by the starting point.

In case of concrete planning the HIP shell initiates a search through the name-consequence links. The goal of the search is some specific situation, and if a subplan that will lead to the wanted goal exists it will be reached in this way.

In case of failure of the above concrete planning the HIP shell initiates the search of a meta-plan by starting a concrete planning from one of the overtypes of the current situation. This is done with all overtypes in the set, and if no solution is found the HIP shell initiates another abstraction and in this way applies concrete planning recursively until the goal situation is found. This will always be the case, even though the final result may be the default plan of attack.

Adaption is used whenever the current plan is not directly executable, mostly due to circumstances that are not controlable by the program, but are due to the human player. Firstly, the HIP shell tries to substitute the present subplan with another one, which will reach the desired goal in the changed situation. Secondly, the HIP shell tries to replan up to the point where the next meta-plan element is situated in the present plan, i.e. the HIP shell tries to fill the gap by constructing a small bridge. Thirdly, the entire plan is replanned if none of the above two options of adaption can be used. This third step will always succeed, as the default plan of attack can be executed in any situation.

6. EXAMPLE

To get an idea of how the intentional game control system will work, when it is implemented in the HIP shell, it might be relevant to look at an extended example.

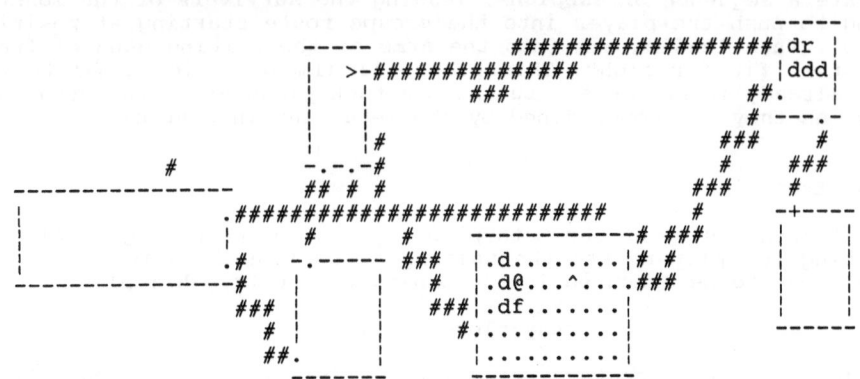

Fig. 7. Nethack game in progress

where the human player @ is in the middle of a game. More precisely
he is in trouble, as the monsters d, d, d, f are trying to frame him
by pushing him away from the stair and towards an arrow trap. The
main setup is that another gang of monsters is waiting at the end of
the most obvious route of escape.

6.1. Identification

The identification of the game situation is done relatively to the
player who will always be at position (0,0). In the game situation
shown in fig. 7. the result of the identification is that the accu-
mulative strength is seven, as one of the monsters has more killing
power as the other four monsters. The positions are good as the monsters are as close as possible (-1,1), (-1,0), (-1,-1), and (0,-1)
to the player. They are in fact all on the right side of the player,
pushing him back against the arrow trap at position (4,0) and the
escape door at position (8,0).

The interesting point is that the situation contains an arrow trap
at position (4,0), and a waiting monster gang at positions (20,9),
(20,10), (20,11), (21,9), and (21,10). This gang is waiting in the
cave at ((20,8),(22,11)), which is situated at the end of the escape
tunnel. This tunnel is at position ((8,0),(19,8)) on the left side
of the player.

6.2. Planning

The present plan is to kill the player through the following meta-
plan of attack,

$$\text{get-close} \rightarrow \text{trap-him} \rightarrow \text{kill-him}$$

which in fact is the default plan of attack with the inclusion of
the trap-him step, as such a trap is available in the present situation. The identification thus supports the current meta-plan step of
pushing the player into the waiting arrow trap or more interesting
into the arms of the waiting monster gang.

In case the player escapes or survives the arrow trap and the subplan of pushing the player into the arrow trap fails, the trap-him
step of the meta-plan has to be replanned. This replanning will generate a sequence of subplans, leading the survivers of the monster
gang to push the player into the escape route starting at position
(8,0), thus leading him into the arms of the waiting gang of fresh
monsters fit for fight. This plan will almost be identical to the
one already in progress - but most attack plans are structured this
way, as they are constrained by the meta-plan in control.

6.3. Execution

The trap-him step of the meta-plan and the corresponding subplan of
pushing the player into the waiting arrow trap is going well. The
next move to be executed is, according to the trap-him plan,

$$\text{stay-close} \longleftrightarrow \text{hit-him}$$

to let the three monsters positioned at (-1,1), (-1,0), and (-1,-1)
attack from the left and letting the fourth monster move down to
wait below at position (1,-2) to intercept one of the possible es-

cape routes. In this way the only open escape route would (hopefully) lead to a disaster for the player.

6.4. Adaption

Adaption can be done at several levels. This is due to the change of goal by goal substitution which is the highest level of adaption, as any higher level of adaption will create a new plan, which cannot be a case of adaption. Another case for adaption is when a monster gets killed and another has to be used instead. The last and most simple case of adaption is the final fitting of the moves to the actual situation. This final fitting means that the controlling meta-plans can be very general and that only a small number of meta-plans is needed, as they can be fitted to suit nearly any situation.

6.5. The Continuing Story

This is the true story of the fall of Bright Brian, a famous Dungeons and Dragons veteran. The actual game will now continue in the following way. The results were obtained through an actual session with this new version of nethack with the author playing the role of Bright Brian.

The player withdraws to the door. Here, he tries to kill the monsters one by one. This is not accomplished, and the player withdraws once more into the tunnel. This has as the result that he ends up being attacked from two sides at the end of the tunnel. This proves to be fatal.

7. EVALUATION

The experiment of applying intentional movement control to the primitive game nethack showed that it is possible to use advanced planning methods to facilitate intelligent games - at least to some limited degree, as the applied intelligence has nothing to do with human intelligence, as it is normally defined (Flavell 1985).

The applied concept of intelligent control can be further developed by the introduction of induction (Holland 1986) and other methods of machine learning (Patterson 1990). These methods can be used to generalize the behaviour of the human player, as this behaviour is usually governed by habits. Once these habits are identified they can be used to predict the moves of the player and in this way the predicted knowledge can be used against him.

8. REFERENCES

Abelson H, Sussman GJ, Sussman J (1985) Structure and Interpretation of Computer Programs. MIT Press, Cambridge MA
Aho AV, Sethi R, Ullman JD (1986) Principles of Compiler Design. Addison-Wesley, Reading MA
Albus JS (1981) Brains, Behaviour, and Robotics. BYTE, Peterborough NH
Dennett DC (1978) Brainstorms. MIT Press, Cambridge MA
Dreyfus HL, Dreyfus SE (1986) Mind over Machine. Free Press, New York NY

242

Flavell JH (1985). Cognitive Development 2.ed. Prentice-Hall, Englewood Cliffs NJ

Holland JH, Holyoak KJ, Nisbett RE, Thagard PR (1986) Induction. MIT Press, Cambridge MA

Johnson-Laird PN (1983) Mental Models. Cambridge University Press, Cambridge

Kernigan BW, Richie DM (1988) The C Programming Language 2.ed. Prentice-Hall, Englewood Cliffs NJ

Kripke SA (1980) Naming and Necessity. Harvard University Press, Cambridge MA

Lewis TG, El-Rewini H (1992) Introduction to Parallel Computing. Prentice-Hall, Englewood Cliffs NJ

Minsky ML (1985) The Society of Mind. Touchstone, New York NY

Patterson DW (1990) Introduction to Artificial Intelligence and Expert Systems. Prentice-Hall, Englewood Cliffs NJ

Piaget J (1968) Six Psychological Studies. Vintage, New York NY

Pribram KH (1971) Languages of the Brain. Prentice-Hall, Englewood Cliffs NJ

Pylyshyn ZW (1984) Computation and Cognition. MIT Press, Cambridge MA

Rich E, Knight K (1991) Artificial Intelligence 2.ed. McGraw-Hill, New York NY

Rosenhead J (ed) (1989) Rational Analysis for a Problematic World. Wiley, Chichester

Rowe NC (1988) Artificial Intelligence through PROLOG. Prentice-Hall, Englewood Cliffs NJ

Sowa JF (1984) Conceptual Structures. Addison-Wesley, Reading MA

Schank RC, Abelson RP (1977) Scripts, Plans, Goals, and Understanding. Lawrence Erlbaum Associates, Hillsdale

Thompson RF (1985) The Brain. Freeman, New York NY

Trans K (1991) An Expert System Shell for Planning with Automatic Feedback Learning. In: Mayoh B (ed) Scandinavian Conference on Artificial Intelligence - 91. IOS Press, Amsterdam, pp 170-175

Trans, K (1992) A Simple Natural Language Interface. In: Leponiemi J (ed) Procedings of NordDATA '92. PITKY, Tampere, pp. 64 - 73

Wilensky R (1983) Planning and Understanding. Addison-Wesley, Reading MA

Winograd T, Flores F (1986) Understanding Computers and Cognition. Addison-Wesley, Reading MA

Kim Trans is assistant professor of computer science at Copenhagen Business School. He is mainly working with the application of hierarchical planning and control to various domains like communication, on-line help facilities, game control, and natural language interfaces. Other areas of interest include artificial intelligence, cognitive modelling and parallel computing.

Trans received his BSc, MSc in computer science from University of Copenhagen, and his Ph.D in computer science from Copenhagen Business School in 1985, 1988, 1992.

Address: Institute of Computer and Systems Sciences, Copenhagen Business School, Rosenørns allé 31, DK-1970 Frederiksberg C, Denmark

Keyframe Animation of Articulated Figures Using Partial Dynamics

KIYOSHI ARAI

ABSTRACT

In this paper, we propose a new method using dynamics to obtain realistic movements of articulated figures used mainly for the generation of human animation. The generation of some portions of the movements in the keyframe animation is accomplished using partial dynamics to enable usage of simpler user-understandable inputs. Experimental results using a human model show that inertial and jumping motions are generated effectively by this method.

Keywords: articulated figures, dynamics, keyframe animation, inertial motion, jumping motion

1. INTRODUCTION

Articulated figures are used mainly for the generation of human animation. There has been much research on the methods applying dynamics to make articulated figures move (Magnenat-Thalmann 1990). Proposed methods using dynamics can be divided into the following classifications:

(1) Specifying forces and torques:
In these methods which are the most fundamental, value inputs of forces and torques are required to control accelerations which generate the motions. Wilhelms (1987) obtained the final motions of a human model by interactive modification of the forces and torques derived from initial motions using keyframes. However, it is not easy to modify forces and torques since they are difficult to grasp for users. There have been some proposed methods not requiring these value inputs for a few particular motions. For example, Bruderlin et al. (1989) generated the walking sequences of a human model by specifying forward velocity, step length and step frequency. Haumann et al. (1992) controlled the hovering flight of a hummingbird by specifying the location and a few properties of the wings of the bird.

(2) Specifying kinematics constraints:
Kinematics constraints such as angles and final joint position enable more user-understandable control than specifying only forces and torques. Isaacs et al. (1987) introduced a matrix which represents the relationships between torques and angular accelerations of all joints. Users can select the easiest input between the torque and the angle which derives the angular acceleration at each joint. Barzel et al. (1988) used forces which guide the object to a specified location. In these methods, however, it is difficult to control the time at which the articulated figure takes the final desired posture. Lee et al. (1990) proposed a method overcoming this drawback by utilizing inverse-kinematics synchronized with inverse-dynamics. Although the trajectory of movement towards the final desired position can be controlled using a load, this method is suitable only for the generation of lifting motions of arms and stand-up motions of legs.

(3) Optimizing a specified function:

Methods using a particular function representing the integral of forces or velocities were also proposed. Realistic motions are obtained by optimizing the specified function. Witkin et al. (1988) showed that this approach enables the generation of springy motions of a simple articulated figure. Kass (1992) constructed an interface which is used for the solutions of general optimizing problems. The weaknesses of the optimization method are the difficulty of specifying the functions for complex motions and the large quantity of optimizing calculations that is required.

(4) Using global dynamics for the entire body:

Girard (1987) used simple dynamics for the postures of the entire body to take into account of the balance of the entire body and its contact with the surroundings. Banking motions to counteract the centrifugal forces and jumping motions governed by gravitational acceleration can be generated. However, this method did not check for interference between the body and the surroundings and thus could not handle collisions.

Usually dynamics is used to simulate the movements governed by muscles. This usage enables the generation of springy motions of articulated figures. Although the motions generated using dynamics are realistic, most of the techniques using dynamics require value inputs of forces and torques which are difficult to grasp for users. Moreover, in the methods using dynamics, it is difficult to give constraints such as keyframes with which the body takes specified postures at specific times. In order to simplify the generation of motion, we propose a new method using partial dynamics for the generation of some portions of the movements in the keyframe animation. Inertial motions are used in which no muscle forces are applied to considerably increase the reality of articulated figures' motion. In addition, inertial motions can be simulated merely with user-understandable inputs, and can be easily inserted into the keyframe animation in which one can directly specify the postures of the articulated figures. Interference is also checked between the body and the surroundings to generate realistic jumping motions. We feel this method is ideally suited for quickly generating animation which does not require full controlled dynamic simulation to achieve the desired realism.

The organization of this paper is as follows. In Section 2 we describe the usage of partial dynamics in the keyframe animation, while in Section 3 we describe the way of deciding the postures of the entire body using inverse-kinematics and interference checks. Experimental results using a human model are presented in Section 4, and a discussion concerning the results is made in Section 5. Concluding remarks are made and further work is discussed in Section 6.

2. PARTIAL DYNAMICS IN THE KEYFRAME ANIMATION

In this section, the usage of partial dynamics in the keyframe animation is described. Users specify angles of joints at the keyframes and values representing joint limits and frictional effects between keyframes. Then partial dynamics is applied on specific parts of the articulated figure during specific intervals between keyframes, and angular accelerations which derive the movements are then obtained automatically.

2.1 Definition of the Articulated Figure

Figure 1 shows the articulated figure used in this method. Let L_c be the link connecting the joint J_c and its neighboring joints J_e at the side facing towards the end. The origin of coordinate system C_c is fixed at the position of joint J_c, and all points within the link L_c are specified using the coordinate system C_c. The relative location of C_c from C_b, which is the coordinate system of J_c's neighboring joint J_b at the side facing towards the base, is represented by a 4x4 transformation matrix M_c. Let J_{base} be the joint at the base. Then M_{base} represents the location of C_{base} relative to the world coordinate system C_{world}. Thus the position of J_c in terms of C_{world} is obtained using a set of transformation matrices such as M_c. L_{end} is the end link attached to J_{end} at the end of the articulated figure.

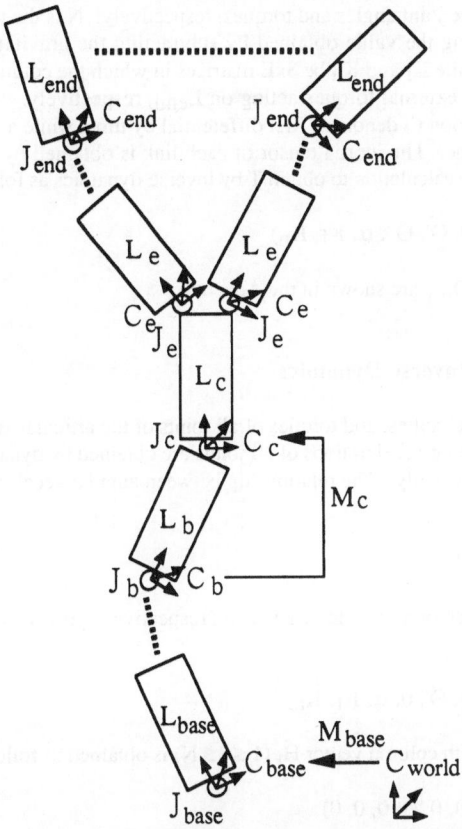

Fig. 1 The articulated figure.

Each joint has one degree of freedom. Joints having two degrees of freedom are treated as two joints each with one degree of freedom connected by one link having no length and no weight. Similarly, joints having three degrees of freedom are treated as three joints connected by two links having no length and no weight. The articulated figure is allowed to branch from the base to the end. For example, in Fig. 1, L_c's neighboring link L_e at the side facing towards the end exists plurally.

Although the articulated figure described here can be used to represent various dynamically-moving objects, we will use it here to represent the moving human body.

2.2   Inverse-Dynamics

When the angles, angular velocities and angular accelerations of all joints of the articulated figure at a specific time are given or calculated, the torques of all the joints are obtained by inverse-dynamics. We adopt the inverse-dynamics methodology proposed by Luh, Walker and Paul (Luh et al. 1980; Walker et al. 1982) based on the Newton-Euler principle. Let Θ and T be $N \times 1$ vectors of which θ_i and τ_i are the i-th components representing the joint angles and torques, respectively. N is the total number of joints. Let α be a 3×1 vector representing the value obtained by subtracting the gravitational acceleration from the acceleration of the base, while K_f and K_n be $3 \times E$ matrices in which the column vectors represent external forces acting on L_{end} and external torques acting on L_{end}, respectively. E is the total number of end joints J_{end}. A single quotation (') denotes a first differential by time, while a double quotation (") denotes a second differential by time. The inertia tensor of each link is obtained by approximating the link as a cylinder. Let us express the calculation to obtain T by inverse-dynamics as follows using a function D_{inv}:

$$T = D_{inv}(\Theta, \Theta', \Theta'', \alpha, K_f, K_n) \tag{1}$$

The details of the function D_{inv} are shown in the Appendix.

2.3   Dynamics Using Inverse-Dynamics

When the angles, angular velocities, and torques of all joints of the articulated figure at a specific time are given or calculated, the angular accelerations of all joints are obtained by dynamics. Calculations are done using inverse-dynamics repeatedly. The relationship between angular accelerations Θ'' and torques T can be expressed as follows:

$$H\Theta'' = T - B \tag{2}$$

B and H are called a bias vector and an inertia matrix, respectively. B is a $N \times 1$ vector and is obtained as follows:

$$B = D_{inv}(\Theta, \Theta', 0, \alpha, K_f, K_n) \tag{3}$$

H is a $N \times N$ matrix and its i-th column vector H_i $(1 \leq i \leq N)$ is obtained as follows:

$$H_i = D_{inv}(\Theta, 0, e_i, 0, 0, 0) \tag{4}$$

In Eq. (4), e_i is a $N \times 1$ unit vector in which only the i-th component is 1 and the others are 0. Let b_i be the i-th component of B. Then b_i represents the torque of the joint J_i if the effect of angular accelerations are neglected. H_i represents the torque of the joint J_i if the effects of gravitational acceleration, acceleration of the base, external forces and external torques are neglected for all components, while the angular acceleration is neglected for all components except for that of J_i, which is set to 1.

2.4   Consideration of Joint Angle Limit and Frictional Effect

When the bias vector B and the inertia matrix H are obtained, Θ'' can be obtained as a function of T. However, the values of T are difficult to grasp for users. Therefore, we generate motions using Θ'' obtained by Eq. (2) in which T is a zero vector. These motions represent passive motions in which inertia must be taken into account for natural and realistic movement. In generating these motions, we consider the limit of joint angles and the effect of friction. Figure 2 shows the process of deciding joint angles. θ_c, θ_t', θ_m', θ_t and θ_d represent respectively the components of Θ_c, Θ_t', Θ_m', Θ_t and Θ_d which are modified forms of the joint angle vector Θ as defined below. Let the current time be t_c, and the next time be $t_d = t_c + \Delta t$, where Δt represents a constant and sufficiently short time duration. The process of deciding each joint angle consists of the following steps:

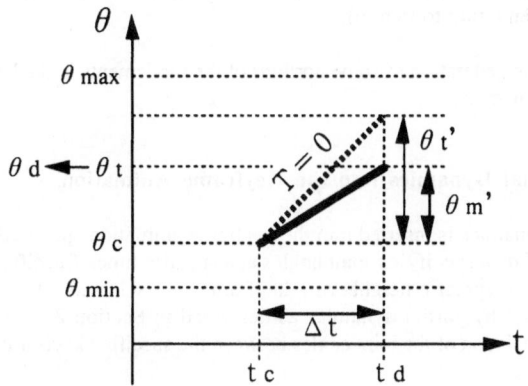

Fig. 2 Process of determining the joint angle using partial dynamics.

(1) Assume that the angle of joints Θ_c and the angular velocity of joints Θ_c' at time t_c are given.

(2) Assign a zero vector to the torque of joints in T at time t_c.

(3) Obtain the bias vector B at time t_c from Θ_c and Θ_c' using Eq. (3).

(4) Obtain the inertia matrix H at time t_c from Θ_c using Eq. (4).

(5) Obtain the angular acceleration of joints Θ_c'' at time t_c using Eq. (2) and the values of T, B and H found in steps (2), (3) and (4), respectively.

(6) Obtain the temporary angular velocity of joints Θ_t' at time t_d from Θ_c' and Θ_c'' using Eq. (5):

$$\Theta_t' = \Theta_c' + \Theta_c'' \Delta t \tag{5}$$

(7) Obtain the modified angular velocity of joints Θ_m' at time t_d by multiplying each component of Θ_t' by a real number in the range of 0 to 1 representing the effects of friction. The joint corresponding to the component multiplied by 0 does not move at all, while the joint corresponding to the component multiplied by 1 moves with absolutely no friction. When returning to this step from step (11) via step (6), the multiplications to the components of Θ_t' corresponding to the components of Θ_t which were assigned new values in step (10) are not executed.

(8) Obtain the temporary angle of joints Θ_t at time t_d from Θ_c and Θ_m' using Eq. (6):

$$\Theta_t = \Theta_c + \Theta_m' \Delta t \tag{6}$$

(9) If every component of Θ_t is within the range between the lower angle limit θ_{min} and upper angle limit θ_{max} of each joint, assign to Θ_t the angle of joints Θ_d at time t_d, and proceed to the next time step.

(10) If there are components of Θ_t not within the range between θ_{min} and θ_{max} of the corresponding joints, assign θ_{min} and θ_{max}, whichever is closest, to the out-of-range components of Θ_t. Then modify Θ_c'' from the modified Θ_t using Eq. (7):

$$\Theta_c'' = ((\Theta_t - \Theta_c) / \Delta t - \Theta_c') / \Delta t \tag{7}$$

(11) Do the following to obtain new values for Θ_c'':
  (a) Assign in Eq. (2) the components of Θ_c'' corresponding to the components of Θ_t assigned new values in step (10).
  (b) Assign in Eq. (2) the components of T corresponding to the components of Θ_t not assigned new values in step (10).
  (c) Using Eq. (2), solve for the remaining components of Θ_c'' and T not assigned new values in (a) and (b). Then return to step (6).

This process is used for the generation of some portions of the movements in the keyframe animation. We call this process partial dynamics.

2.5 Insertion of Partial Dynamics into the Keyframe Animation

In this method, partial dynamics is inserted into the keyframe animation specified by a set of keyframes, each of which consists of data specifying joint angles at a specific time. Specific parts of the articulated figure in intervals between specific neighboring keyframes are selected. The joint angle data of the selected parts are obtained by partial dynamics as described in Section 2.4. The rest of the data are obtained by smooth interpolation of the joint angles between the specified keyframes.

An example of keyframe animation using this method is shown in Figure 3. The keyframes at the times t_1, t_2, t_3 and t_4 are given, and part P of the articulated figure in the interval $[t_2, t_3]$ is selected as the section where partial dynamics is executed. Let the angle and the angular velocity of the joint J at time t_i be θ_i and θ_i', respectively ($1 \leq i \leq 4$). The movement of joint J in P is generated by the following steps:

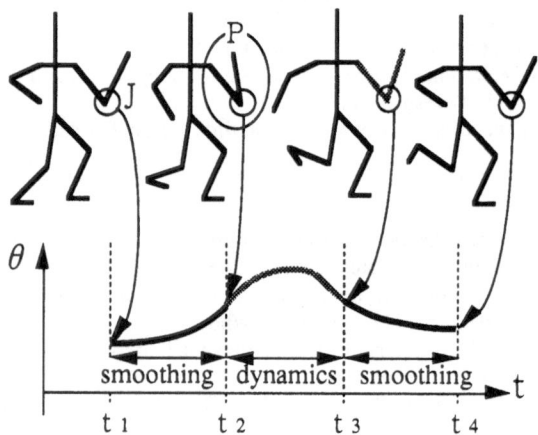

Fig. 3 Insertion of partial dynamics into the keyframe animation.

(1) Obtain the movement in the interval $[t_1, t_2]$ by quadratic interpolation using θ_1, θ_1' and θ_2. Otherwise, obtain the data by cubic interpolation using θ_1, θ_1', θ_2 and specified θ_2'. The angle of the joint θ_2 and the angular velocity of the joint θ_2' at time t_2, which is the beginning of the interval where partial dynamics is executed, can be easily controlled by changing the keyframes. The results of this control affect the calculated results of the partial dynamics.
(2) Obtain the movement in the interval $[t_2, t_3]$ by partial dynamics described in Section 2.4 using θ_2 and θ_2' as the initial values. The values of θ_3 and θ_3' are found from the obtained movement.

(3) Obtain the movement in the interval [t_3, t_4] by cubic interpolation using θ_3, θ_3', θ_4 and specified θ_4'.

In this way, partial dynamics can be easily inserted into the keyframe animation where realistic movements are required.

3. CONSTRAINTS TO DECIDE THE POSTURES OF THE ENTIRE BODY

In this section, the way of deciding the postures of the entire body is described. Users specify simple constraints in specific intervals between keyframes such as fixing the position of joints. The postures are then obtained automatically using inverse-kinematics while considering gravity and interference effects.

3.1 Fixing the Position of Joints Using Inverse-Kinematics

In keyframe animation, it is necessary to calculate the postures of the entire body of the articulated figure in the world coordinate. When the articulated figure comes in contact with the surroundings, forces are applied both to the figure and to the surroundings. However, instead of dealing with these forces, we determine the posture of the entire body by specifying simple constraints. These constraints are used together with the partial dynamics described in Section 2 in the keyframe animation. One constraint involves fixing the position of joints. For example, in the case of generating a walking sequence of a human model, the position of the toe's joint which comes in contact with the ground is fixed. If the movements of the torso in the world coordinate is specified in advance, we use inverse-kinematics to fix the toe's joint.

3.2 Considering Gravity and Interference Effects

The other constraint involves considering the effect of gravity and interference with the surroundings as illustrated in Figure 4. Let the current time be t_c, and the next time be $t_d = t_c + \Delta t$, where Δt represents a constant and sufficiently short time duration. F_c and F_d are the postures of the articulated figure F at times t_c and t_d respectively. The articulated figure is either separated or in contact with the surroundings. In most cases of separation, the gravity is the only external force acting on the articulated figure, while in most cases of contact, at least one joint of the articulated figure is fixed in the world coordinate. Accordingly, the constraint considering gravity and interference effects is given as follows:

(1) Assume that the posture F_c is given.
(2) Let F_t be the temporary posture of F at time t_d which is obtained by tracing the position of F's center of gravity on the assumption that only gravity acts on F as the external force.
(3) As shown in Figure 4(a), if both F_c and F_t interfere or come in contact with the surroundings, modify the position of F_t so that the position of the joint contacting the surroundings is fixed, and let the modified F_t be F_d.
(4) If only F_c interferes or comes in contact with the surroundings, let F_t be F_d without modification.
(5) If neither F_c nor F_t interfere or come in contact with the surroundings, let F_t be F_d without modification.
(6) As shown in Figure 4(b), if only F_t interferes or comes in contact with the surroundings, shift the position of F_t's center of gravity along the line which connects F_c's and F_t's centers of gravity until F_t makes contact with the surroundings, and let the shifted F_t be F_d. If in the next iteration condition (3) is true, then the position of the joint which is the nearest to the contact position will be fixed.

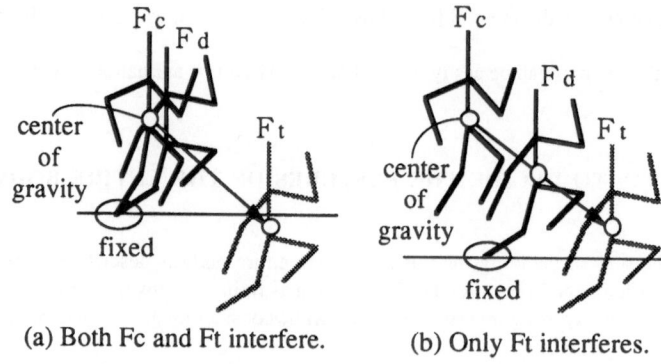

(a) Both Fc and Ft interfere.　　　(b) Only Ft interferes.

Fig. 4 Constraints considering gravity and interference.

Incorporating gravity and interference effects enables the generation of jumping motions of the articulated figure. In checking for interference, each link of the articulated figure is approximated by a cylinder to which hemispheres are attached at both ends, as shown in Figure 5. The surface of the approximated shape is a set of points which are equidistant from the center axis of the cylinder. Therefore, each interference check can be executed rapidly by estimating the distance between the center axis and the surroundings.

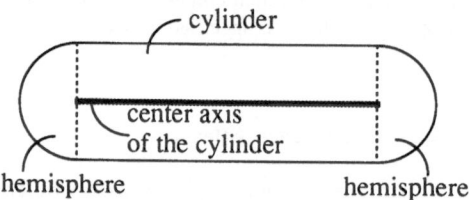

Fig. 5 The approximated shape of each link for interference checks.

4. EXPERIMENTAL RESULTS

Generation of three kinds of motion using a human model was tested by applying the proposed method. A HP9000/835TurboSRX workstation was used for calculating motions and displaying results. Each joint of the human model had initially three axes of rotation. The degrees of freedom and range of joint rotation were then specified by applying limits to the angle of each axis. The time step between neighboring frames was 1/30 second, i.e., each motion was represented in a 30 frames per second format. In the following description, let F_n be the n-th frame, and let K_n be the n-th keyframe. $[K_n, K_{n+1}]$ represents the closed interval between keyframe K_n and keyframe K_{n+1}.

(1) Throwing motion:
A generated result of a throwing motion using the right arm is shown in Figure 6, where the inertial motions of the right arm thrown forward and the left arm swung backward were simulated. The data for this motion consisted of 31 frames from F_0 to F_{30}. It took approximately 3 seconds to generate these data. F_0, F_5, F_{15} and F_{30} were specified respectively as K_1, K_2, K_3 and K_4. In $[K_1, K_2]$, the movements of the body above the waist were obtained by quadratic interpolation, while the movements of the legs were obtained by fixing the joints of both toes using inverse-kinematics. In $[K_2, K_3]$, both arms between the shoulders and the hands were selected and their movements were obtained by partial dynamics described in Section 2.4. The posture of the entire body was determined by fixing the joint of the left toe. In this partial dynamics example, real numbers representing the effects of friction at the joints of the selected parts were set to 0.8 except for that at the joint of the right wrist, which was set to 0.4. In $[K_3, K_4]$, all movements were obtained by cubic interpolation, and the joint of the left toe was specified as fixed.

(2) Walking motion:
A generated result of a walking motion is shown in Figure 7, where the inertial motions of arms were simulated and the motions of legs were adjusted automatically not to slide on the ground. The data for this motion consisted of 41 frames from F_0 to F_{40}. It took approximately 4 seconds to generate these data. F_0, F_{10}, F_{20}, F_{30} and F_{40} were specified respectively as K_1, K_2, K_3, K_4 and K_5. In $[K_1, K_2]$ and $[K_4, K_5]$, partial dynamics was applied on the left arm, while in $[K_2, K_3]$ and $[K_3, K_4]$, partial dynamics was applied on the right arm. Real numbers representing the effects of friction at the joints of the selected parts were set to 0.9 except for that at the joint of the wrists, which were set to 0.4. In $[K_1, K_2]$ and $[K_2, K_3]$, inverse-kinematics was applied on the left leg to fix the joint of the left toe, while in $[K_3, K_4]$ and $[K_4, K_5]$, inverse-kinematics was applied on the right leg to fix the joint of the right toe.

(3) Jumping motion:
A generated result of a jumping motion from a stand to the floor is shown in Figure 8, where the height of the jump, the location of the landing and the time of the landing were obtained automatically. The data for this motion consisted of 31 frames from F_0 to F_{30}. It took approximately 3 seconds to generate these data. F_0, F_{10} and F_{30} were specified respectively as K_1, K_2 and K_3. In $[K_1, K_2]$, the joint of the right ankle was specified as fixed until there was no longer any interference with the surroundings. In $[K_2, K_3]$, the joint of the right ankle was specified as fixed when interference with the surroundings would arise. The constraint described in Section 3.2 was applied. The human model parted from the stand at F_6, reached its highest location at F_{10}, and landed on the floor at F_{18}.

In Figs. 6 - 8, the top row of figures labeled K_i ($i = 1, 2, 3, ...$) represent keyframes, while the bottom row labeled F_j ($j = 0, 1, 2, ...$) represent frames of the generated motions using the method presented in this paper.

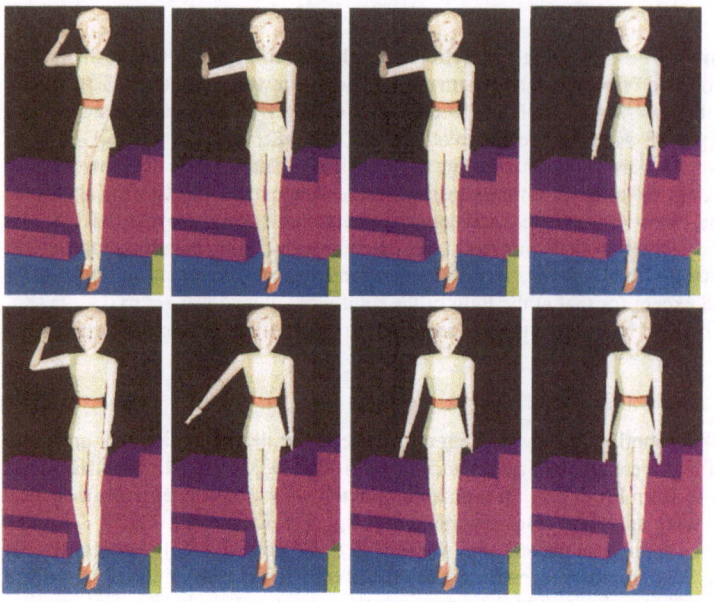

K₁	K₂	K₃	K₄
F_0	F_5	F_{15}	F_{30}
F_3	F_{10}	F_{15}	F_{25}

Fig. 6 Generated result of a throwing motion.

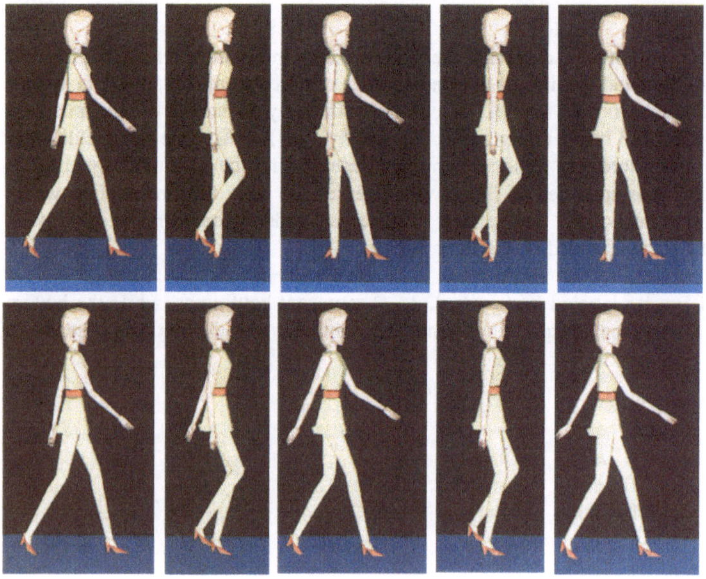

K₁	K₂	K₃	K₄	K₅
F_0	F_{10}	F_{20}	F_{30}	F_{40}
F_0	F_{10}	F_{20}	F_{30}	F_{40}

Fig. 7 Generated result of a walking motion.

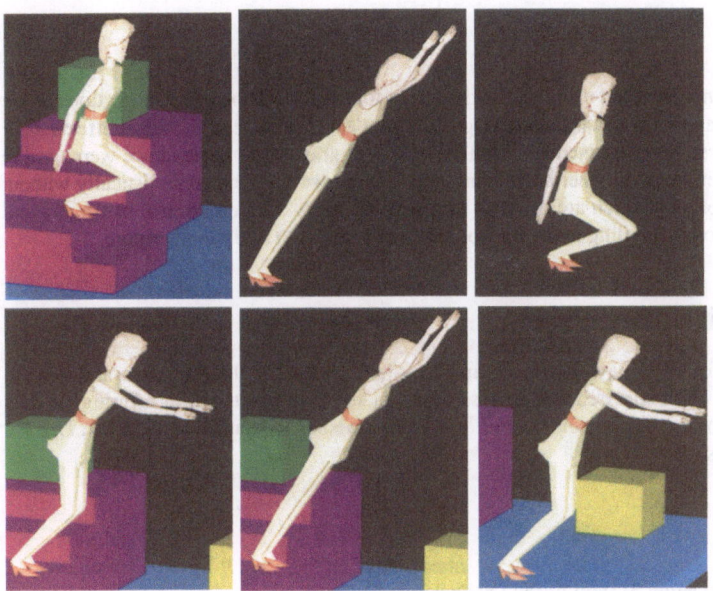

K₁	K₂	K₃
F_0	F_{10}	F_{30}
F_6	F_{10}	F_{18}

Fig. 8 Generated result of a jumping motion.

5. DISCUSSION

In the proposed method, the quantity of the calculations to generate inertial motions is proportional to the cube of the total number of joints included in the parts where partial dynamics is used. Therefore, a large quantity of calculations is required if partial dynamics is used treating the entire body of the human model as one part. However, only a few calculations are required if partial dynamics is used only for a few specific parts, such as arms and legs where joints have large flexibility and inertial motions are generated effectively.

In the experiments using a human figure, finger joints were not controlled. Fingers have many joints, and they are not independent when they move, such as when grasping objects. Therefore, it is difficult to apply the proposed method to the motions of fingers. In order to generate realistic motions of hands, new functions such as that proposed by Magnenat-Thalmann et al. (1988) need to be incorporated.

Motion control using keyframes is more user-understandable than using inputs of forces and torques, and it enables efficient generation of motions. However, making animation can be divided into two cases where movements reflecting the user's intentions are specified in detail or only through global specifications. The proposed method is suitable for the former case, but lacks sufficient functions to satisfy the users' specifications in the latter case. In order to realize such functions, we have to study automatic generation of motions according to the environment such as that proposed by several authors (Haumann et al. 1992; McKenna et al. 1990).

6. CONCLUSION

In this paper, we proposed a new method using partial dynamics for the generation of some portions of the movements in the keyframe animation of articulated figures. Joint angle limits and frictional effects were considered in partial dynamics. Inverse-kinematics and the effects of gravity and interference were used to determine the posture of the entire body. Inertial and jumping motions were generated realistically without using inputs of forces and torques which are difficult to grasp for users. Motion control of fingers and automatic generation of motions according to the environment are subjects to study in the future.

ACKNOWLEDGMENTS

The author would like to thank Tsuneya Kurihara and Ken-ichi Anjyo for their support and helpful discussions. Appreciation is also expressed to Kazuhisa Machida and Seiji Futatsugi for offering the data of the human model used for the experiments. The author also wishes to thank Dr. Peter M. Lee for proofreading and suggestions.

REFERENCES

Barzel R, Barr AH (1988) Modeling System Based On Dynamic Constraints.
ACM Computer Graphics, 22, 4 (SIGGRAPH '88), pp.179-188.
Bruderlin A, Calvert TW (1989) Goal-Directed, Dynamic Animation of Human Walking.
ACM Computer Graphics, 23, 3 (SIGGRAPH '89), pp.233-242.
Girard M (1987) Interactive Design of 3D Computer-Animated Legged Animal Motion.
IEEE CG&A, 7, 6, pp.39-51.
Haumann DR, Hodgins JK (1992) The Control of Hovering Flight for Computer Animation.
Computer Animation '92, pp.3-19.
Isaacs PM, Cohen MF (1987) Controlling Dynamic Simulation with Kinematic Constraints, Behavior Functions and Inverse Dynamics. ACM Computer Graphics, 21, 4 (SIGGRAPH '87), pp.215-224.
Kass M (1992) Inverse Problems in Computer Graphics.
Computer Animation '92, pp.21-33.
Lee P, Wei S, Zhao J, Badler NI (1990) Strength Guided Motion.
ACM Computer Graphics, 24, 4, (SIGGRAPH '90), pp.253-262.
Luh JYS, Walker MW, Paul RPC (1980) On-line Computational Scheme for Mechanical Manipulators.
J. Dynamic Systems, Measurement, Control 102, pp.69-76.
Magnenat-Thalmann N, Laperriere R, Thalmann D (1988) Joint-Dependent Local Deformations for Hand Animation and Object Grasping. Graphics Interface '88, pp.26-33.
Magnenat-Thalmann N (1990) New Trends in the Direction of Synthetic Actors.
CG International '90, pp.17-35.
McKenna M, Pieper S, Zeltzer D (1990) Control of a Virtual Actor: The Roach.
ACM Computer Graphics, 24, 2 (1990 Symposium on Interactive 3D Graphics), pp.165-174.
Walker MW, Orin DE (1982) Efficient Dynamics Computer Simulation of Robot Mechanisms.
J. Dynamic Systems, Measurement, Control 104, pp.205-211.
Wilhelms J (1987) Using Dynamic Analysis for Realistic Animation of Articulated Bodies.
IEEE CG&A, 7, 6, pp.12-27.
Witkin A, Kass M (1988) Spacetime Constraints.
ACM Computer Graphics, 22, 4 (SIGGRAPH '88), pp.159-168.

APPENDIX

The details of the function D_{inv} introduced in Section 2.2 are shown below.

(1) In inverse-dynamics, each link of the articulated figure is approximated as a cylinder. Link L_c's inertia tensor I_c in coordinate system C_c is a 3x3 matrix and its components I_{jk} are obtained as follows:

$$I_{11} = (m_c h_c^2 + 3m_c w_c^2) / 12 \tag{8}$$
$$I_{22} = (m_c w_c^2) / 2 \tag{9}$$
$$I_{33} = (m_c h_c^2 + 3m_c w_c^2) / 12 \tag{10}$$
$$I_{12} = I_{13} = I_{21} = I_{23} = I_{31} = I_{32} = 0 \tag{11}$$

where m_c, h_c and w_c represent respectively the mass, the height and the radius of the cylinder approximating link L_c.

(2) Initial values for the base (J_{base}) are given as follows:

$$\omega_{base} = 0, \quad \omega_{base}' = 0, \quad v_{base}' = \alpha \tag{12}$$

where ω_{base} and v_{base} are 3x1 vectors and represent respectively the rotational velocity and the straight velocity of the base. The value obtained by subtracting the gravitational acceleration from the acceleration of the base is represented by a 3x1 vector α.

(3) The following calculations are executed repeatedly from the base toward the end:

$$\omega_c = \omega_b + z_c \theta_c' \tag{13}$$
$$\omega_c' = \omega_b' + z_c \theta_c'' + \omega_b \times z_c \theta_c' \tag{14}$$
$$v_c' = \omega_b' \times r_c + \omega_b \times (\omega_b \times r_c) + v_b' \tag{15}$$
$$u_c' = \omega_c' \times s_c + \omega_c \times (\omega_c \times s_c) + v_c' \tag{16}$$

where ω_c, ω_b, v_c, v_b, r_c, u_c, s_c and z_c are 3x1 vectors and represent the following values:
ω_c, ω_b : the rotational velocity of joint J_c, J_b
v_c, v_b : the straight velocity of joint J_c, J_b
r_c : the vector from joint J_b to joint J_c
u_c : the straight velocity of link L_c's center of gravity
s_c : the vector from joint J_c to link L_c's center of gravity
z_c : joint J_c's axis of rotation

(4) Initial values for the i-th end are given as follows ($1 \le i \le E$):

$$f_{ext} = K_f e_i, \quad n_{ext} = K_n e_i \tag{17}$$

where f_{ext} and n_{ext} are 3x1 vectors and represent respectively the external force and the external torque acting on each L_{end}. In Eq. (17), e_i is a Ex1 unit vector in which only the i-th component is 1 and the others are 0. E is the total number of end joints J_{end}.

(5) The following calculations are executed repeatedly from the end toward the base:

$$f_c = m_c u_c' + \Sigma f_e \tag{18}$$
$$n_c = A_c I_c A_c^T \omega_c' + \omega_c \times (A_c I_c A_c^T \omega_c) + s_c \times m_c u_c' + \Sigma ((r_e \times f_e) + n_e) \tag{19}$$

where f_c, f_e, n_c, n_e, and r_e are 3x1 vectors and represent the following values:

f_c, f_e : the force acting on L_b from L_c, and on L_c from L_e (f_e is f_{ext} when f_c is f_{end}.)

n_c, n_e : the torque acting on L_b from L_c, and on L_c from L_e (n_e is n_{ext} when n_c is n_{end}.)

r_e : the vector from joint J_c to joint J_e (r_{ext} is the vector from J_{end} to the end of L_{end}.)

A_c is a 3x3 matrix which represents the rotational transformation from coordinate systems C_c to C_{world}. This matrix corresponds to the subset of the product of 4x4 transformation matrices M_{base} to M_c. The superscript T denotes the transpose of a matrix or a vector.

(6) Finally, the torque is found by:

$$\tau_c = z_c^T n_c \qquad (20)$$

Thus T can be obtained from Θ, Θ', Θ'', α, K_f and K_n.

Kiyoshi Arai is a researcher at the Central Research Laboratory, Hitachi, Ltd. He received the B. E. and M. E. degrees from Tokyo Institute of Technology, Tokyo, Japan, in 1987 and 1989, respectively. His research interests include geometric modeling, facial animation and articulated figure animation.
Mr. Arai is a member of IPS of Japan.
Address: Central Research Laboratory, Hitachi, Ltd., 1-280 Higashi-Koigakubo, Kokubunji, Tokyo 185, Japan.
E-mail: arai@crl.hitachi.co.jp

Legged Locomotion Using HIDDS

STEPHANIA LOIZIDOU and GORDON J. CLAPWORTHY

ABSTRACT

The aim of the project was to experiment with the use of dynamic analysis in the manipulation and control of articulated figures for application in computer animation. A hybrid direct/inverse dynamics method was constructed and ground reaction forces were included by use of a virtual leg. Gait determinants were used to provide a parametric description of bipedal walking.

Keywords : figure animation, dynamic modelling, gait determinants, ground reaction forces, virtual leg.

1. INTRODUCTION

The problem of creating an animated motion sequence is quite complicated. Activities of articulated bodies, such as humans, are intricate mainly due to the complexity of the model, which has a large number of joints each with several degrees of freedom and interactions between these joints controlled by muscles. Simplifying the form of the model is an attractive approach to this complex situation, but this is likely to have a detrimental effect on how the model will look, and how realistic its motion will be.

A possible approach, to the research of human figure locomotion, is to combine work on the study of animals (biological systems), Alexander (1983), and the construction of machines and control theory (laboratory robots), as discussed by Raibert (1978, 1986), Craig (1989) and Vukobratovic et al (1990). Although the fields are related, the problems involved are not identical.

The study of **biological systems** proves to be much more complicated than one would expect. It is difficult to formulate experiments that will include and control the numerous variables involved. On the other hand, simple **laboratory robots** are easy to build. Experiments with precise control are possible when careful measurements and manipulations are used. They are easy to study, and the style of their motion is not relevant.

The models used in animation are more complex than most robots and, therefore, present more difficult problems. Moreover, in animation the style of motion is important, as the eye is unwilling to accept even mildly unrealistic motion for bodies as familiar as humans and animals.

Analysis of living systems and synthesis of laboratory systems are complementary activities. In solving the problem for robotics, we can generate a set of plausible algorithms for the biological system. On the other hand, in understanding the biological behaviour, we can enhance the control of the behaviour for the machine.

We have already considered the concept of ground reaction forces (Loizidou 1992), which was aided by research in legged machines. The idea was drawn from research in robotics which led to the development of a one-legged hopping machine by Kearney et al (1991) at the University of Iowa.

A similar approach has been followed for the development of a locomotor-gait controller. Data from biomechanics, prosthetics and anthropometry - Thorstensson et al (1984, 1985), Grillner et al (1979), Nilsson et al (1985) - provided the original estimations and simplifications of motion, which were combined with the use of a direct dynamics algorithm, borrowed from research in robotics (Featherstone 1983, 1987) to develop a model for human walking.

The most serious problem with dynamic motion specification is **motion control**. To allow the user to specify motion under internal muscular control, a reliable, convenient, and positionally-based method must be found. For reasons of clarity, we can split the problem into distinct, but related, levels of control which are described in the next section.

2. LEVELS OF CONTROL

Knowledge about a dynamically-based animation cycle could be considered at three levels : low, middle and high. The lowest level should calculate the joint angles using the dynamic equations of motion. This would then need higher levels of control, where the values of the locomotion parameters could be determined. At the top level, the form of the motion should be specified easily and conveniently using a flexible set of movement commands that generate a variety of motions. The various levels could be specified as follows.

At the **lowest level**, the dynamic equations of motion need to be formulated and solved. The motion is described directly in terms of the generalised coordinates and, depending upon whether an inverse or direct dynamics problem is being solved, either the accelerations or the forces and torques need to be specified explicitly.

The **middle level** is responsible for the definition of gait-specific rules. It determines the locomotion parameters that 'guide' the dynamic simulation of the limbs, it employs the gait determinants, their attributes and rules associated with them. It is used to define and adjust the character of the movement.

The **high level** is responsible for the creation and coordination of the motion. At this level, the motion is specified generically, employing everyday concepts to determine the style of the movement, such as '*walk happily*' or '*walk vigorously*'. These commands would be translated automatically into the corresponding parametric descriptions of the motion, so that even a non-expert user could control the movement. For this, a good user interface and a well-defined, unambiguous specification language are essential. Of course, the animator will always be able to adjust the form of motion by specifying parameters at the middle level, which will then be translated into the lower level of control, for the solution of the dynamic equations of motion.

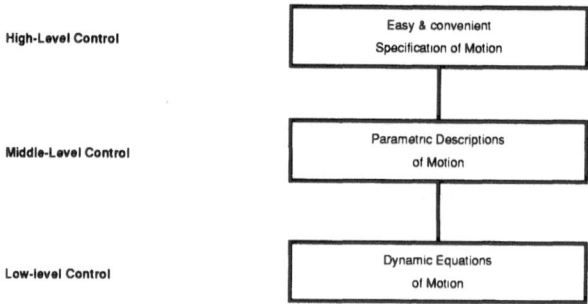

Fig.1 - Levels of the Control Hierarchy

Figure 1 gives a structural outline of the levels of control as they are described above. Such a high-level control system inevitably involves considerable complexity, and in the literature associated with this field of study, no-one as yet has tried to implement such a system. The work described in this paper is particularly concerned with the design and implementation of the middle level of control, i.e. describing the motion parametrically, but the construction of a high-level system is a goal for future development.

3. A GENERIC LOCOMOTION PATTERN

In legged locomotion, the body translation results from rotational movements in the lower limbs. Certain problems need to be addressed, such as the coordination of the legs, the balancing of the upper body with respect to the movement and the correct timings of the individual leg motions (Bruderlin & Calvert, 1989).

To reduce the amount of detail necessary to define a motion, a system should possess **goal-directed control** so that tasks can be specified at a high level, in order to produce fine control of the style of motion. Our initial attempts, based on the hierarchical model of Figure 1, have concentrated on walking, for which the parameters are quantities such as velocity, step-length, step-frequency, and a variety of gait determinants.

Human Locomotion

Motion is an important activity of our every-day life, but the manner of motion, the *'how?'*, is a question that is asked very rarely. All people move constantly, though few realise how complex their movements are, and even fewer stop to analyse how these movements come about. Yet it is through their movements that people have the means to interact with their environment, to express their feelings and to relate meaningfully to one another.

Human locomotion is a phenomenon of most extraordinary complexity. Because of this complexity, the study of human movement in all its forms may be conducted from many points of view. Human walking produces a translation from one location to another by means of a bipedal gait. Many individual motions occur simultaneously, making analysis difficult without the possession of some unifying principle. The concept of gait determinants and the different parameters involved will be introduced and examined, to enable a higher level of control to be developed.

We, therefore, need to study carefully the primary determinants of human locomotion, as well as to record and measure the magnitudes, directions and rates of change of the translations, rotations and forces occurring in the body. These will be the main topics of discussion of the next sections.

4. HIGHER LEVELS OF CONTROL IN HUMAN WALKING

Walking is a smooth, highly-coordinated, rhythmical, symmetric movement in which the body moves step by step in the required direction at the necessary speed. It incorporates the concepts of **gait**, the manner of walking, and of **locomotion**, the act of moving from place to place.

One of the chief attributes of a normal gait is the wide range of safe and comparatively comfortable walking speeds available. Speed is variable as a person hurries, hesitates, stops or starts. All gaits have certain common characteristics. The lower extremities provide the major action in walking, with additional involvement of the head, trunk and arms.

For simplification, walking is broken into two phases - the stance and the swing phase - and these are further broken into subphases. The **stance phase** is the period of double support where both feet are on the ground, whereas the **swing phase** is the single support state where one foot is off the ground. Accordingly, since each lower limb goes through a stance and a swing phase, we can define a stance and a swing leg. In walking, one foot is in contact with the ground at all times.

For bipedal walking, a locomotion (or gait) cycle consists of a step each by the right and left lower limbs. That is, the limbs pass through both the stance and the swing phases and return to their original relative position at the beginning of the cycle. The stance and swing phases of a locomotion cycle are examined separately, which greatly simplifies the control as well as the numerical integration process. For practical purposes, this can be reduced to one step if a symmetric gait in a straight line is assumed, with left and right sides performing symmetric movements shifted in time.

The high-level concepts need to be applied before the impending step, whereas low-level motion control takes place during the step. In this way, locomotion parameters can be changed from step to step. The dynamics formulation is subject to the step constraints and produces the desired motions during a phase by applying rules about walking directly at the low level. This is the reason why phases are further divided into subphases.

In the following sections, we examine in more detail how this control hierarchy has been implemented in our system **AnthroPI** (Anthropomorphic Programming Interface) which is the graphics editor (Loizidou 1992).

Control Principles

The execution of the different components in AnthroPI is based on the four principles identified below.

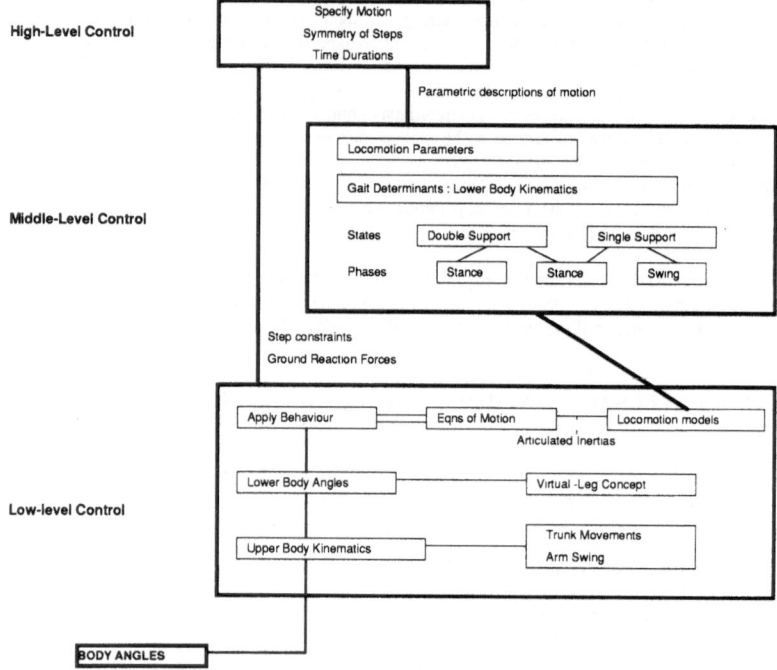

Fig.2 : Levels of Control Hierarchy in AnthroPI

1. The control hierarchy as illustrated in Figure 2 is applied to each step of a walking sequence, where a step is defined as the double plus the single support state (see also Figure 3). High-level instructions are decoded before the impending step, and low-level actions are executed during the step. The system offers the capability of changing the locomotion parameters from one step to the next.

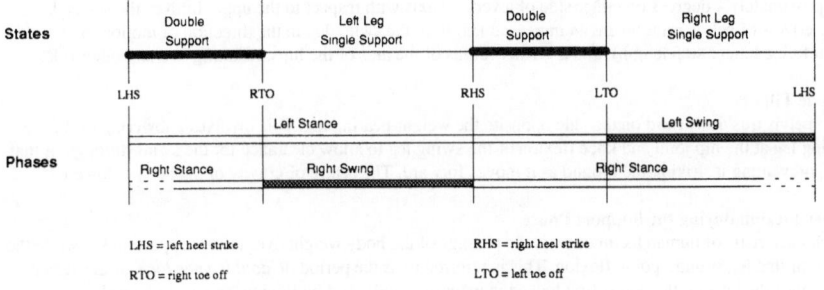

Fig.3 : Locomotion Cycle for Bipedal Walking

2. The dynamic equations of motion guide the lower body kinematics, but the kinematic computations, such as the gait determinants, may affect the dynamics. Of course, it is always the case that dynamics is at the very heart of the control because it guarantees natural-looking rotational movements of the legs and of the whole hierarchical structure of the body, though it is aided by the use of kinematic principles.

3. The upper body movements follow and depend upon the lower body movements. For example, the movements of the torso and arms need to be expressed relative to the movements of the legs (e.g. right arm swings forward at the same time as the left leg is pushed forward). This is the reason why the root of the structure needs to be changed to the corresponding foot in contact with the floor before starting the dynamic analysis.

4. The stance and swing phases of each individual leg are considered separately which greatly simplifies the control. Therefore, for each leg, the simulation of the stance phase is executed first followed by the swing phase dynamics. The symmetry of steps is applied here for the next dynamics calculation. Note that while one leg is in the swing phase, the other is in the stance phase.

Upon definition of the above specific rules, the concept of **determinants of gait** needs to be introduced. Although there is no unique convention in describing the motions of the links during walking, one description given by Saunders et al (1953), and discussed by McMahon (1984a, b), involves the consideration of six major determinants which are related to the function of the hip, knee and ankle during walking. Theoretical definitions of the gait determinants based on Saunders' work are introduced in the following section.

The Determinants of Gait

The gait determinants mainly describe the movements of the pelvis during locomotion. Careful observations of these determinants provide insight into individual variations of the gait.

For analytical purposes, we also consider the behaviour of the centre of gravity in a bipedal model, in which the lower extremities are represented by rigid limbs. This knowledge is needed to link the ground reaction forces with the concept of gait determinants.

The major determinants in normal gait of human locomotion are : pelvic rotation, pelvic tilt, knee motion during the support phase, foot and ankle motion, knee motion during the swing phase, and lateral motion of the pelvis.

Pelvic Rotation
The pelvis rotates alternately to the right and to the left at each hip joint, relative to the line of progression (approximately 4 degrees on either side of a vertical axis with respect to the upper limb of the stance leg). The effects of pelvic rotation are an increased length of the swing leg in the direction of motion (and therefore a longer step length), and a greater radius of the arcs of the hips, resulting in a smoother ride.

Pelvic Tilt
The pelvis tilts downward on the side opposite the weight-bearing leg. This involves a lowering of the swing leg at the hip joint and knee flexion of the swing leg to allow clearance for the swing-through of that leg, preventing it striking the ground as it moves forward. The centre of gravity of the body is lowered.

Knee Flexion during the Support Phase
A characteristic of human locomotion is the passage of the body weight over to the supporting leg while the knee of that leg is undergoing flexion. This is referred to as the period of '*double knee lock*' of the stance leg, since the knee of that leg is first locked in extension, unlocked by flexion, and again locked in extension prior to its final flexion.

Foot and Ankle Motion
This involves the transition from double-support phase to swing phase by smoothing out the path of the centre of gravity. It comprises the relation of the rotation of the ankle about a radius formed by the heel, and the rotation of the foot about a centre established at the fore part of the foot in association with heel rise.

Knee Flexion during the Swing Phase
At heel contact the knee joint is fully extended, so that the extremity is at its maximum length and the centre of gravity reaches its lowest point in downward displacement. Rapid plantar flexion of the foot, associated with the initiation of knee flexion, maintains the level of the centre of gravity. The termination of this is associated with flexion of the second knee at heel rise.

Lateral Displacement of the Pelvis
The body rocks from side to side since weight bearing is alternately transferred from one limb to the other. The centre of gravity is displaced laterally over the weight-bearing leg, twice during the cycle of motion.

The three determinants of gait : **pelvic rotation**, **pelvic tilt** and **knee flexion**, all contribute to the flattening of the arc through which the centre of gravity of the body is moved. Pelvic rotation elevates the extremities of the arc, whereas pelvic tilt and knee flexion depress its summits. The deviations of the centre of gravity in the horizontal and the vertical planes are almost equal.

The relative lengthening of the extremities considerably reduces the range of flexion and extension, at the hip joint, required to maintain the same length of stride. It also plays an exceedingly important role in permitting increased velocities of gait, since greater velocities of locomotion are achieved by the lengthening of the stride rather than by increases in cadence.

Individual variations in locomotion are due to exaggerations in one, or another, of the six determinants. Owing to the interactions between the various factors, exaggerations in the range of one determinant are compensated for by reductions in another, so that the final pathway of the centre of gravity remains essentially the same in that it is the most economical to maintain.

We have experimented with the application of subsets of these parameters, building on the early work of Vasilonikolidakis & Clapworthy (1991). To construct a model which corresponds as closely as possible to the results produced from physiological and photographical studies, as well as biological research, the gait determinants and the correct time durations were introduced and included in the implementation of the dynamic analysis.

The gait determinants taken into consideration included the pelvic rotation, pelvic tilt, knee flexion during the support phase and knee flexion during the swing phase. In particular, the motion of the trunk was determined by the rotations that propagated from the root of the motion to the kinematic chains, i.e. the torso and the lower body, in addition to the application of the gait determinants. These were introduced in the model as kinematic constraints if the motion of the anthropomorphic figure was outside the specific, allowable, range. Upper and lower limits were employed. In this way, the gait determinants restricted the motion to the specified limits. Similar techniques were employed for the motion of the legs and arms.

Implementation of the pelvic rotation involved the left and right rotation at the hip joint where the pelvic angle was in the predetermined range of -4..4 degrees. Similarly, the pelvis was allowed to tilt on the side opposite the weight-bearing leg (-5..5 degrees), and an internal force was applied to generate these movements. The rotation of the pelvis is a maximum at foot contact and a minimum at mid-step, whereas the pelvic tilt is a maximum at mid-step and a minimum at foot contact. Linear interpolation was used to obtain the intermediate angles, which is justified since the absolute displacements produced by the determinants are rather small.

Knee flexion during the support phase introduced a kinematic constraint at the knee angle which made the leg flex, lock and flex again. The angle of the knee flexion was dependent upon the step length or the step frequency of the particular gait. For example, a larger step length resulted in a larger knee angle. Knee flexion during the swing phase was necessary in maintaining the level of the centre of gravity and depended upon the step length or the step frequency.

Time Durations and Locomotion Parameters

Walking can be varied by changing the values of the step length and step frequency

$$\text{velocity} = \text{step\_length} * \text{step\_frequency}.$$

To specify conveniently a desired locomotion we need to define two of the three locomotion parameters : velocity, step length and step frequency. We therefore need to transform the three locomotion parameters into the step constraints for low-level control. Experimental results, Inman et al (1981), relate walking speed to the time needed to perform a cycle. Correct time durations of a locomotion cycle have also been calculated by Bruderlin & Calvert (1989) and Boulic et al (1991).

Experimental data (Inman et al, 1981) shows that,

$$\text{step\_length} = 0.004 * \text{step\_frequency} * \text{body\_height}$$

and therefore

$$(\text{step\_frequency})^2 = 250 * \text{velocity} / \text{body\_height} .$$

Measurements imply that the maximum value of step_frequency is 182 steps per minute. From the step frequency, we can calculate the time for a cycle

$$t_{cycle} = 2 * t_{step} = 2 / \text{step\_frequency},$$

and the times for the double support, t_{ds}, and single support phases (see Figure 3), since,

$$t_{step} = t_{stance} - t_{ds} \qquad \text{and} \qquad t_{step} = t_{swing} + t_{ds} .$$

Furthermore, from experimental results (Inman et al, 1981),

$$t_{ds} = (-0.0016 * \text{step\_frequency} + 0.2908) * t_{cycle} .$$

In this fashion, the step frequency is used together with symmetry of steps to calculate the time for each phase of a step. This will sufficiently represent the movements of one cycle.

Virtual-Leg Concept

An algorithm for controlling a one-legged hopping model (Kearney et al, 1991) was adapted for use in evaluating ground reaction forces. During the double support phase of bipedal walking, both legs are in contact with the ground. The method thus has to deal with the situation in which there are two points of contact. This led to the creation of a **virtual leg** which represents the pair of legs acting in unison and which is active only during the double-support phase. Similar proposals have been made by Raibert & Hodgins (1990) and Raibert (1986), who also referred to work by Sutherland (1983).

The two physical legs behave like one virtual leg, located between them. The forces and torques exerted on the body by the two physical legs and by the virtual leg are equal, so the behaviour of the body is the same in both cases. For the implementation of the virtual-leg concept, a set of operations needs to be defined : positioning, synchronisation and force equalisation.

Force-equalisation for the double-support phase, for example, locates the virtual leg between the two physical legs that it represents. It makes the resulting behaviour simple to analyse and similar to that of the one-legged systems. **Positioning** places the physical feet which determine the location of the virtual foot. **Synchronisation** ensures coordination of the behaviour of the physical legs.

The virtual-leg approach discards the passive stability that the two legs can provide, in favour of active stability. In this fashion, the control system must coordinate the low-level behaviour of the physical legs and must provide locomotion algorithms that specify the desired behaviour for the virtual leg. This is summarised in Figure 4.

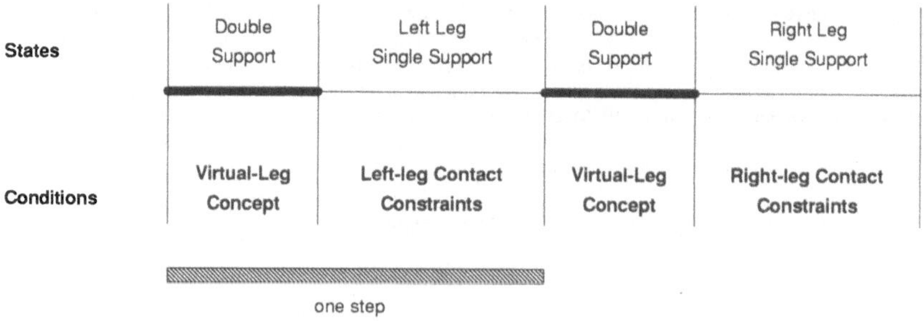

States	Double Support	Left Leg Single Support	Double Support	Right Leg Single Support
Conditions	Virtual-Leg Concept	Left-leg Contact Constraints	Virtual-Leg Concept	Right-leg Contact Constraints

one step

Fig.4 : Virtual-Leg Concept

In Figure 5, r_r represents the virtual leg of the right leg, and similarly r_l the virtual leg of the left leg. To achieve a smooth transition of the virtual leg from the double to the single support phase, the following expression is introduced which relates the positions of the left and right physical legs, that is,

$$r = a\,r_l + (1\text{-}a)\,r_r$$

where the coefficient a, takes values in the range $0 < a < 1$. Further, a is time dependent and its value is chosen to change linearly with time.

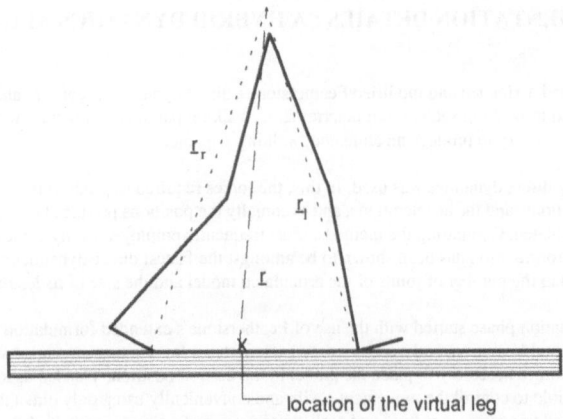

location of the virtual leg

Fig.5 : Double-Support Phase

Figure 6 illustrates the position of the virtual leg when the two physical legs are in contact with the ground. In Figure 6(a), the left leg is ready to touch the ground and become the stance leg whereas the right leg is in contact with the ground. The virtual leg is positioned at the right leg, and therefore a = 0.

Similarly, transition from the double-support position to the case where only the left leg is in contact with the ground, Figure 6(c), will result in having the position of this leg identical to the position of the virtual leg (a = 1). Transition from single support to double support will result in an in-between position, Fig.6(b), and this can be further interpolated to consider intermediate stages.

Defining a to be linear in time is a straightforward approach, but a smoother transition from the single- to the double-support phase could possibly be achieved by use of a cosine or a cubic function.

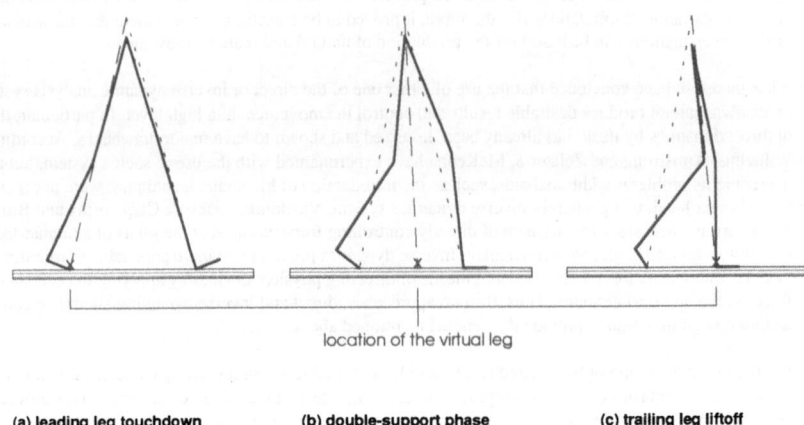

location of the virtual leg

(a) leading leg touchdown   (b) double-support phase   (c) trailing leg liftoff

Fig.6 : The Virtual Leg - Two Legs with Ground Contact

5. IMPLEMENTATION DETAILS : A HYBRID DYNAMICS ALGORITHM

Having described, extended and modified Featherstone's direct dynamics algorithm and examined the concepts related to walking such as gait determinants, walking parameters together with the time durations, the next step was to try to produce an animated, walking sequence.

Initially, purely direct dynamics was used. In this, the forces required to produce the motion are entered into a system of equations, and the accelerations, and eventually the positions produced under the influence of these forces, are calculated. Comparing the methods. most frequently employed for dynamic analysis, Featherstone's formulation has been shown to be amongst the fastest direct-dynamics algorithms, as it is linearly related to the number of joints of the articulated model and the size of its leading coefficient is small.

The implementation phase started with the use of Featherstone's extended formulation which, although producing acceptable motion, had a serious drawback in that a lot of experimentation was required to determine the forces necessary to place the model in the desired position. This led us to the conclusion that it was not possible to control the movement easily and conveniently using only direct dynamics. Additional aids were needed to guarantee natural and realistic motion, and a simple method of motion specification.

Thus HIDDS (Hybrid Inverse and Direct Dynamics System) was developed to achieve a fully dynamically-animated walking sequence. HIDDS included the use of both the inverse and direct dynamics equations of motion. Featherstone's direct dynamics algorithm had to be reformulated and used as an inverse dynamics system. Once this reformulation was applied and tested, it was combined with the direct dynamics approach.

The resulting hybrid system therefore consists of two sub-systems, the direct and the inverse one, Loizidou & Clapworthy (1992) . A call of HIDDS initialises the values of the inertia tensors, the masses, dimensions and coordinates of all the links and joints of the model, and then transfers the control to the inverse dynamics sub-system. This sub-system requires the determination of the final positions of all the links of the hierarchical structure of the model. It calculates the forces necessary to be applied to each link of the hierarchy, then initialises the evaluation of the direct dynamics sub-system for the calculation of the accelerations. From these, the positions of the model for the next iteration are found. Once the initial stage of the motion is reached, HIDDS needs to be used as an experimental tool to provide the 'guide' as to where the motion has to be directed to provide the required results.

The introduction of HIDDS solved most of the problems associated with the use of either one of the direct, or inverse dynamics formulations. Furthermore, it proved to be a useful and convenient tool on which further investigations can be based for the production of natural and realistic movements.

It has therefore been concluded that the use of either one of the direct or inverse dynamic analysis systems, on its own, cannot produce desirable results and control the movement at a high level. In particular, the use of direct dynamics by itself, has already been discussed and shown to have major drawbacks. Accordingly, Wilhelms, Armstrong and Zeltzer & McKenna have experimented with the use of such a system, but to overcome its problems additional aids, such as the introduction of kinematic techniques, were necessary. On the other hand, using a purely inverse dynamics system, Vasilonikolidakis & Clapworthy and Bruderlin & Calvert, the necessary requirement of directly controlling forces/torques at the joints of a human-like model was very difficult and inconvenient. Inverse dynamics proved to be more applicable to robotics models, where actuators can be used as a means of directing physical devices by applying the calculated forces at the appropriate joints. Thus, the two approaches, direct and inverse dynamics, should be combined and used in conjunction to provide the benefits mentioned above.

For the implementation of the desired results and for the production of a walking cycle, an animation environment, AnthroPI (Anthropomorphic Programming Interface) has been constructed. This provided a convenient system for, firstly, specifying the motion required and initialising the dynamics equations of motion and, secondly, presenting the results graphically. The system is completely interactive and allows its user to specify the motion at any level of control that he/she wishes.

It employs configuration files for initial estimates of all the parameters necessary, such as masses and inertia tensors; it enables the coordinate systems and dimensions to be defined, likewise the position of the root and the order of traversal of the tree; it presents the model as a hierarchical structure; it permits the locking of degrees of freedom; it provides menus for selecting different options, calling the system and its sub-systems, as well as displaying the sequence at the required pace. The motion can be stored in, or read from, files, allowing a sequence to be replayed. A play-back facility enables individual frames to be stored in different files and played back successively, in almost real time.

The human model used for this purpose had the necessary links and joints to be recognised as anthropomorphic, and therefore, to enable the visualisation of its movements. Anthropometric data and biological studies provided the correct values for the dimensions of the model.

6. CONCLUSIONS AND FUTURE DIRECTIONS

The use of dynamics showed that such a system has the potential, with further development, to produce realistic, natural and coordinated human motion. The results proved that it is feasible to create an animation system, in particular an animated walking sequence, for articulated figures that offers an easy user interface, and it is independent of the configuration of the model. Such a system can be used as the basic platform from which further investigations can take place.

Research needs to be directed towards the development of a learning control system, possibly an expert database. The useful mechanism of correcting and refining the motion needs to be incorporated. Furthermore, figures could interact in parallel through message passing, to reduce computational costs. Such a proposed, high-level system could be used to create visual worlds through the use of a computer, and aid the large list of applications related to this area. The topic has still broad and fertile prospects for future research. The possibilities are endless.

References

Alexander R (1983) *Animal Mechanics*. Blackwell Scientific Publications

Boulic R, Renault O (1991) 3D Hierarchies for Animation. In : N Magnenat-Thalmann, D Thalmann (eds), *New Trends in Animation and Visualization*, John Wiley & Sons

Bruderlin A, Calvert T (1989) Goal-Directed Dynamic Animation for Human Walking. *ACM Computer Graphics*, 23(3):233-242

Craig J (1989) Introduction to Robotics Mechanics and Control (2nd ed). Addison-Wesley Publishing Co.

Featherstone R (1983) The Calculation of Robot Dynamics Using Articulated Body Inertias. *International Journal of Robotics Research*, 2(1):13-30

Featherstone R (1987) *Robotic Dynamic Algorithms*. Kluwer Academic Publishers

Grillner S, Halbertsma J, Nilsson J, Thorstensson A (1979) The Adaptation to Speed in Human Locomotion. *Brain Research*, 165:177-182

Hodgins J, Raibert M (1990) Biped Gymnastics. *International Journal of Robotics Research*, 9(2):115-132

Inman V, Ralston H, Todd F (1981) *Human Walking*. Williams & Wilkins, Baltimore/London

Kearney J, Hansen S, Cremer J (1991) *Programming Mechanical Simulations*. 2nd Eurographics Workshop on Simulation and Animation, Vienna.

Loizidou S (1992) *Dynamic Analysis of Anthropomorphic Manipulators in Computer Animation*. Ph.D. Dissertation, University of North London.

Loizidou S, Clapworthy G J (1992) *HIDDS - Hybrid Inverse and Direct Dynamics System for Human Figure Animation*. 3rd Eurographics Workshop on Animation and Simulation, Cambridge

Loizidou S, Clapworthy G J (1991) *Dynamic Analysis with Recursive Propagation for Motion Control in Human Figure Animation.* Proc. CompuGraphics '91, Sesimbra, Portugal

McMahon T (1984a) *Muscles, Reflexes and Locomotion.* Princeton University Press, Princeton NH.

McMahon T (1984b) Mechanics of Locomotion. *International Journal of Robotics Research*, 3(2):4-28

Nilsson J, Thorstensson A, Halbertsma J (1985) Changes in Leg Movements and Muscle Activity with Speeds of Locomotion and Mode of Progression in Humans. *Acta Physiol Scand*, 123:457-475

Raibert M (1978) Manipulator Control using the Configuration Space Method. *The Industrial Robot*, 69-73

Raibert M (1986) *Legged Robots that Balance.* The MIT Press, Cambridge, Massachusetts

Saunders J, Inman V, Eberhart H (1953) The Major Determinants in Normal and Pathological Gait. *Journal of Bone and Joint Surgery*, 35-A(3):543-558

Sutherland I (1983) *A Walking Robot.* Pittsburgh : The Marcian Chronicles, Inc

Thorstensson A, Oddsson L, Carlson H (1985) Motor Control of Voluntary Trunk Movements in Standing. *Acta Physiol Scand*, 125:309-321

Thorstensson A, Nilsson J, Carlson H (1984) Trunk Movements in Human Locomotion. *Acta Physiol Scand*, 121:9-22

Vasilonikolidakis N, Clapworthy G J (1991) Design of Realistic Gaits for the Purpose of Animation. In : N Magnenat-Thalmann, D Thalmann (eds), *Computer Animation '91*, Springer-Verlag, 101-114

Vukobratovic M, Borovac B, Stokic D (1990) *Legged Locomotion.* Springer-Verlag, Berlin

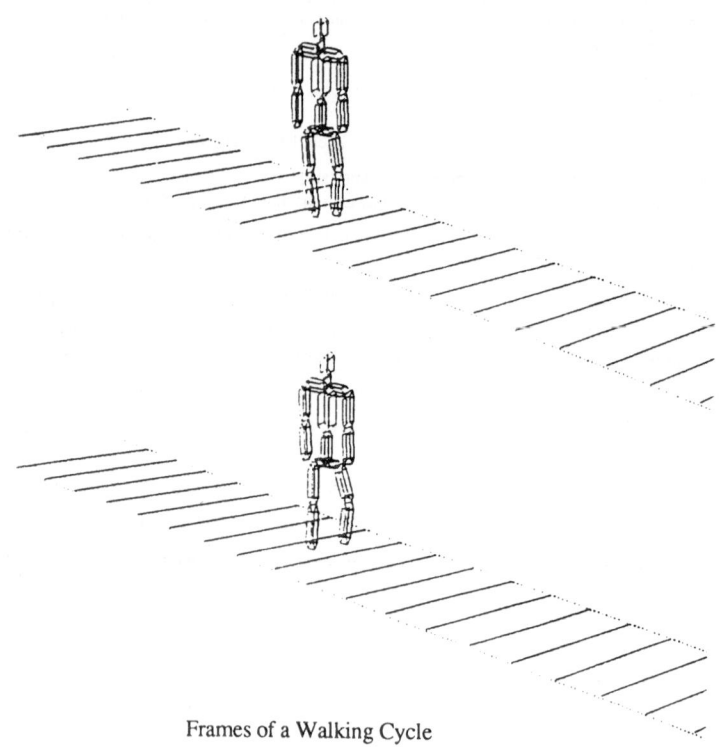

Frames of a Walking Cycle

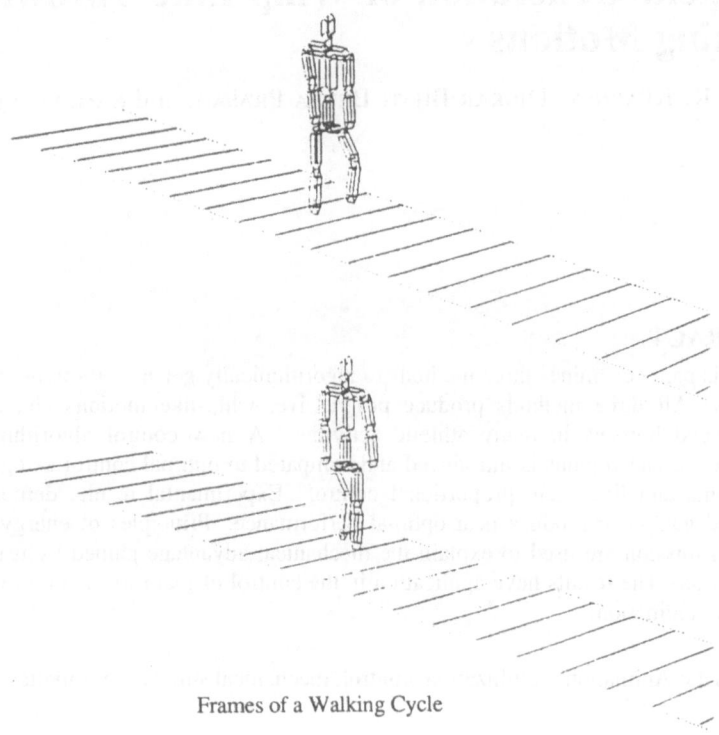

Frames of a Walking Cycle

BIOGRAPHY

Stephania Loizidou received her BSc in Computer Science and Mathematics from the Polytechnic of North London in 1988 and a PhD in Computer Science from the University of North London in 1992. Her research interests include computer animation, particularly of human-like, articulated bodies, and animation using physical modelling.
Address : P. O. Box 1589, Limassol, CYPRUS.

Gordon Clapworthy is Principal Lecturer in Computing and Mathematics at De Montfort University, Milton Keynes, having previously been at the Polytechnic of North London. He received a BSc in Mathematics and a PhD in Aeronautical Engineering from the University of London and an MSc in Computer Science from the City University. His research interests include computer graphics and computer animation, in particular figure animation. His publications include work on transonic aerodynamics in addition to computer graphics. Clapworthy is a committee member of the British Chapter of ACM and a member of Eurographics.
Address : De Montfort University, Hammerwood Gate, Kents Hill, Milton Keynes MK7 6HP, U.K

Efficient Generation of Whip-Like Throwing and Striking Motions

Joseph K. Kearney, Dinkar Bhat, Bevra Prasad, and Samuel Yuan

ABSTRACT

This paper examines three methods to algorithmically generate throwing and striking motions. All three methods produce progressive, whip-like motions characteristic of experienced humans in many athletic activities. A new control algorithm based on dynamic, cascaded gains is introduced and compared to optimal control using space-time constraints and fixed-gain proportional control. Experimental results demonstrate that cascaded gains can produce near-optimal performance. Principles of energy generation and transmission are used to explain the mechanical advantage gained by using a whip-like motion. The results have application in the control of real robots and in motion synthesis for animation.

Keywords: Animation, optimization, control, mechanical simulation, robotics

1. INTRODUCTION

The transmission of energy to objects around us is an essential part of many human activities. Performance in golf, tennis, baseball, soccer, and karate is largely determined by the effectiveness with which we impart kinetic energy to a ball, board, or opponent. To be proficient at these activities, we must move our body at high rates of speed. It is widely reported that in a variety of throwing and striking activities, the movements of competent athletes progress from the proximal to the distal end of an appendage (Cavanagh 1976, Joris 1985, Jorgensen 1970, Kreighbaum 1990). In this manner, the down-swing of a golf club begins with movement of the torso followed by the arms and then the club. This pattern of progressive movement is called a whip-like motion and can be applied to either an arm or a leg. It is conjectured that such a cascaded motion is naturally preferred because it is efficient. However, there is scant quantitative evidence to support this conclusion.

In this paper, we present three methods for synthesizing whip-like motions in simulated robots. Our goal is to devise efficient algorithms for controlling real and modeled robots. We use these control algorithms to create realistic animations of throwing and striking motions. In one approach, we specify space-time constraints that give the boundary conditions for throwing (initial position and velocity and final position and velocity) and then, using numerical optimization, compute a trajectory that minimizes an objective function based on effort (Witkin 1988, Prasad 1990, Cohen 1992, van de Panne 1990, Bhat 1992). The optimal trajectory is estimated through an iterative search process. The motions generated with this technique are smooth, efficient, and consistent with models of human motions. However, as a method for control, optimization has some significant disadvantages. Because optimization requires search, it is inefficient. The trajectory found by the optimization algorithm may only be a local minima and the solution to which the algorithm converges may depend on the trajectory from which the search process is initiated. Moreover, the optimal solution gives little insight into the underlying dynamic principles that govern the behavior the linkage. The optimal controller is a black box that produces a least cost solution satisfying initial and final conditions. Each problem instance is treated as an independent problem. Sometimes the results are counterintuitive and produce unexpected motions that appear inappropriate in an animation. We would like to understand the mechanical advantage gained with whip-like motions and discover general principles that govern the efficient control of motion.

To the end of developing practical, adaptive control methods we derive two control methods that generate high tip velocity in link chain and produce a whip-like motion characteristic of human throwing and striking motions. We discuss how these techniques apply principles of energy generation and transfer to gain mechanical advantage and achieve efficient performance. The first method uses proportional position controllers (analogous to simple springs) to control joint actuators. Cochran and Stubbs (1968) proposed using a controller based on springs to model a golf swing. We show how the effort expended is related to the tuning of controller gains. The second method accentuates the progressive motion by creating a dependency between the springs gains and the motion of the link below. By using dynamic, cascading gains we achieve motions that approach the efficiency of the optimal motion.

2. PROBLEM STATEMENT

Our goal is to find efficient methods to generate high velocity at the tip of an open chain of links. High tip velocity is important in a wide variety of athletic tasks that require transmission of energy to other objects. The transmission can be accomplished by releasing a grasped object (i.e. throwing) or striking another object as in golf, karate, tennis serving, and baseball batting. We want to achieve high velocity with minimal effort so that we conserve resources, avoid potential damage from high strain, and maximize performance within the bounds of actuator output.

There has been substantial debate in the human movement literature about the best way to quantify the cost of a movement (Aleshinsky 1986a, Aleshinsky 1986b). The controversy is, in part, related to the cancellation of positive and negative quantities over a periodic motion with many measures based on concepts of mechanical work. Effort has also been defined in a variety of ways in animation systems that generate motions through effort minimization (Witkin 1988, van de Panne 1990, Cohen 1992). To evaluate the effort required to produce a motion, we estimate the sum of the squared torques applied to move the linkage. Thus, for a two link arm with joint torque values $\tau_1(0),\dots \tau_1(n), \tau_2(0),\dots \tau_2(n)$ calculated at discrete time steps, $0, \Delta t, 2\Delta t,\dots, n\Delta t$, our measure of effort is:

$$R = h \sum_{i=1}^{2} \sum_{t=0}^{n} \tau_i(t)^2 \, \Delta t$$

We call this measure the total torque.

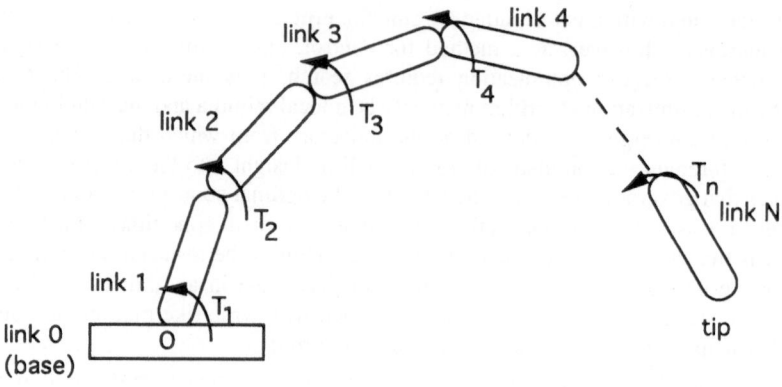

Figure 1. The N-link chain model. Our goal is efficiently achieve high tip velocity.

A general model of the two-dimensional link chain to be controlled is pictured in figure 1. Links are indexed from the immobile based labeled link 0. The moving components are labeled links 1 through link n. We refer to base end of the chain as the proximal end and to the free end as the distal end. The linkage may correspond to the arm or leg of a human. The analysis also applies to virtual chains that are coordinated to behave as a link chain. In an overhead throw, for example, the legs, torso, and arms act together as if they are a single chain.

We are concerned with planar motion in a gravity free environment. We assume that the component links are rigid and have uniform density. Links are interconnected by frictionless, revolute joints. Each joint has a limited range of motion. This disallows full circular rotations as in a windmill softball pitch.

We will examine control strategies for which the predominant motion is in the same direction at all joints. This style of motion, called a swinging motion and illustrated in figure 2, is naturally preferred by experienced humans for many throwing and striking tasks. The entire throwing or striking motion may contain a backswing phase in which the links are rotated into position for a forward rotation. When the tip of the linkage reaches maximal velocity an object is released or contact is made. There may also be a dissipation phase after maximal velocity is reached to bring the linkage back to rest. We focus on the middle segment of the motion that begins with a stationary linkage prepared for forward motion and ends when the tip reaches maximal velocity.

Within these constraints on the motion, there are many ways in which the limbs could be rotated through their range to generate large velocity. Effective throwing requires coordination of the joint motions to best utilize all actuators and exploit mechanical advantages.

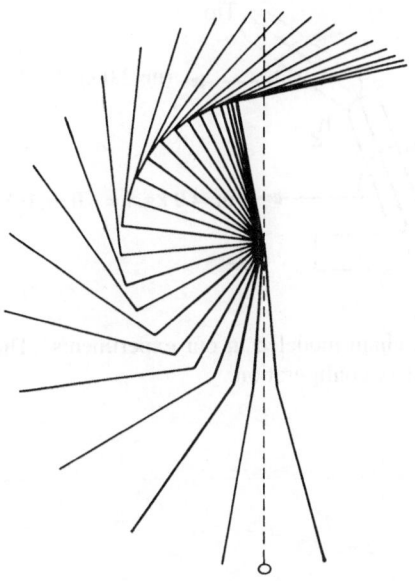

Figure 2. A golf swing as approximated from a stroboscopic photograph of a golfer swinging a driver. (reprinted with permission from Jorgensen, 1970.)

3. Three Approaches

We examine three methods to synthesize whip-like motions for virtual links chain of arbitrary length. In this section, we define the methods and compare their performance on a two-link chain.

3.1 Proportional Position Control

We begin by demonstrating how proportional controllers on joint position can be coordinated to produce a whip-like motion and achieve high tip velocity. The torque applied at each joint is proportional to the difference between the current angle and the set point.

$$\tau_i = K_i(\phi_i^d - \phi_i)$$

where τ_i is the torque applied at joint i, K_i is the gain on the controller at joint i, ϕ_i^d is the set point of the controller at joint i, and ϕ_i is the current joint angle. The proportional controller models an undamped spring.

We demonstrate proportional control with a two link chain. The set point at the base joint is placed midway through the joint range. Interior joints reach their set point when the joint angle is 0, that is, when the two links connected by the joint have the same orientation. The masses, lengths, and moments of inertia for the components of the two link chain are shown in figure 3. The gain for the base link, K_1, is set to 1000.0. The gain for the second joint, K_2, is set to 50.0. This value was chosen to achieve maximal tip velocity for a motion that starts from the configuration illustrated in figure 3. The variation in maximal tip velocity for a range of K_2 values is shown in figure 4. The maximal tip velocity increases with the gain on joint 2 until the gain is about 50. As the gain is increased

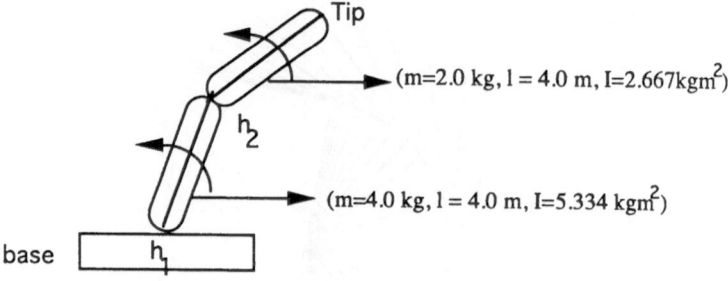

Figure 3. The two-link chain modeled in our experiments. The chain is shown in the initial, stationary configuration.

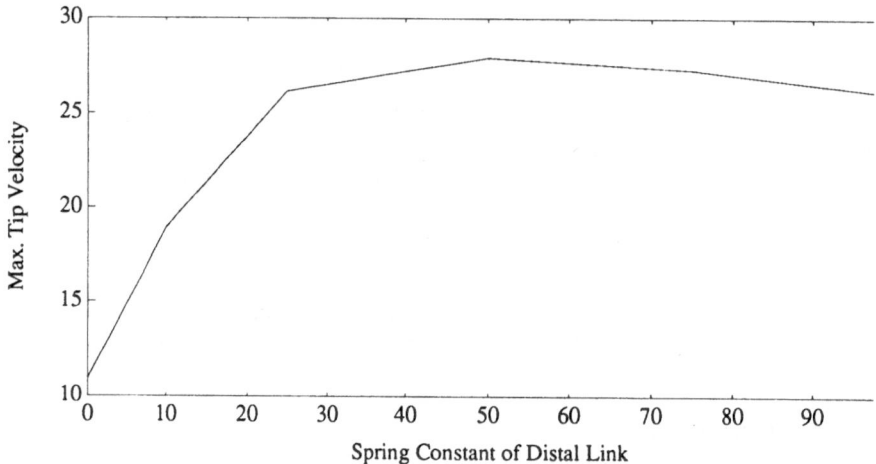

Figure 4. The influence of the gain on the proportional controller at joint 2 on tip velocity. The gain on joint 1 was fixed at 1000.0.

The motion of the two link mechanism was simulated using the model-based, dynamic simulator **Newton** (Cremer 1989, Hoffmann 1987). A sequence of frames from an animation of the motion are overlayed in figure 5. Profiles of joint angles, angular velocities, joint torques, and the tip velocity are presented in figure 6. The lower link leads the upper link in the early portion of the sequence. The progressive nature of the movement is evident in both the joint angle profiles and in the overlayed image. To measure the efficiency of the method, we calculate the total torque required to move from the stationary starting configuration to the configuration at which the maximal tip velocity is achieved. The value of the total torque R for the torque profiles in figure 6 is 57,530 Nm. This value provides a basis of comparing proportional control to other methods.

Figure 5. A sequence of frames from the simulation of the proportional controller.

3.3 Cascading Gain

The progressive motion of the proportional controller can be accentuated by defining a time-varying gain at the second joint that is initially small and gradually grows during the course of the movement. As the gain increases, we are effectively increasing the stiffness of the spring. The initially low gain will cause the forward rotation of the second link to be delayed with respect to the movement of the first link. We define the controllers for joints $2, 3, .., n$ to be

$$\tau_i = \kappa_i(\phi_i^d - \phi_i)$$

where κ_i is a variable gain that depends on the angle ϕ_{i-1}, the set point ϕ_{i-1}^d, and the initial angle ϕ_{i-1}^I at joint $i-1$. At any instant, the variable gain is defined as:

$$\kappa_i = K_i \frac{(\phi_{i-1} - \phi_{i-1}^I)}{(\phi_{i-1}^d - \phi_{i-1}^I)}.$$

The base link drives the system and is controlled by a simple, proportional controller. When applied to an n-link chain, the gains increase progressively along the linkage as each successive joint nears its set point.

The cascaded-gain controller was simulated with the two-link model previously described. Gain parameters were chosen so that the maximum tip velocity was approximately the same as in the previous experiment. These parameters were determined experimentally. With $K_1 = 600.0$, we found that the greatest maximum tip velocity was obtained when $K_2 = 100.0$. The resultant tip velocity was approximately equal to that found with the proportional controller described in the previous section. A sequence of frames from an animation of the motion are overlayed in figure 7. Profiles of joint angles, angular velocities, joint torques, and tip velocity are presented in figure 8.

As with the proportional controller, the cascaded-gain controller leads to a progressive, whip-like motion. The overall effort as measured by the total torque was 28,848 Nm. The effort expended is a substantial improvement over the proportional controller (57,530 Nm).

3.2 Optimal Motion Analysis

To evaluate the performance of the proportional and cascaded-gain controllers, we determined the optimal trajectory satisfying the initial and final conditions of the motion

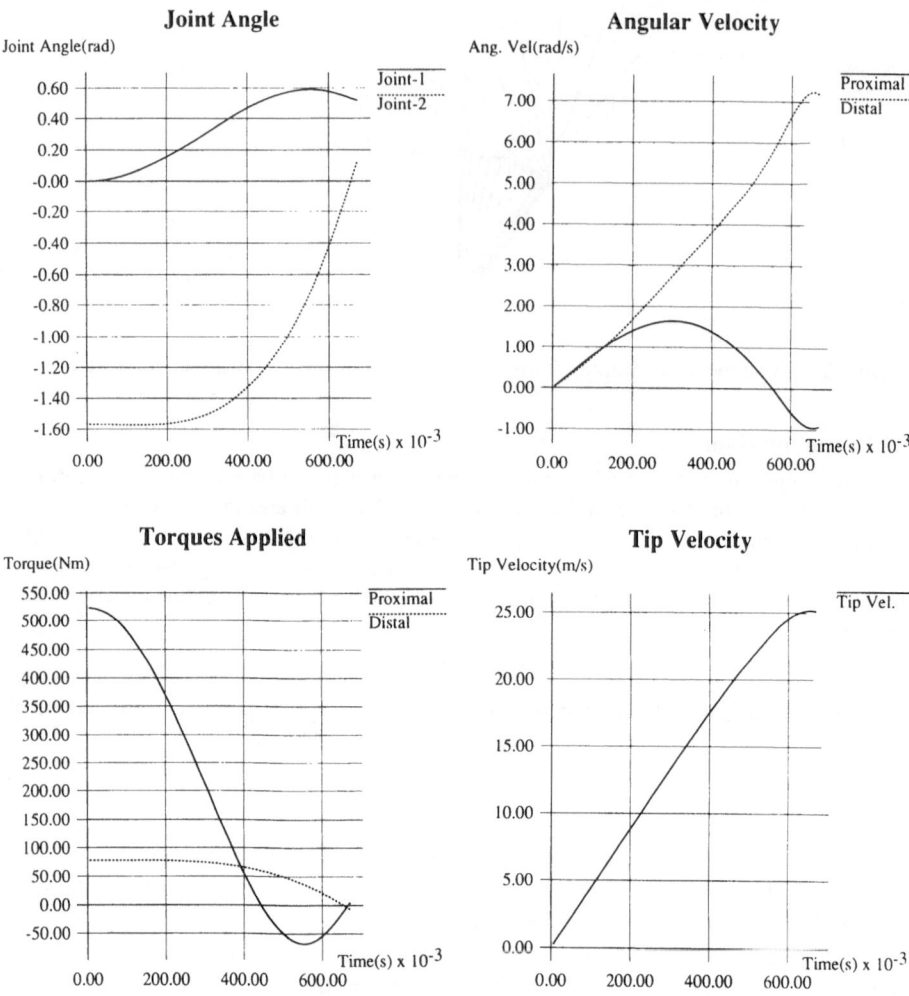

Figure 6. Simulation results for the proportional controller. The graphs show the joint angles, the angular velocities of the links, the joint torques, and the velocity of the tip of the distal link.

determined with the cascaded-gain controller. The tool employed for optimal motion analysis is a system called **Optimizer** (Prasad 1990). Optimizer solves for optimal motions by discretizing a continuous motion into a sequence of time-varying positions. Given a set of constraints on positions and velocities and an initial sequence, Optimizer formulates a nonlinear least squares problem which is solved with a version of the Levenberg-Marquardt algorithm. The constraints on our optimization problems were derived from the simulation results for the cascaded-gain controller. As in the simulation, the initial joint velocities were zero and the initial joint angles were poised for a forward swing. The final joint angles and velocities were constrained to match the joint angles and

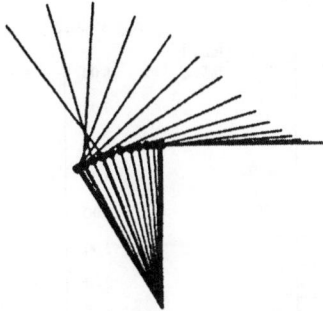

Figure 7. A sequence of frames from the simulation of the cascaded-gain controller.

velocities at the time when the simulation achieved maximal tip velocity.

The results of the optimization are presented in figures 9 and 10. A whip-like motion is evident in the optimal motion. The total torque for the optimal motion was 29,450 Nm. While the trajectory differs somewhat from the trajectory generated by cascaded-gain controller, the total torques are nearly identical. Given that different methods where used to compute the trajectories and that the results contain numeric error, the slight difference in efficiency should not be considered significant. Note also that the torque profile of the cascaded-gain controller has a qualitative similarity to the torque profile of the optimal controller. In particular, the torque on the second joint gradually increases and then decreases. In contrast, the torque curve for the fixed gain spring is monotonically decreasing over the same range of joint angles.

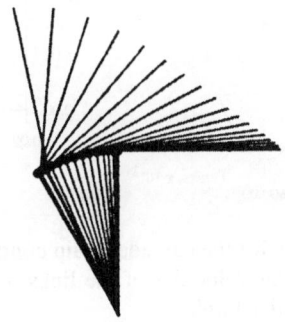

Figure 9. A sequence of frames from the optimization.

4. ENERGY TRANSFER ANALYSIS

What is the nature of the mechanical advantage gained by a progressive motion? The energy in a link chain is distributed across its component links. Within a link, energy can be partitioned into translational, rotational, and potential fractions. (Aleshinsky 1986, Aleshinsky 1986b). Links interact through the constraint forces at joints. The force

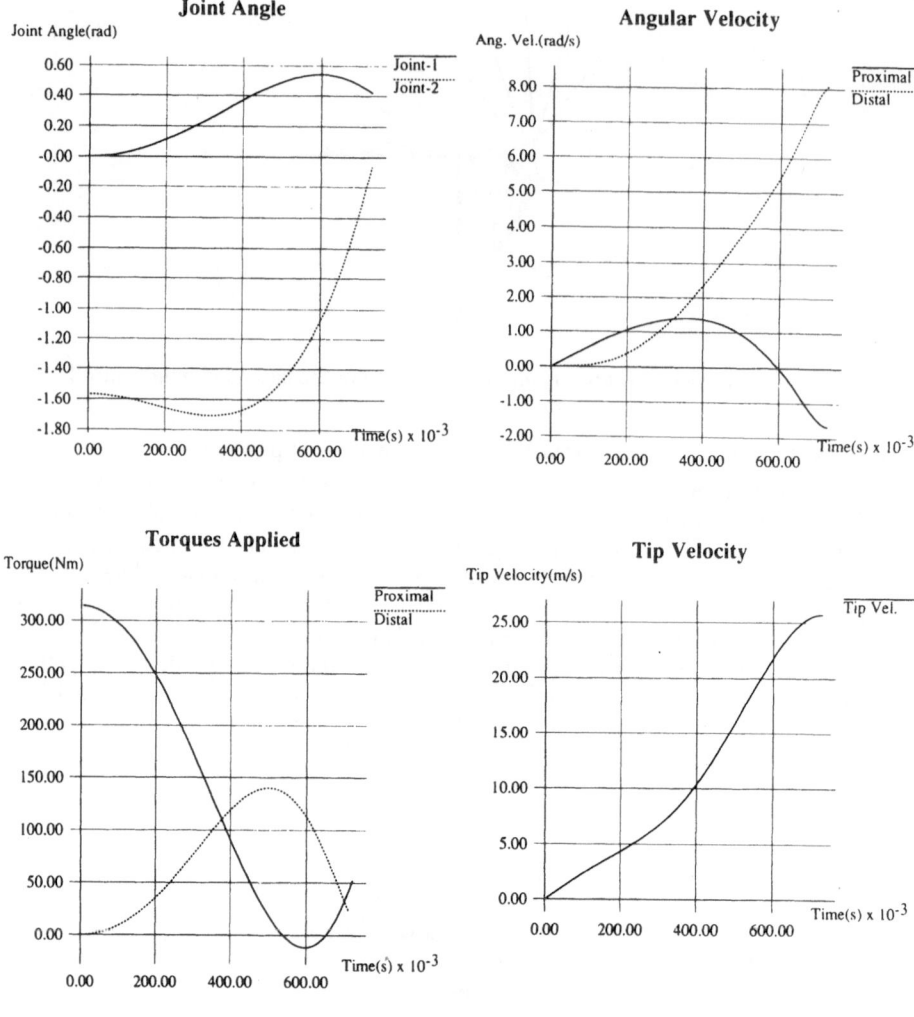

Figure 8. Simulaton results for the cascaded-gain controller. The graphs show the joint angles, the angular velocities of the links, the joint torques, and the velocity of the tip of the distal link.

applied by link i to link $i+1$ can cause the energy in link $i+1$ to increase or decrease. It can also convert energy from one fraction to another to another. Energy conversion, from translational to rotational fractions, plays a crucial role in whip-like motions.

In both the proportional and cascaded-gain control models, the motions of a link can be decomposed into two phases. In the first phase, the force applied by a link to the adjacent link at its distal end is in the direction of the desired rotation. During this phase, the torque and angular velocity at the proximal joint have the same sign. This torque contributes to an increase in the energy of the entire linkage distal to the joint by increasing angular momentum about the joint. In the second phase, the link applies a force opposing

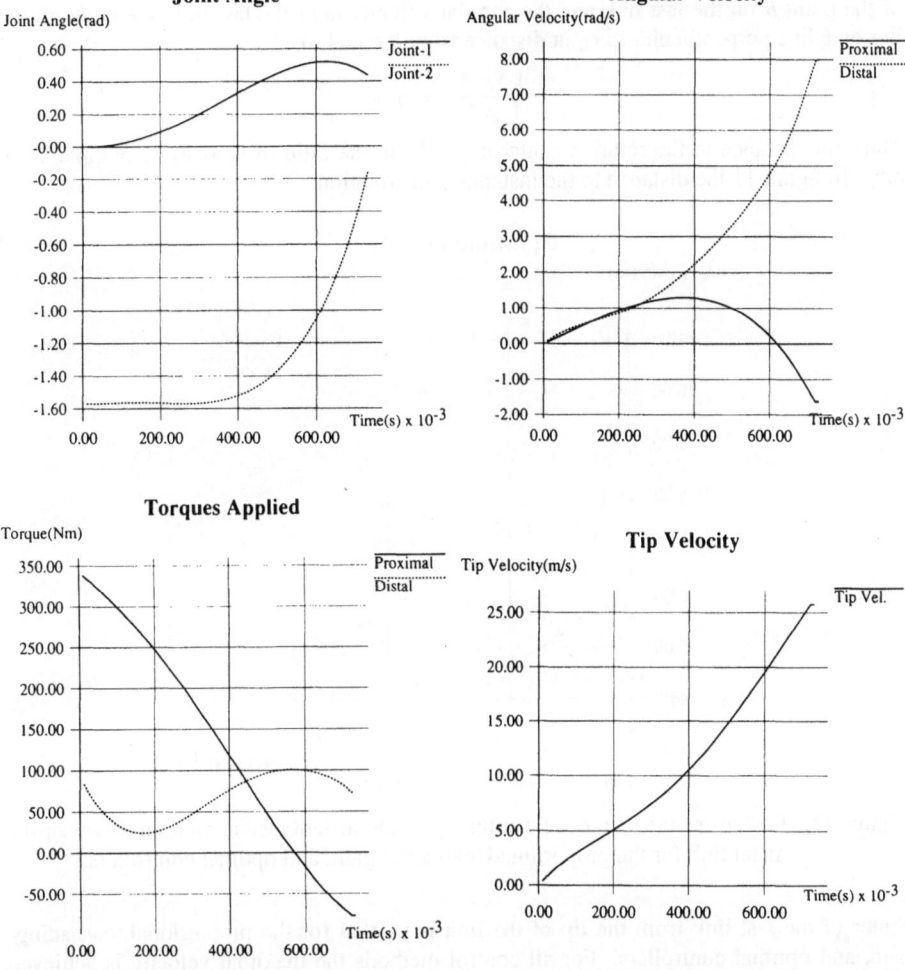

Figure 10. Optimization results. The initial and final constraints for the optimization
were taken from the results of the simulation of the cascaded-gain controller.
The graphs show the joint angles, the angular velocities of the links, the joint
torques, and the velocity of the tip of the distal link.

exchange of energy from translational to rotational fractions in the linkage distal to the
upper joint. The increase in angular velocity leads to a net increase in the magnitude of
the velocity of the distal end point. The overall effect is that the instantaneous center of
rotation of the last link moves progressively closer to the tip of the linkage during the
motion.

For a body in two-dimensional space, the instantaneous axis of zero velocity, IA, is
the axis about which the body's velocity is described as pure rotation. For any point, B,
on the body

where IC is the point at which the IA intersects the plane of motion. Given the velocity v_B of the point B on the last link and the angular velocity ω of the last link, we know the IC lies on a line perpendicular to v_B at distance from B equal to

$$\frac{\parallel v_B \parallel}{\parallel \omega \parallel} = r_{B/IC}.$$

Thus, the distance to the rotation center depends on the ratio of velocity to angular velocity. In figure 11 the distance to the instantaneous rotation

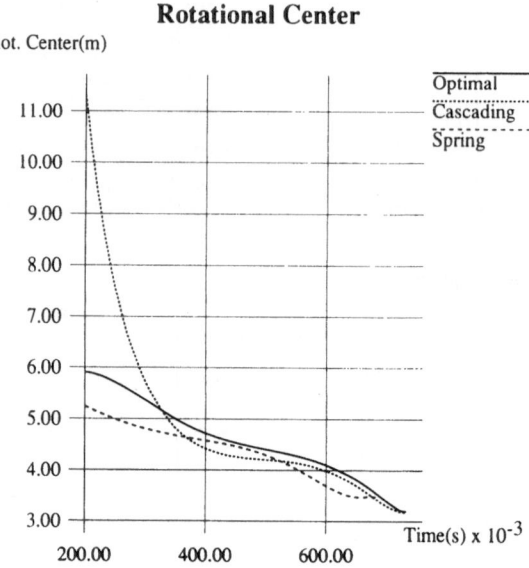

Figure 11. Profiles of the distance from the tip to the instantaneous rotation center of the distal link for the proportional, cascaded-gain, and optimal controllers.

center of the last link from the tip of the link is plotted for the proportional, cascading-gain, and optimal controllers. For all control methods the maximal velocity is achieved when the rotation center is nearest the tip. The rotation center changes more dramatically and reaches a lower level with the cascaded-gain controller. We believe a principle source of the efficiency for the cascaded-gain controller is an improvement in the conversion of translational to rotational energy as indicated by the reduction in the distance of the rotation center.

5. CONCLUSIONS

Efficient generation and transmission of energy is critical to accomplishing many tasks. It is believed that the consistent preference of whip-like motions by competent athletes for a wide variety of throwing and striking tasks is due to mechanical advantages inherent in a progressive motion. The optimization results presented here provide strong evidence that a whip-like motion is mechanically efficient with respect effort as measured by the sum of squared torques.

All of the three control methods examined in the paper produce, to some extent, a whip-like motion and provide adequate capability to control a robot arm or to algorithmically synthesize biomechanically plausible motions for animation. The computational simplicity and near-optimal performance of the cascaded-gain controller are attractive features. Because the computations at each joint depend only on local state information, the method generalizes to link chains of arbitrary length. In this way, the cascaded-gain controller is device and task independent; it can be applied to any virtual chain in an articulated body and any task that requires high tip speed. Thus, a human's two lower legs and upper legs could be treated as a part of virtual chain that continues with the torso and head. This virtual chain could be controlled to "head" a soccer ball.

Lastly, analysis of the energy distribution in the linkage reveals that the efficiency of whip-like motions is related to the conversion of translational to rotational energy. As the chain whips, the instantaneous center of rotation of the last link moves progressively closer to the tip. Maximal tip velocity is achieved when the rotation center is closest to the tip. The more efficient methods move the rotation center over a greater distance to a point closer to the tip. We believe concepts of energy generation and transfer are critical to understanding how to control complex mechanisms.

6. Acknowledgement

This work was supported, in part, by National Science Foundation Grant IRI-8808896 and Office of Naval Research Grant ONR 00014-88K-0632.

7. References

Aleshinsky, S. Y., "An Energy Sources and Fractions Approach to the Mechanical Energy Expenditure Problem - I. Basic Concepts, Description of the Model, Analysis of a One-Link System Movement," *Journal of Biomechanics*, vol. 19, no. 4, pp. 287-293, 1986.

Aleshinsky, S. Y., "An Energy Sources and Fractions Approach to the Mechanical Energy Expenditure Problem - II. Movement of the Multi-Link Chain Model," *Journal of Biomechanics*, vol. 19, no. 4, pp. 295-300, 1986.

Bhat, D., "Development of Control Models Using Concepts of Energy Generation and Transfer for a Whip-Type Motion in Multi-Link Systems," M.S. Thesis, University of Iowa, December, 1992.

Cavanagh, P.R. and Landa, J., "A Biomechanical Analysis of the Karate Chop," *The Research Quarterly*, vol. 47, no. 4, pp. 610-618, 1976.

Cochran, A. and Stobbs, J., *The Search for the Perfect Spring*, J. P. Lippincott Company, Philadelphia, PA, 1968.

Cohen, M. F., "Interactive Spacetime Control for Animation," *Computer Graphics (Proc. SIGGRAPH)*, vol. 26, no. 2, pp. 293-308, 1992.

Cremer, J., "An Architecture for General Purpose Physical Simulation -- Integrating Geometry, Dynamics, and Control," Ph.D. Thesis, TR 89-987, Cornell University, April,

1989.

Hoffmann, C. M. and Hopcroft, J. E., "Simulation of physical systems from geometric models," *IEEE Journal of Robotics and Automation,* vol. RA-3, no. 3, pp. 194-206, June 1987.

Jorgensen, T. Jr., "On the Dynamics of the Swing of a Golf Club," *American Journal of Physics,* vol. 38, no. 5, pp. 644-651, May 1970.

Joris, H. J. J., Edwards van Muyen, A. J., van Ingen Schenau, G. J., and Kemper, H. C. G., "Force, Velocity, and Energy Flow During the Overarm Throw in Female Handball Players," *Journal of Biomechanics,* vol. 18, no. 6, pp. 409-414, 1985.

Kreighbaum, E. and Barthels, K. M., in *Biomechanics, A Qualitative Approach for Studying Human Movement,* Macmillan Publishing Company, New York, NY, 1990.

van de Panne, M., Fiume, E., and Vranesic, Z., "Reusable Motion Synthesis Using State-Space Controllers," *Computer Graphics (Proc. SIGGRAPH),* vol. 24, no. 4, pp. 225-234, 1990.

Prasad, B., "Optimizer: A Model Driven System for the Study of Optimal Motions," M.S. Thesis, University of Iowa, August, 1990.

Witkin, A. and Kass, M., "Spacetime Constraints," *Computer Graphics (Proc. SIGGRAPH),* vol. 22, no. 4, pp. 159-168, 1988.

Figure 12. Rendered images from an animation of the proportional control method. The transparency of the objects increases as the motion progresses.

Figure 13. Rendered images from an animation of the cascaded-gain control method. The transparency of the objects increases as the motion progresses.

Figure 14. Rendered images from an animation of the trajectory estimated through optimization of space-time constraints. The transparency of the objects increases as the motion progresses.

Joseph K. Kearney is an Associate Professor of Computer Science at the University of Iowa, Iowa City and has been a member of that faculty since 1983. He spent a year as a Visiting Scientist in the Computer Science Department at Cornell University, Ithaca, NY in 1986 and 1987. His research interests include animation, control, computer vision, mechanical simulation, robot programming, and robot locomotion, and virtual environments. He is an associate editor for*ACM Computing Surveys*. Kearney received the B.A. degree in psychology from the University of Minnesota in 1975, the M.A. in psychology from the University of Texas 1979, and M.S. and Ph.D. degrees in computer science from the University of Minnesota in 1981 and 1983.
address: Department of Computer Science, University of Iowa, Iowa City, IA, 52242; kearney@cs.uiowa.edu

Dinkar N. Bhat was born in Bangalore,India on June 16, 1967. He received his B.Tech in Electrical Engineering from the Indian Institute of Technology, Madras, India, in 1988. From July 1988 to August 1990 he worked as a Software Engineer in TELCO, India. He received his M.S. in Computer Science from the University of Iowa, Iowa City in 1992 and since then has been working on his Ph.D. at Columbia University, New York. His research interests are in computer vision, graphics, animation and mathematical tools for optimization.
address: Department of Computer Science, Columbia University, New York, NY, 10025; bhat@cs.columbia.edu

Bevra Prasad is a consultant at LCG Consulting in Mountain View, California. He is currently involved in the design and development of intuitive graphical interfaces in the Windows environment, that can access a wide range of services over LANs and WANs, using client/server technology. One of the projects he is currently working on is a Natural Language Interface to a variety of databases. His interests include graphics, user-interfaces and networking. He received his Master's in Computer Science from the University of Iowa in 1990, and Bachelor's in Computer Science and Engineering from the Indian Institute of Technology, Bombay, India, in 1988.
address: 3500 Granada Avenue, #123 Santa Clara, CA 95051; prde001@dsis.epri.com

Samuel S. M. Yuan recieved the B.S. degree in industrial engineering from the Feng Chia Uiniversity in Taiwan in 1972. He recieved the M.S. degree in industrial engineering from the Kansas State University in 1980. From 1980 to 1985, he worked as an industrial engineer and a process engineer for the Electronics Component Division of AT&T in kansas City, Missouri. He is currently a senior industrial engineer in the Collins Avionics and Communication Division of Rockwell International in Cedar Rapids, Iowa. He is in charge of automatic component insertion operations for circuit boards. Mr. Yuan is also working towards his Master's degree in computer science in the University of Iowa in Iowa City. His main interests are in robotic animation and simulation.
address: Department of Computer Science, University of Iowa, Iowa City, Iowa, 52242; yuan@cs.uiowa.edu

Movement Definition from Conceptual Curve Sketches

Olov Fahlander

Summary

We propose an animation specification methodology to be used in an interactive environment, primarily intended for articulated figure control. The method is based on many techniques used earlier, but now integrated into a flexible parameter-driven specification framework. It is very similar to parametric keyframe animation, but with each parameter designed separately. The user is free to "slide" different design parameters relative to each other in time and thereby accomplish coordination. The lack of this feature has been considered a main limitation and disadvantage of keyframe-based techniques. In our case there is a decoupling between the parameters, which are correlated to each other at the very last stage of the design. Only then keyframes are considered to coordinate the behaviours.

As a trajectory modeling primitive we use parabolics, which in contrast to many well known curve techniques, has a low polynomial complexity, so that algebraic derivations such as inversions can be done more easily. The usual inflexibility of parabolics is alleviated through the use of a "tweak" factor, which blends a pair of segments together so that more degrees of freedom are obtained, but without the cost of a higher polynomial complexity. This implies that the approach described here is that of "piecewise constant force", which is relevant at least in free fall. For non-falling objects it may be approximately true, provided that the time interval is sufficiently small. The extension to non-constant forces is however rather obvious. For one-dimensional parametric specifications this might often be appropriate, where angles of an articulated figure is an obvious application. For general path specifications in 3D space, good methods already exist that might well be incorporated into the framework described here.

For parabolic trajectories we derive the expressions to relate kinematic trajectory properties to forces and accelerations. Potentially, there is a possibility through techniques such as the P-curves (by Baecker), to accomplish the same results as with our method. But again, we see the weakness of these techniques in that they require of the user to determine the timing for each of the selected parameters.

Our intention is to demonstrate through an example, how an animation can be prepared through the use of conceptual curve sketches. Using these, the exact timing requirement is replaced by either interactive on-line design using a real time display, or by exploiting a natural law such as Newton's force-law. We suggest a very flexible methodology, which gives the user the freedom to parameterize his model in a way he/she feels appropriate. The central part of the specification is done by filling in a well-defined table, preferably done as a spreadsheet. Primarily the curve sketches only specify the essential behaviour of the objects such as their "waving" motion, not their actual locations in time or amplitude. These properties are instead evaluated and "tuned" to each other at a later moment when the actual animation is available on screen in a preview form. The example used is a swimdiver performing a few jumps on the trampoline, tumbling in the air and finally leveling with the water surface. To gain further understanding of the process during the specification phase, a simple dynamic simulation of the same situation is also demonstrated.

A full paper of this report can be obtained from this author on request.

Address: Department of Electrical Engineering, University of Linköping, S-581 83 Linköping, Sweden

Interactive Design of Animation with Knowledge Based Moving Controls

Syuichi Sato, Kunio Kondo, Daisuke Ojiro, Hisashi Sato, Shizuo Shimada, and Mitsuru Kaneko

A computer assisted painting apparatus was developed by Kaneko(1991) for generating 'cels' for a motion picture. The term 'cel' here is a word taken from a celluloid sheet which is traditionally used in animation film. In the above system, however, a cel does not mean a physical sheet but a digitalized static frame in the moving picture. In order to activate the system, computer animation technology has been demanded among well experienced animators to assist skilled painters to save their repetitive works about a moving object.

One of difficulties to create animation is the design of a moving object step by step and how realistically it seems when played back. During the stage of drawing cels, no one can imagine what may happen in the effect. An idea proposed by Kaneko is to move an object in a graphic screen before the data of movements are sent to the system. He insists that the system should contain knowledge of movements in some classified categories, which can be applied to any kind of objects whenever played basically with the same moving characteristics.

Our research started with analyzing the fundamental techniques of motion adopted in the past works of animation films. We agreed to classify the motion of an object into nine patterns of velocity controls as shown in Figure 1. Each curve analogically represents the velocity of an object along a moving path. The gradient of curve shows at the same time an acceleration force which plays an important parameter to show an exaggerated object along the path(as shown in Figure 2).

An interactive procedure is quite popular among painters, however, our target procedure is to make the whole system more clever as to understand natural language, such as 'come like a dog run', 'jumping walk like a little girl',etc., while watching the monitoring CRT.

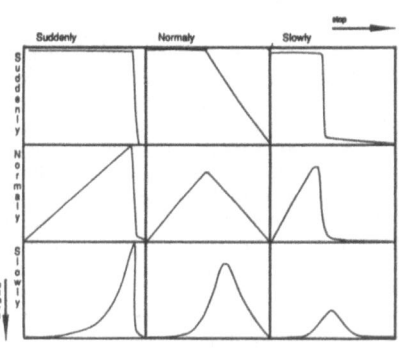

Figure 1: Velocity Characteristics

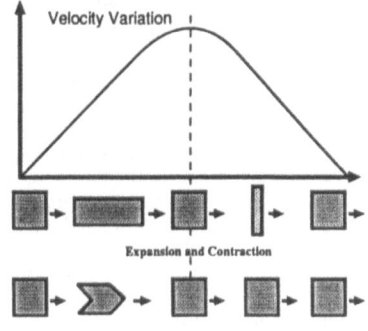

Figure 2: Shapes with Exaggeration

REFERENCE

Mitsuru KANEKO (1991) A Process of Making Animation, CG-ARTS

Address: Dept. Information and Computer Sciences, Saitama University, 255 Shimo-okubo, Urawa, 338, Japan

Route Planning in Animation Using a Language Interpreter

A. Cavusoglu and A. L. Thomas

Abstract

The objective of this work is to explore extensions to high level programming languages which will help to extend the power of animation systems. The construction of program libraries of animation facilities is clearly the first step in such a programme. However, if we wish to raise the level of abstraction at which such an exercise can be attempted, we quickly reach a threshold above which the semantics of the commands we wish to employ become complicated.

To help us to make progress in this, we chose an area where much low level work has already been done. This provided us with the support which we needed to experiment with alternatives; giving the freedom to seek our objectives, without being blocked: for example, by impossible geometric tasks. For the initial studies, we chose to investigate the 'apparently' simple command "walk". However, if we wish to say "Walk over to that wall", as a command in an actor based animation environment, we are making a statement open to a wide variety of lower level interpretations.

Expecting to develop a hierarchical language structure, we looked to implement the walk command using a repeat statement of the form:

REPEAT Step UNTIL Goal END ;

Two outcomes of this approach appeared immediately. Firstly, the step command becomes a complex conditional command, where the conditions depend on the goal, but also on the situation found in the environment. Secondly, the goal can be considered as a test on the current state, or it can be used to set up a strategy or structure by which its target can be achieved.

Two lines of investigation are being followed. The first is an artificial intelligence approach: restructuring the goal and the conditional aspects of commands which depend on it to create a plan for the overall repeat command to adhere to.

The second is an exploration of alternative ways of implementing conditional actions, which depend on local events inside the repeat loop, in other words, which are aspects of the behavior of the environment, not of the goals. We have started the study of language facilities which will allow us convenient access to, and control of an environment-generated-event mechanism. We are initially exploring the use of hardware triggered, object-interference-events generated from CSG models of the environment, in the control of motion commands.

Address: The University of Sussex, School of Engineering and Applied Sciences, Brighton BN1 9QT, England

Route Planning in Animation Using a Language Interpreter

A. Dawson and A.J. Thomas

Abstract

The objective of this book is to explore extensions to high level programming languages, which will help to extend the power of animation systems. The communication between an animated animal or character can help either step in such a programming. However, if we wish to raise the level of abstraction at which humans operate, we can recommend, we only try reach a threshold above which the semantics of the commands we wish to employ be more comprehensive.

[body text largely illegible]

NATURAL LANGUAGE COMMAND

[text illegible]

Conference Organization

Cochairs
Nadia Magnenat Thalmann, University of Geneva
Daniel Thalmann, Swiss Federal Institute of Technology

International Program Committee

Norman Badler	University of Pennsylvania, USA
Eugene Fiume	University of Toronto, Canada
David Haumann	IBM, Yorkton Heights, USA
Michael Kass	Apple Computers, USA
Tosiyasu L. Kunii	University of Tokyo, Japan
Gavin Miller	Apple Computers, USA
Nadia Magnenat Thalmann	University of Geneva, Switzerland
Fred Parke	IBM, Austin, USA
Alex Pentland	MIT, USA
Peter Stücki	University of Zürich, Switzerland
Demetri Terzopoulos	University of Toronto, Canada
Daniel Thalmann	Swiss Federal Institute of Technology

External Reviewers

Bezault Laurent
Boulic Ronan
Breiteneder Christian
Cohen Michael F.
Gibbs Simon
Gobbetti Enrico
Gotoda Hironobu
Hafner Michel
Kalra Prem
Lee Myeong Wee
Max Nelson

Moccozet Laurent
Noser Hansrudi
Pintado Xavier
Renault Olivier
Reynolds Craig
Sakagawa Y.
Sato Hideyuki
Schleich Robert
Takahashi Tokiichiro
Watanabe Yasuhiko

Organized by: **Computer Graphics Society**
University of Geneva
Swiss Federal Institute of Technology

In Cooperation with: **IEEE Computer Society**
British Computer Society
Eurographics
IFIP WG 5.10

Author Index